Code-IT Primary Programming

How to Teach Primary Programming using Scratch

A complete Computer Science study programme for Key Stage 2 using the free programming language Scratch

Phil Bagge

First published in Great Britain in 2015 by
The University of Buckingham Press
Yeomanry House
Hunter Street
Buckingham MK18 1EG

CIP catalogue record for this book is available at the British Library.

ISBN 9781908684530

Acknowledgements

Thank you:

Thanks to my wife Rachael, who has put up with me dropping salary and leaving a secure teaching job to pursue primary computing science. Thanks also to my wonderful children Antonio and Marissa who have put up with far less family Minecraft and been my first guinea pigs for many new ideas.

Thanks to the School of Electronics and Computer Science at the University of Southampton, for organising Computing CPD activities. Thanks also to Professor Les Carr, who has put up with an endless string of questions about computational thinking, programming, networks and the Internet. I would never have arrived at this book without your patience.

Thanks to Sally-Ann Evans, Brendan Carroll, Steve Summerton, Trevor Walker, Lisa Marshal & Lynne Thorne, who saw something in what I was trying to achieve and employed me to teach computing science in their schools. Without your belief many of the ideas in this book would not have been attempted, let alone refined and improved.

Thanks to my ICT friends in Hampshire, Emma Goto, Jon Audain, Sue Savory and Ian Addison, who have put up with me expounding the benefits of computing science and still talk to me!

Thanks to the many passionate advocates of computing science in CAS that I have had the pleasure of working with over the years, Mark Dorling, John Woollard, Miles Berry, Simon Peyton Jones, Simon Humphries, Graham Hastings, Chip Chippindal, Jane Waite, Alan O'Donohoe, Jo Badge, Dave Ames & Sarah Zaman.

Thanks also to my publisher Christopher Woodhead for asking me to write the one book I really wanted to write.

Phil Bagge 11th October 2015

Foreword

We live in interesting times! From the 1980s until the 2000s PCs dominated the computing landscape and, despite their gradual appearance in our homes for education, entertainment and hobbies, it was business programming for the corporate environment that was the order of the day. It was only natural that our National Curriculum reflected that, by emphasising the business uses of information and computing technology (ICT). However, the last decade has seen the emergence of the Web, the Cloud and mobile devices with an insatiable demand for new kinds of programs – Web sites, social networks, media players, fitness and health trackers, apps for smartphones, tablets and watches as well as notebook, laptop and desktop PCs. The information revolution that was predicted in the 1970s has just hit top gear, and our National Curriculum has been revised to reflect that our children will need to be able to understand, control and create these new technologies – that they need to learn how to program.

This book is a fantastic introduction to computing and programming, giving primary school children the basic skills and tools of programming. It distils some brilliant classroom experiences of creating new things (quizzes, games, calculators, simulators, displays, musical instruments) and solving new problems (in arithmetic, geometry, literacy and control). It provides educators with the resources to create valuable learning experiences of their own that draw out computational understanding through computational practice and it encourages children to join the information revolution as creative programmers able to take full advantage of all the opportunities of a connected society.

Professor Leslie Carr

Web Science Institute & Department of Electronics and Computer Science

University of Southampton

Contents

Chapter 2

Chapter 3

Chapter 4

Chapter 5

Author introduction

I have been a primary school teacher, lead teacher and advanced skills teacher in Information and Communication Technology for many years and in that time I have tried many new technologies in the classroom. Looking for something that would stretch my pupils' thinking, in 2012 I joined CAS (Computing at Schools), a grassroots organisation dedicated to promoting Computer Science. There I discovered the challenge of programming and computational thinking. I was so impressed with pupils' positive responses to this more challenging work that I approached a group of Hampshire primary head teachers and asked them if they would employ me to teach a strand of computing science.

For the last three years I have taught over 1300 hours of Computer Science in six schools. In these years I have made plenty of mistakes while discovering what works and what helps develop resilience and problem solving skills in my pupils. I set up my own website, code-it.co.uk, to record my journey and help others benefit from my experiences. These resources have been edited and revised many times and downloaded by teachers tens of thousands of times for use within classrooms across the country. It has been a real joy writing this book as it has given me the chance to do one definitive version reflecting the way I teach computing science now. The Scratch resources on my website will remain there but this book is the best, most up to date version of these.

0A. Ways to use this book

This book can be used by:-

- Experienced teacher - programmers as a guide to what works in the classroom when delivering the National Curriculum
- Teachers with little experience of programming, who would value a "way in" to teaching computing with confidence
- Parents who want to help their children gain important skills and work on a topic that they have an enthusiasm for

This book can be used:-

- As a full programming strand for KS2 (7-11 year olds) for all four year groups
- As a resource book of programming planning that emphasises computational thinking
- As a supplementary strand of programming that emphasises Music, Maths, Literacy or Gaming
- As a starting place to think through and create your own programming planning
- As a home tutoring guide to develop Computer Science knowledge and skills through programming
- As a set of projects to work through with your child if their school has chosen to teach only the barest minimum Computer Science or teach lots of it in an unplugged fashion. Please ask your school if they are using or intend to use the scheme first.

0B. Teacher Book & Pupil Workbooks

This volume goes alongside four pupils' workbooks. These are printed in black and white and are priced so they can be bought for each child as a workbook, saving teachers and support staff time.

Pupil Workbooks

Each programming module has reference to resources in the pupil workbooks when pupils need to use them. Each Scratch module also has an overview page in the pupil workbooks briefly describing the project and key computational thinking ideas. These pages also contain further home projects that pupils could complete independently once they have fully completed the module at school. Pupils could take the book home to complete these. Projects are graded.

First Steps ☆ These are reinforcement activities

Next Steps ☆ ☆ These require more investigation

Further Steps ☆ ☆ ☆ Designed to challenge the more able

You may also wish to point out the pupil parent guidance sheet found at the front of the pupil workbooks the first time you send one of the further challenges home, as it stresses the independent nature of the tasks.

0C. Hint Cards & Video Support

Many projects contain hint cards. These can be photocopied and folded to make A4 booklets. Some contain code samples that pupils can use to help them debug errors and some contain hints that help to trigger the next step in learning. It is worth printing these before the lesson and using with those pupils who need them.

The author is working on a set of videos to support many of the modules found in the book.

You can find these and other online files mentioned in the book at:

http://code-it.co.uk/bookmedia

0D. Why Scratch and why mainly Scratch in KS2?

When I first started teaching Computer Science in five schools I flitted about between Logo, Scratch, Kodu, Python and a few other programming languages. I found that I was wasting time covering the basics over and over again as pupils struggled to come to terms with new ways to do the same things. I realised that if pupils were truly to design and write their own programs with sequence, selection, repetition and variables I needed to develop depth in one programming language first before dipping into others. When evaluating which language to use as my core language I was looking for an ability to create a wide variety of programming types not just games (Kodu) or drawings (Logo) and a language that used the programming basics of sequence, selection, repetition and variables well and are which aided pupils' understanding of these foundational concepts. Scratch with its bright colourful blocks and excellent design was really the only choice. It was just the cherry on the top that it has an excellent user community and was created and supported by one of the world's premier computing universities, the Massachusetts Institute of Technology.

Limits of this volume

This work is only concerned with the first two aims of the English Computing National Curriculum worked out through the first three aims of the KS2 programs of study.

The aims are:-

The National Curriculum for computing aims to ensure that all pupils:

- can understand and apply the fundamental principles and concepts of computer science, including abstraction, logic, algorithms and data representation.
- can analyse problems in computational terms, and have repeated practical experience of writing computer programs in order to solve such problems.

The first three aims of the programs of study in KS2 are:

Pupils should be taught to:

- design, write and debug programs that accomplish specific goals, including controlling or simulating physical systems; solve problems by decomposing them into smaller parts.
- use sequence, selection, and repetition in programs; work with variables and various forms of input and output.
- use logical reasoning to explain how some simple algorithms work and to detect and correct errors in algorithms and programs.

0E. Computational Thinking in the National Curriculum

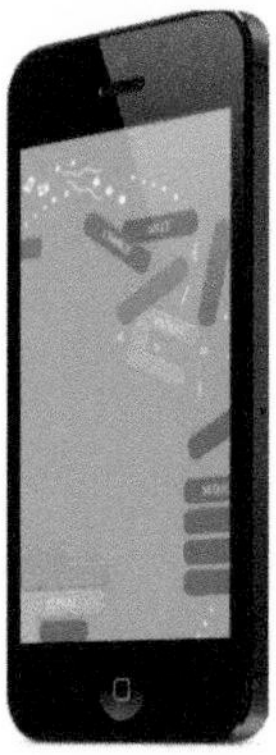

The opening statement of the introductory paragraph of the 2014 English computing National Curriculum[1] says, *"A high-quality computing education equips pupils to use computational thinking and creativity to understand and change the world."* This is a wonderful opening statement which highlights the importance of computational thinking. I also like the way it highlights that computer science is both a science and an engineering discipline. Understanding the world is a scientific endeavour and changing it is an engineering one. Computer Science doesn't just think about things, it turns this thinking into digital artefacts to be tested and evaluated by society.

What is Computational Thinking like?

Computational thinking – the ability to think about solving problems with a computer. This is like scientific thinking (how to use experimental methods) or mathematical thinking (using equations, logic, algebra and trigonometry) or historical thinking (using documentary evidence and cross-checking written sources). Although programming (or coding) is often talked about, it is the wider ability to use a variety of programming, analysis and modelling techniques that is important.

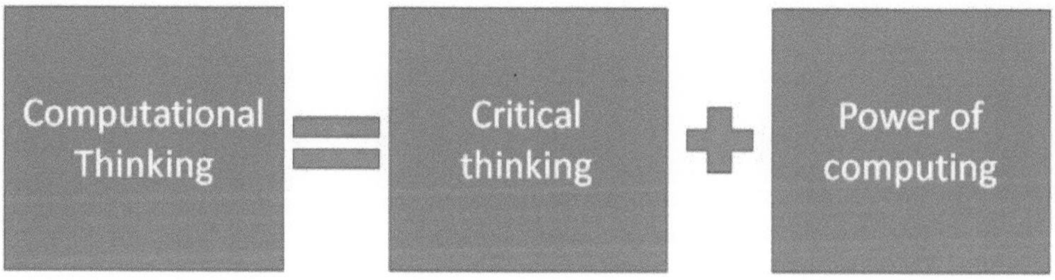
Computational Thinking
Critical thinking
Power of computing

Computational Thinking is

Wikipedia[2] describes it as "problem solving method that uses computer science techniques."

ITSE[3], the International Society for Technology in Education, in their article on computational thinking describe computational thinking as critical thinking ideas combined with the power of computing. Computational thinking is not thinking like a computer. Computers are un-intelligent devices, all the things they do they do because a human has thought through a set of instructions (algorithm) and then converted this into code that a computer can follow precisely.

Who first thought of the term?

The first[4] person to popularise computational thinking and call for computational thinking skills to be taught to all was Jeanette Wing,[5] a prominent American computer scientist. She argued that, *"To reading, writing, and arithmetic, we should add computational thinking to every child's analytical ability."*[6]

Is it a new idea?

The idea that problem solving methods used by computer scientists should be taught to every child is relatively new (2006), however the toolkit of useful critical thinking tools are much older.

What thinking skills are included?

A recent CAS working group included algorithmic thinking, evaluation, decomposition, abstraction and generalisation in their framework document[7]. These are specific thinking skills that have particular meanings for primary pupils and teachers. (Note that they are important for other areas of the curriculum too!)

Algorithmic Thinking

Algorithms define a precise set of instructions or rules to achieve an outcome or solve a problem. A recipe can be an algorithm, musical score can be an algorithm and instructional writing can be an algorithm. All working computer programs started life as human ideas that were expressed as algorithms in thoughts, words, symbols or flow charts. Programming is the challenge of turning precise ideas (algorithms) into code that can be read by a machine. When we define a precise set of instructions we save time as this algorithm can be reused to solve a problem over and over again and adapted (generalised) to solve similar problems.

Evaluation

Evaluation is how we look at algorithms and determine how useful they are, how adaptable, how efficient and how correct they are. There may be many algorithmic solutions to a problem, evaluation asks which one was best and why? Evaluation is also concerned with the people who use an algorithm. Did it solve their problem? Was it better on paper than in practice? Evaluation is also a very useful skill to extend into programming as well. Getting pupils to think about an end user in the design (algorithm) stage can help focus ideas. I think there is a lot of links between logical thinking in the National Curriculum and evaluation.

Decomposition

Decomposition is the skill of breaking a complex problem up into smaller manageable chunks and solving these chunks separately. I have found this to be a wonderfully useful skill in games design. Faced with the task of creating a new game[8] pupils are often overwhelmed by the amount to think through. We use a decomposition planner where they jot down what they want the game to do first before circling objects and ideas and describing these in greater detail. This allows them to focus on designing small parts of the game separately before recomposing these ideas into the whole. Before pupils can usefully use this type of decomposition they need to see it modelled. In this scheme we do this at various points, decomposing an introductory project such as the Smoking Car [p26], Showing pupils a working copy of what they will create without showing them the code and asking them what they would need to create and what they would need to make it do. At the early stages this can be done verbally but it is important as projects become more complex to insist on written decomposition as we do in the Times Table Game [p142].

Abstraction

Abstraction is the skill of reducing complexity by hiding irrelevant detail and focussing on the most important element. This is a really useful computational skill as once the irrelevant detail has been stripped away computer scientists can focus on what really needs doing. Imagine I wanted to turn the card game Pairs into a computer game. The most important element is; you win if items are the same. This can be abstracted further into A = B win, A ≠ B lose. In the Music Abstraction module [p100], we use abstraction to turn a musical sound track on a video into an algorithm and then into musical programming in Scratch. We start by listening to a video and identifying all the elements on the video, singing, high and low pitch notes, moving pictures, backing track etc. We then look at what detail is important to turn into notes on Scratch and what is irrelevant. We ended up identifying pitch as the most important element to keep. We swapped to a much simpler music track where pitch was more obvious and listened to this to write a musical algorithm before converting this into code.[9]

Generalisation

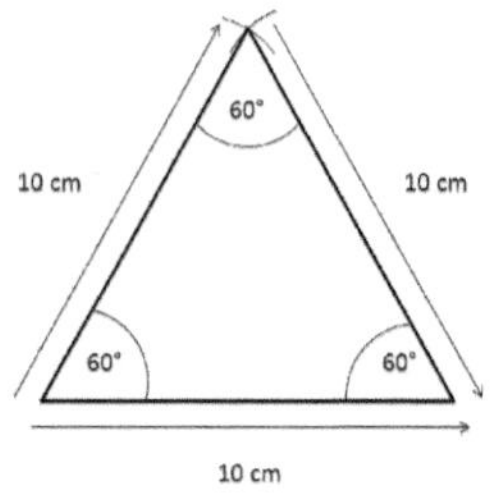
60°
10 cm
10 cm
60°
60°
10 cm

Generalisation is adapting a solution that solved one problem to solve another. In our abstraction example earlier we reduced matching pairs to A = B win A ≠ B lose. We could then use generalisation to adapt this solution to think about creating a quiz. In a quiz, if the answer we have thought of is the same as the user's answer we say it is correct. If the answer is not the same we say it is wrong. This is almost identical to A = B win A ≠ B lose, so we can adapt one solution to solve a similar problem. In our Scratch perimeter program [p157][10] we discover simple ways to calculate the perimeter of an equilateral triangle. Pupils then use the principle of generalisation to adapt this solution to calculate the perimeter of other regular 2D shapes.

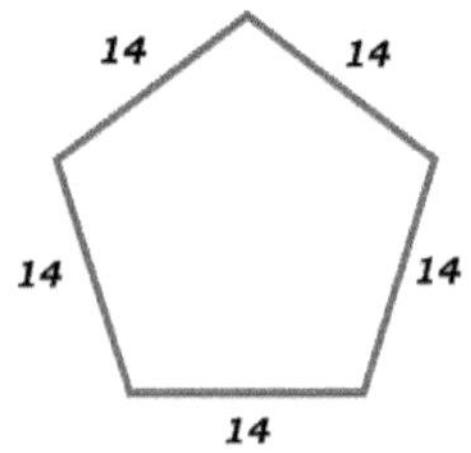
14
14
14
14
14

In KS1 we find mention of algorithms and logical reasoning. In KS2 we find decomposition and logical reasoning. In KS3 abstraction, algorithms and logical thinking are included. The National Curriculum is a minimum entitlement and in this book we will be making use of the full range of computational thinking skills when they are appropriate.

References

1 Computing National Curriculum https://www.gov.uk/government/publications/national-curriculum-in-england-computing-programmes-of-study

2. Wikipedia Computational Thinking http://en.wikipedia.org/wiki/Computational_thinking#cite_note-1

3. David Barr, John Harrison, and Leslie Conery (2011). "Computational Thinking: A Digital Age Skill for Everyone"

4. Seymour Papert mentions computational thinking but doesn't really expand what it means or call for these skills to be taught to all. However I haven't read all of his works so am happy to be corrected. He mentions computational thinking in "An exploration in the space of mathematics educations". International Journal of Computers for Mathematical Learning (1996) http://www.papert.org/articles/AnExplorationintheSpaceofMathematicsEducations.html I couldn't find a comprehensive treatment of computational thinking in this journal.

5. Jeanette Wing http://en.wikipedia.org/wiki/Jeannette_Wing

6. Jeanette M Wing Viewpoint (2006) https://www.cs.cmu.edu/~15110-s13/Wing06-ct.pdf

7. Professor Paul Curzon, Mark Dorling, Thomas Ng, Dr Cynthia Selby & Dr John Woollard (2014) Developing computational thinking in the classroom: a frameworkhttp://community.computingatschool.org.uk/resources/2324 (second document link on right)

8. Primary Games maker planning including decomposed games planner http://code-it.co.uk/scratch/primarygamesmaker/primarygamesmakeroverview

9. Scratch music as code planning http://code-it.co.uk/scratch/musicscore/musicscoreoverview

10. Scratch perimeter program http://code-it.co.uk/scratch/perimeter/perimeteroverview

0F. Computational Doing

Debugging and Resilience

Computing isn't just about thinking, it's about doing. Learning to program means learning how to think about a problem, design an algorithm and then translate that algorithm into a form that the computer will understand. Like any creative process, it has lots of steps and many potential mis-steps. One of THE MOST IMPORTANT skills in practical computing is to be able to spot your errors, your typing mistakes, your logical errors and your wrong assumptions and to correct them. Debugging (so-called because of the story that errors in 1940s computer programs were caused by bugs and moths flying into the computers and short-circuiting the valves) is a learned skill of logical thinking and deduction. E.B. White (the author of Charlotte's Web) said that "writing is rewriting" – it's just as true that "programming is debugging".

Debugging in the National Curriculum

Finding and fixing errors in algorithm and code is a key part of the new computing curriculum. Pupils are exhorted to *'create and debug simple programs'* in KS1 and *'detect and correct errors in algorithms and programs'* in KS2. This emphasis on the importance of a process is in stark contrast to many pupils experiences in ICT where the finished product was often seen as paramount. Debugging is an excellent way to promote independence, resilience and move pupils away from learned helplessness.

Don't debug for pupils

Everywhere I teach I have seen teachers jump in and debug things for pupils. I think this often comes from fear that something really has gone wrong combined with too heavy a focus on the finished product over the process. If you do this you are denying your pupils' essential problem-solving experiences and the opportunity to develop resilience. When I first started teaching Computer Science I had to train myself out of doing this. We need to facilitate pupils debugging themselves by suggesting strategies and giving them time to find errors themselves. Make it clear that you or their peers debugging their code or fixing their algorithms is not an option. The sense of achievement when they find errors is tangible. On a technical note we only debug code but I have heard pupils talk about debugging their sentences or maths problems and I don't correct their use of the word elsewhere as they have the essential sense of it.

It is normal to make mistakes in Computer Science

When I first started teaching programming a Y6 pupil burst into tears. When I enquired as to what was wrong she informed me that she had never made a mistake in ICT before. Apart from the obvious horror at discovering a pupil who had gone through the whole of primary education without ever having been stretched enough in ICT to make a mistake there is the need to reassure pupils that it is ok to make mistakes. I often find this can take quite a few weeks before pupils really believe me. As always they are judging to see if my words match up to my actions in the classroom. Once they realise that if is acceptable to make mistakes they take more risks and become better problem-solvers.

Praise Debugging and Problem-Solving

I save my highest praise for pupils who debug and problem-solve. I reward their resilience and problem-solving with stickers, or names on a wall display. On occasion I have had younger pupils deliberately make and fix bugs just to get recognised but as long as the habit of debugging combined with the idea of personal responsibility to fix things themselves is ingrained I am happy.

06. Combating Learned Helplessness

In my experience learned helplessness is particularly prevalent in Computing. Learned helplessness is a strategy for getting other people to solve problems for you. In the classroom, for pupils, these others may be the teacher, LSA, classroom assistant or other pupils.

In computing learned helplessness can be seen in various ways. Sweet helplessness often manifests to the teacher as a pupil putting on a sweet helpless voice and declaring they are stuck. Aggressive helplessness manifests with a cross tone and the implication that they think the work is 'stupid' or they don't get it. Being stuck is never a problem but if you ask what they are stuck on and the pupil cannot tell you or describe the problem or they give vague indications that they are stuck on everything then there is a good chance they are using learned helplessness to get you to solve their problem. Similar strategies will often be used with their peers, tailored to make the problem-solver feel valued, superior or pressured into helping.

The problem is that many teachers and pupils will respond to this strategy in computing by solving the problem for the pupil. Often excellent teachers, who wouldn't dream of doing work for pupils in other areas of the curriculum, will jump in and solve the problem for the pupil. The fact that so many pupils use learned helplessness suggests that it has been a successful strategy for many.

Getting someone else to do your work for you would be an issue in any subject, but it is the antithesis of Computer Science with its emphasis on problem-solving and debugging. In fact to solve a problem for a child is to deny them the opportunity to debug code or fix algorithm and as such is debilitating.

How has it become so prevalent in computing? I suspect that it has grown out of teacher fear or unfamiliarity with the subject material coupled with a belief that pupils know more about technology than adults combined with an emphasis on the finished product rather than the process. All of these factors lead teachers to fix things for pupils rather than steer them to find solutions for themselves.

Steps to counter learned helplessness

1. Establish a positive class attitude towards problem solving. Computer Science is very useful in that it calls errors bugs and finding errors debugging. Although all bugs are caused by humans, the language is much more impersonal than mistakes which imply blame or fault. Using bug and debugging language is helpful. It is also important to let pupils know that mistakes/bugs are a normal part of computing, that they are to be expected, that professional programmers write code that have bugs all the time and that you will not be cross or upset if their work has bugs/mistakes. This for me is a mantra for new classes for the first few weeks and once they know I mean it there is a collective sigh of relief!
2. Promote the idea that it is not your job to fix their algorithms or debug their code. It is your job to promote useful strategies that they can use to fix things themselves and we will come onto those very soon. So when they come to you they know they are looking for strategies to find and fix things themselves.

3. Challenge pupils' helplessness and expose it for what it is. I have asked pupils' "are you trying to get me to fix your code?" "Are you trying to get me to solve the problem for you?" In the same way that we couldn't move on until we recognised the issue, some pupils won't either. Of course good teachers do this tactfully, and with regards to pupils' known issues, but an element of challenge is inevitable to identify the issue.

4. Recruit your pupils to combat helplessness. Encourage the class to join you in this by putting a ban on doing things for other people. They can describe what to do but are not allowed to do it for them or give them a full solution to programming solutions. As you model this they will reflect this attitude to their peers. Having a ban on touching anyone else's mouse, keyboard or touchscreen is a good start. I often compare this to writing in someone else's maths or literacy exercise book.

5. Move pupils away from language that personifies digital machines. "My computer hates me," is typical. Computers are deterministic which means that if all the inputs are the same you will always get the same output. Personification encourages pupils to think that an answer might not be available due to the capriciousness of the machine, an attitude that is anti-problem solving and frankly incorrect.

6. Don't neglect the other adults in the class, all your good work could be being undone by your LSA or classroom assistant. Train them to help using good strategies and hints rather than solutions. Each module has useful debugging strategies share these with support staff before the lesson. If you are providing training on the new curriculum don't neglect your class room assistants, they are important.

7. Explain why resilience is important. Unless pupils know why this life skill is important they won't value it.

8. Finally you may notice learned helplessness in teachers and learning support assistants. Is it worth the hassle to challenge this? As a parent I know that my children don't do what I say but what I do. I lead mostly by example or lack of it as my wife will testify. This is just as true in the classroom or computer suite. Of course we need to be tactful and recognise the good practice of teachers and the excellent problem solving strategies in other curriculum areas, but if we don't identify the problem, nothing will change. I have found that talking about my own struggle to change has enabled others to do likewise.

Scratch Debugging Strategies

Possible teacher responses to encourage debugging in brackets:

Comparing their code with that of their neighbour or teacher to see if it is the same.

Looking for simple colour differences if using blocks. (Are the colours of your blocks the same as the colours of teachers or neighbours?)

Looking for different shapes. (Are your code blocks the same shape as teachers or neighbours)

Looking for things that are missing (How many blocks have you got, is that the same as teachers or neighbours?)

Looking for patterns and shapes in the blocks. (Is your block shape the same as teachers or neighbours?)

Pupils read code aloud to see if it does what they wanted it to do.

Pupils read code to a partner to see if it sounds right or is in the right order.

Pupils read code to see if it is the same as teacher or peer. (Why not read teacher's or peer's code. Now read your code, are they the same?)

Teachers read code written in abbreviations in full.

Pupils ask questions of the code that doesn't work. These can take the form of asking a question such as "if I do *x* why doesn't *y* happen?" Or "why doesn't this code section work all of the time?" (Teachers often need to model these before pupils will think to ask them themselves.)

Pupils step through more complex code which could include loops, selection and variables. They describe to a peer or teacher what is happening in each stage. (Can you describe to your partner what is happening in each step of your code, point to it as you describe it)

A variation on stepping through is to list what is happening at each stage. This is particularly useful when dealing with multiple variables or variables which change within loops. (Can you list what is happening inside each variable after each repeat?)

Pupils use divide and conquer where they break up longer sequences of code and run parts of it separately to try and find out where the error is. This strategy can be difficult to use if parts of the code are dependent on other parts functioning correctly. (Can you save your work and then split it up into parts and run each part separately to try to find the bug?) (Run each block one at a time: is there any block that is not working as you thought it should?)

Pupils explain the code out loud to an inanimate object. This is often called rubber ducking.

There is a pupil version of these in the beginning of each pupil workbook.

Providing Hints not Solutions

On a practical note, if you have provided a debugging hint, walk away from the pupil. If you linger, pupils will delay using the hint just in case you provide a better one or give them a full solution. If you are not clear what the bug is, use a tablet or phone to take a quick photo of the screen. You can then examine this away from the child to inform your next hint.

0H. Programming elements of the National Curriculum Expanded

- Sequence
- Selection
- Repetition
- Variables
- Input and outputs
- Control or simulate physical systems

Sequence

Sequence (FIRST do this THEN do that THEN do the other) is the most basic programming idea. All programming will have some form of sequence even if these are as basic as linking a key to a single action. Basic doesn't mean simple though as the context of any code gives it its complexity.

pen down
move 50 steps
turn 90 degrees
move 50 steps
turn 90 degrees
move 50 steps
turn 90 degrees
move 50 steps
turn 90 degrees
move 50 steps
turn 90 degrees

*What shape would this sequence draw?

**Stairs but many teachers and students after a quick glance will say a square.*

Repetition

Repetition or loops are a way of repeating an element or elements many times. The use of repetition makes a program more efficient by reducing the number of programming elements. It helps to use real life loops such as those found in music or dance to introduce repetition.

Loops are either repeated a specific number of times, or until a predetermined condition is reached. Scratch also uses a non-terminating loop called a forever loop. Programming elements inside this loop continue to loop until the program or programming block are stopped.

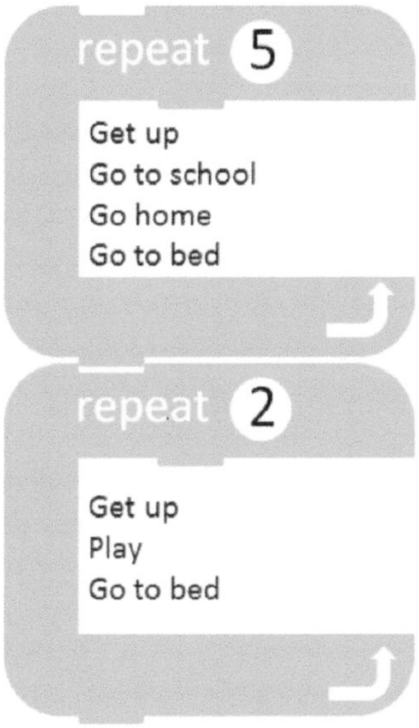
repeat 5
Get up
Go to school
Go home
Go to bed
repeat 2
Get up
Play
Go to bed

A school week in repeat loops

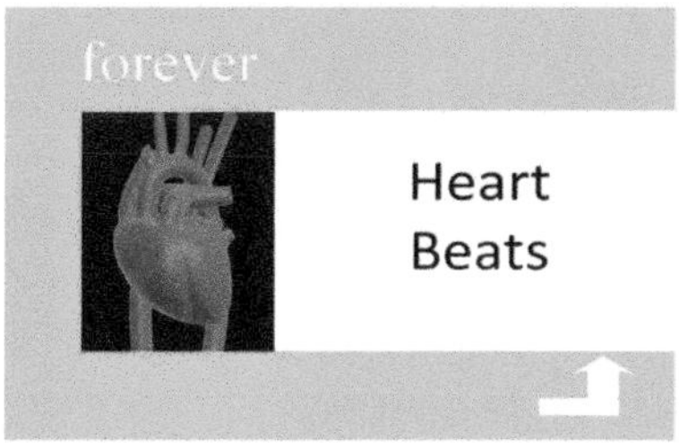
forever
Heart
Beats

A forever loop in the real world

This would be considered an error in any other programming language where the norm would be to have a while loop that would have a means of exiting the loop built in. Removing the exit condition means that younger pupils can use this type of loop at an earlier stage. Scratch has this type of terminating on a condition loop as well, called a repeat until loop.

Selection

Selection is about choice – a program can decide to take different pathways depending on current conditions. Scratch has two conditional selection blocks.

In the simplest *if* selection block a piece of code is run *if the condition is* met. If the condition is *not met* then the code is ignored.

In the *if else* selection block if the condition is met the top if code is run but *if* the condition is not met the bottom *else* code is run.

if key right arrow pressed?
turn 15 degrees

If the key right arrow is pressed turn right 15 degrees: if the key is not pressed then nothing happens

if key space pressed?
turn 15 degrees
else
turn 15 degrees

Either **if** or **else** will be run

Forever if

Scratch 1.4 has a hybrid block called a *forever if* block that combines a *forever* loop with an *if* selection block. I never use these as it is far better to combine a *forever* loop with an *if* block. It makes more sense to your pupils to start with the if block and then add a *forever* loop if you want it checked over and over again. Scratch 2.0 doesn't include this block.

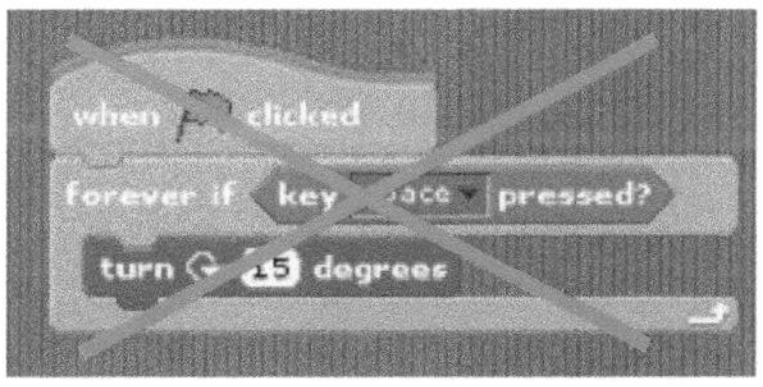
when clicked
pressed?
degrees

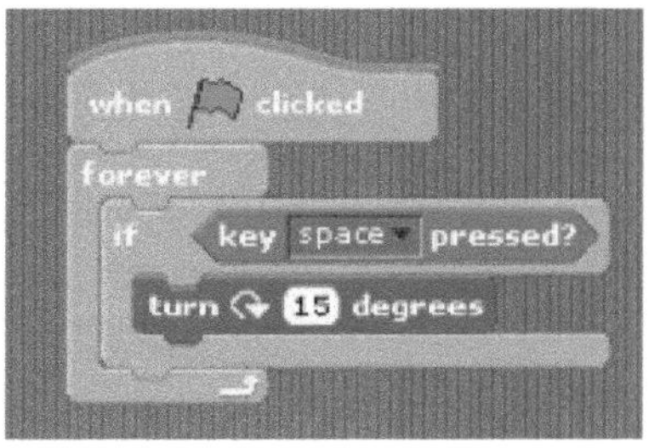
when clicked
forever
if key space pressed?
turn 15 degrees

Variables

Variables are spaces in the computer memory where information is held. They can be named whatever the programmer wants although it is useful to name them after what you want them to do. They can hold numbers or text. Once a variable has been set up and information put inside, the program remembers what is inside and can use it just by referring to the variable name. If a number is stored inside a variable it can be changed by a mathematical operation.

Inputs and Outputs

Inputs are pieces of information that are put into a computer or digital device. A keyboard, mouse or touch screen is an input device. An output is just a way of getting information out of a digital device such as a screen, printer and speakers.

Control or Simulate Physical Systems

*Can you spot the design flaw with this otherwise excellent fan?

This book includes three modules that control physical systems using the Scratch programming language and Lego Wedo. The Toilet Fan involves pupils designing a Lego fan and then programming it to respond to different stimulus including a distance sensor.

The car barrier involves pupils designing and creating a car park barrier and then programming it to raise and lower slowly responding to a range of different inputs.

Finally the tilt switch encourages pupils to use a tilt switch inside a variety of projects of their own choosing

> If schools can't afford Lego Wedo then I recommend Crumble, a cheap programming board that can control up to two motors and respond to a range of different inputs. At the time of going to press Crumble doesn't work directly with Scratch but uses a free Scratch inspired program.

For more Crumble teaching resources see
http://code-it.co.uk/crumble/crumble

You can buy the Crumble from
http://redfernelectronics.co.uk/crumble/

**Answer: The fan blade is far too near the user's Lego head*

01. Design Strategies

The projects in this book all draw out aspects of computational thinking. As you can see from the programming design elements diagram, they also start from a variety of different starting points to help pupils build up a range of programming and thinking skills. Where a formal algorithm is used, created or adapted this can take many forms such as the symbols used within Training Your Computer To Do Maths or flowcharts used in the Coin Sorter or Clock. Some projects such as the Slug Trail game are clearly at the teacher's direction whereas projects like the selection investigation and primary games maker has a much higher element of pupil ideas and exploration.

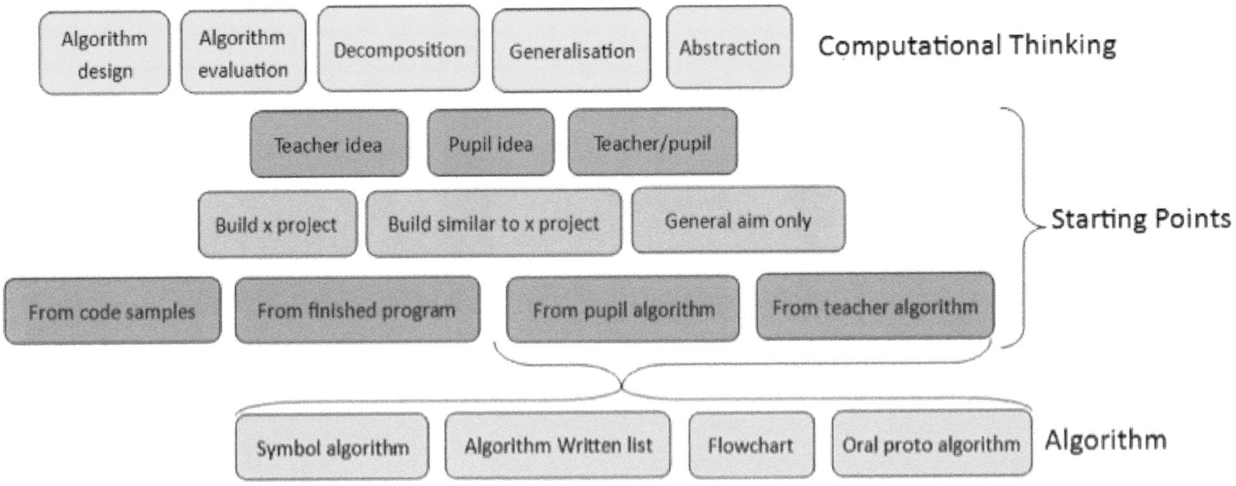
Algorithm design
Algorithm evaluation
Decomposition
Generalisation
Abstraction
Computational Thinking
Teacher idea
Pupil idea
Teacher/pupil
Build x project
Build similar to x project
General aim only
Starting Points
From code samples
From finished program
From pupil algorithm
From teacher algorithm
Symbol algorithm
Algorithm Written list
Flowchart
Oral proto algorithm
Algorithm

Programming design elements found in this scheme of work

0J. Teaching Methods

New concepts are often introduced through direct instruction: the author has found that it is rare for a pupil to independently discover how more complex ideas such as changing a variable inside a loop or how to use selection or manipulate variables without seeing concrete examples first. However, it is important to move to re-purposing or exploration soon after, as these challenge pupils to use ideas in other contexts and help the teacher to ascertain what has really been understood. It is also important to let pupils know that if they have completed the directed task set, including any extensions, then it is good for them to explore aspects independently as long as it is not in the same code block. This means that if they generate code that doesn't work they can disable it by detaching the start block. Most of the projects have exploration or re-purposing time built in. Don't be tempted to reduce this time as it what motivates pupils and gets them self-studying.

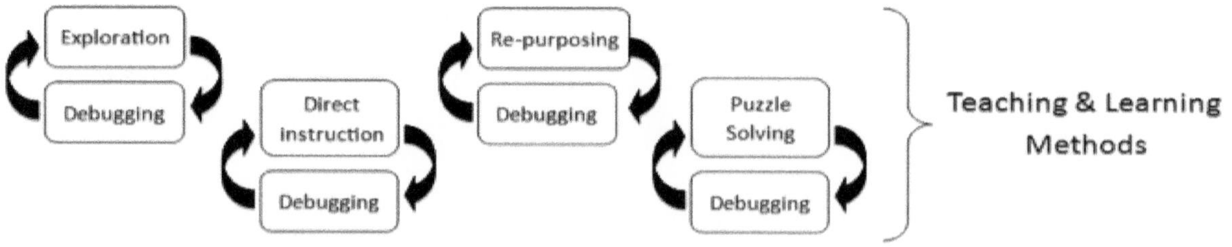
Exploration
Debugging
Direct instruction
Debugging
Re-purposing
Debugging
Puzzle Solving
Debugging
Teaching & Learning Methods

Balance between Direct Instruction & Exploration/Re-purposing

Direct instruction assumes that you as the teacher are driving the learning forward by introducing new concepts and methods. Exploration and re-purposing give pupils the chance to discover nuance, consolidate learning and make it their own. Too much direct instruction without enough exploration or re-purposing leads to shallow learning, concepts grasped at but not fully internalised. Conversely, too much exploration without a hard enough challenge leads to tinkering in the traditional understanding of the word "an unskilled worker." Unskilled because they don't have enough tools or ideas in their toolkit to achieve anything substantial. Most of my work in the last year has been fine - tuning this balance across a range of schools and this book is the result.

0k. Maths Complexity

Although Maths concepts used in this book are broadly in line with the Maths National Curriculum, there are occasions where some pupils may use a concept before being secure in this area in Maths. In these cases you are providing a layer of understanding often linked to a concrete application which will aid their understanding in the future. For example, pupils who have explored and listened to the length of a note using tenths in the Music Machine module undoubtedly have a greater understanding of the difference between 0.2 and 0.5. This type of knowledge enriches their mathematical understanding.

You may notice that there are no projects that directly investigate angles of shapes in this book. This is for two reasons. Firstly, Scratch is often not the best programming language for this as sprites bounce off the edges of the screen obscuring programming that is mathematically correct. In my opinion Logo is far better for this type of work. Secondly, teachers and pupils need to be clear that in Maths you will be measuring the internal angle (a) but in computing you are using a part of the external angle (b). This is not insurmountable and could make a good exploration of the differences but does add extra complexity to the task.

Modules with a clear Maths focus such as the Coordinates module are often best taught following on from using these within Maths lessons if at all possible.

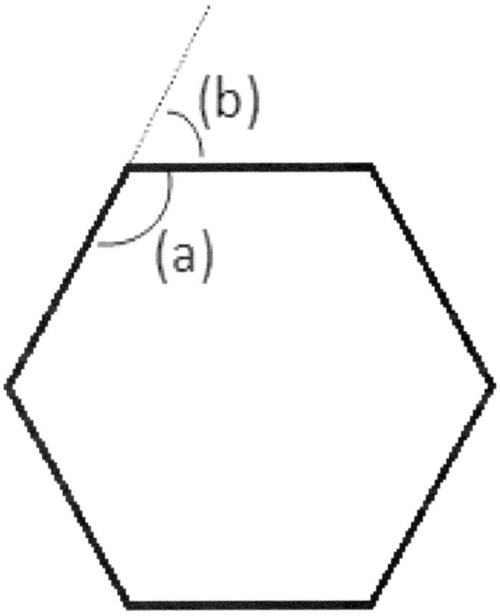
(b)
(a)

FMS logo can be downloaded from

http://sourceforge.net/projects/fmslogo/

Work through projects first

As a computing inspector I occasionally encounter a teacher who picks up Computing planning three minutes before the lesson and then attempts to wing it. The reason Computer Science is included in the National Curriculum is because it is challenging and thought provoking. You will need to create these projects yourself before teaching them if you are not to be left floundering. You don't need to be the expert who knows everything, in fact that can be counterproductive, but you do need to be a fellow learner engaged alongside your pupils with the programming and thinking behind it.

01. Versions of Scratch

Practical Issues with Scratch

Scratch has two versions: 1.4 which MIT have been refining since 2007 and 2.0 which came out in May 2013. Scratch 1.4, the older version, is available as a program download for Windows, Mac and Linux from the Scratch website at https://scratch.mit.edu/scratch_1.4/. Unlike Scratch 2.0 it will work in 800 x 600 resolution and therefore is better for schools that purchased netbooks with limited screen size or older data projectors that are clearest in the lower resolution. This author would contend that the painting editor is also easier for younger pupils to use. This progression uses 1.4 in Years 3 and 4 before switching to Scratch 2.0 for Years 5 and 6 but teachers will find that either version can be used for all year groups' projects with a little adaptation.

Scratch 2.0 is available online on an up to date browser. Users can use Scratch 2.0 online either by setting up a free account or by accessing the program without logging on. Whilst logged on with a free Scratch community account files are saved online. If used without an account files must be downloaded before the browser is closed or work is lost. The offline version of Scratch 2.0 can be downloaded for free here http://scratch.mit.edu/scratch2download/. It needs Adobe Air installed first but the instructions are easy to follow. As the current version is always being updated, pupils and staff will get used to requests to update the program, which for most locked down school networks is not a real option.

Online Community

Scratch has a vibrant online community where projects can be shared and other peoples' projects modified. It is a good idea as a teacher of pupils in lower KS2 to setup your own teacher account and use this to upload pupils' work to embed or link to on your school website. Pupils can create programs in 1.4 and these will be converted to Scratch 2.0 when uploaded to the online community. In upper KS2 you can either help pupils to set up their own accounts after seeking parents' approval or notify parents and pupils and encourage them to do this at home. Pupils who don't want an online account can always use the offline editor meaning no one is disadvantaged. The site is good natured as rude or abusive commenters are blocked and banned. You can join or login from this page https://scratch.mit.edu/.

Limitations

Scratch 2.0 has the ability for the user to create a procedure that can be used repeatedly. However, this is not a fully working function that returns data back into the original script/block. Working with a limited set of blocks by definition limits choice although on the whole I think MIT have done an excellent job of keeping the essentials without overpowering the user. All programming choices/blocks are on display. This is great when pupils are exploring as armed with curiosity and reading skills, basic functions unfold. However it can also be harder to focus pupils on the elements you want them to explore.

> I still use Logo when exploring angles of 2d shapes as pupils can be easily limited to a lesser set of code.

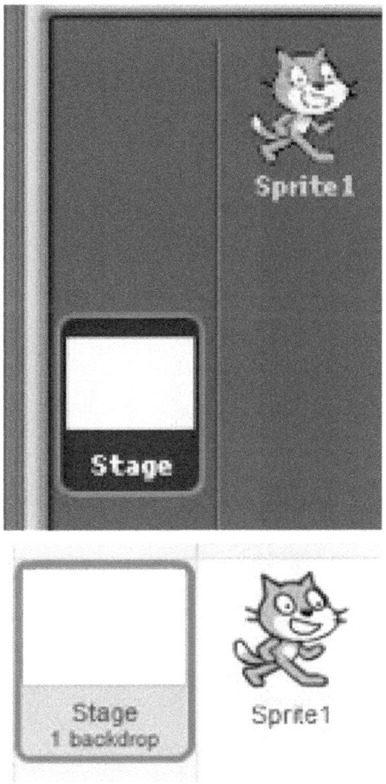
Sprite1
Stage
Stage
1 backdrop
Sprite1

Stage and Sprite are very close and it is easy to draw something on the stage and then be left looking at the stage scripts area

Common errors every teacher should know about

Every pupil will click on *stage* and wonder where their code has gone. This is easily fixed by asking them if they are programming the stage or the sprite.

Every child will "lose" their sprite as it moves off the visible stage or is hidden by the hide block. This is very easy to remedy in Scratch 1.4 as you can right click on the sprite icon and click *show*. In Scratch 2.0 drag out a go to x:0 y:0 motion block and click on it.

Lots of children will delete a sprite mid-project to replace it with a "better" one, thus deleting all their code. If pupils have just deleted their sprite, then click on *edit* and *undelete* will restore the last action. In the early sessions it is easier to ban changing sprites mid-project than cope with the ramifications of deleted work.

show
export this sprite
duplicate
delete
Sprites
info
duplicate
delete
save to local file
show
Sprite1

Right click and select *show* to view a hidden sprite

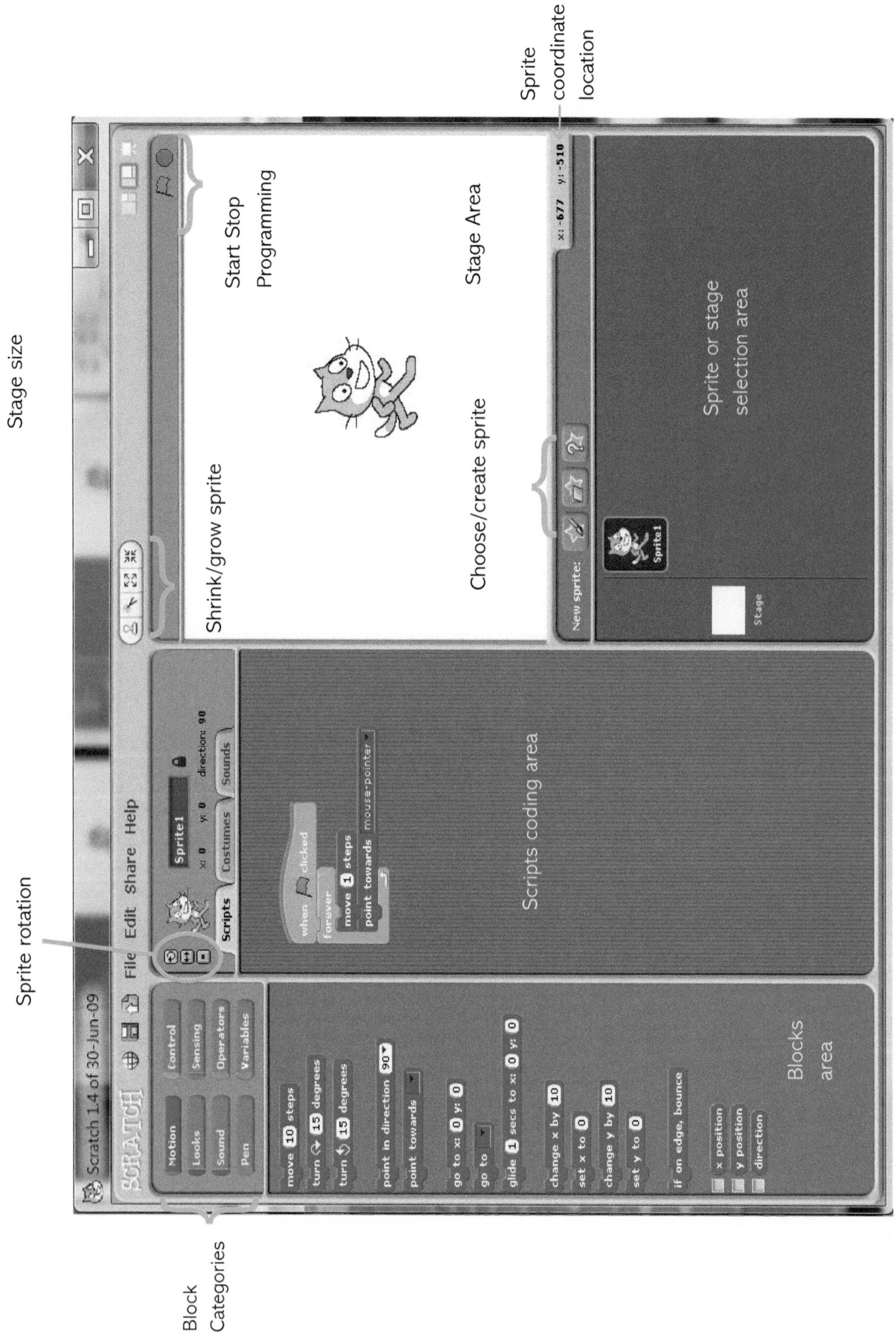
Stage size
Sprite rotation
Block Categories
Shrink/grow sprite
Start Stop Programming
Stage Area
Choose/create sprite
Sprite coordinate location
Sprite or stage selection area
Scripts coding area
Blocks area
Scratch 1.4 of 30-Jun-09
File Edit Share Help
Motion Looks Sound Pen
Control Sensing Operators Variables
Sprite1
Scripts Costumes Sounds
New sprite:
Stage

Scratch 1.4

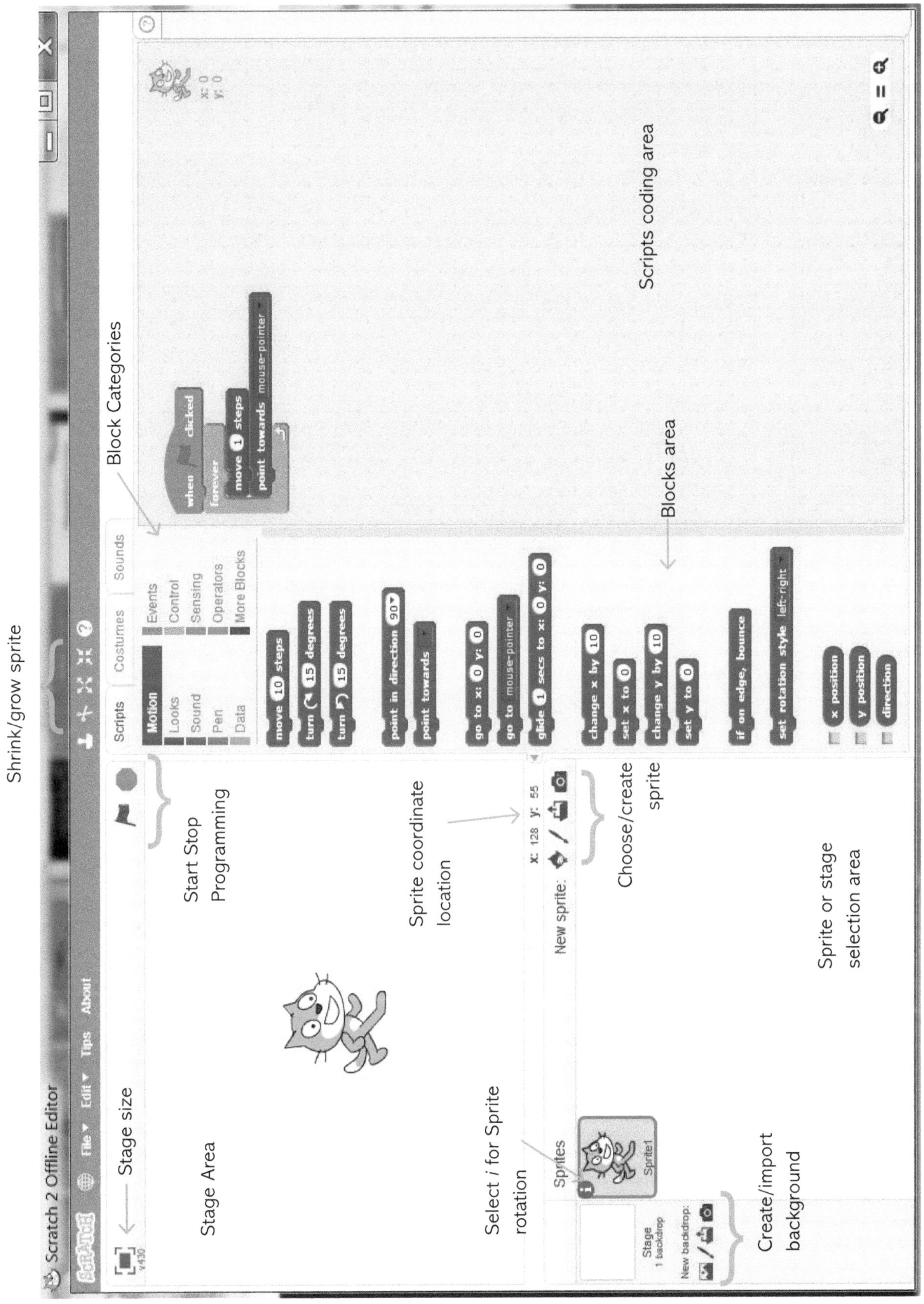
Shrink/grow sprite
Stage size
Stage Area
Start Stop Programming
Sprite coordinate location
Select i for Sprite rotation
Choose/create sprite
Create/import background
Sprite or stage selection area
Block Categories
Blocks area
Scripts coding area

Scratch 2.0

0M. Module Overview

Name	Brief Description
Smoking Car	A simple game to move a car around a screen leaving a smoky trail as it goes.
Music Machine	Explore the wonderful world of sound by creating your own music machine.
Conversation	Gossip, argument, discussion, persuasive pitch. You decide the focus of this simple conversation.
Interactive Display	Turning facts learnt in any subject into an interactive display that could be uploaded to your school website.
Dressing Up Game	Click on the character to see their costume change. Or click on their accessories to see them animate or change colour.
Year 3 Assessment	Design a program based on the ideas learnt in previous modules.
Maths Quiz	Create a scoring quiz.
Music Algorithm to Music Code	Follow musical notation to program Twinkle Twinkle Little Star before choosing your own musical notation to decipher.
Slug Trail Game	Can you keep the slug inside the track? There will be consequences if you can't!
Selection Investigation	Discover lots of the features of Scratch as you investigate what happens when your character touches a colour.
Train your Computer to do Maths	Train your computer to add, subtract, multiply and divide. Break up a more complex maths problem and solve it with the power of programming.
Counting Machine	Train the computer to count in whole numbers, fractions, backwards etc before creating a countdown timer for your teacher.
Music Abstraction	Discover what is important and what is not when you convert a music video into Scratch notes.
Random Word	Create random words that follow real spelling patterns, program multiple story starts using the same code or just gaze into the future and choose a job for everyone.
Coin Program	Program a function machine that sorts money totals into all the correct coins and notes.
Crab Maze	Can the crab make it through the maze collecting coins as it goes? Will it make it to the next level or will it hit the maze wall and end the game?
Toilet Fan	Design and build a Lego fan model before programming it to turn on when someone approaches the toilet and off when they leave.
Angle Sorter	Type in the number of degrees your angle has and the program will tell you what type of angle it is and its properties. It may even draw it.
Car Park Barrier	Design and build a Lego car park barrier before programming it to lift when it senses a car approaching.
Times Table Game	Can you click on the moving balls which are part of the table in question and earn points or will you click the wrong ball and lose points?
Perimeter Program	Design and create a program that calculates perimeters of regular shapes.
Clock	Program a working digital and analogue clock.
Cartesian Coordinates	Practise plotting Cartesian coordinates before turning them into Scratch code that draws the shapes you planned. Simply the best Cartesian coordinates supporting activity there is!

Translation, Enlargement & Rotation	Don't just stop at plotting coordinates in all four quadrants discover the power of translation, enlargement and rotation.
Primary Games Maker	Design and program a complex game based around either a platform game, scrolling background game or snail trail game. Be astounded by the ability of all pupils to adapt, repurpose and invent with Scratch.
Tilt Switch	Here is a tilt switch. This is how it works. What can you do with it? Sit back and watch the fun!
Chatbot	Compete against your classmates to design a program that interacts with the user like a human.

ON. Module Dependency Chart

Whilst it is possible to take some of the modules and teach them independently from each other, pupils will get the most out this scheme of work where concepts are built up gradually. The module dependency chart will help you plan your own route.

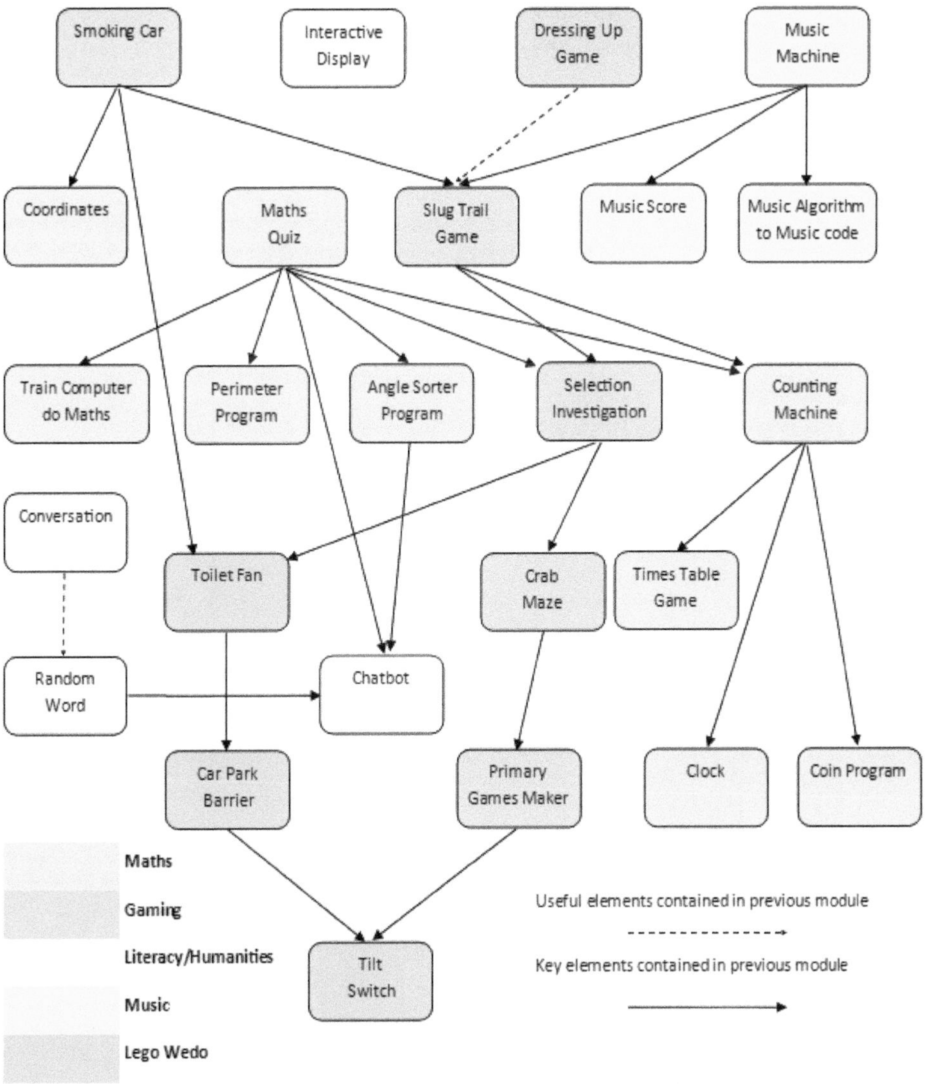
Smoking Car
Interactive Display
Dressing Up Game
Music Machine
Coordinates
Maths Quiz
Slug Trail Game
Music Score
Music Algorithm to Music code
Train Computer do Maths
Perimeter Program
Angle Sorter Program
Selection Investigation
Counting Machine
Conversation
Toilet Fan
Crab Maze
Times Table Game
Random Word
Chatbot
Car Park Barrier
Primary Games Maker
Clock
Coin Program
Tilt Switch
Maths
Gaming
Literacy/Humanities
Music
Lego Wedo
Useful elements contained in previous module
Key elements contained in previous module

0o. Progresion Chart

Algorithm	Algorithm (programming) Evaluation	Decomposition	Generalisation	Pattern Spotting	Abstraction
Write simple sequence algorithms using words. (Maths Quiz) read and decode musical algorithms (Music Score) use rules algorithms	Identify if an algorithm does what you want it to do. Is Scratch conversation easy to read?	Observe a working program and decompose its elements as a class (Smoking Car, Slug Maze)	Recognise where an idea is adapted and used again as directed by the teacher (Perimeter)	Spot patterns in algorithm or code and continue the patterns (Coin Machine, program a clock)	Define all the elements in something and then remove the ones that are not needed (Music as code)
Read and follow algorithms with selection and repetition (Number Machine)	Recognise that there is more than one algorithm to do the same thing (Smoking Car movement)	Observe a working program and decompose its elements as an individual (Tables Game)	Pupil chooses to adapt ideas that they have used to solve similar problems (Selection investigation, primary games maker, Random word)		
Complete unfinished algorithms with selection and or repetition (Coins sorter, Program a clock)	Recognise that one algorithm may be better (less instructions)	Create a program by decomposing it into parts and solving parts separately (Primary games maker)			
Create an algorithm with selection or repetition	Design an algorithm/code for a specific person or group of people (design a Scratch program for younger pupils)				
	Evaluate more complex code that does the same thing (Scratch code with loops and without)		Light Yellow Column Heading Indicates more complex aspects that are introduced after Year 3	Reading the Grid Aspects that are in the same row are not of equivalent difficulty	Reading the Grid Top row skills are the easiest becoming harder as you move downwards

'atch sign	Sequence	Selection	Repetition	Variable Use	Input Output	Debugging
lowing :ructions :reate ıoking ; Music chine, ıssing Up ne)	Create sequence of simple code that can be easily read	Use single simple selection condition	Create simple repeat x times loop (music machine)	Variable used to hold number or word and reported (Quiz, Counting machine)	Simple inputs (keys, mouse click, switch etc) control on or off (Lego Wedo toilet fan, car park barrier)	Identify where in the code or algorithm bug/ problem occurs
d small ı critical ıptations ıoking ; Music chine, ıssing Up ne)	Create multiple sequences running concurrently (Scratch music machine notes and beat in separate blocks)	Create selection within a loop (Slug maze, selection investigation)	Create non terminating continuous (forever) loop (making sprite move slug maze, selection investigation, crab maze)	Multiple non connected variables used	Changing state other than on off such as fast slow bright dim etc (Lego Wedo toilet fan, car park barrier)	Debug simple sequence errors independently
ıpt a given sign for a v teacher en purpose nes Tables ne)	Create sequences or multiple sequences where timing is critical (control sprite on Times Tables Game)	Use single maths operator condition within selection (Maths quiz)	Loops within loops for a reason (clock)	Variables that change inside a loop (Counting machine)	Use sensors to control or report (Lego Wedo tilt switch)	Debug simple repetition, selection & variable errors independently
ɔurposing ıs for a il chosen ɔose ection stigation, ıary games ker)		Multiple selection beyond if and else (perimeter)	Create and use loops that terminates when condition met (repeat until loop in coin program)	Variables interacting with other variables (train computer to do maths)		Debug repetition, selection & variable errors independently
		Multiple conditions using AND OR NOT (Maths Quiz extension)				Dividing up code to find where the error is or running Scratch sets of blocks separately

Pupil Progression

We need to build up pupils' understanding gradually regardless of their age. When I first started teaching Computer Science I attempted far too complex programming projects with upper KS2 pupils with no prior knowledge. Since those disasters I have built up knowledge incrementally starting all pupils with the Smoking Car and Music Machine before moving on to the Maths Quiz and Slug Trail Game regardless of their age. These take less time with older pupils but they build basic understanding necessary to make real progress later on. This also makes it easier to roll out training for teachers following a model of Continuing Professional Development training followed by teaching, reflection and then more CPD.

Gender Balance in Computing

Traditionally a very small percentage of women have found jobs in the tech industries. Whilst we can't hope to address all the issues that discourages them in primary schools we can make a good start. I have noticed that a greater percentage of boys than girls are excited about gaming projects. This is one of the reasons that I ensure that gaming is only one of my programming strands. Many of my boys treat the computer as a toy to be played with whilst a greater proportion of my girls see it as a tool and this is often reflected in the programming projects they seek to create independently. I am always careful to make sure that I am consistent in my approach to all my students and that I am not enforcing stereotypes by solving problems for my girls whilst challenging my boys to think for themselves.

Op. Assessment

To aid our understanding of pupil progression and help with assessment I have included an adapted version of my progression grid[1] focussing on KS2 and Scratch on page 22 and 23.[2]

I have purposely not tried to create these into any sort of levels. Skills and knowledge in the same row may not be of equivalent difficulty. Yellow headed columns indicate skills that are not introduced in Year 3 and start in later years.

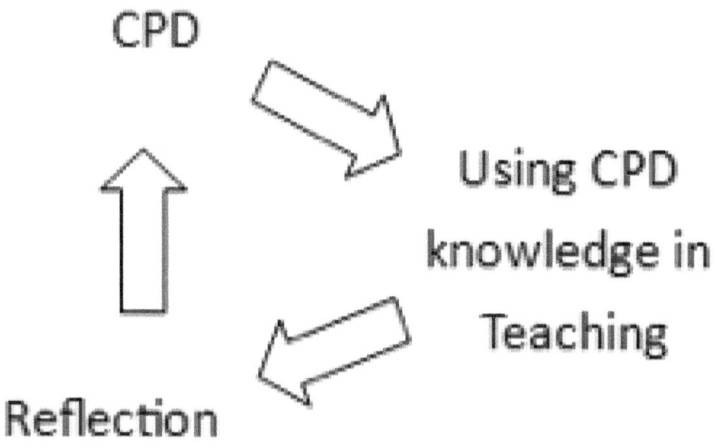
CPD
Using CPD knowledge in Teaching
Reflection

CPD Training Triangle

[1] http://code-it.co.uk/assessment-progression/

[2] For more advice on inclusion in computing see CAS Include http://casinclude.org.uk/

Pupil Self-Assessment

The most important thing to start assessing straight away is pupil progress and understanding within each lesson. To this purpose you will find a learning objective and pupil feedback sheet in the pupil workbook for each module. Pupils annotate these with smiley faces at the end of each lesson to help teachers determine who needs more support or challenge in the next lesson. Teachers can also annotate these in the top right corner circle if pupils needed lots of extra support or were discovering new things to use or re-use.

End of Module Assessment

At the end of each module I also record an average attainment based on the programming seen and pupils' feedback. These can be tracked in a spreadsheet[1] to record an average across the year and help with report writing.

End of Year Assessments

In Year 3 there is an open-ended assessment and in Year 4 the selection investigation provides good information about what pupils can achieve independently. In Year 5 there is no obvious end of year assessment and I normally use an aggregate of all modules used. In Year 6 the obvious choice is the primary games maker as pupils will need to use many of the computational thinking skills independently to succeed. The Chatbot could also be used in Year 6 if you didn't want to use the gaming strand.

Final Word

Over the last three years every day has been a privilege to encourage pupils to become resilient independent problem-solvers through the wonderful medium of Scratch programming. Pupils never fail to surprise me with their enthusiasm for programming, willingness to self-learn and speed they move from users to creators. I hope you and your pupils enjoy the modules and become infected with the digital maker bug. Remember nothing worthwhile was ever created quickly, vive la struggle!

Phil Bagge

[1]Recording progress spreadsheet http://code-it.co.uk/wp-content/uploads/2015/08/ScratchComputingAssessmentKS2.xlsx

1A. Smoking Car Puzzle Game

Time to complete module

3-4 hours

National Curriculum Programs of Study

Pupils should be taught to:

- ***design, write and debug programs that accomplish specific goals,*** including controlling or simulating physical systems; ***solve problems by decomposing them into smaller parts***
- ***use sequence***, selection, and repetition in programs; work with variables and ***various forms of input and output***
- ***use logical reasoning*** to explain how some simple algorithms work and ***to detect and correct errors in algorithms and programs***

Debugging Hints

Compare teacher code with pupil's code. Read code aloud. Hand out debugging cards.

Computational Thinking

Decomposition: breaking a program into smaller chunks and solving each chuck separately

Module Aim Create a car that travels round a roadway emitting smoke as it goes. Can the user keep the smoke trail on the roadway?

Module Learning Focus

- By the end of the module children will be able to:
- Write code to create a simple game
- Begin to break processes down into smaller parts (decomposition)
- Learn simple techniques for debugging
- Learn new Computer Science terms such as bug and debugging
- Create code using keyboard inputs

Assessment for Learning

At the end of each session direct pupils to page 4 of pupil workbook 1 to help them reflect on what they have learnt. It is often worth working through this line by line to avoid pupils filling in everything with a smiley face. You can also annotate this during the lesson to record pupils who have needed much more support or have demonstrated greater understanding.

Computer Science Concepts

- Using keyboard inputs to control aspects of the game
- Simple Sequence of code

Maths Concepts

Up, Down, Left & Right link to degrees (0, 90, 180 & -90).
Move distances negative number for reverse.

Adult Focus

All adults need to be clear that they are to support using hints only and not solve things for pupils.

Resources

Print out and fold three copies of every card to help pupils debug their work. These can be found after the planning.

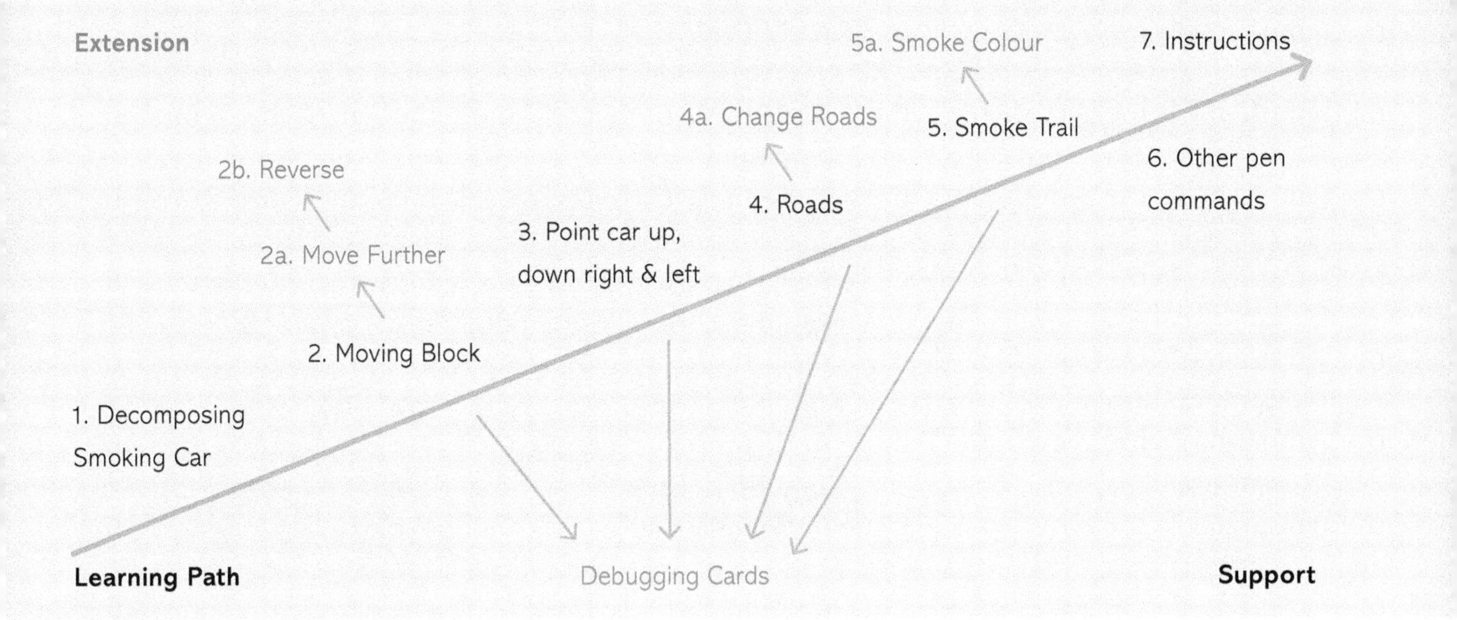
Extension
5a. Smoke Colour
7. Instructions
4a. Change Roads
5. Smoke Trail
2b. Reverse
6. Other pen commands
4. Roads
3. Point car up, down right & left
2a. Move Further
2. Moving Block
1. Decomposing Smoking Car
Learning Path
Debugging Cards
Support

1. Decomposing Smoking Car

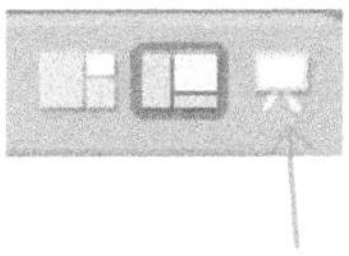

Presentation mode

Download the Scratch 1.4 file from http://code-it.co.uk/bookmedia or navigate to http://scratch.mit.edu/projects/43651270/. Put the program into presentation mode so the code cannot be seen. Explain to your pupils that before they can make a game like this one they will need to think through what objects they will need to make and what they will need to make those objects do. You can do this with the class, listing all the elements on a whiteboard or use the decompose planner from page 5 of pupils workbook 1. You will need to play the game lots of times and describe what keys you are pressing.

2. Create a moving block

Choose new sprite from file

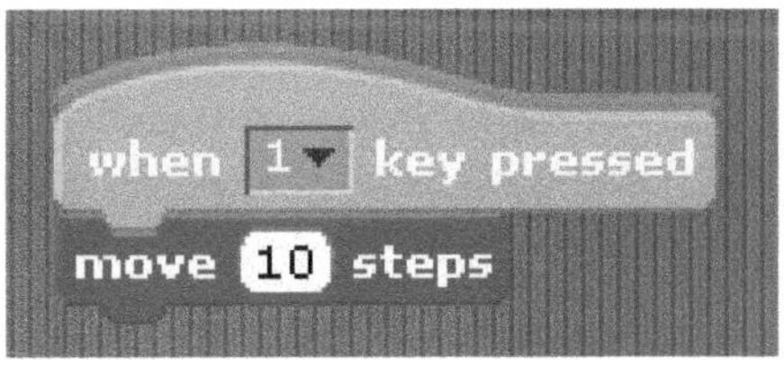
when 1 key pressed
move 10 steps

First demonstrate how to import the car sprite by choosing new sprite from file. Remind pupils that this is an object they decomposed earlier. Throughout the module link each stage to their initial decomposition. Open the star folder called choose new sprite from file then open the Transportation folder. Then drag out a keyboard input block and a Move 10 steps block. Show pupils how a white snap-to line appears when you join blocks together. Demonstrate how to snap the blocks together carefully and change the *space* key to a *1* using the black triangle menu. Get the whole class to read the block together. Encourage pupils to test their code before asking for an extension activity.

2a. Move Further Extension

Ask pupils who have created a move block and tested it to create more blocks where:

the 2 keyboard input moves 20 and the 3 key moves 30. Make sure pupils know that these should be separate blocks of code which are not attached to the first block of code.

2b. Reverse

Can they also make another block of code that moves the car backwards?

Before moving onto the steering blocks it is worth going over these extensions with the whole class. Drag out two blocks of code like this.

Computational Thinking
Algorithm Evaluation asks which algorithm is best, most efficient or most correct.

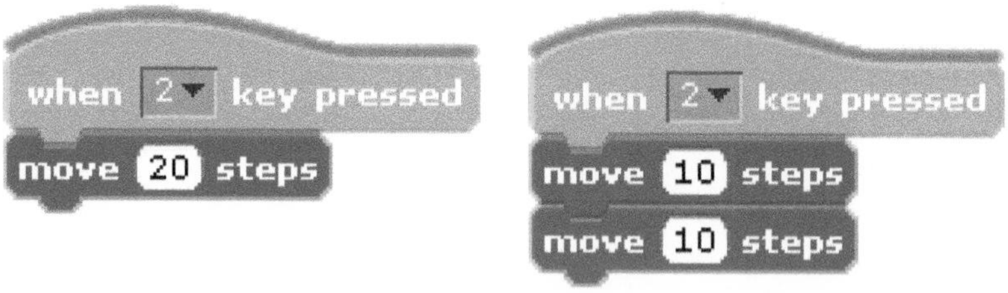
when 2 key pressed
move 20 steps
when 2 key pressed
move 10 steps
move 10 steps

Explain that both blocks of code are correct because they both work. There are many different ways to do the same thing when programming. However if we were looking at which solution is best or most efficient, we might be looking at which used the least amount of coding blocks.

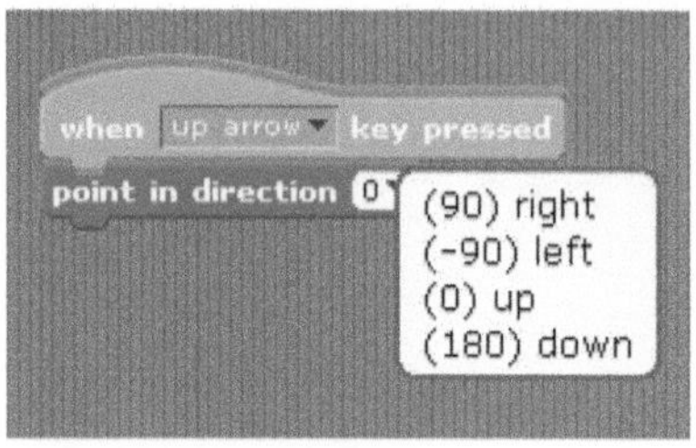
when up arrow key pressed
point in direction 0
(90) right
(-90) left
(0) up
(180) down

3. Point Car Up Down Right & Left

Drag out four keyboard input starting blocks. Click on the menu triangle of the point in direction block. Read the whole connected block with the class and pause when you get to the direction. What should they choose? Will anyone link the up arrow with the up direction? Repeat with the other three blocks.

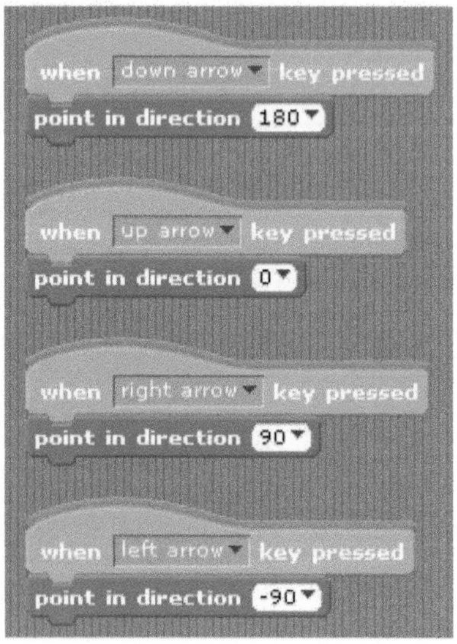
when down arrow key pressed
point in direction 180
when up arrow key pressed
point in direction 0
when right arrow key pressed
point in direction 90
when left arrow key pressed
point in direction -90

Pupil Extension Question

If pupils finish early and have tested their car by taking it for a drive; ask them if there is any limitation with our steering method? Give them time to go away and think about that. If anyone comes back and indicates that you can only travel in four directions then ask them if they could make more blocks to help fix that.

when a key pressed
point in direction 45
when b key pressed
turn 15 degrees

4. Road Creation

Click on Stage

Click on Background

Click Edit on Background1

Use the paintbrush tool and a grey colour to draw a road.

Use the fill tool and a green colour to fill in the background.

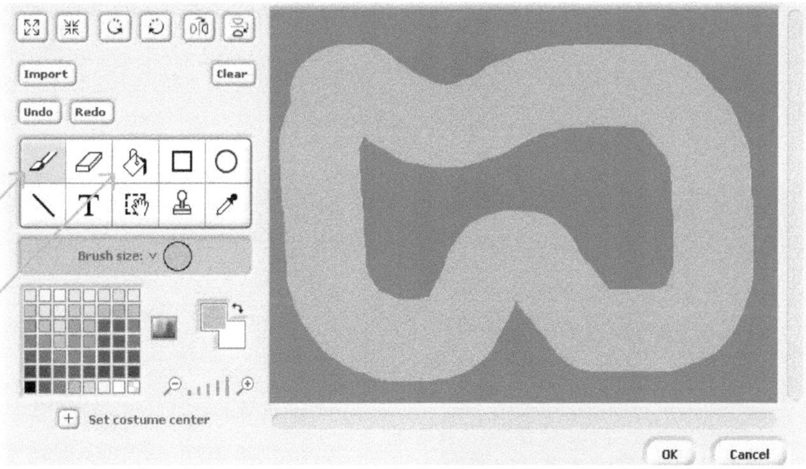
Import
Clear
Undo
Redo
Brush size:
Set costume center
OK
Cancel

4a. Change Roads

Challenge pupils to link a keyboard input to change the background in the stage area

next background

Found in looks blocks

5. Smoke Trail

Drag out three more keyboard input blocks and show pupils where the pen blocks are. Link pen up, pen down and clear as shown. Explain that pen down will put an invisible pen down on the screen, when the car is driven away it will drag the pen with it leaving a line. They will only see this line when the car drives away. Ask pupils what keyboard inputs would be good to choose? They can't all use the same key!

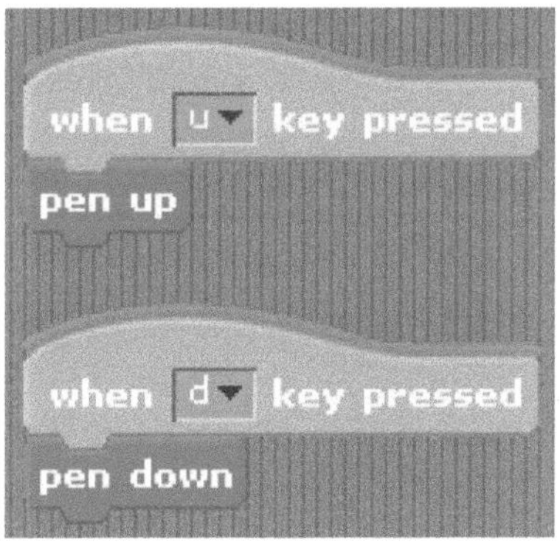
when u key pressed
pen up
when d key pressed
pen down

when c key pressed
clear

5a. Smoke Colour

Can pupils link keyboard inputs to change the colour of the line? Ask them if they can make the Y key draw a yellow line or G key draw a green line

6. Other Pen Commands

Can pupils investigate what could happen if they use other pen commands linked to other keys? What can they discover?

Stress that their exploration needs to be in separate blocks of code so that bugs can be quickly neutralised by removing the starting block. Allow pupils plenty of time for this.

4. Road Creation (continued)

Show pupils how to click *Copy* to make more than one roadway. Can they make the second roadway more challenging to drive round? Allow time for pupils to make multiple roadways.

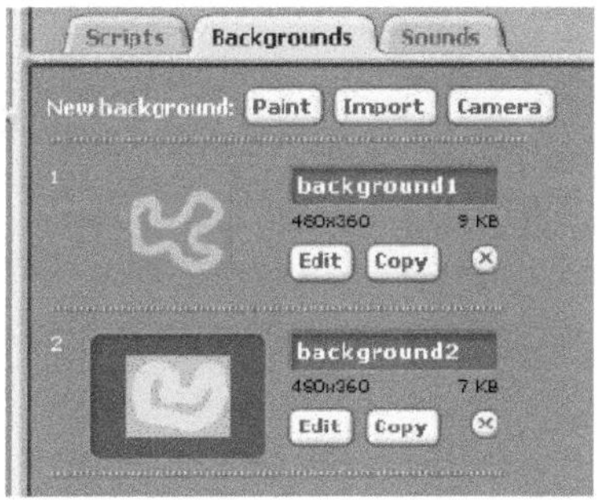
Scripts
Backgrounds
Sounds
New background:
Paint
Import
Camera
background1
480x360
5 KB
Edit
Copy
background2
480x360
7 KB
Edit
Copy

Hints

Sometimes pupils forget to select the sprite or stage they want to code before coding and end up writing code in the wrong place. These pupils will often report that blocks are missing. A teacher reminder asking them if they are coding the car or the stage can help.

7. Instructions

Can they write a key to their game? Demonstrate painting a sprite, zooming right out, opening the text tool and dragging it to the top left of the screen. Now type the first few instructions.

i=instructions

1=move 10

up arrow=point up

Can they find a way that instructions pop up when the i key is pressed and then hide after 10 seconds? After a while, drag out *show*, *hide* and *wait* blocks but let them work out the order.

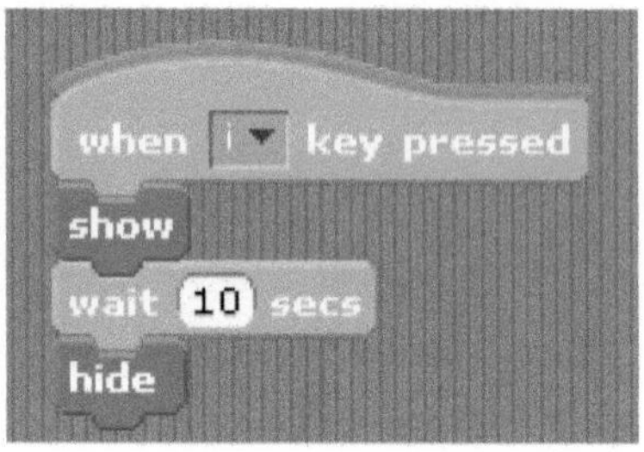
when i key pressed
show
wait 10 secs
hide

Hints

Pupils occasionally drive a car completely off the screen or hide it using the hide command. To get this back right click on the car and select show.

show
export this sprite
duplicate
delete

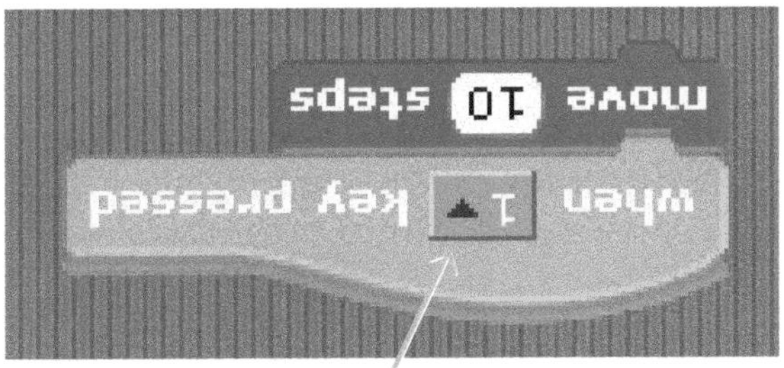

when ↑ key pressed
move 10 steps

Click here to change key

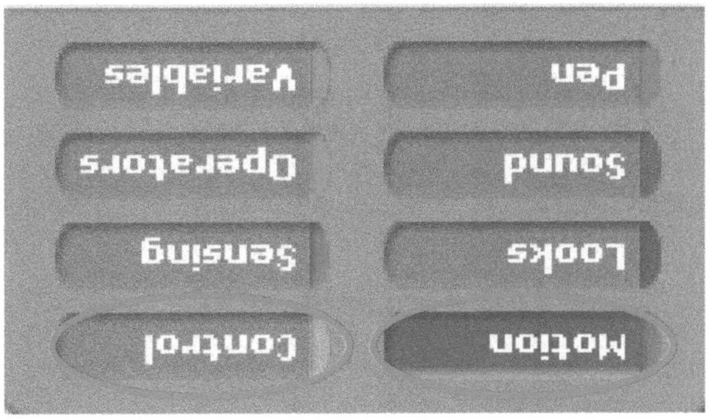

Motion
Control
Looks
Sensing
Sound
Operators
Pen
Variables

car

code-it.co.uk

Smoking Car

Debugging Card

Move

Car

Smoking Car

Debugging Card

code-it.co.uk

Change Car Direction

code-it.co.uk

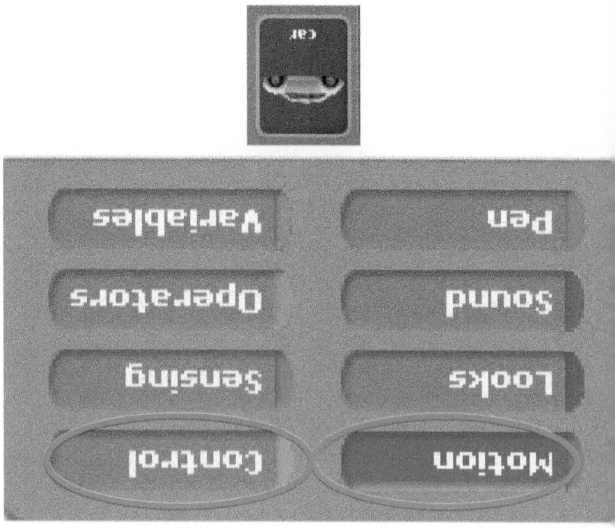

Motion
Control
Looks
Sensing
Sound
Operators
Pen
Variables
car

code-it.co.uk

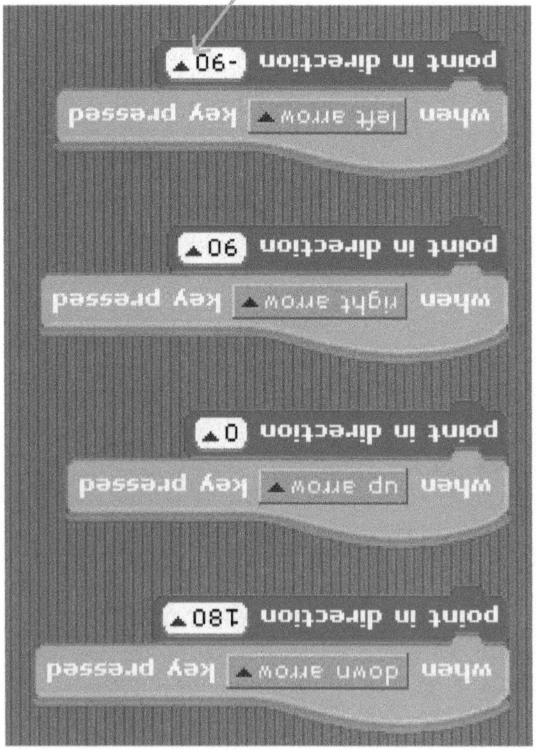

when down arrow key pressed
point in direction 180
when up arrow key pressed
point in direction 0
when right arrow key pressed
point in direction 90
when left arrow key pressed
point in direction -90

Click here to change direction

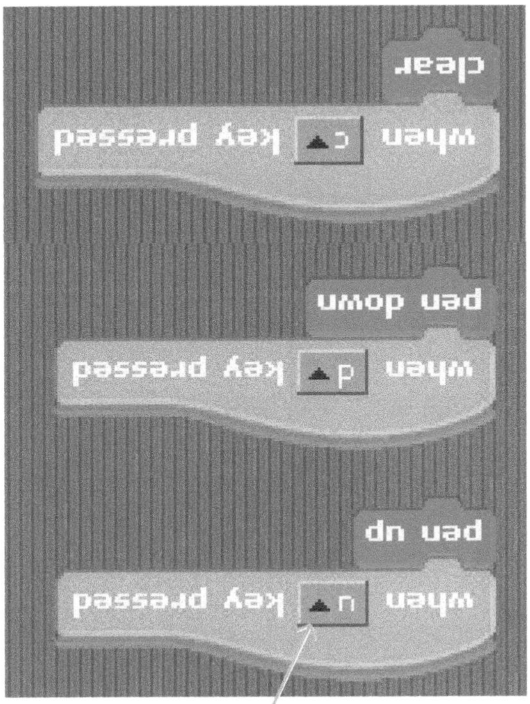
when c key pressed
clear
when d key pressed
pen down
when u key pressed
pen up
Click here to change key

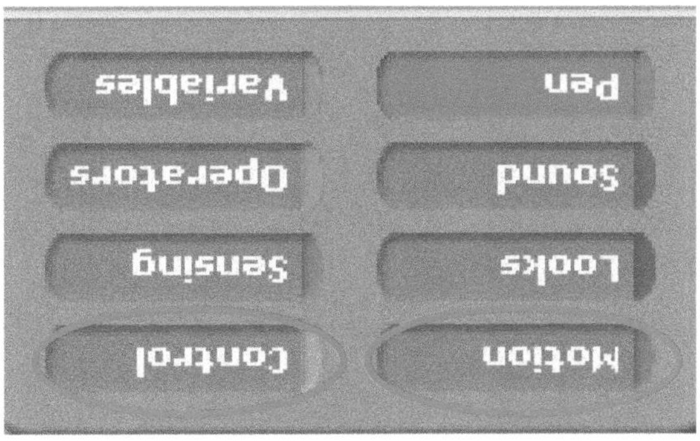
Motion
Looks
Sound
Pen
Control
Sensing
Operators
Variables

car

code-it.co.uk

Smoking Car

Debugging Card

code-it.co.uk

Pen Up

Pen Down

Clear

code-it.co.uk

1B. Music Machine

Time to complete the module

2-3 hours without composing music for another area of the curriculum

Module Aim Pupils draw simple buttons and program them to play sequences of sounds when they are clicked with the left mouse button. They could use their knowledge gained to compose music for another area of the curriculum.

National Curriculum Programs of Study

Pupils should be taught to:

- ***design, write and debug programs that accomplish specific goals***, including controlling or simulating physical systems; solve problems by decomposing them into smaller parts
- ***use sequence***, selection, ***and repetition in programs; work with*** variables and ***various forms of input and output***
- ***use logical reasoning to*** explain how some simple algorithms work and to ***detect and correct errors in algorithms and programs***

Computational Thinking

Algorithm Programming Evaluation

Pupils are evaluating each other's code and asking if it is fit for purpose and feeding back any bugs

Module Learning Focus

By the end of this module pupils will be able to:

- Understand and use the mouse click input to start code
- Be able to draw their own simple sprites
- Use the music code blocks independently
- Start to understand the importance of repetition in computing
- Evaluate their peers' programming
- Create their own music using Scratch

Computer Science Concepts

- Using a mouse click & keyboard inputs to control aspects of the game
- Simple Sequence of code
- Repeat x times loops

Maths Concepts

Decimal fractions

Assessment for Learning

At the end of each session direct pupils to page 7 of pupil workbook 1 to help them reflect on what they have learnt. It is often worth working through this line by line to avoid pupils filling in everything with a smiley face. You can also annotate this to record pupils who have needed much more support or have demonstrated greater understanding.

Adult Focus

Adults need to be clear that they are here to provide hints only and not full solutions.

Debugging Hints Read the code aloud - does it make sense? Hand out debugging cards

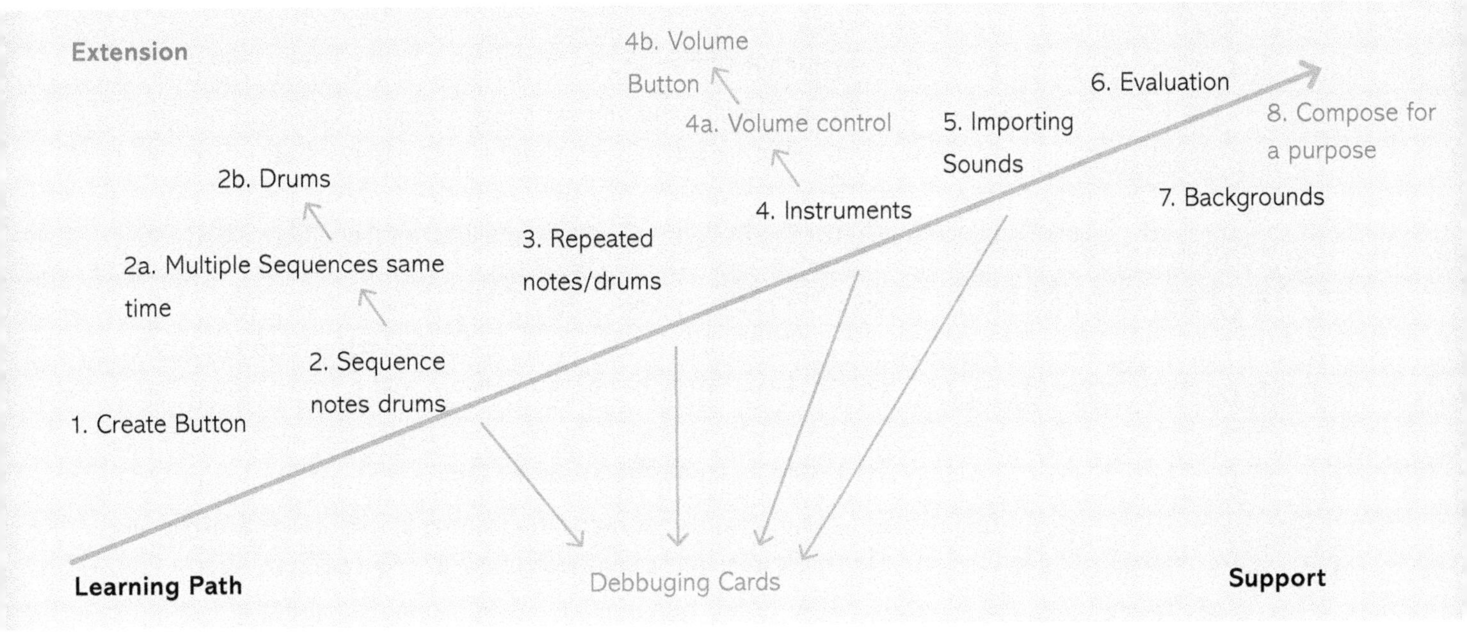

Extension
4b. Volume Button
4a. Volume control
6. Evaluation
5. Importing Sounds
8. Compose for a purpose
2b. Drums
7. Backgrounds
4. Instruments
3. Repeated notes/drums
2a. Multiple Sequences same time
2. Sequence notes drums
1. Create Button
Learning Path
Debbuging Cards
Support

1. Create Button

Right click and delete the cat sprite
Left click on the Paint new sprite button
Using the solid rectangle tool
or ellipse tool and a bright colour paint a single square
Click ok to close the paint editor
Rename your sprite button1 (above costume tab)

> **Alternative Method** You could create a button then duplicate until you have four buttons

button1
x: -175 y: 72 direction:
Scripts
Costumes
Sounds

Pupils can create as many buttons as they can in a limited time.
Once everyone has created at least three, move on.

A common mistake is to create more than one button in the same painting editor. These will all be joined together and act as one button. Warning pupils not to do this can be helpful.

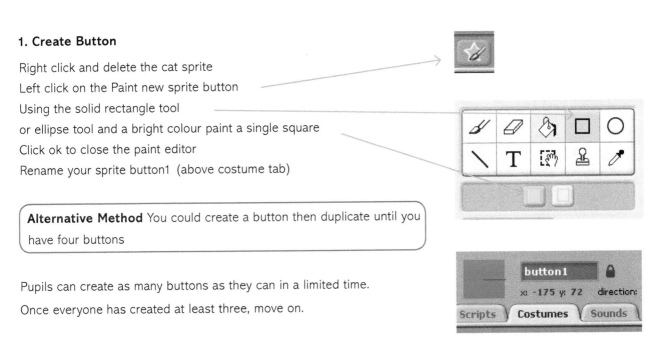

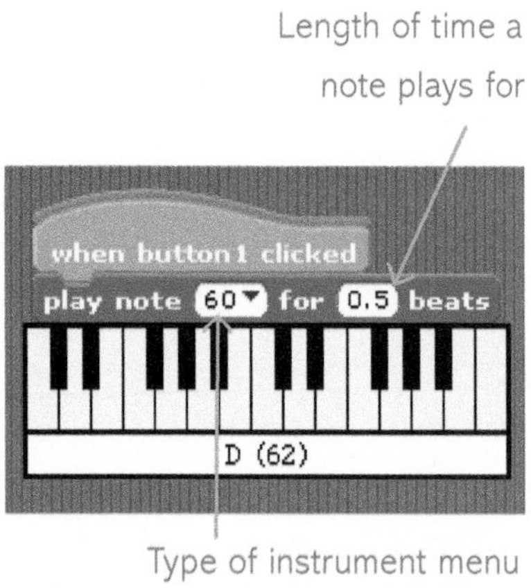
Length of time a note plays for
when button1 clicked
play note 60 for 0.5 beats
D (62)
Type of instrument menu

2. Sequence of notes

Open up control blocks and ask pupils which block we can use so that the code will be started from a mouse click? Show pupils how the name of this will change if you rename the sprite.

Show pupils how they can play a sequence of notes. Demonstrate changing the note and how long it plays for. There is a decimal number line in the pupil workbook page 9 that you can refer to.

Give pupils time to experiment with these notes. It is worth restricting younger pupils to any number between 0.1 and 1.

when pink clicked
play note 59 for 0.5 beats
play note 60 for 0.5 beats
play note 62 for 0.5 beats
play note 64 for 0.5 beats
when pink clicked
play drum 48 for 0.2 beats
play drum 48 for 0.2 beats
play drum 48 for 0.2 beats
play drum 48 for 0.2 beats
play drum 48 for 0.2 beats
play drum 48 for 0.2 beats
play drum 48 for 0.2 beats
play drum 48 for 0.2 beats
play drum 48 for 0.2 beats
play drum 48 for 0.2 beats

2a. Multiple sequences at same time

Show all pupils how they can have multiple blocks playing at same time. All starting from the same when button is clicked block.

2b. Drums

Some pupils may already have found these but it is worth pointing them out if not.

3. Repeated notes/drums

Introduce the idea of things being repeated you could use this resource http://code-it.co.uk/wp-content/uploads/2015/05/loops.pdf. You could also use dance to help you. Get pupils to show you a few dance moves to a popular song. Create a symbol to represent each one of these.

Pupils then create dances for each other and record the notation in their pupil workbook 1 page 8 using your notation x number of times to repeat. Pupils then dance each other's dances following the notation.

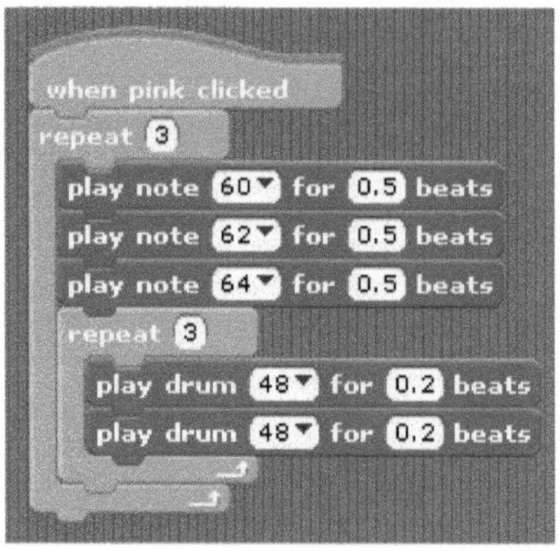
when pink clicked
repeat 3
play note 60 for 0.5 beats
play note 62 for 0.5 beats
play note 64 for 0.5 beats
repeat 3
play drum 48 for 0.2 beats
play drum 48 for 0.2 beats

Now show pupils how a repeat x loop works

Place some notes in a repeat 3 loop and run the code.

Now place some drums inside another repeat loop and place it inside the first loop. Ask pupils to explain to each other how the notes and drums will play. They can make up their own challenges that need the order explaining by a partner.

4. Instruments

Demonstrate how to change the instrument type for the note blocks by clicking on the menu triangle and selecting another instrument.

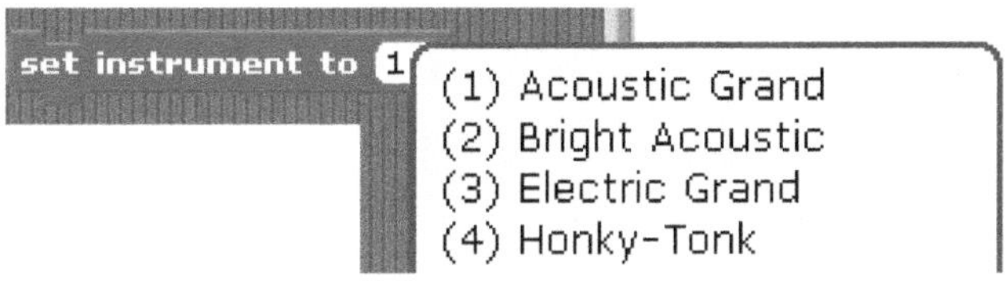
set instrument to 1
(1) Acoustic Grand
(2) Bright Acoustic
(3) Electric Grand
(4) Honky-Tonk

4a. Volume control

Can pupils change the volume of a short part of their musical composition?
You can only control the volume on a single sprite and the volume will return to a previous volume when you program in a new sprite.

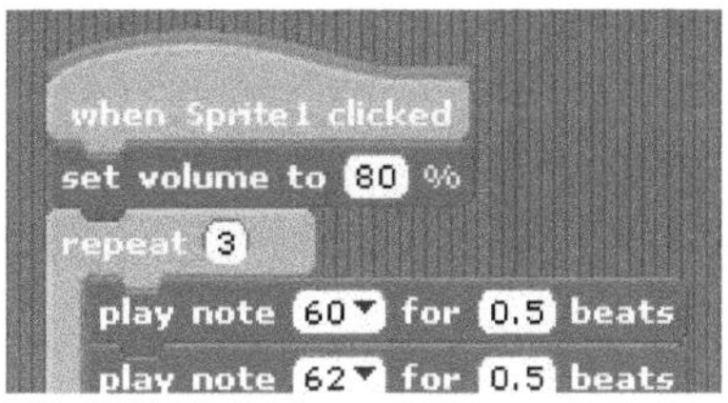
when Sprite1 clicked
set volume to 80 %
repeat 3
play note 60 for 0.5 beats
play note 62 for 0.5 beats

4b. Volume button

Can pupils change volume using keys?

5. Importing sounds from Music Loops folder

Sounds tab import

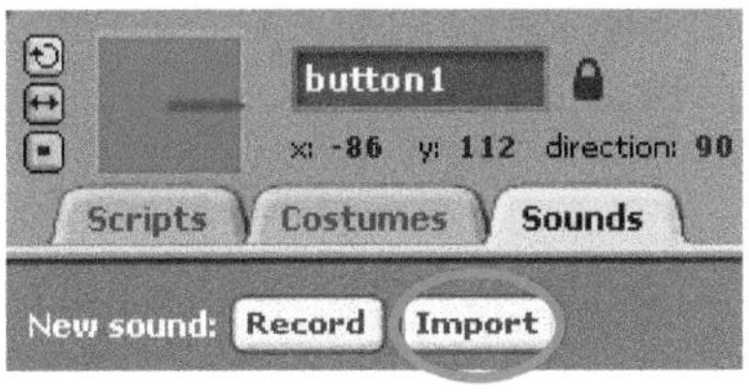
button1
x: -86 y: 112 direction: 90
Scripts
Costumes
Sounds
New sound: Record Import

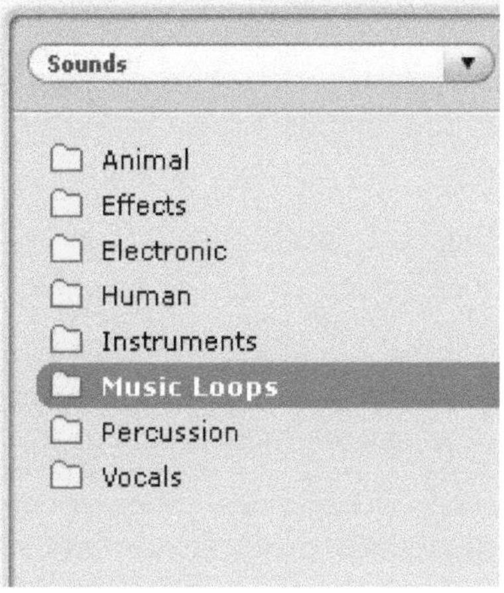
Sounds
Animal
Effects
Electronic
Human
Instruments
Music Loops
Percussion
Vocals

New sound: Record Import
1
DrumSet1
0:00:02
91 KB

Note you can only select a sound to play once it has been imported and then only for that sprite

Once the sound has been imported it can be used in the play sound code blocks. The play sound **until done** block will play the whole sound through before moving on to the next block. The play sound block will start the sound and then continue with other coding blocks before the sound has finished.

when button2 clicked
play sound HumanBeatbox1 until done
play sound HumanBeatbox2 until done

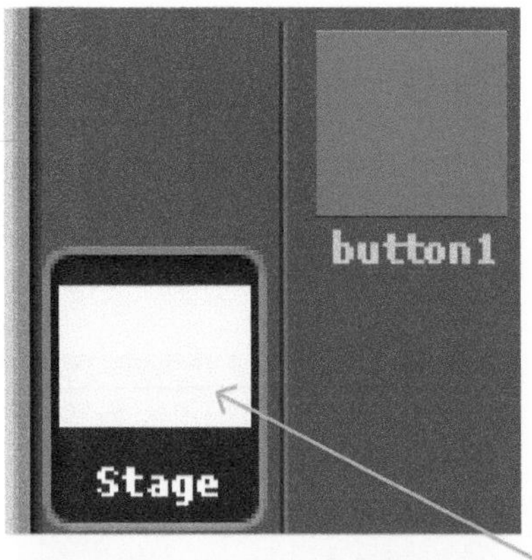
button1
Stage

6. Informal Evaluation

It is useful for pupils to help each other by evaluating each other's programs and looking for bugs. Set projects to presentation mode and evaluate either using post it notes on the desk or turning to page 10 of the pupil workbook 1 to leave written evaluation. If you are using the pupil workbook there are three opportunities for evaluation. You could use the other two when pupils are composing for a purpose.

Scripts
Backgrounds
Sounds
New background:
Paint
Import
Camera
background1
480x360
Edit
Copy

7. Background Design

Left click on stage

Left click on backgrounds

Left click on edit

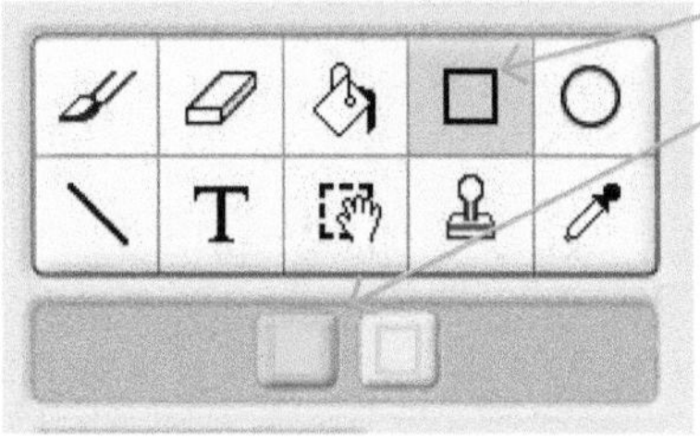

Choose the rectangle tool

Choose the solid colour

Draw a large rectangle that almost fills the whole screen

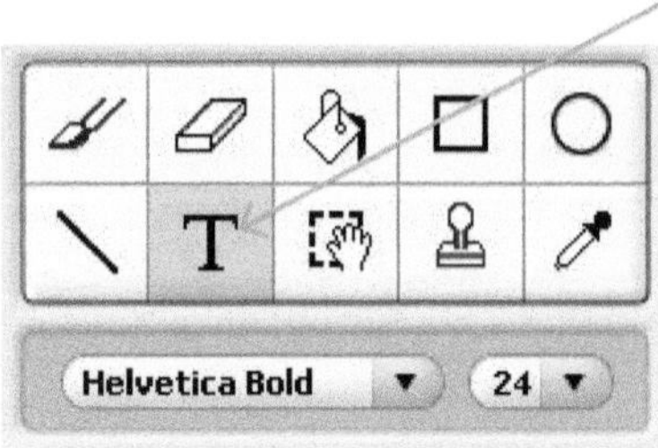
Helvetica Bold
24

Select the Text button

Music Machine

Use the small black square to move the text

Write Music Machine or pupil's own equivalent name

If you have time they could create a more colourful machine background and even make it flash (Hint cards) as an extension.

Music National Curriculum

Pupils should be taught to improvise and compose music for a range of purposes

8. Compose for a purpose

The real challenge comes after pupils have an idea of what can be programmed. Find a real context for their new skills in composing music that links to another area of the curriculum or in creating a musical instrument that sounds like it is from a certain era if linking to History.

Print extra independent extension activities in the pupil books and send them home.

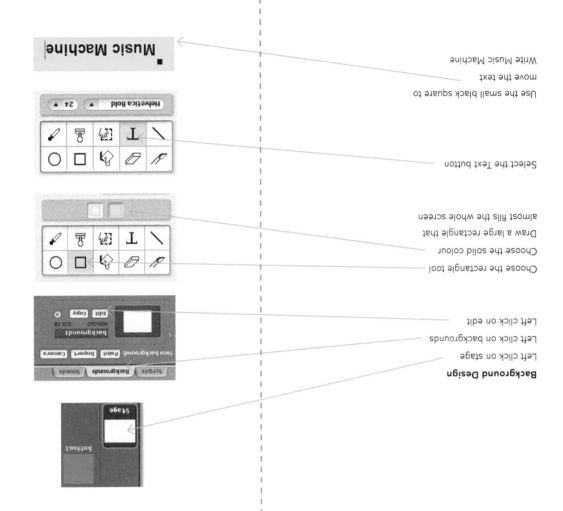

Background Design

Left click on stage

Left click on backgrounds

Left click on edit

Choose the rectangle tool

Choose the solid colour

Draw a large rectangle that almost fills the whole screen

Select the Text button

Use the small black square to move the text

Write Music Machine

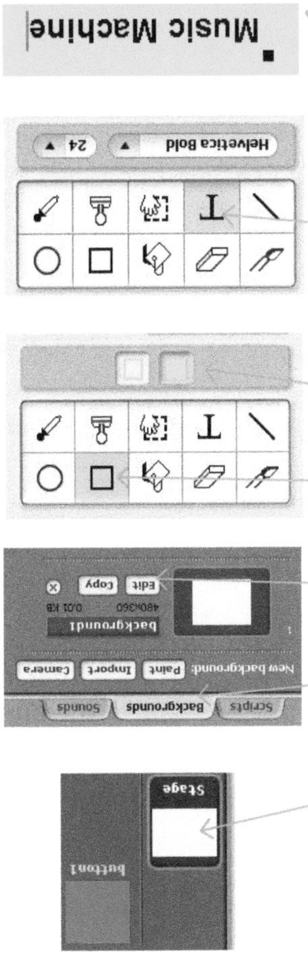

Music Machine
Helvetica Bold
24
Scripts
Backgrounds
Sounds
New background:
Paint
Import
Camera
background1
480x360
0.01 KB
Edit
Copy
Stage
button1

Scratch

Music Machine

Help Card

code-it.co.uk

Background

code-it.co.uk

Scratch
Music Machine
Extension Cards

code-it.co.uk

Flashing
Background Part 1

Open the stage and background tab and click copy

New background:
Paint
Import
Camera
1
background1
480x360
10 KB
Edit
Copy

Choose a new colour and use the fill tool to change the colour

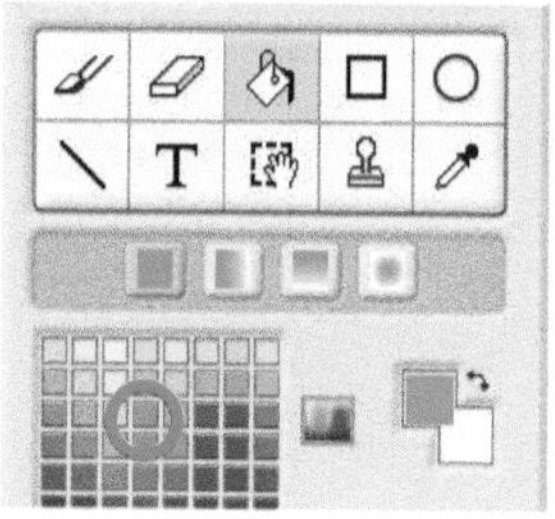

Music

code-it.co.uk

Copy the background twice and edit to change the background colour

Stage

code-it.co.uk

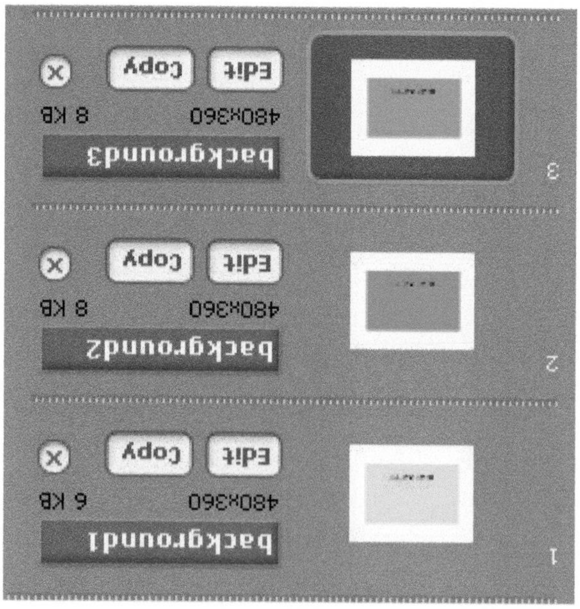
1
background1
480x360
6 KB
Edit
Copy
2
background2
480x360
8 KB
Edit
Copy
3
background3
480x360
8 KB
Edit
Copy

Now ask for part 2

Teacher Note Staple card shut and challenge pupil to solve without looking at the solution

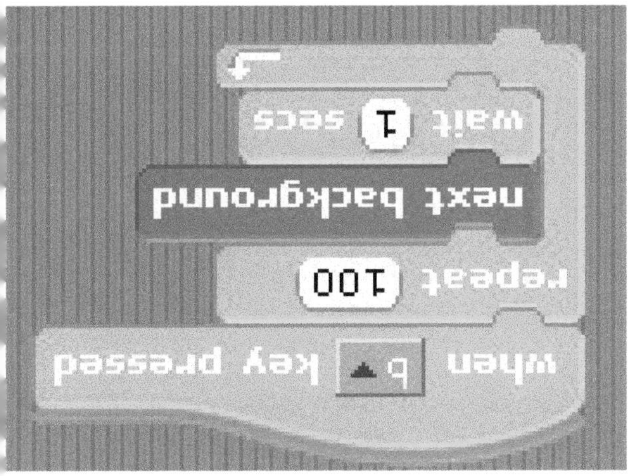

when b key pressed
repeat 100
next background
wait 1 secs

Can you find another way of making the background flash?

hint

switch to costume costume2

code-it.co.uk

Stage

Scratch

Music Machine

Extension Cards

code-it.co.uk

Flashing Background Part 2

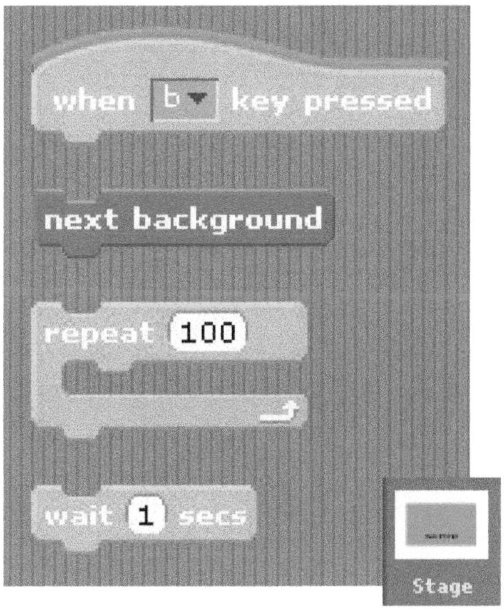

when b key pressed
next background
repeat 100
wait 1 secs
Stage

Can you use these code blocks in the stage to make the backgrounds flash?

code-it.co.uk

Import Sound

start

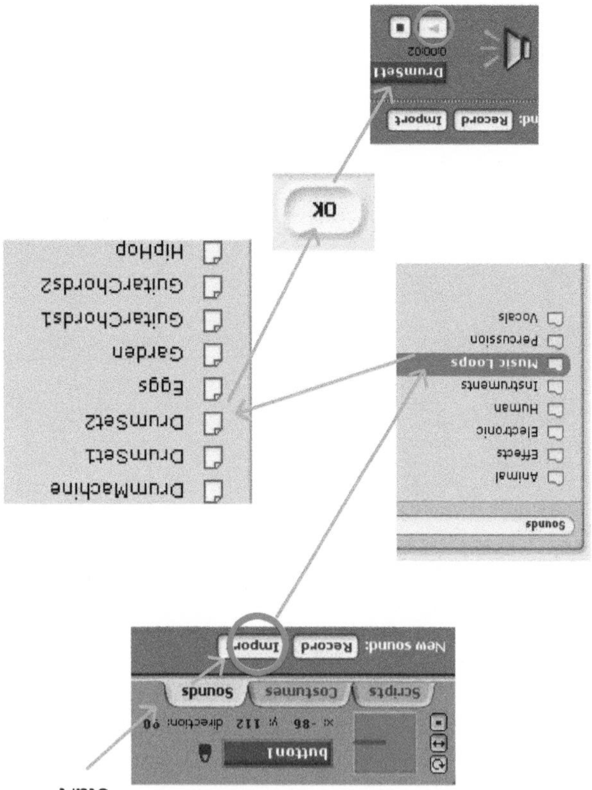
button1
Scripts
Costumes
Sounds
New sound: Record Import
Sounds
Animal
Effects
Electronic
Human
Instruments
Music Loops
Percussion
Vocals
DrumMachine
Drumset1
DrumSet2
Eggs
Garden
GuitarChords1
GuitarChords2
HipHop
OK
Record Import
Drumset1

code-it.co.uk

Scratch Music Machine Catch Up Cards

code-it.co.uk

Import Sound

code-it.co.uk

Needs to be coded in
every button to work
fully

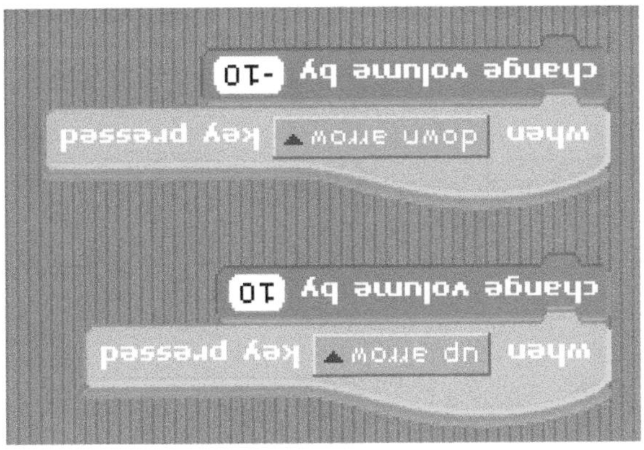
when up arrow key pressed
change volume by 10
when down arrow key pressed
change volume by -10

code-it.co.uk

button1

Motion
Control
Looks
Sensing
Sound
Operators
Pen
Variables

Scratch Music Machine Extension Cards

code-it.co.uk

Volume Control

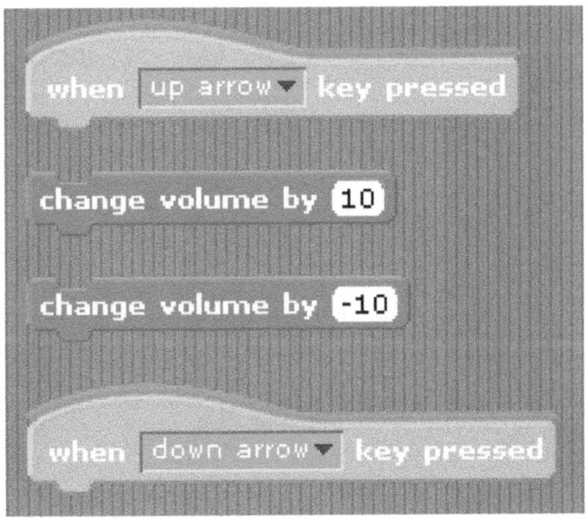
when up arrow key pressed
change volume by 10
change volume by -10
when down arrow key pressed

Can you use these blocks to make the volume increase (go up) and decrease (go down) when keys are pressed?

code-it.co.uk

1c. Conversation

Time to complete the basic module

2 hours

Module Aim: Program two or more characters to take part in a conversation

National Curriculum Programs of Study

Pupils should be taught to:

- ***design, write and debug programs that accomplish specific goals,*** including controlling or simulating physical systems; solve problems by decomposing them into smaller parts
- ***use sequence, selection,*** and ***repetition in programs; work with*** variables and ***various forms of input and output***
- ***use logical reasoning to*** explain how some simple algorithms work and to ***detect and correct errors in algorithms and programs***

Module Learning Focus

By the end of the module children will be able to:

- Create an algorithm to plan a conversation between two or more characters
- Convert an algorithm into Scratch code
- Test and debug a program

Computer Science Concepts

- All programming is turning an algorithm into code

Maths Concepts

- Time in seconds
- Optional extension degrees and X Y coordinates

Cross Curricular Focus

The basic premise can be adapted for use across many areas of the curriculum. It could be a dentist explaining dental hygiene techniques or a pair of stone age characters talking about their new tools - a powerful farewell at a train station as part of a WW2 evacuation scene or a campaigner trying to persuade a shopkeeper to stock Fairtrade produce.

Assessment for Learning

At the end of each session direct pupils to page 12 of pupil workbook 1 to help them reflect on what they have learnt. It is often worth working through this line by line to avoid pupils filling in everything with a smiley face. You can also annotate this to record pupils who have needed much more support or have demonstrated greater understanding.

Adult Focus

All adults need to be clear that they are to support using hints and strategies only and not solve things for pupils.

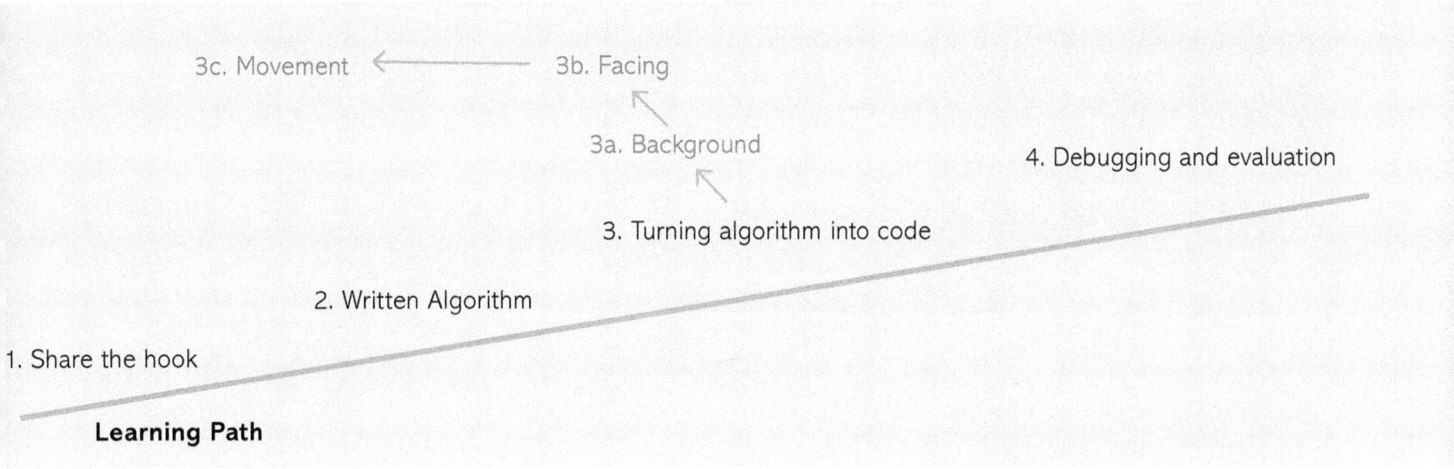
3c. Movement
3b. Facing
3a. Background
4. Debugging and evaluation
3. Turning algorithm into code
2. Written Algorithm
1. Share the hook
Learning Path

1. Share the Hook

Take a few moments to excite and enthuse your pupils about the conversation hook you or they have chosen.

2. Written Algorithm

Ask two children to have a conversation about a topic you know they will have lots to talk about. Ask the rest of your pupils to watch them carefully. After a minute stop them and ask the class what the pattern is? Draw out how when one child is speaking the other is waiting. Emphasise that the length of time one child waits is exactly the same as the other child speaks. Share the conversation algorithm template, you can find this on page 13 of the pupil workbook 1. I recommend that you model a conversation using the teacher template that you can find online http://code-it.co.uk/wp-content/uploads/2015/08/template.png. You can import this into Smart or Promethean notebook. Now give pupils time to complete their written algorithm. Check their algorithms to make sure they have matched the wait times to the speech times.

Debugging Hints

A common bug whilst pupils are converting their algorithms into code is where both sprites start talking at the same time. Direct pupils back to checking their algorithm line by line to find the fault. Encourage them to read their algorithm out loud and then check to see if it is the same as their code.

3. Turning Algorithm into Code

Import two sprites using the choose new sprite from file button.

Add a when green flag clicked starting block to each sprite and ask the pupils where the green flag is.

when clicked
say Welcome to my lair for 3 secs
wait 2 secs

Drag out a say hello for two seconds block and a wait block and start to turn your algorithm into code. Frequently refer back to your conversation and make a great play over matching the times and order of the conversation to the algorithm.

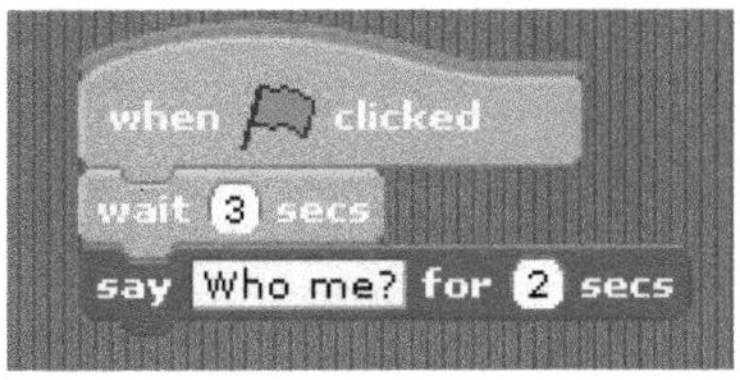
when clicked
wait 3 secs
say Who me? for 2 secs

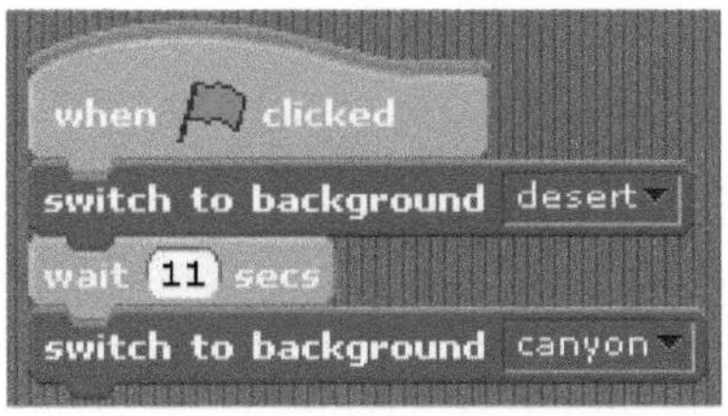
when clicked
switch to background desert
wait 11 secs
switch to background canyon

3a. Background

Show pupils how they can use import a background.

-Stage

-Backgrounds

-Import

You may also wish to demonstrate how a background can be changed after a period of time through the use of a script.

Sprite1
Scripts
Costumes

3b. Facing

In a natural conversation characters look away occasionally. Scratch can program that as well.

First set the character to left and right only.

Note you can flip the character manually by moving the blue direction of travel line to left or right.

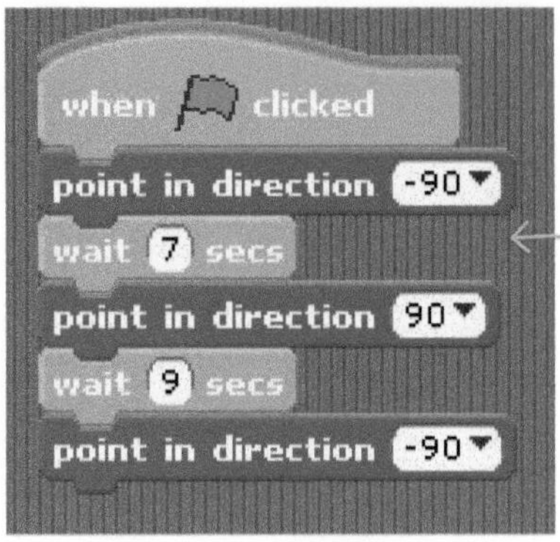
when clicked
point in direction -90
wait 7 secs
point in direction 90
wait 9 secs
point in direction -90

Now you can build up a script using waits and point in direction blocks.

3c. Movement

The scratch stage area is mapped to a 480 x 360 grid set out in four quadrant Cartesian coordinate system.

Pupils can use X & Y coordinate glide to blocks to move characters. This would normally be beyond most Year 3 pupils however you can place a sprite any where you want and double click on it and the coordinates blocks will change in the Motion blocks area.

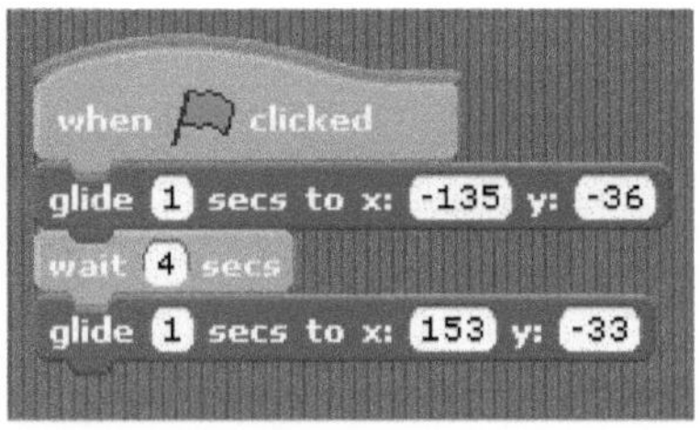
when clicked
glide 1 secs to x: -135 y: -36
wait 4 secs
glide 1 secs to x: 153 y: -33

> **Experiment**
>
> This stage provides a perfect opportunity to give pupils time to experiment and discover new effects they can script whilst the conversation is running. Encourage them to build these using new green flag blocks running alongside existing code but not inside existing speech code. This keeps the speech code from being compromised.

4. Debugging & Evaluation

Instruct pupils to save their work, tidy up code by right mouse clicking in each script area and selecting clean up.

clean up
save picture of scripts
add comment

Direct them to open their evaluation page 14 of their pupil workbook 1 and leave this open by their computer. Give them time to evaluate their peers' work using the checklist. It is good to allow at least two evaluations by different pupils. The teacher could fill in the third.

Make sure you allow pupils time to correct bugs after the evaluation.

1D. Interactive Display

Module Aim: Pupils make an interactive display which tells the user what a picture is or does. This could be a museum display screen or any interactive display linked to any subject. You will need to decide a focus before starting.

Time to complete module

3-4 hours

Module Learning Focus

By the end of the module children will be able to:

- Write code to create an interactive display that links to another area of the curriculum
- Plan what pictures they will need and what they will program the picture to say (Algorithm)
- Learn simple techniques for debugging
- Create code using the mouse click as an input
- Increase their knowledge of copyright
- Know how to clean up a sprite by removing unwanted background

Computer Science Concepts

- Writing an algorithm (idea to turn into a program)
- Mouse click as an input
- Understand that all programming is turning an algorithm into code

Assessment for Learning

At the end of each session direct pupils to page 16 of pupil workbook 1 to help them reflect on what they have learnt. It is often worth working through this line by line to avoid pupils filling in everything with a smiley face. You can also annotate this to record pupils who have needed much more support or have demonstrated greater understanding.

Adult Focus

All adults need to be clear that they are to support using hints only and not solve things for pupils.

Computational Thinking- **Algorithm:** ordered ideas that can be turned into a program.

Cross Curricular Focus The basic premise can be adapted for use across all areas of the curriculum. It could be a Roman centurion's equipment, reflections on the properties of solids, liquids and gases, local landmarks described or musical instruments classified.

National Curriculum Programs of Study

Pupils should be taught to:

- ***design, write and debug programs that accomplish specific goals,*** including controlling or simulating physical systems; solve problems by decomposing them into smaller parts
- ***use sequence,*** selection, and repetition ***in programs; work with*** variables and ***various forms of input and output***
- ***use logical reasoning*** to explain how some simple algorithms work and ***to detect and correct errors in algorithms and programs***

Debugging Hints

- Compare teacher code ideas with pupils code
- Read code aloud
- Compare code with original algorithm (ideas in the mind map): does it do what you wanted it to do?

5.Adding Information

4. Cleaning up Sprites

3. Importing Sprites

6. Evaluating Program

2. Mind Map Algorithm

1. Share the hook

Learning Path

Copyright Hints

If pupils are only sharing creation within schools then they don't need to worry about what pictures they choose.

If they are intending to share on the Scratch website then they will need to be much more careful and avoid pictures that have a watermark (text) over them or those that block right click and save picture as commands.

Schools have been fined for posting copyright pictures on websites.

1. Share the Hook

Take a few moments to excite and enthuse your pupils about the Interactive display hook you or they have chosen. Explain that they are going to draw or import pictures of the objects needed and then program them so that when they are clicked on they will provide information about the picture. It helps to have made a simple version yourself first to show pupils.

2, Mind Map Algorithm

Ask pupils to turn to their pupil workbook planners page 17 and use the mind map area to help them decide on the type of sprites they might need. Writing their theme in the centre and then mind mapping object ideas and what they might code these to say or do.

3. Importing Sprites

The world wide web is a great source of pictures to use in a project like this. If you intend to share your projects online then it is worth avoiding pictures with watermarks. This is a great opportunity to initiate a discussion around copyright.

From Google Images

Right click on image

Save image as _ _ _

Give it a useful name in your pictures folder

Give pupils lots of time to import many useful pictures before importing them into Scratch

You could get pupils to fill in there mind map after they have found useful pictures online.

Inside Scratch

Click on paint new sprite

Click on import

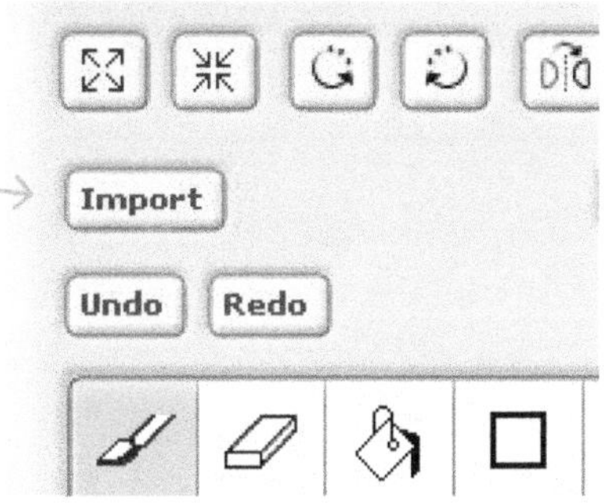
Import
Undo
Redo

You will need to navigate to where you saved your picture which will be different for each school network.

You could always draw your sprites but that will take a lot longer.
Only import one picture at a time. Click ok before painting a new sprite and importing a new picture.

4. Cleaning up Sprite

Pictures from the world wide web will often have too much white space or a background. You can clean them up inside the Scratch paint editor.

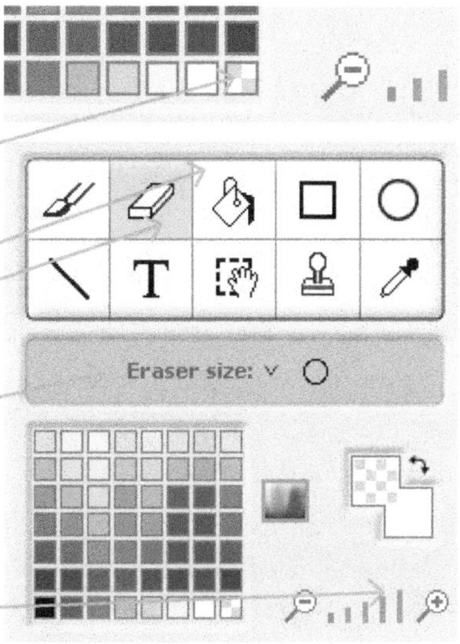
T
Eraser size:

Whitespace

Select the grey and white no colour option.
Use the fill tool to replace the white background with nothing.

Background picture

Select eraser (rubber)
Adjust the size
Zoom into the image
Carefully go round the edges and remove excess back-ground

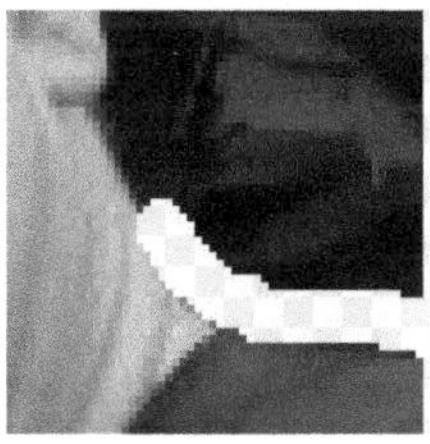

5. Adding information

You now want the sprites to say information about the object when they are clicked on.

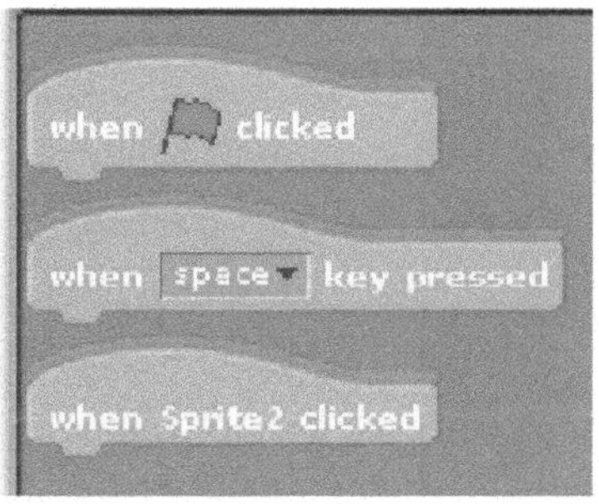
when clicked
when space key pressed
when Sprite2 clicked

Three out of the four curved starting blocks

Show pupils the three top curved starting blocks Ask them which block you should use to start speech if the block is clicked on by the mouse? Many will say the top green flag block because it has the word clicked in it. Point out where the green flag is and that this is not the same as clicking on the sprite. Also point out that the name may be different if you have renamed the sprite and show them where to do this.

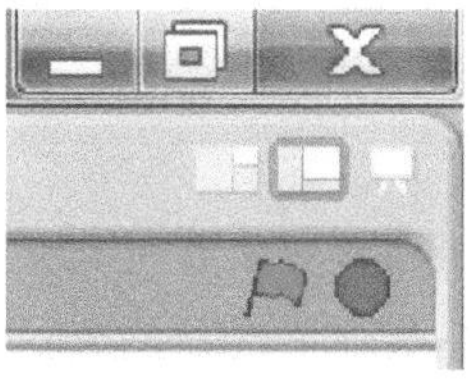

Green flag found at top right of window on Scratch 1 .4

File Edit Share Help
scutum
x: 0 y: 0 direction: 90
Scripts
Costumes
Sounds

Rename a sprite by typing into this box

If they have completed the conversation module they should have no problem with finding a way of bringing up speech using the say or think blocks.

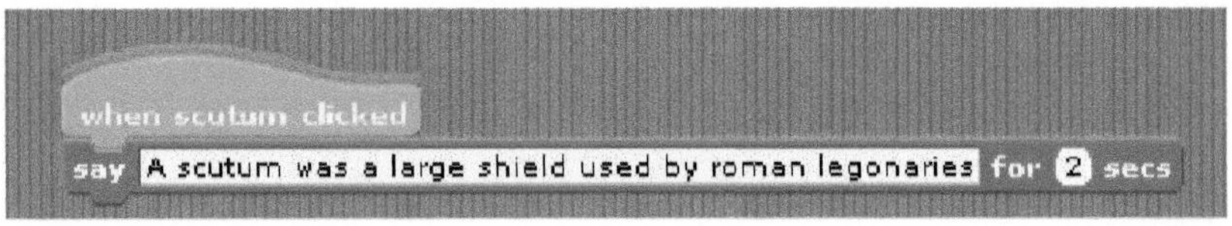
when scutum clicked
say A scutum was a large shield used by roman legonaries for 2 secs

Speech linked to a when sprite is clicked block

Alternatively they could record a message using the sound recording tool found in the sound tab of every sprite.

They can then link this to the starting block using the play sound block. If they have completed the music machine they may have discovered this themselves.

Scripts
Costumes
Sounds
New sound: Record Import
meow
0:00:01
37 KB
Sound Recorder
OK

Record brings up a sound recorder.

Once a sound is recorded you can rename it here

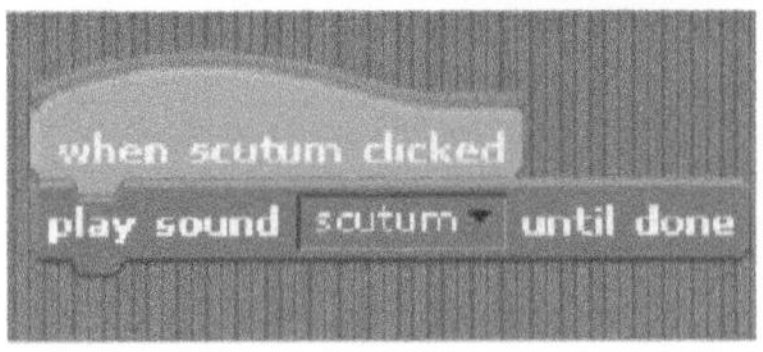
when scutum clicked
play sound scutum until done

Play sound block

Top right for presentation mode

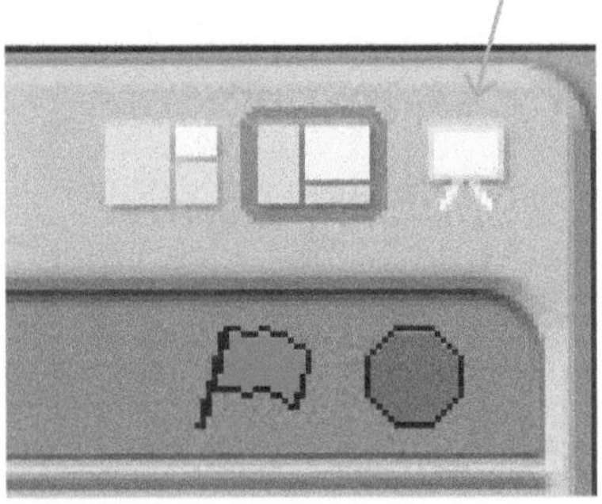

Click esc on keyboard to exit presentation mode

6. Evaluating the Program

Ask pupils to save their work.

Get them to set their project to display mode.

Encourage everyone to try each other's work.

You can also do a quick survey about most information or best design by asking pupils to stand by the work they think meets that criteria. They are not allowed to choose their own work!

1E. Dressing Up Game

Module Aim: Pupils create a dressing up game where the characters' costumes change when they are mouse - clicked on. They can also draw accessories which change colour or animate when they are clicked on.

Time to complete module

3-4 hours

Computer Science Concepts

- Using a mouse click input to change costumes
- Using a mouse click input to change the colour of items of clothing or accessories
- Instructions can be repeated using a repeat x times loop

Digital Literacy

- Using the fill tool to change clothing colours
- Zooming in and working at pixel level

Maths Concepts

- Decimal fractions tenths of a second

Assessment for Learning

At the end of each session direct pupils to page 19 of pupil workbook 1 to help them reflect on what they have learnt. It is often worth working through this line by line to avoid pupils filling in everything with a smiley face. You can also annotate this to record pupils who have needed much more support or have demonstrated greater understanding.

Adult Focus

All adults need to be clear that they are to support using hints only and not solve things for pupils. It helps to cement computing concepts if adults ask pupils to explain how a code block works.

Computational Thinking- **Generalisation:** adapting a solution that worked in one place to work in another. Pupils take the idea of changing the costume inside a loop and use this for different animations of varying time lengths.

National Curriculum Programs of Study

Pupils should be taught to:

- ***design, write and debug programs that accomplish specific goals,*** including controlling or simulating physical systems; solve problems by decomposing them into smaller parts
- ***use sequence, selection, and repetition in programs; work with*** variables and ***various forms of input and output***
- ***use logical reasoning*** to explain how some simple algorithms work and ***to detect and correct errors in algorithms and programs***

Debugging Hints

- Compare teacher code ideas with pupils' code
- Read code aloud
- If providing debugging hints with an animation pretend to be the animation and step through the code actions physically to help pupils see the fault

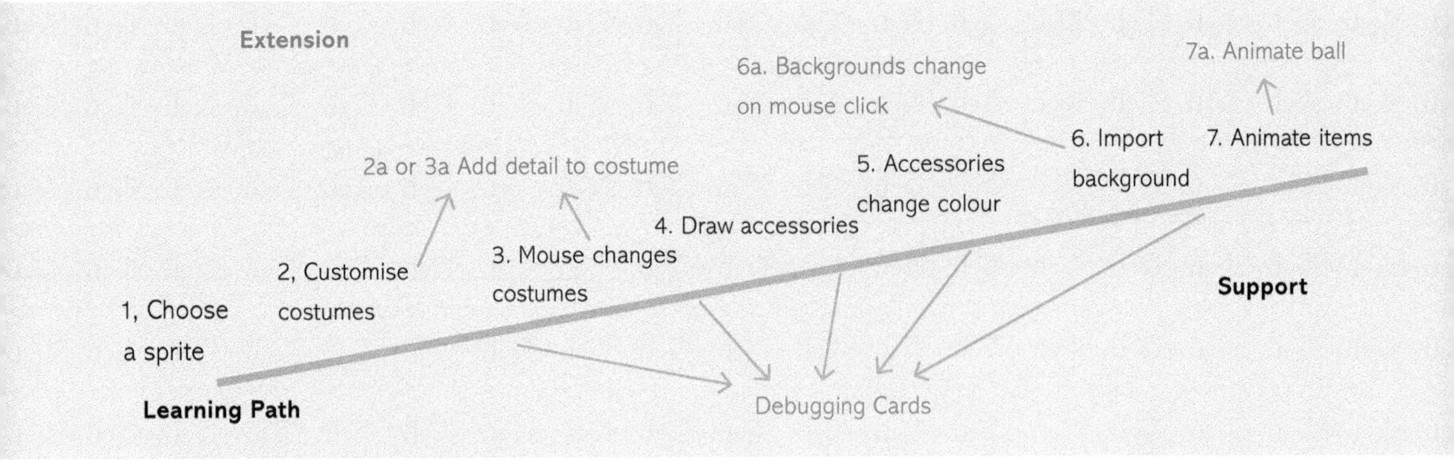
Extension
6a. Backgrounds change on mouse click
7a. Animate ball
2a or 3a Add detail to costume
5. Accessories change colour
6. Import background
7. Animate items
4. Draw accessories
3. Mouse changes costumes
2, Customise costumes
1, Choose a sprite
Support
Learning Path
Debugging Cards

show
export this sprite
duplicate
delete

1. Choose a Sprite

Show pupils how to right click and delete the cat sprite and then choose a new one. Instruct pupils to choose these sprites as they are really easy to colour and accessorise. If you do allow free choice steer clear of photos as they don't colour easily.

girl3-standing
breakdancer-1

People

Left click on the choose new sprite from file button and then navigate to the people folder

2. Customise Costumes

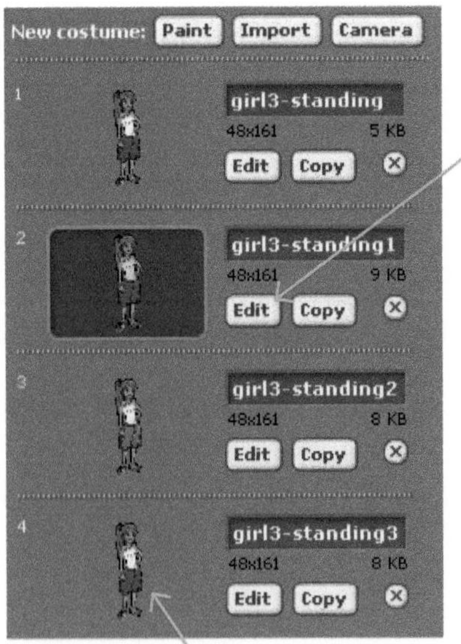
New costume: Paint Import Camera
girl3-standing
48x161 5 KB
Edit Copy
girl3-standing1
48x161 9 KB
Edit Copy
girl3-standing2
48x161 8 KB
Edit Copy
girl3-standing3
48x161 8 KB
Edit Copy

Example costumes

Demonstrate how to navigate to sprite costumes and how to copy a costume. Edit the copied costume.

Show pupils how to select a colour and then using the fill tool colour in an item of clothing. Repeat this for a couple of costumes and then send them off to do likewise.

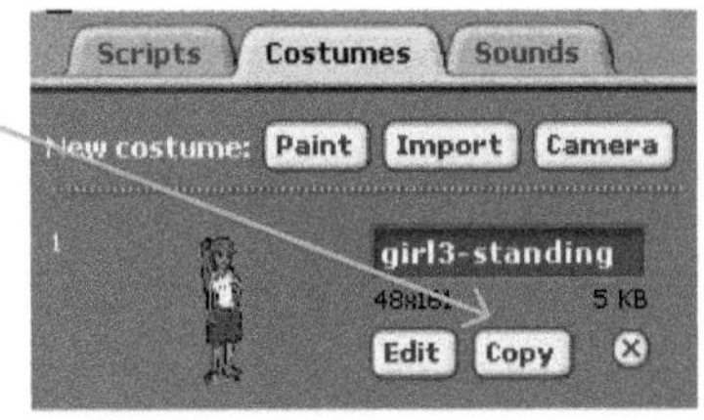
Scripts Costumes Sounds
New costume: Paint Import Camera
girl3-standing
5 KB
Edit Copy

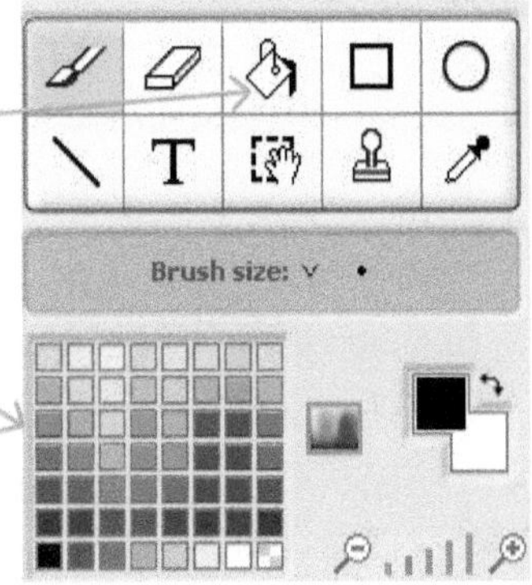
Brush size:

Fill tool

colour chooser

2a. Add detail to costume

Show pupils how to zoom in on the sprite and write a word using the smallest brush at single pixel level. This is a good opportunity to talk about the colours on screen being made up of tiny dots called pixels. These colours are made from mixing quantities of red, green and blue light.

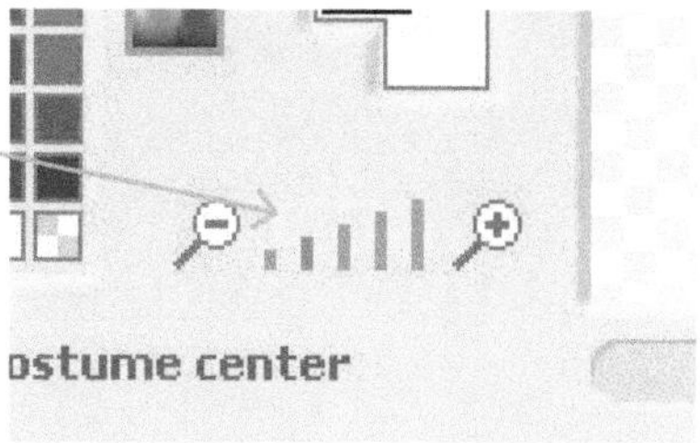
ostume center

3. Mouse changes costume

Show pupils how this code can change the costume once the sprite is clicked on.

when Ruby clicked
next costume

3a. Add detail to costume

(see comments made in 2a)

Ruby

4. Draw Accessories

Demo drawing an accessory or item of clothing. Show pupils how you need to grow or shrink it as well as rotate or re-draw to get it looking good. Stress the need to draw it with one colour inside an outline. This is necessary so we can code it to change colour later. For best results use a vibrant base colour.

5. Code item to change colour

Navigate to the purple looks blocks. Ask pupils if they can see which block might change the colour?

Include this code in the scripts area.

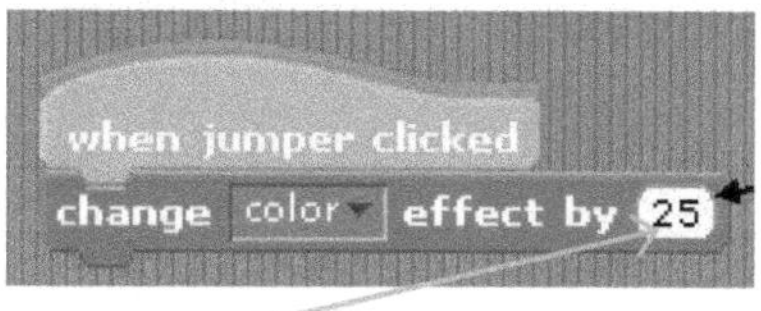
when jumper clicked
change color effect by 25

6. Import a background

Although you could draw your own background I think it is good to import one so that your drawn items stand out.

Click on Stage

Click on backgrounds

Click on import

Find a background you like. Repeat to make more backgrounds using import button

Stage

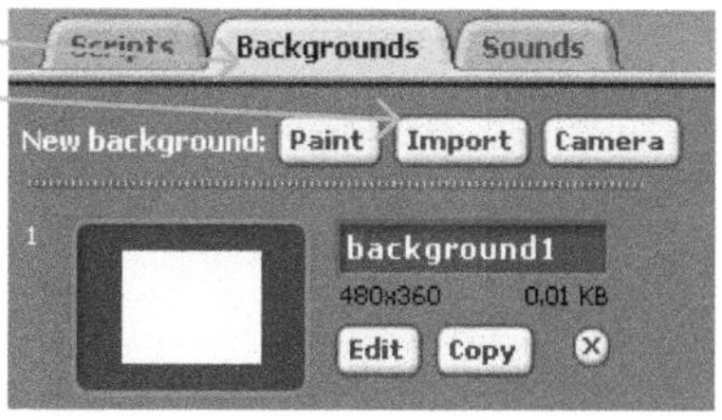
Backgrounds
Sounds
New background:
Paint
Import
Camera
background1
480x360
0.01 KB
Edit
Copy

when Stage clicked
next background

6a. Code your background to change when clicked

Challenge pupils to work out which code to use to go to next background when stage is clicked.

You may wish to give block colour hints. (Yellow and purple blocks)

7. Animate Item

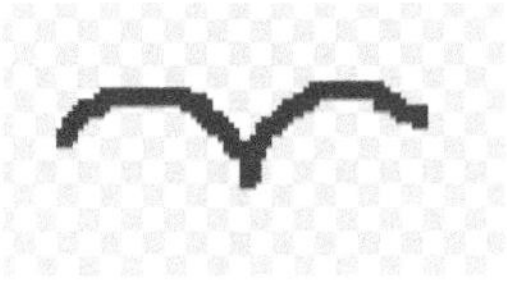

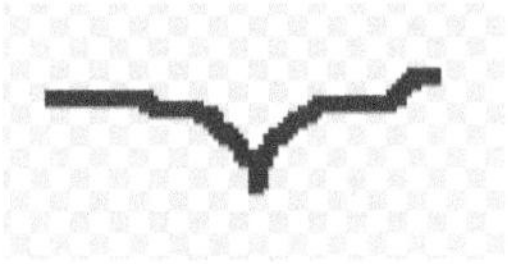

Paint new sprite

Hand draw a simple bird

Rename the sprite

Click on the costume tab

Click copy

Edit the second costume

Using the eraser tool rub out the wing tips and redraw these in a different position

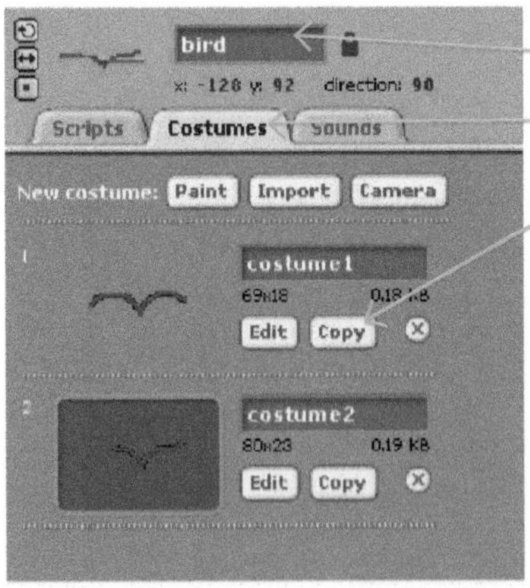
bird
x: -128 y: 92 direction: 90
Scripts
Costumes
Sounds
New costume: Paint Import Camera
costume1
69x18
Edit Copy
costume2
80x23
0.19 KB
Edit Copy

In the scripts area add the scripts underneath If you haven't introduced repeat loops use either some dance steps, music loops or my online loop examples.

See P37 in the Music Machine for a detailed explanation and online loop link.

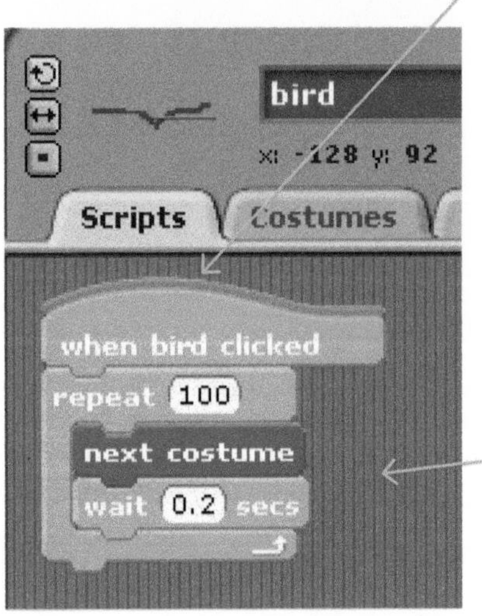
bird
x: -128 y: 92
Scripts
Costumes
when bird clicked
repeat 100
next costume
wait 0.2 secs

The wait one second is a great chance to extend pupils' decimal fraction knowledge. Draw a simple 0 to 1 line and place the tenths on it. Get pupils to experiment with lengths of time and tell you what is slower and what is quicker in their creations. Once they have made a bird they can let their imaginations run wild.

7a. Animate Ball

Choose new sprite from file. Choose a ball from the things folder. In the costumes tab copy the ball once. Change the centre of the second ball sprite as shown using set costume centre button. Now add similar code to that above and the ball will look like it is bouncing as the centre of the costume changes inside the loop.

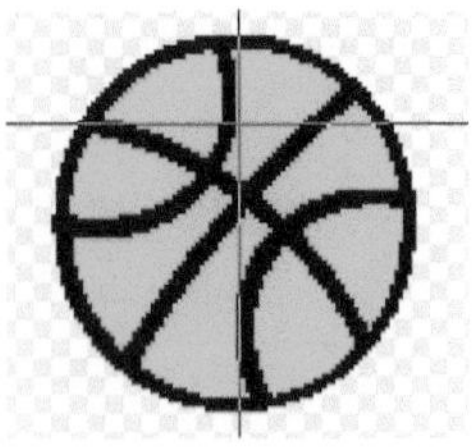

Set costume center

Ruby

1, Click on sprite

Scripts
Costumes
Sounds

2, Click on costumes

3, Click on copy

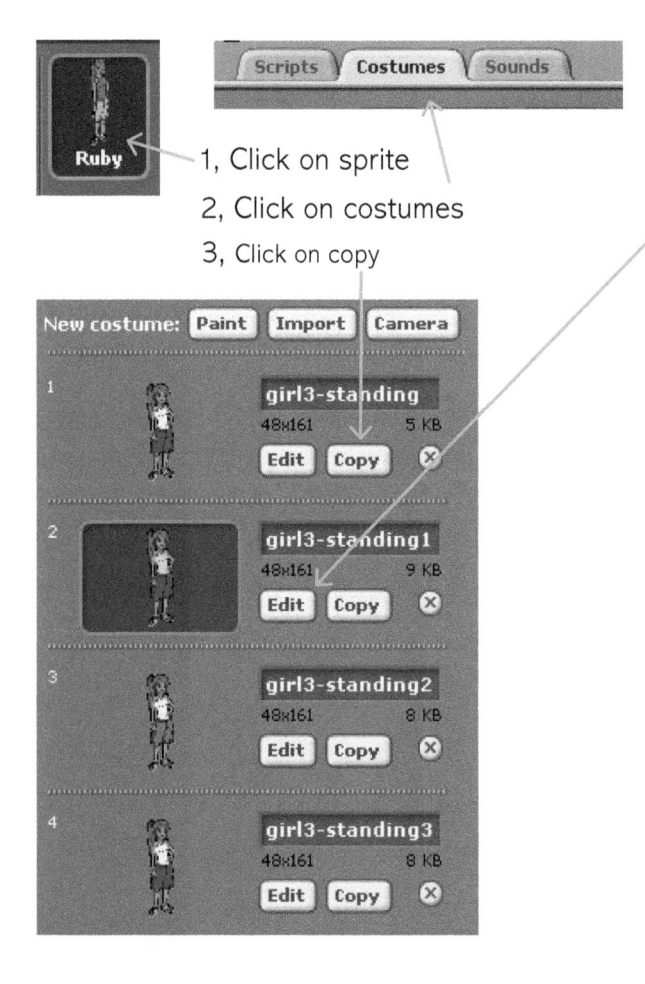

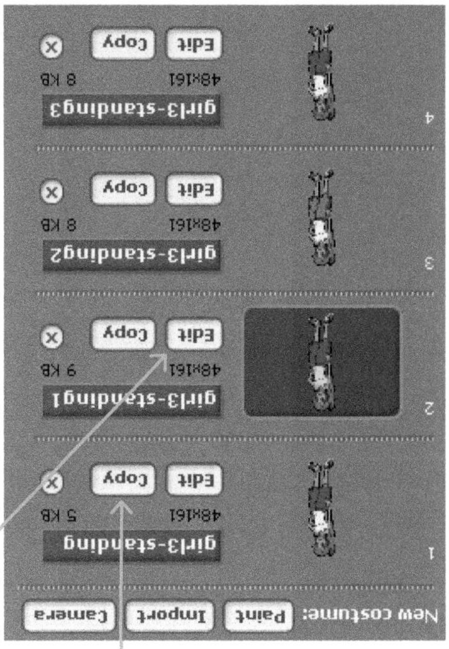
New costume: Paint Import Camera
girl3-standing
48x161 5 KB
Edit Copy
girl3-standing1
48x161 9 KB
Edit Copy
girl3-standing2
48x161 8 KB
Edit Copy
girl3-standing3
48x161 8 KB
Edit Copy

4, Click on edit

5, Click on paint bucket (fill tool)

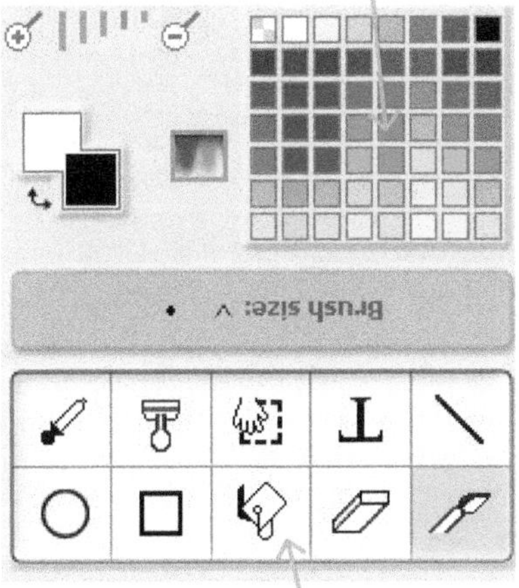
Brush size:

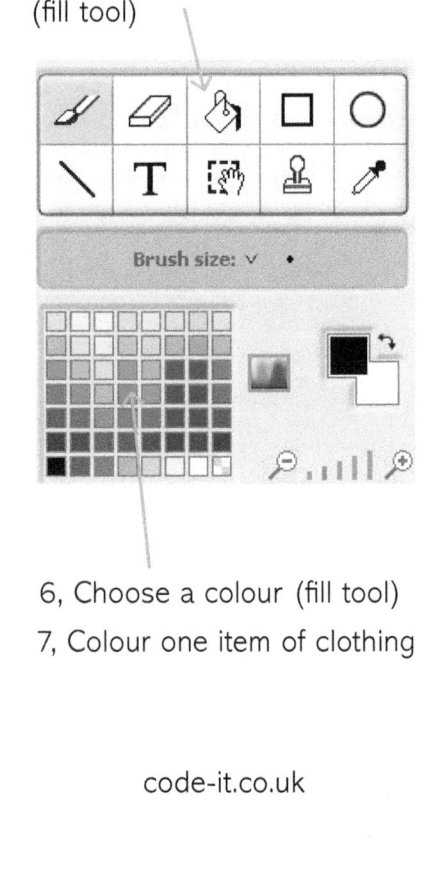

6, Choose a colour (fill tool)

7, Colour one item of clothing

code-it.co.uk

Dressing Up Help Card

code-it.co.uk

Customise Sprite

code-it.co.uk

Import Backgrounds Help

code-it.co.uk

Dressing up Help Cards

code-it.co.uk

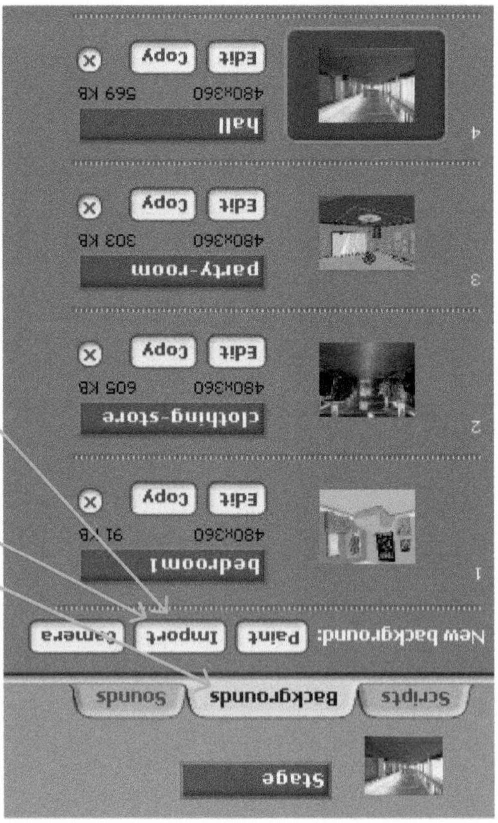
Stage
Scripts
Backgrounds
Sounds
New background:
Paint
Import
Camera
bedroom1
480x360
clothing-store
480x360
605 KB
party-room
480x360
303 KB
hall
480x360
569 KB
Edit
Copy

Stage

1. Click on stage
2. Click on backgrounds
3. Click on Import
4. Choose a background from one of the folders (Indoors, Nature, Outdoors, Sport)
5. Click OK
6. Go back to import and choose another background

Code-it.co.uk

1F. Action Planning Assessment

Module Aim: This module is designed to give pupils who have completed some of the other Y3 projects such as the Smoking Car, Music Machine, Conversation, Interactive Display and Dressing Up Game an independent challenge which can then be assessed.

Time to complete module

Planning time plus 2 hours

Module Learning Focus

By the end of the module children will be able to:

- Describe how they have used Scratch blocks in the past
- Describe a simple project that they wish to create
- Created a meaningful project independently
- Debug code independently

Adult Focus

All adults need to be clear that this is an assessment and that they need to avoid fixing code for pupils. It is all alright to remind pupils how to create sprites or access backgrounds etc. Reminders that are not code-related are permitted but be wary of providing too much help lest you encourage dependence.

However you could allow pupils a single code question per session as long as that was agreed with all adults.

3. Creation

2. Algorithm Idea

1. Reflection

Learning line

National Curriculum Programs of Study

Pupils should be taught to:

- ***design, write and debug programs that accomplish specific goals,*** including controlling or simulating physical systems; ***solve problems by decomposing them into smaller parts***
- ***use sequence,*** selection, ***and repetition in programs; work with*** variables and ***various forms of input and output***
- ***use logical reasoning*** to explain how some simple algorithms work and to ***detect and correct errors in algorithms and programs***

Useful Hints

Read code aloud: does it make sense? Save your work and have a look at ways you have solved this issue in other Scratch creations

1. Reflection

Project - block sheet
http://code-it.co.uk/wp-content/uploads/2015/08/y3blocks.pdf

Direct pupils to workbook page 21. Explain that these are blocks that they have used in their modules of Scratch work.

Ask them to work together to say what each block does and what they used it for. Explain that they may need to share these explanations with the rest of the class.

Give pupils 5 minutes then ask pairs to report on different blocks. Be sure that you remind pupils what they did with these blocks in the other programs if they don't mention this themselves.

2. Algorithm Idea

Explain that they can use these blocks to program a project of their choosing. Mention that they can use other blocks than these but that these are the best blocks to start with. Pupils then go off in small groups to discuss their own ideas before filling in the simple planner on pupil workbook page 21 Please note that the blocks on their workbook sheet are in black and white and are arranged differently. This is to encourage them to read the blocks and not just rely on the colour coding. Teachers need to check that their ideas involve some coding and that the projects are suitably simple to start with.

3. Creation

It is a good idea to have the help/debugging cards available from the other projects for independent use. It also helps to have the blocks displayed on the interactive whiteboard screen. Allow time during the module for pupils to show their work to each other. You could use the chart below as a basis for assessing independent work.

Above	Pupils combine blocks in ways they haven't before - such as when sprite is clicked it moves; music is played from a key or from using new programming blocks or pupils use a loop successfully in a new or an old way.
Within	Pupils re-use programming elements such as keys to move or point in a direction or sprites that when clicked on produce sound. There is a proto theme to the project other than just random sprites that do things.
Below	Pupils' finished projects have little usable code often characterised by lots of sprites that don't do anything.

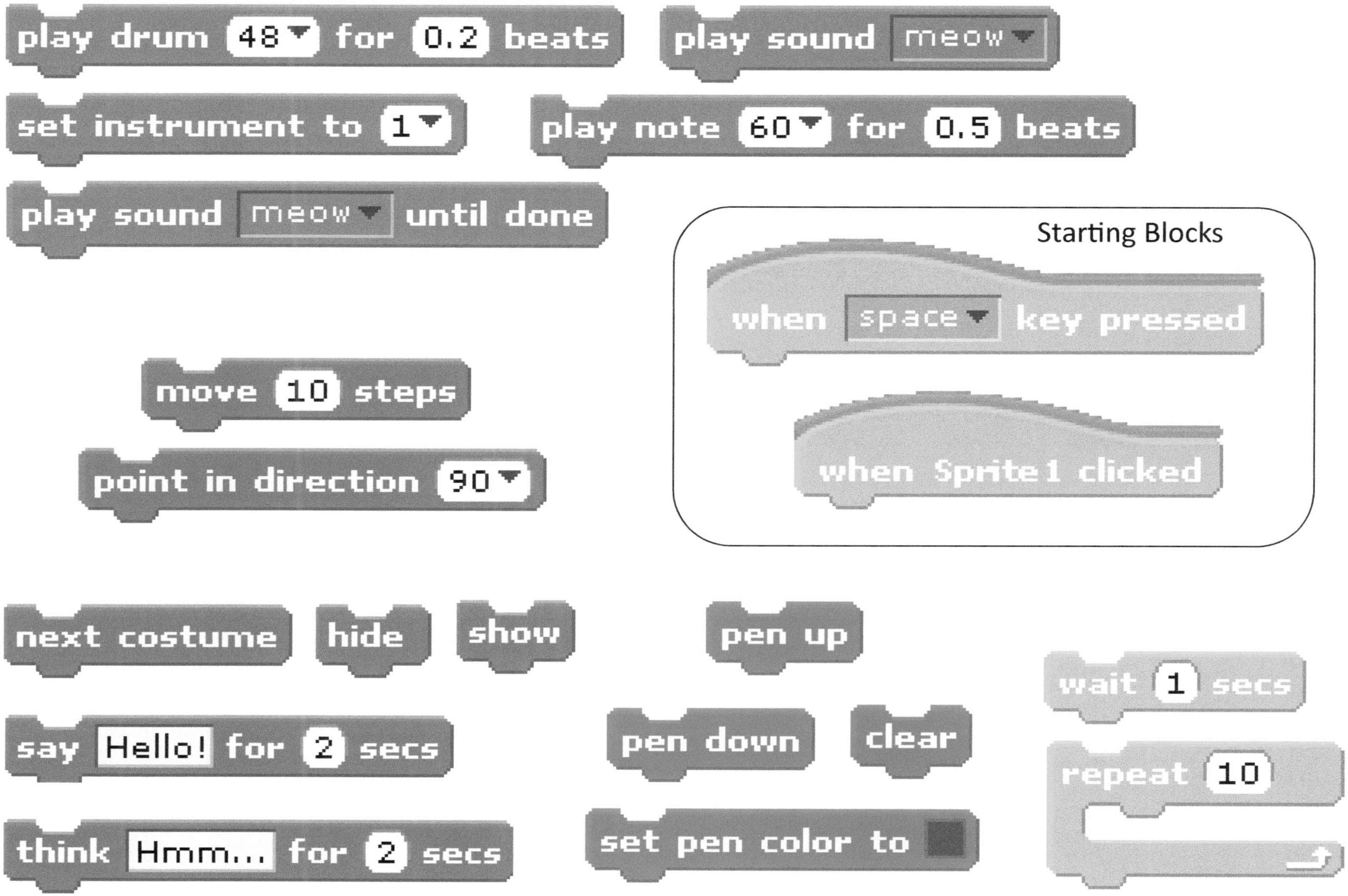
play drum 48 for 0.2 beats
play sound meow
set instrument to 1
play note 60 for 0.5 beats
play sound meow until done
Starting Blocks
when space key pressed
when Sprite1 clicked
move 10 steps
point in direction 90
next costume
hide
show
pen up
wait 1 secs
say Hello! for 2 secs
pen down
clear
repeat 10
think Hmm... for 2 secs
set pen color to

2A. Maths Quiz

Time to complete module

3-4 hours

Module Aim: Design a quiz algorithm and convert this into Scratch code

National Curriculum Programs of Study

Pupils should be taught to:

- ***design, write and debug programs that accomplish specific goals***, including controlling or simulating physical systems; solve problems by decomposing them into smaller parts
- ***use sequence, selection,*** and ***repetition in programs; work with variables and various forms of input and output***
- ***use logical reasoning to explain how some simple algorithms work and to detect and correct errors in algorithms and programs***

Debugging Hints

- Compare teacher code with pupils code
- Read code aloud including signs = < > + -
- Compare code line by line
- Break long sequence into parts and test each part (question)
- Explain code to a partner
- Point to the code as it runs

Module Learning Focus

By the end of the module children will be able to:

- Design a quiz algorithm
- Identify which parts of the algorithm became which parts of the code
- Code a quiz

Computer Science Concepts

- If else selection
- Broadcasting to trigger other blocks
- Variable for score
- Algorithm to code
- User typed input into program

Maths Concepts

- Equals means the same as

Assessment for Learning

At the end of each session direct pupils to page 4 of pupil workbook 2 to help them reflect on what they have learnt. It is often worth working through this line by line to avoid pupils filling in everything with a smiley face. You can also annotate this to record pupils who have needed much more support or have demonstrated greater understanding.

Adult Focus

All adults need to be clear that they are to support using hints only and not solve things for pupils.

Video Support Maths Quiz walk-through for teachers
https://youtu.be/U2P5_GhACeg

Computational Thinking- **Algorithm:** a precise step by step guide to achieving a specific outcome.

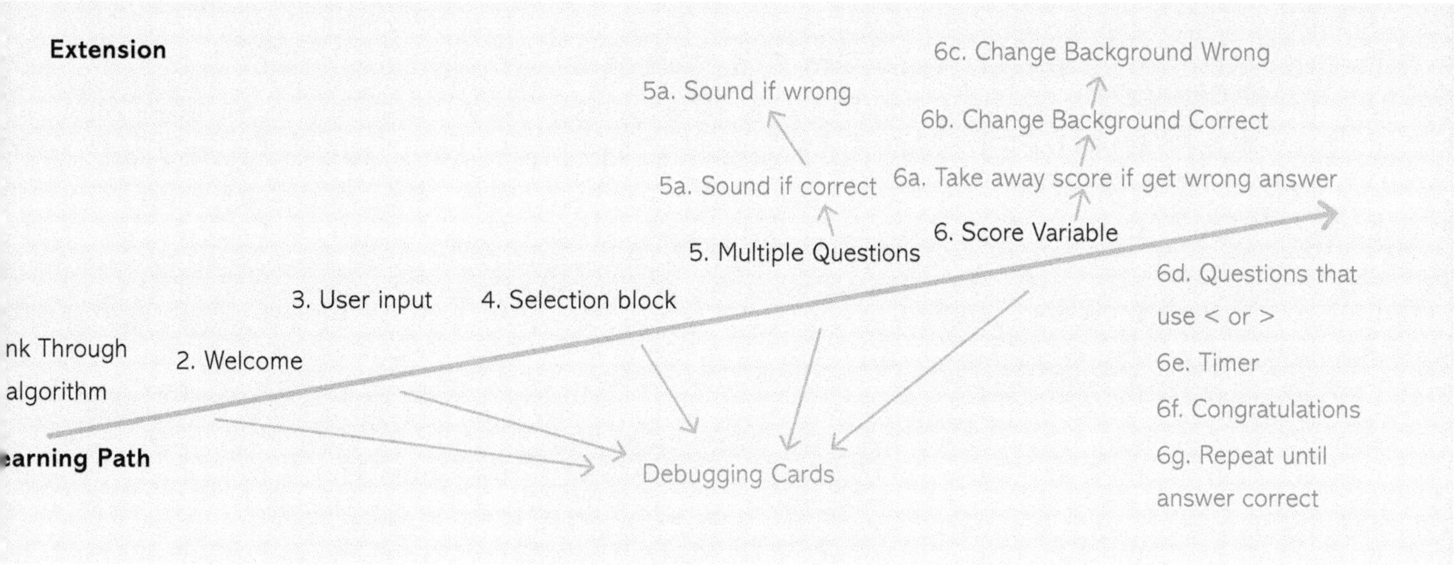
Extension
6c. Change Background Wrong
5a. Sound if wrong
6b. Change Background Correct
5a. Sound if correct
6a. Take away score if get wrong answer
6. Score Variable
5. Multiple Questions
3. User input
4. Selection block
6d. Questions that use < or >
nk Through algorithm
2. Welcome
6e. Timer
6f. Congratulations
earning Path
Debugging Cards
6g. Repeat until answer correct

1. Think through steps (algorithm) to ask a quiz question

Ask a simple maths quiz question to the class. Get them in pairs to work out the steps to think and ask that question and record them in their pupil workbook page 5. Make sure they realise that this is nothing to do with code and it is what a human would do if asking this question as part of a quiz. Once they have completed this; draw out that the quiz master would need to think of the question and then think of the answer before they can ask the question. Once the user has answered the question ask them how they will know if the question is right or wrong. Indicate that the quiz master has got the original thought - through answer and the answer the quiz user gave them. To hold one in each hand and look alternately at both like you are examining them helps pupils. You could write MY QUIZ ANSWER on one piece of paper and USER ANSWER on another. You are looking for a pupil to indicate that they need to be the same. Often pupils will come up with the idea of comparing the answers which is a step in the right direction. Push pupils to be more specific and ask for a type of comparison as they need to be identified as the same. You can then ask what the maths symbol for the same is (=). Then go through http://code-it.co.uk/wp-content/uploads/2015/05/quiz.pdf which highlights the process graphically.

2. Welcome

Explain that this program will mostly be one sequence of instructions from start to finish. Can pupils choose a good starting block and a way to welcome users to their quiz? Have they tested their code?

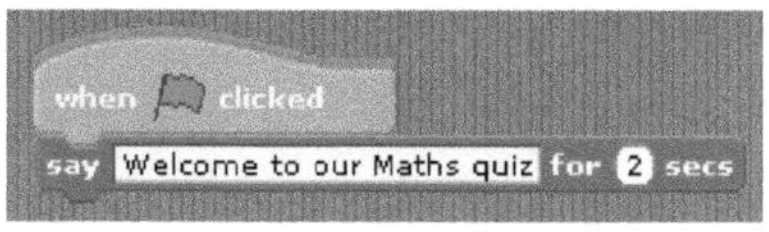
when clicked
say Welcome to our Maths quiz for 2 secs

Example Question

What is 3x3?

After a count of 3 all shout out your answer

1 2 3

If you shouted 9 then well done and give yourself a point.

If you shouted anything else you are wrong and receive no points.

Computers are built on Maths

I don't share this with all pupils at this age but it is useful for teachers to know that all computers are built on Maths.

High and low voltages are converted in to binary 0s and 1s.

Binary 0s and 1s are converted into binary maths.

Then there are lots of other layers before we interact with a modern computer.

So at a fundamental layer if you can relate anything to mathematical functions you can program it.

Common Errors

Pupil types in word answer instead of using the blue answer block

answer

Ticked box

3. User Input Ask Block

Drag the ask and the answer blocks out. Explain that this is a user **input** block. It **puts in** information from the person taking the quiz. Now tick the answer block so that it is visible on the screen. Explain that whatever is typed into the ask input block goes inside the answer block. Type in a maths question that everyone will know the answer to and watch as it appears in the answer block after you tick to accept it. Give pupils time to create this and try it out.

answer 9
What's your name?
when clicked
say Welcome to our Maths quiz for 2 secs
ask 3x3=? and wait
answer
9

Answer box displayed as it is ticked in sensing blocks

Input box on screen

This will be used in the next step

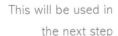

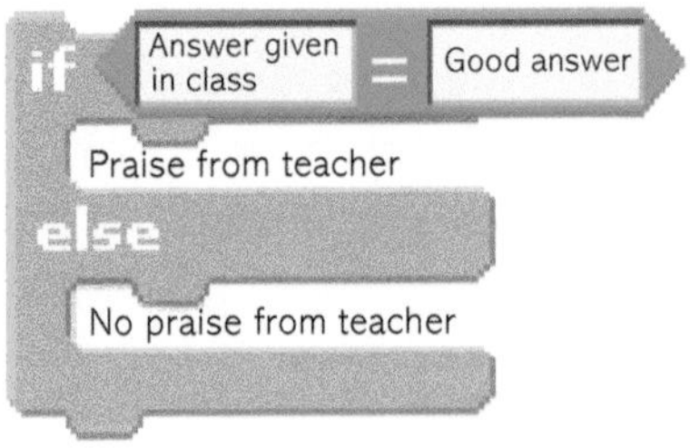
if
Answer given in class
=
Good answer
Praise from teacher
else
No praise from teacher

Selection in the real world last example

4. Selection

If this is the first time that pupils have met the idea of selection it is worth explaining using some real world examples first which you can find at http://code-it.co.uk/wp-content/uploads/2015/05/selectioninrealworld.pdf. The last example is important as it paves the way for the code. Make sure in the last example you draw out that equals means the same as.

Drag out these blocks and arrange them like this. Make sure you draw attention to the shape especially when inserting the equals block. Notice that the equals block goes inside the if else block and then the answer block goes inside the left hand side of the equals block.

If you are not sure how this works watch the walk-through for teachers before the lesson https://youtu.be/U2P5_GhACeg

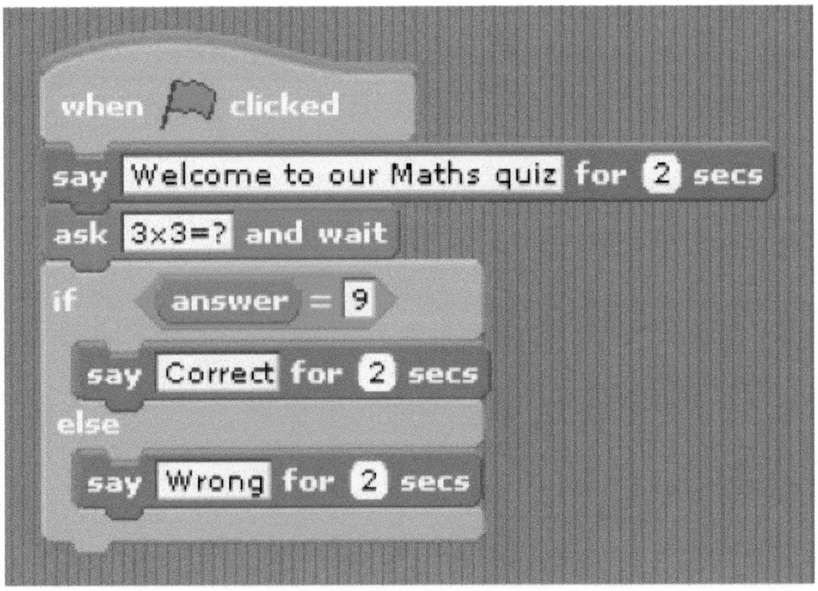
when clicked
say Welcome to our Maths quiz for 2 secs
ask 3x3=? and wait
if answer = 9
say Correct for 2 secs
else
say Wrong for 2 secs

Algorithm to Code Answers

Talk through the program line by line before running it to help pupils understand what is happening. Pretend to be a user who gets an answer right then. Pretend to type the answer and ask the pupils where the answer has gone in to, within the code? (The blue answer block.)

The program then checks to see if it is the same (point to equals sign) as the right answer: this means that the condition has been met and only the top correct block is run. Do the same for a wrong answer pointing out that the answer is not the same as the right answer so only the else block is run.

After pupils have coded and tested a quiz question, check their understanding of how their algorithm matches to the code through the pupil activity on page 6 of the pupil workbook. This can be a good activity to allow paired working as it facilitates discussion. You might want to save this activity to the end of the lesson as a plenary.

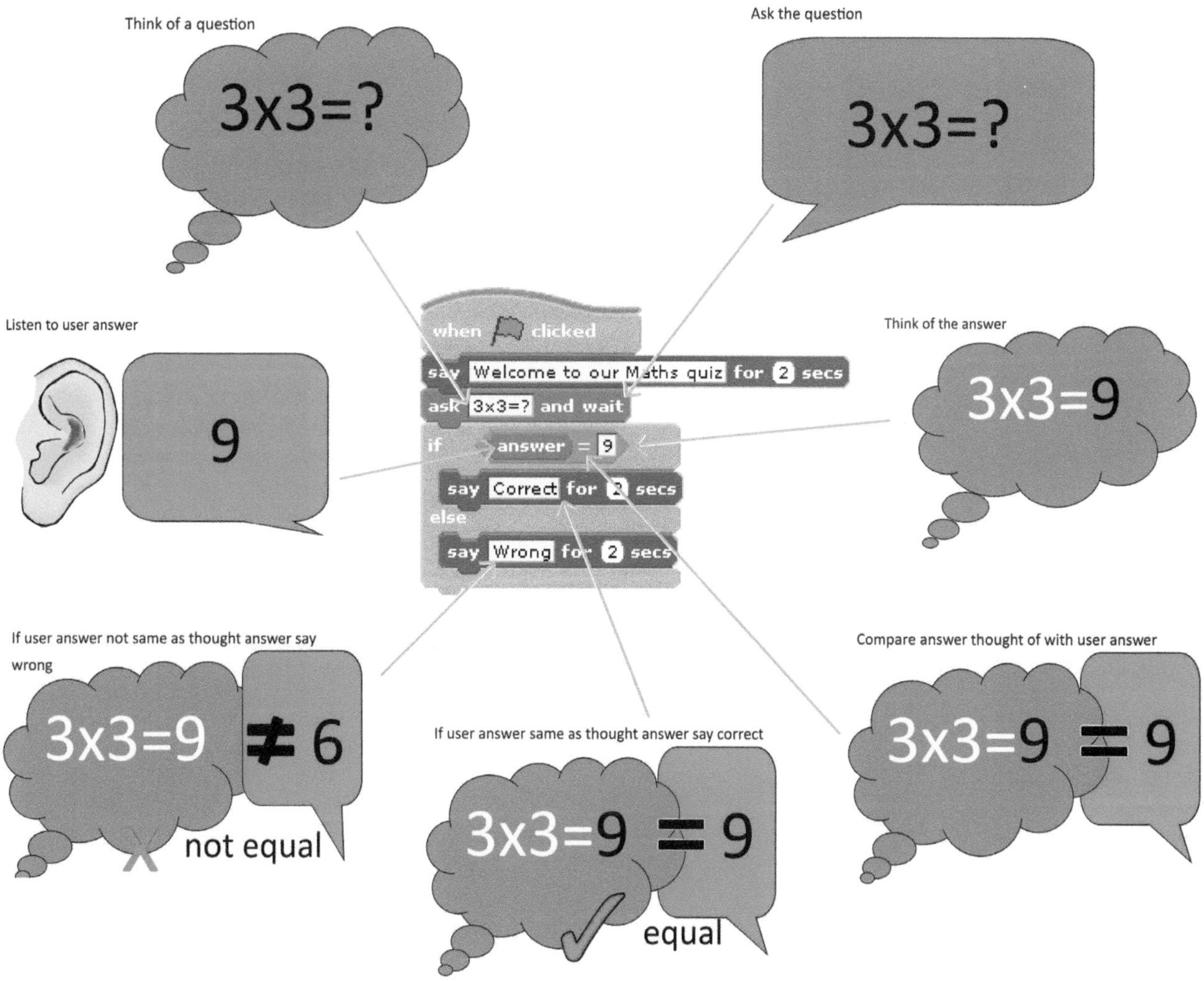
Think of a question
3x3=?
Ask the question
3x3=?
Listen to user answer
9
when clicked
say Welcome to our Maths quiz for 2 secs
ask 3x3=? and wait
if answer = 9
say Correct for 2 secs
else
say Wrong for 2 secs
Think of the answer
3x3=9
If user answer not same as thought answer say wrong
3x3=9 ≠ 6
not equal
If user answer same as thought answer say correct
3x3=9 = 9
equal
Compare answer thought of with user answer
3x3=9 = 9

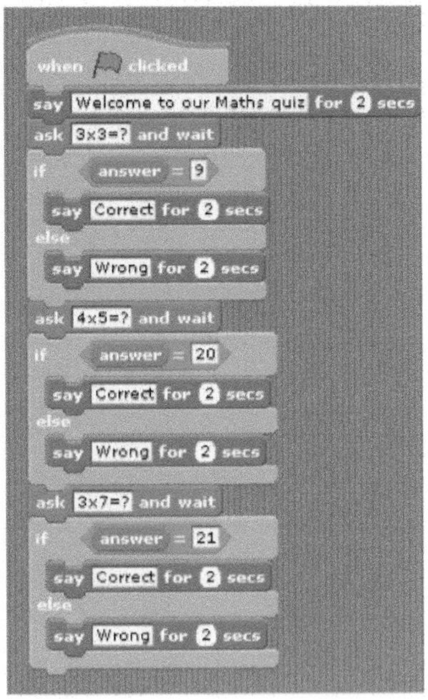
when clicked
say Welcome to our Maths quiz for 2 secs
ask 3x3=? and wait
if answer = 9
say Correct for 2 secs
else
say Wrong for 2 secs
ask 4x5=? and wait
if answer = 20
say Correct for 2 secs
else
say Wrong for 2 secs
ask 3x7=? and wait
if answer = 21
say Correct for 2 secs
else
say Wrong for 2 secs

5. Multiple Questions

Demonstrate how to build another question underneath the first and ask pupils to create as many questions as they can in the time.

Don't show pupils how to duplicate the blocks until they have done a few more questions block by block.

Now demonstrate how to duplicate blocks by dragging out a single question and right clicking on the top - most blue ask block and choosing duplicate. Always right click on the top block of the code section you want duplicated.

Common Errors

Once pupils have started to duplicate it is very easy to snap the question inside the bottom else part of the selection block. Demonstrate this; can they tell you when the second question would be asked? ANSWER Only if you got question 1 wrong. For most pupils this is an error but an exceptional pupil may be making an adaptive quiz that responds to the user.

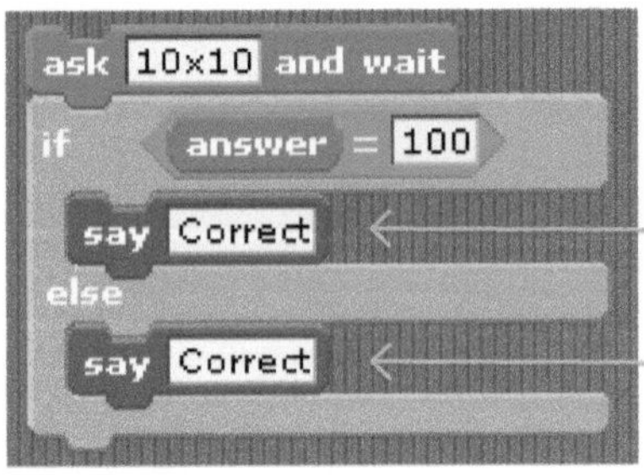
ask 10x10 and wait
if answer = 100
say Correct
else
say Correct

Common Errors

Another common error is to use say blocks without timings. This runs the say blocks so fast that the user can't see them at all. Comparing their code with yours is normally enough for most pupils to identify the error.

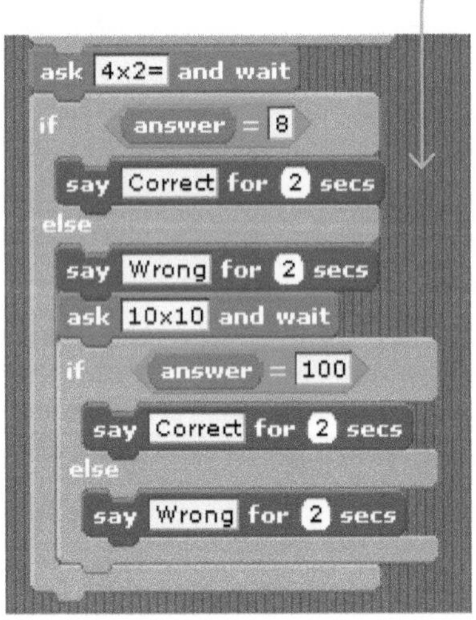
ask 4x2= and wait
if answer = 8
say Correct for 2 secs
else
say Wrong for 2 secs
ask 10x10 and wait
if answer = 100
say Correct for 2 secs
else
say Wrong for 2 secs

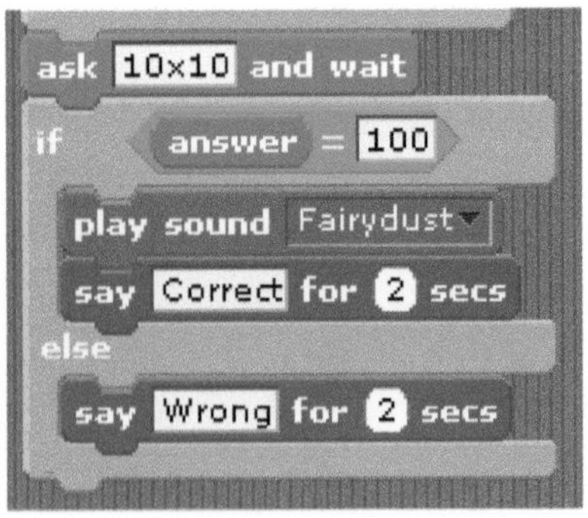
ask 10x10 and wait
if answer = 100
play sound Fairydust
say Correct for 2 secs
else
say Wrong for 2 secs

5a. Sound if Correct

Ask pupils to make the quiz play a sound if the quiz question is correct. This is a further test to see if they understand what is happening inside the selection process. Many pupils will choose to add this without your prompting especially if they completed the music machine in the past.

5b. Sound if incorrect

6. Score Variable

Ask pupils what it means if we say that the weather is variable? Draw out that it means changeable. Explain that we can get the program to keep score for us by creating a variable which is like a pencil pot which we can put pencils/numbers in to to help us keep score.

Ask pupils what possible scores the user could get from a three question quiz if each question is worth one mark each? (0, 1, 2 or 3) Ask them if we know what score a user will get before they take the quiz? This is important as many pupils won't have considered the range of possibilities and may have already awarded a 'mark' via a say command at the end of each question.

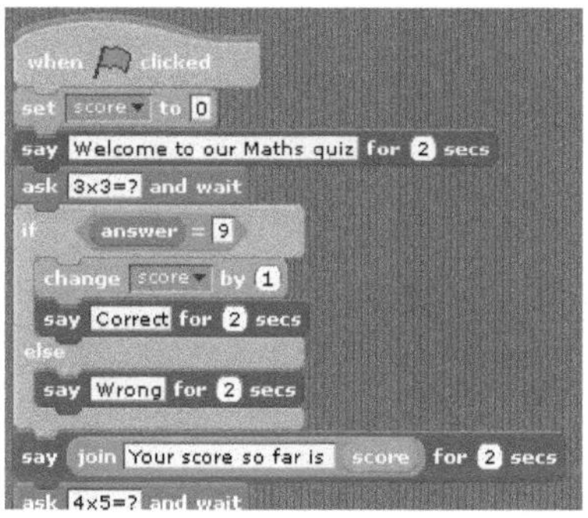
when clicked
set score to 0
say Welcome to our Maths quiz for 2 secs
ask 3x3=? and wait
if answer = 9
change score by 1
say Correct for 2 secs
else
say Wrong for 2 secs
say join Your score so far is score for 2 secs
ask 4x5=? and wait

You may also wish to show pupils how you can get the sprite to say the score through the use of a say, join and score variable. Pupils love the cleverness of this.

Create a variable called score

Click on orange variable block

Click on make a variable

Type in a name like score

Select for all sprites

Click ok

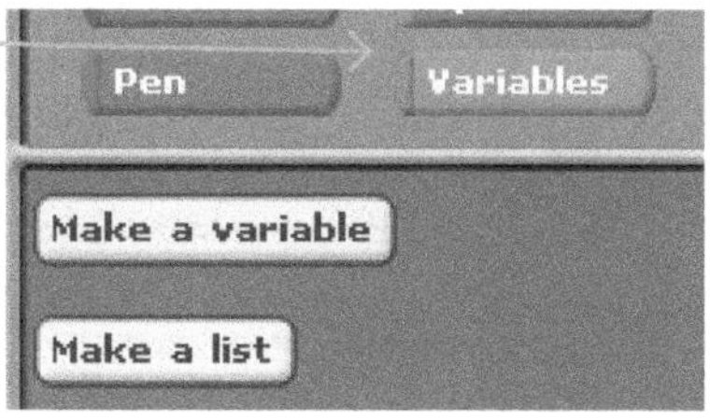
Pen
Variables
Make a variable
Make a list

Ask pupils what score the user should start with? Drag out the **set score to 0** block and ask pupils where it should go? (At the top so the quiz always starts with zero points). The set score block is like always emptying the pot first before filling it with whatever is set.

This video explains the difference between setting and changing a variable in Scratch https://youtu.be/D01vMX7HUu4

Now drag out multiple **change score by 1** blocks and ask pupils to decide where they should go to put a point into the variable pot if the user gets the question correct.

If pupils come up with the wrong location go with it and run the program to show them otherwise. A common one is after each question.

When pupils have come up with the right location talk through the code to explain it before running it. A great way to do this is with a box labelled score for the variable containing 4 pencils that a pupil holds. Model setting the score to 0 by removing all the pencils. Model adding a pencil into the box if you get the answer right.

Finally run the code getting some answers right and some wrong before encouraging them to create their own score.

6a. Takeaway score point if user gets answer wrong. Add a change score by -1 into the else section. Challenge pupils to solve this independantly.

Common Bugs

Inserting **set score to 1** blocks instead of **change score by 1**. This sets the score back to 1 every time it is used.

Missing out a **set score to 0** block

This means that when the quiz is run the second time the old score is still inside the variable and will be added to instead of having an empty score when you start.

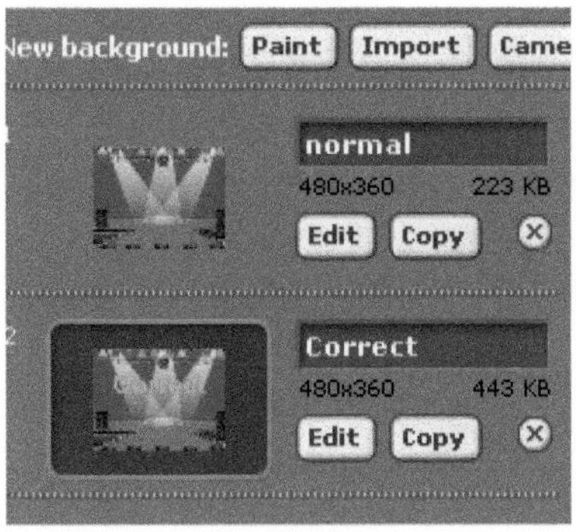
New background: Paint Import Came
normal
480x360 223 KB
Edit Copy
Correct
480x360 443 KB
Edit Copy

6b. Change Background to Correct if Answer Correct

As this might be their first experience with broadcasts I normally take a break-away group aside to go through this. Get pupils to import two backgrounds and change one by adding the word correct on it. Change the names of the backgrounds to normal and correct. Give pupils a few minutes to do this.

Broadcasts explained in this video https://youtu.be/BwFT6dYAUz0

Gather pupils back and whisper in two pupils' ears that if you say the word correct, they must jump up and down twice and then sit down. Explain to the group that we are going to use a broadcast command to change the background when the users gets a question correct. When you say correct the two pupils will jump up and down. Make sure you use correct more times. Explain that we can all hear the broadcast command but only those who have the code instructions will know what to do with it.

Now setup the code as shown starting with broadcast in sprite and then moving on to stage/screen code.

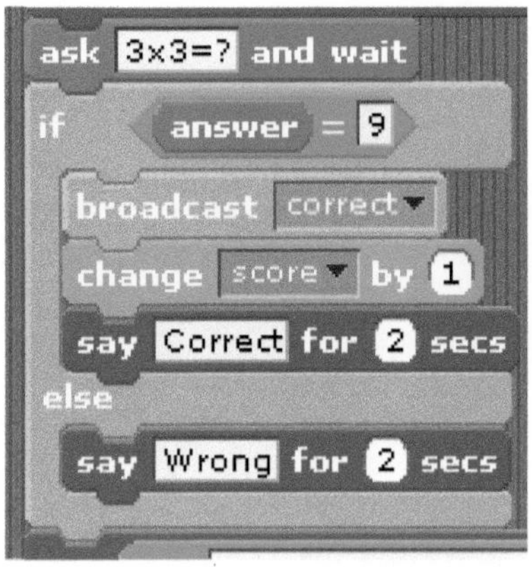
ask 3x3=? and wait
if answer = 9
broadcast correct
change score by 1
say Correct for 2 secs
else
say Wrong for 2 secs

Broadcast in sprite

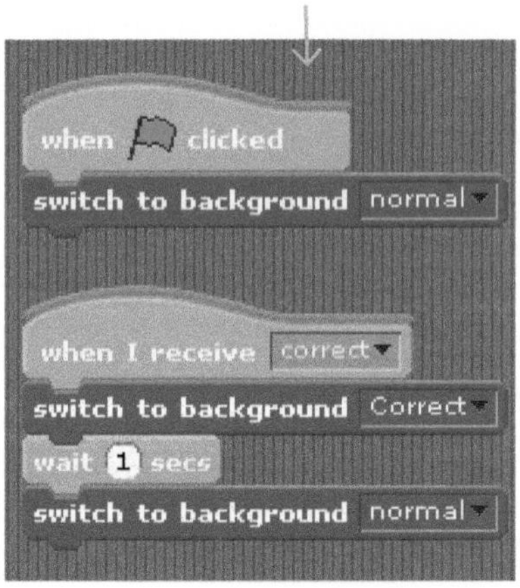
when clicked
switch to background normal
when I receive correct
switch to background Correct
wait 1 secs
switch to background normal

Stage/Screen code

6c. Change Background if User Gives Wrong Answer

This is a good independent task to see who understood the use of a broadcast

6d. Code that uses less than or greater than

Can pupils create questions such as type a number less than 56. Use a > or < block instead of an = one

Note

If pupils have used Scratch Junior, broadcasts are like the colourful letter icons that can be used to trigger code elsewhere.

6e. Timer

Can pupils create a timer for the quiz which ends the game after a set period of time? This could be further extended so that the user could select a difficulty level which results in a longer or shorter time period. Pupils could use simple wait for x seconds time blocks although this will not show the user the time counting down or a time variable inside a loop which is the better solution.

when clicked
wait 28 secs
say 2 seconds to go for 1 secs
say 1 seconds to go for 1 secs
stop all
when clicked
set timer to 30
repeat 30
wait 1 secs
change timer by -1
stop all

6f. Congratulations

Add code at the end of the quiz that congratulates the player IF they got all of the questions correct ELSE it tells them their score. Pupils would need to use an if else selection blocks.

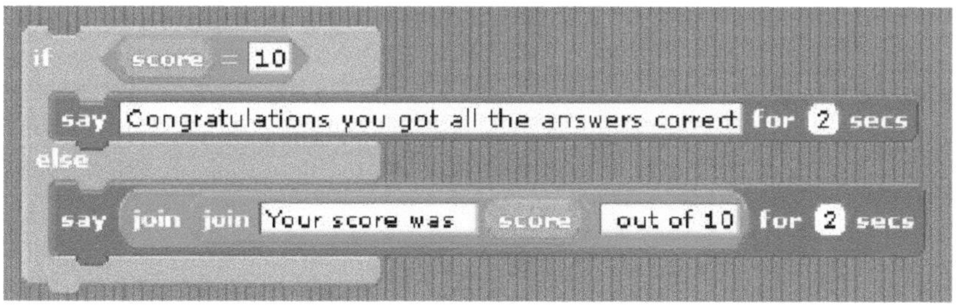
if score = 10
say Congratulations you got all the answers correct for 2 secs
else
say join join Your score was score out of 10 for 2 secs

6g. Repeat until answer correct

Can pupils get a question to repeat until the user answers it correctly? Ask if this solution would affect a scoring variable.

Please note this is not the only way of doing this but most methods affect scoring.

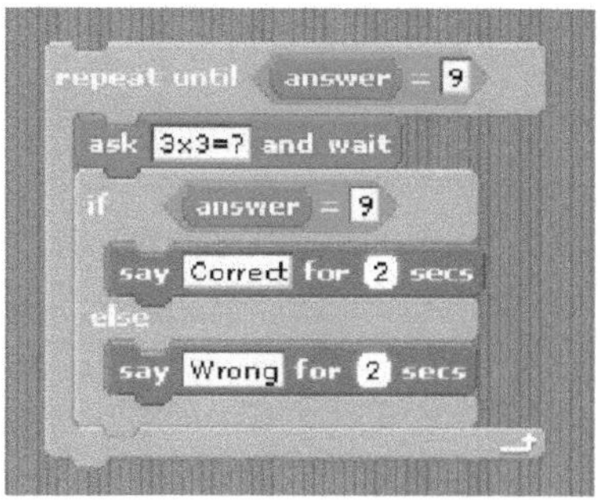
repeat until answer = 9
ask 3x3=? and wait
if answer = 9
say Correct for 2 secs
else
say Wrong for 2 secs

> **Cross Curricular Opportunities**
>
> **Maths**
>
> Pupils create a quiz for other members of their set or maths group based on recent maths topics. Pupils directed to create questions of a specific type geared to the needs of their immediate Maths curriculum.
>
> **Other areas of the curriculum**
>
> Pupils instructed to create a quiz around a specific topic such as Roman or Neolithic Britain, light and sound, keeping safe on the web or sacred texts from the great world religions.

My thanks to Vikki Dodd Head of Computing Queen Elizabeth's Grammar School Blackburn for these extra challenges 6e and 6f

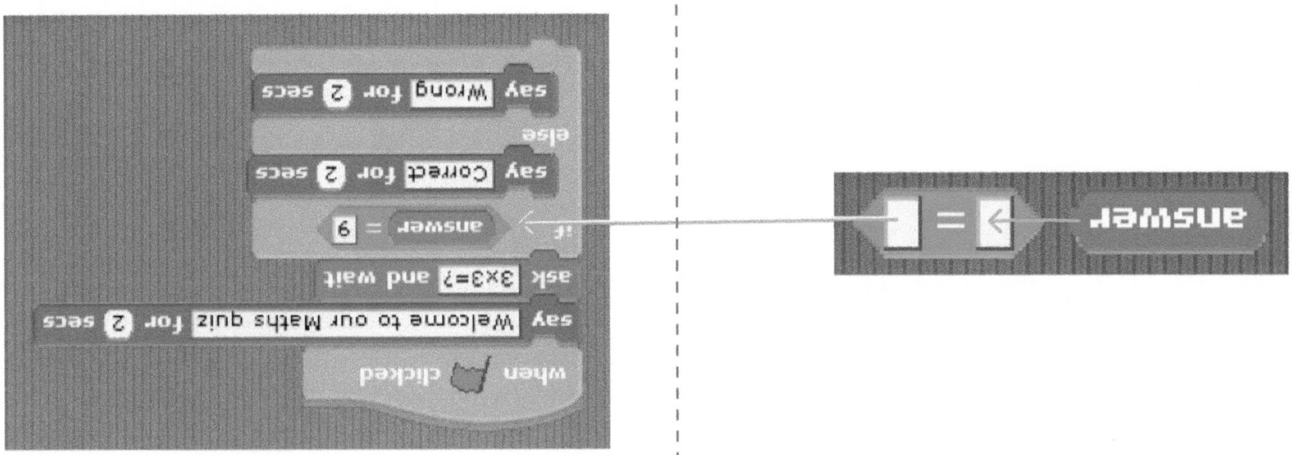
when clicked
say Welcome to our Maths quiz for 2 secs
ask 3x3=? and wait
if answer = 9
say Correct for 2 secs
else
say Wrong for 2 secs
answer
=

Question

Scratch

Maths Games

Help Card

code-it.co.uk

code-it.co.uk

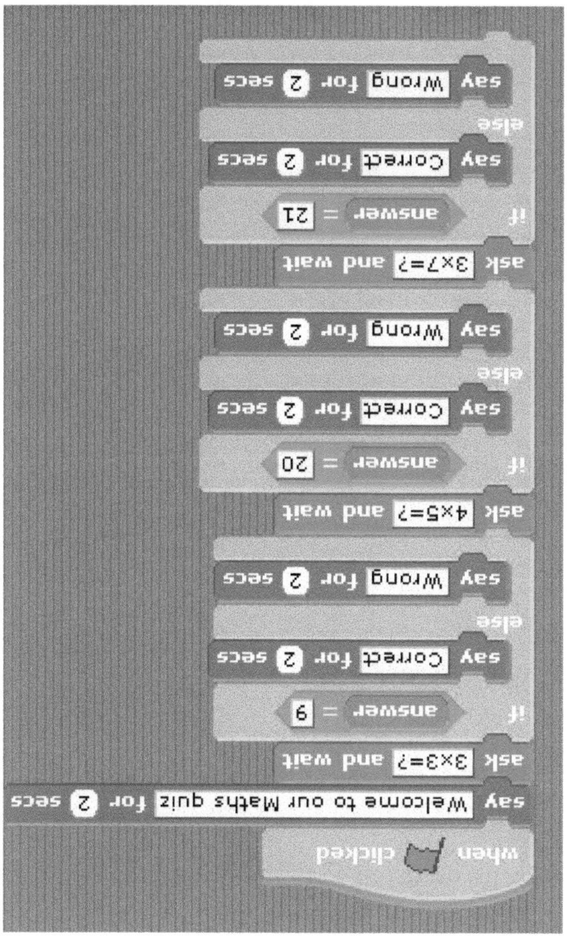
when clicked
say Welcome to our Maths quiz for 2 secs
ask 3x3=? and wait
if answer = 9
say Correct for 2 secs
else
say Wrong for 2 secs
ask 4x5=? and wait
if answer = 20
say Correct for 2 secs
else
say Wrong for 2 secs
ask 3x7=? and wait
if answer = 21
say Correct for 2 secs
else
say Wrong for 2 secs

code-it.co.uk

Multiple Questions

Scratch

Maths Games

Support Card

2B. Music Algorithm to Music Code

Time to complete module
1 hour

Module Aim: Can pupils convert musical score (algorithm) into musical code?

National Curriculum Programs of Study

Pupils should be taught to:

- ***design, write and debug programs that accomplish specific goals***, including controlling or simulating physical systems; solve problems by decomposing them into smaller parts
- ***use sequence***, selection, ***and repetition in programs;*** work with variables and various forms of input and output
- ***use logical reasoning to*** explain how some simple algorithms work and to ***detect and correct errors in algorithms and programs***

Precondition: It is advisable that all pupils have completed the Music Machine to familiarise themselves with the music blocks.

Module Learning Focus

By the end of the module children will be able to:

- Decode musical score into Scratch numbers
- Convert these numbers into Scratch note blocks
- Listen to the code to find and correct bugs
- Start to apply this idea to other musical scores

Computer Science Concepts

- Sequence
- Repeat loops
- Converting algorithm to code

Maths Concepts

- Decimal Fractions

Adult Focus

All adults need to be clear that they are to support using hints only and not solve things for pupils.

Useful Hints: Listen to the code: does it sound right? Trace the code with your finger as it plays to spot the location of bugs. Break long sequence into parts and test each part.

Computational Thinking: **Algorithm** - A set of steps or rules to accomplish a set task or solve a problem.

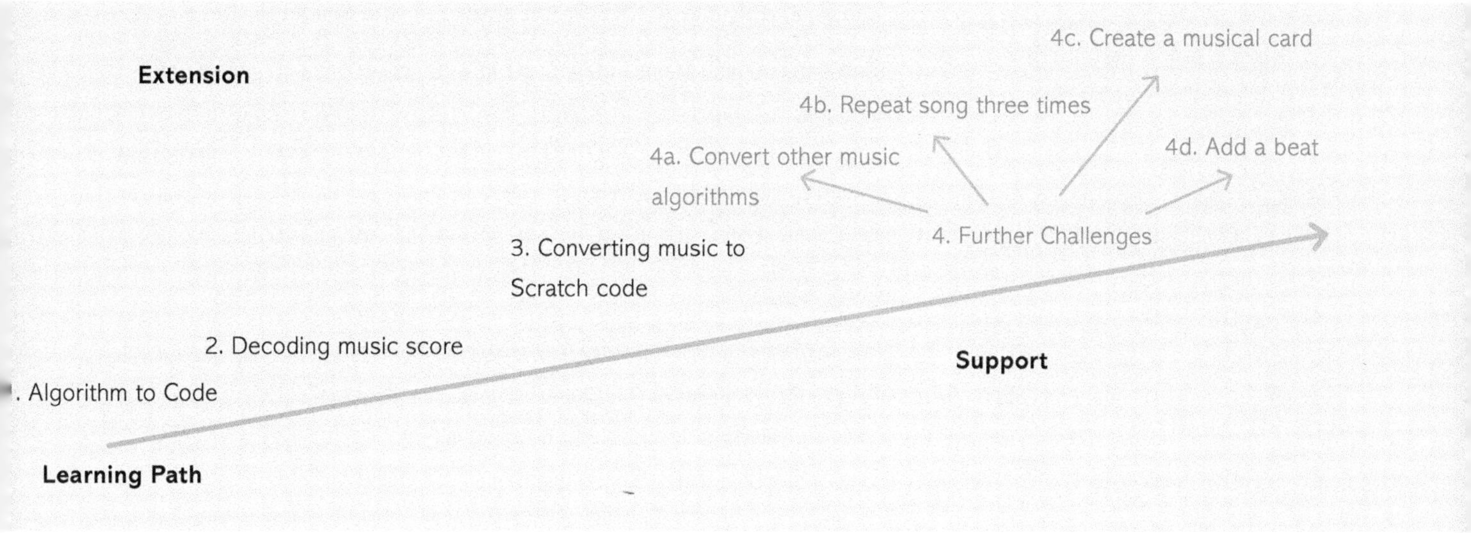
4c. Create a musical card
Extension
4b. Repeat song three times
4a. Convert other music algorithms
4d. Add a beat
4. Further Challenges
3. Converting music to Scratch code
2. Decoding music score
Support
. Algorithm to Code
Learning Path

1. Algorithm to Code

Remind pupils that all programs begin life as algorithms. The algorithm could be an informal one in the programmer's head, a flowchart or a list of written instructions.

Score Help Sheet
http://code-it.co.uk/wp-content/uploads/2015/05/scorehelp.pdf

Our task is to program Twinkle Twinkle Little Star using note blocks so that it will play the whole tune. We could create our own algorithm but fortunately someone helpful has provided a ready made algorithm for us to use. Ask them what that might be? Answer a musical score.

2. Decoding music score

Explain how musical notes are an algorithm to help people play exactly the same tune. People follow the musical score turning the algorithm into music.

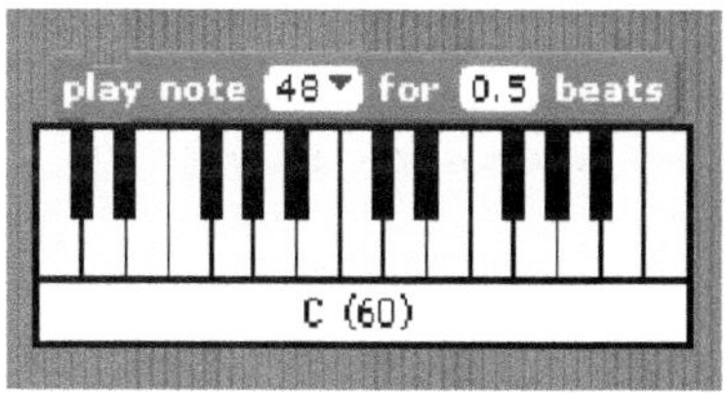
play note 48 for 0.5 beats
C (60)

Open Scratch and drag out a play note block. Remind them where they may have used this before (Music Machine). Open the score help sheet and explain how each half a line up on the stave is the next white note along the keyboard to the right. Some pupils get stuck because they are looking at the stem of the note and not the dot. Focus pupils on where the dot is.

Now demonstrate decoding the first few notes. Can they use the key on the bottom of the help sheet to help them decode the rest of the notes?

At some point as pupils are decoding go over the difference between a quarter and a half note. Can they see how they might change the length of note in Scratch (beats) to make half and quarter notes?

Encourage pupils to decode all the score before converting it into Scratch code.

Note Scratch beat lengths don't match classic notation so 0.5 beats matches a quarter note. 1 beat matches a half note.

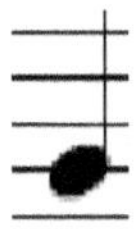

Quarter notes

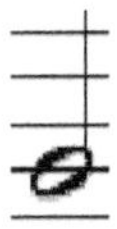

Half notes

Computational Thinking

Algorithm Evaluation is concerned with efficiency. For a professional programmer this would mean how much computing resources are used such as processor power, RAM memory or hard drive space. We can help pupils to start thinking efficiently by using the least amount of code.

Debugging Hint

Divide and conquer can be a very useful strategy for discovering bugs in their musical code.

Split the code into two parts and listen to both. When you have ascertained which half has the bug split this half in half again. Repeat until you have found the bug.

3. Converting music to Scratch code

Challenge pupils to use their decoded algorithm (Scratch note numbers) to program Twinkle Twinkle Little Star in the most efficient way they can using the least number of note blocks. You may also wish to remind them about repeat x type loop blocks.

More Support

Give everyone the base help score sheet which is in the pupil's workbook and in teacher's workbook on p73 but if anyone is really struggling I give them the easier score help sheet on page 74.

3a. Convert other musical algorithms

Can they program another piece of music? There is some free downloadable sheet music including Happy Birthday and Jingle Bells at http://www.letsplaykidsmusic.com/tag/free-sheet-music/ You may need to steer them away from music with different types of notes than the ones used or challenge them to find out how they might be different and the code adapted for the more able.

3b. Repeat song three times

Can they find a way to play the song through three times? The repeat loop is one way or they could use a broadcast command or if using Scratch 2.0 they could make their own block/procedure and refer to it three times.

3c. Create a Musical Card

Can they create a musical card to cheer someone up or celebrate their birthday?

3d. Add a beat alongside your tune

This is a good one to do if pupils didn't get much exploration time when you taught the Music Machine.

Twinkle Twinkle Little Star

Mozart

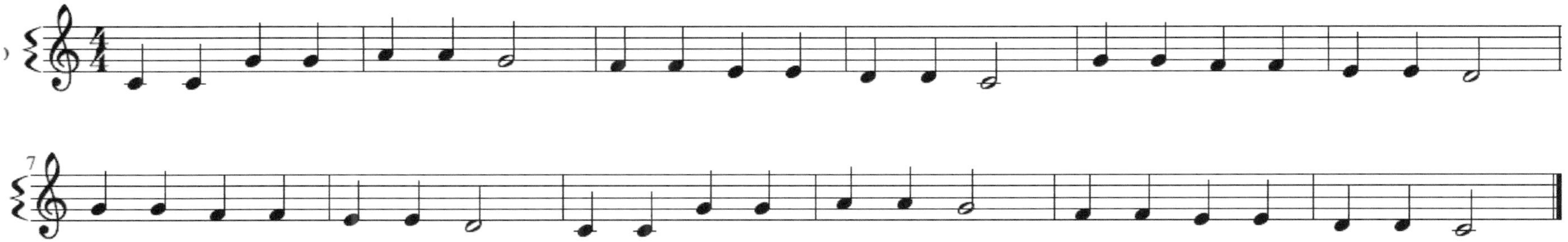

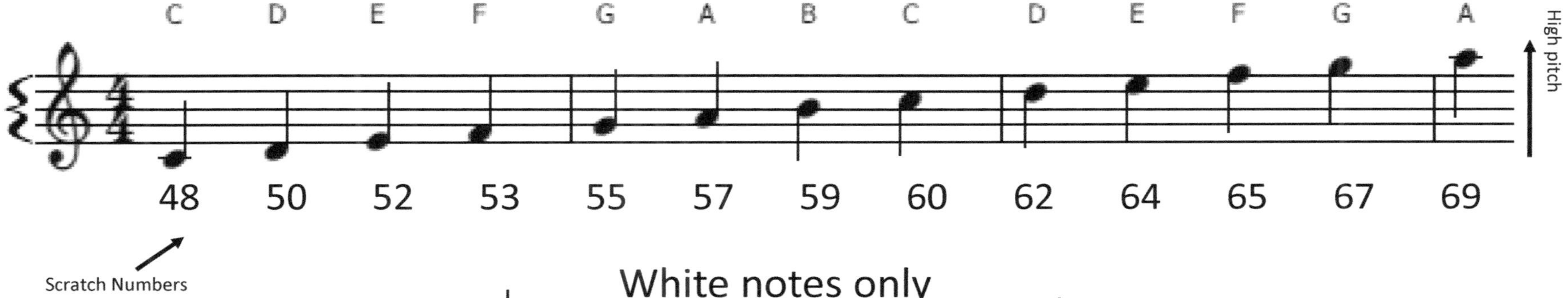
C D E F G A B C D E F G A
High pitch
48 50 52 53 55 57 59 60 62 64 65 67 69
Scratch Numbers

White notes only

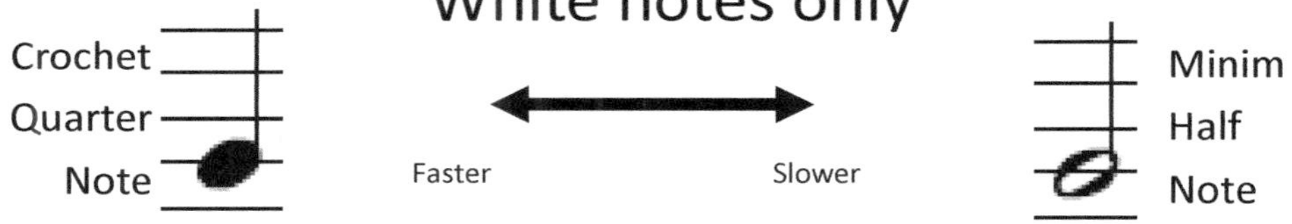
Crochet
Quarter
Note
Faster
Slower
Minim
Half
Note

code-it.co.uk

Twinkle Twinkle Little Star

Mozart

C C G G A A G F F E E D D C G G F F E E D
7
G G F F E E D C C G G A A G F F E E D D C

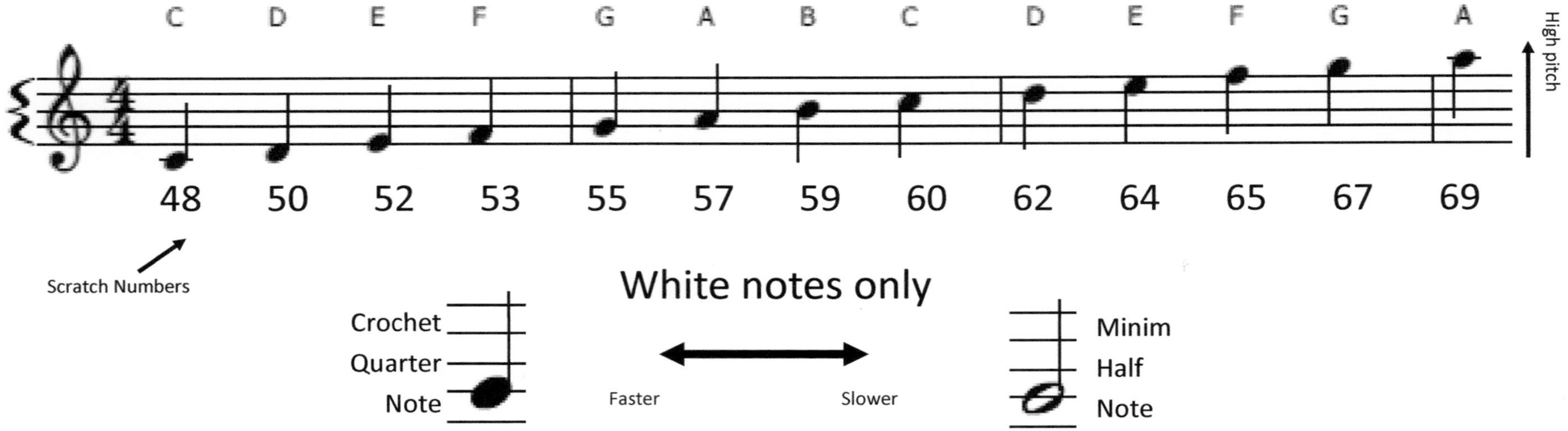
C D E F G A B C D E F G A
48 50 52 53 55 57 59 60 62 64 65 67 69
High pitch
Scratch Numbers
White notes only
Crochet
Quarter
Note
Faster
Slower
Minim
Half
Note

code-it.co.uk

2c. Slug Trail

Module Aim: Pupils create a slug that travels round a roadway leaving a trail behind. Can the user keep the slug on the road or suffer its hideous shrieks?

Time to complete module

2-3 hours

Module Learning Focus

By the end of the module children will be able to:

- Decompose the program as a class
- Build a game that uses continuous loops
- Investigate pen blocks within continuous loops
- Generalise selection within a loop to reuse a concept for a similar function

Computer Science Concepts

- Introducing the power of a continuous repeat loop
- If else selection within a loop

Assessment for Learning

At the end of each session direct pupils to page 11 of pupil workbook 2 to help them reflect on what they have learnt. It is often worth working through this line by line to avoid pupils filling in everything with a smiley face. You can also annotate this to record pupils who have needed much more support or have demonstrated greater understanding.

Adult Focus

All adults need to be clear that they are to support using hints only and not solve things for pupils.

Computational Thinking- **Decomposition:** breaking up a complex challenge into smaller parts and solving them separately before recomposing to solve the whole challenge

National Curriculum Programs of Study

Pupils should be taught to:

- ***design, write and debug programs that accomplish specific goals,*** including controlling or simulating physical systems; ***solve problems by decomposing them into smaller parts***
- ***use sequence, selection, and repetition in programs; work with*** variables and ***various forms of input and output***
- ***use logical reasoning*** to explain how some simple algorithms work and ***to detect and correct errors in algorithms and programs***

Debugging Hints

- Compare teacher code with pupil's code
- Read code aloud
- What code works? Click/ run scratch blocks of code one by one
- Read your code now - read teacher's or peers'
- Hand out hint cards

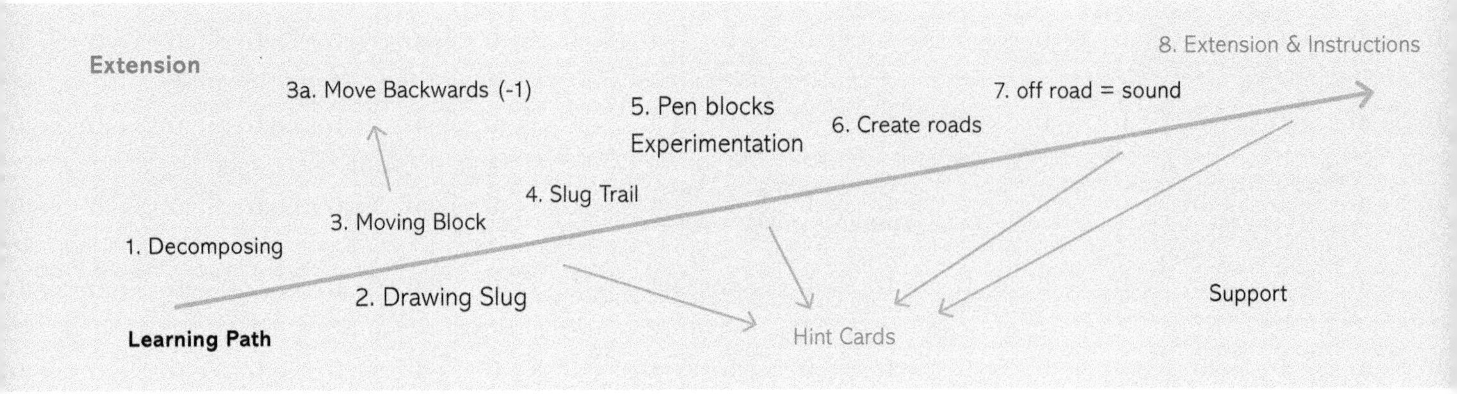
Extension
3a. Move Backwards (-1)
5. Pen blocks Experimentation
6. Create roads
7. off road = sound
8. Extension & Instructions
4. Slug Trail
3. Moving Block
1. Decomposing
2. Drawing Slug
Learning Path
Hint Cards
Support

1. Decomposing the key elements of the game

Load Slug Trail Example File on Scratch 1.4 http://code-it.co.uk/wp-content/uploads/2015/05/slugtrail.sb

Play the game without showing pupils the code (presentation mode, top right).

Ask pupils to work in pairs to identify (decompose) all the features of the game. (Moving, follow mouse, leave trail, make sound if leave road, roads, instructions etc.)

Ask them what they will need to make, and what they will need to make it do?

Pupils can record their decomposed elements in their pupils workbooks page 12 or decompose verbally as a class. Collate their decomposed elements on a board in the class or suite so it can be referred to during the project. A nice touch is to include initials for pupils who first tell you an element. When you get to build these later you can refer to 'Adina's moving slug' or 'Ben's track'.

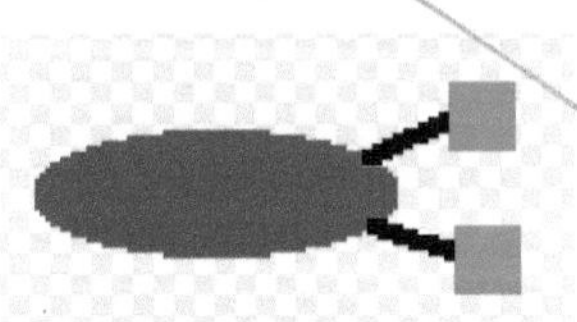

2. Drawing the Slug

Click on the paint new sprite button.

Draw slug using ellipse tool for the body, the line tool for the antenna and the pen tool for the ends of the antennae.

Make sure you draw it facing right or it will travel in the wrong direction.

Common Bugs

Line is not drawing from underneath the slug

Common cause

Pupils have included a dot away from spite when painting it

Fix

Edit sprite, delete dot and then re centre sprite using set costume centre button at bottom of paint editor

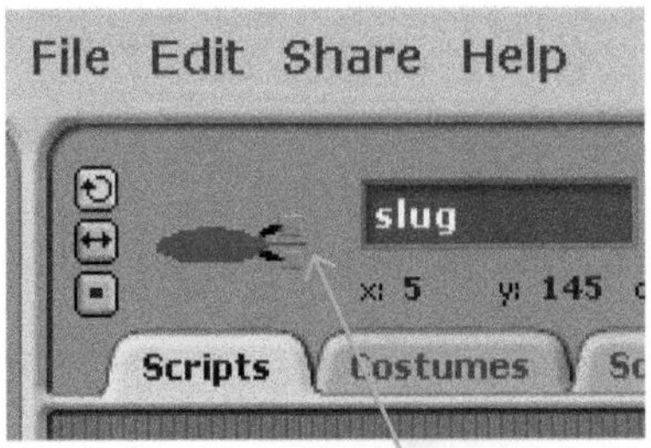
File Edit Share Help
slug
x: 5 y: 145
Scripts
Costumes

The blue line shows direction of travel

Set costume center

Set costume centre button

3. Moving Block

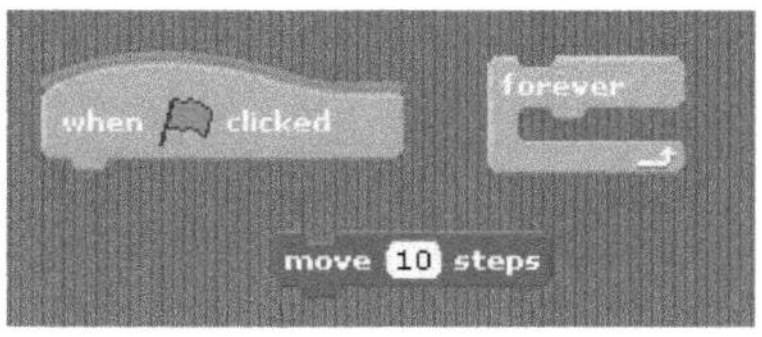
when clicked
forever
move 10 steps

Explain that they are now going to make their slug move continuously. Link this to their decomposed list. If this is the first time pupils have encountered forever loop show them everyday examples http://code-it.co.uk/wp-content/uploads/2015/05/foreverloops.pdf. Drag out these blocks of code and encourage them to snap these together and click the green flag. When they get it right the slug will shoot across the screen. If they don't get it right re-assemble it and try again.

As pupils get their slugs to move, challenge them to reduce the speed without adding any extra blocks.

After they solve this by reducing their move 10 steps block to a smaller number. Drag out the point towards block and select the mouse pointer from the menu triangle.

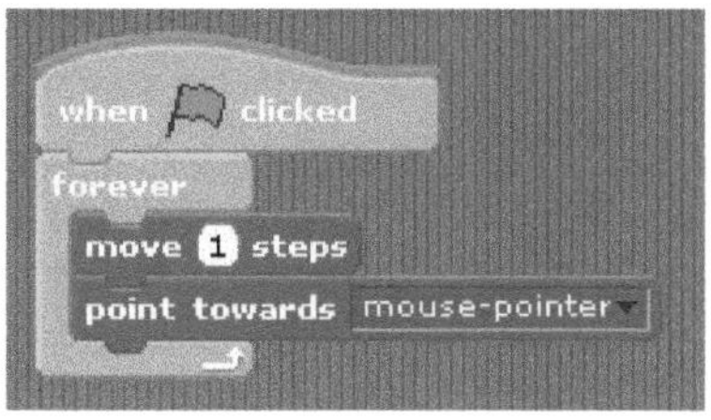
when clicked
forever
move 1 steps
point towards mouse-pointer

Can they find a place for this block so the slug moves continuously towards the mouse pointer?

Once they have got the code working, model what is happening physically by pretending to be the slug. Start off by moving across the room saying move one step repeatedly, reach the wall and continue to try to move just like the slug in the first stage before the point towards the mouse pointer block is introduced. Then invite a child up to be the mouse pointer and instruct them not to be caught by you. Move one step and then change direction to point towards the mouse pointer/ child repeatedly. The slug will then chase the mouse pointer/child. If a child asks why the slug seems to shake when it catches the mouse pointer put a sheet of paper on the floor and explain that this represents the mouse pointer. Now move one step over the paper and then turn round to point towards the paper/mouse pointer. Repeat this to make the point.

3a. Moving Backwards

Can pupils change the block so the slug travels backwards without adding any extra blocks? Answer is to change move 1 step into move -1 step.

4. Slug Trail

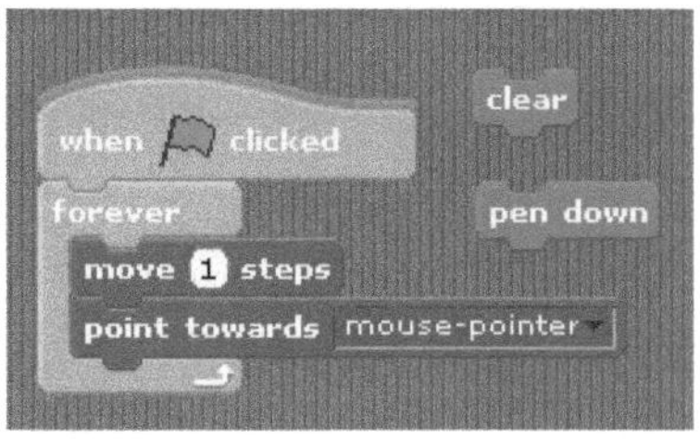
when clicked
clear
forever
pen down
move 1 steps
point towards mouse-pointer

Go back to the decomposed planner and find the references to the slug trail. Can anyone think of a coding block that they can use to draw lines? If you completed the Smoking Car they may remember the pen down block. If not drag the pen down block out and ask pupils if they can find a place for it so it gets run once only.

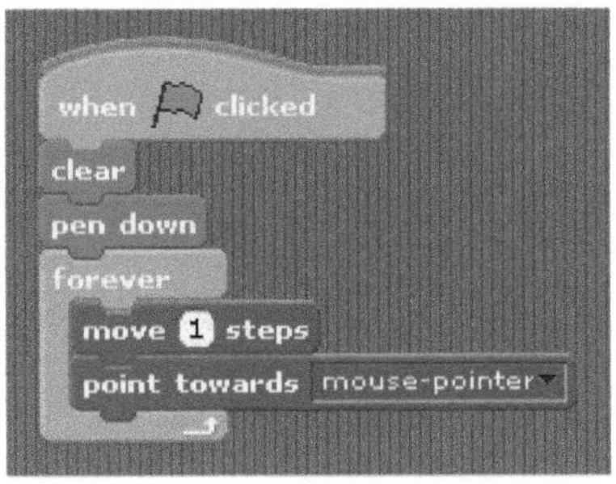
when clicked
clear
pen down
forever
move 1 steps
point towards mouse-pointer

Popular Solution

Many pupils will put it inside the forever loop. Point out that this works but that it is not the most efficient coding as the pen down runs over and over inside the loop.

Next drag out the clear block and ask pupils to find a place to put it so that when the game is started all the previous lines will be cleared. Sometimes pupils will drag out another green flag block and place the clear in its own block of code. This is a perfectly valid solution.

5. Pen Blocks Experimentation

Encourage pupils to save their work at this point. Explain that if they make any bugs that are difficult to fix they have a working copy of the game to restore/bring back.

Now point to the pen blocks and encourage pupils to experiment with them. Can they set keys to change the colour? Can they draw a multi-coloured line? What happens with some of the blocks if used inside the loop as well as before it? Does all the code need to go inside the main block?

Note

The change pen size by block if put in a loop will very quickly grow the pen size to cover the whole screen. If a pupil does this they can fix it by dragging out the set pen size to 1 and double clicking on it.

Don't forget however, to remove the original change pen size by block! Can they explain to you why it has happened?

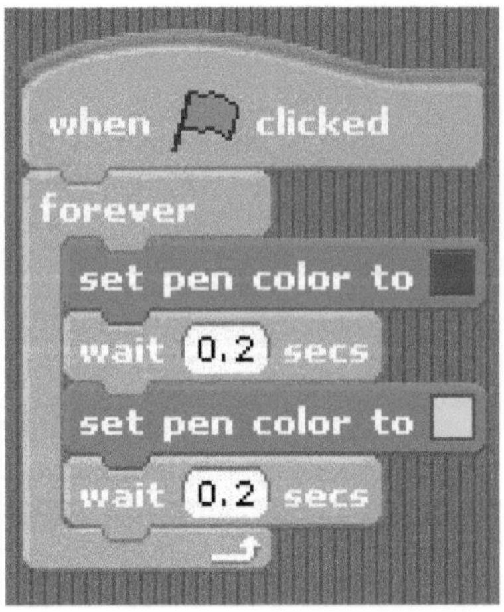
when clicked
forever
set pen color to
wait 0.2 secs
set pen color to
wait 0.2 secs

A possible multi-coloured solution. Many pupils will put these colours into the main move loop but the addition of waits in there will stop the moving blocks from working properly. (Hint card available.)

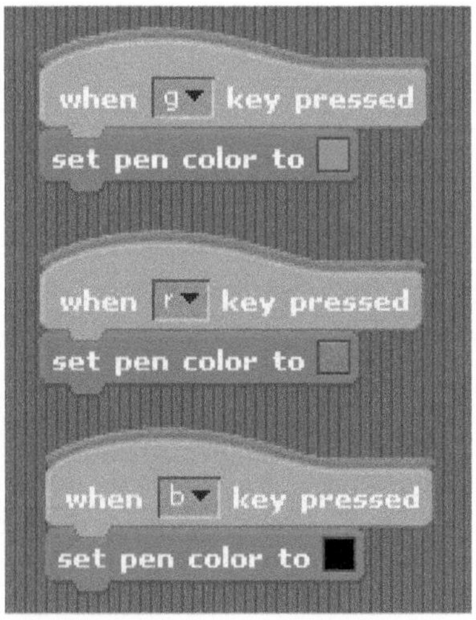
when g key pressed
set pen color to
when r key pressed
set pen color to
when b key pressed
set pen color to

Possible pen colour solution

6. Create Roads

Remind pupils of the roads they created in the smoking car game. Remind them how to select stage then backgrounds tab and then edit to draw a slugway trail.

Some may need a reminder of the copy button to draw multiple slugway trails.

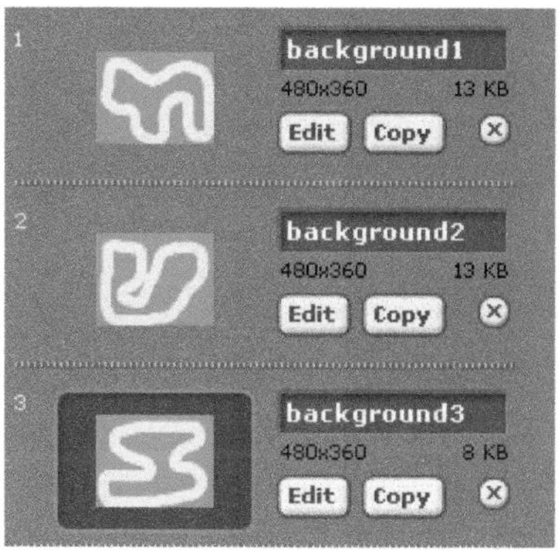
background1
480x360 13 KB
Edit Copy
background2
480x360 13 KB
Edit Copy
background3
480x360 8 KB
Edit Copy

Same colour backgrounds

The most important thing is that they must keep all the backgrounds exactly the same colour as they will be using the colour to code later.

> **Note** Warn pupils that sprite should not be same colour as the road or background to avoid the slug looking like it has disappeared.

6. Off road leads to sound

Give pupils 2 minutes to import an annoying sound such as screech (which you can find in Sounds tab, import, electronic, screech.)

Scripts Costumes Sounds
New sound: Record Import
Screech
0:00:03 57 KB

Now drag out an if selection block and insert a touching colour block as shown. Click in the colour and then onto the background colour to change the colour.

if touching color ?
play sound Screech

Remind pupils that this selection block will only play the sound if it is touching the colour. Drag the slug so that it is touching the background colour. Explain that you can run one block just by mouse clicking on that block once. Ask pupils if screech will play when you mouse click on it.

Repeat the process when the slug is not touching the background colour.

This condition will only be checked once. Ask pupils where they could put the code so it gets checked over and over and over again. This can either go in its own forever loop or inside the move forever loop.

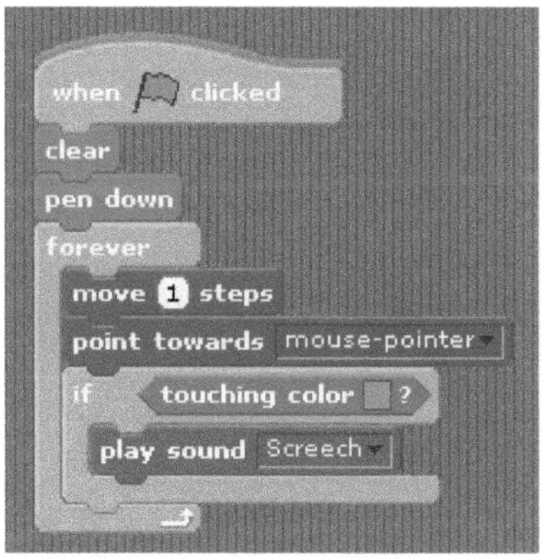
when clicked
clear
pen down
forever
move 1 steps
point towards mouse-pointer
if touching color ?
play sound Screech

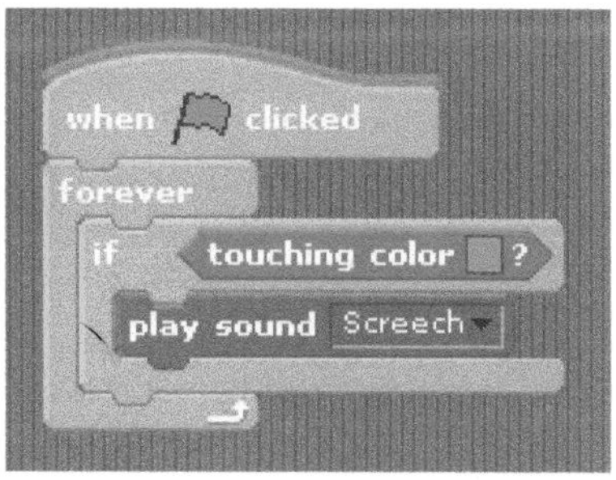
when clicked
forever
if touching color ?
play sound Screech

when x key pressed
next background

Solution

8. Extensions & Instructions Change Background (easy)

Challenge pupils to see if they can work out the right code to make x key change background. Code must go in stage area.

Stop All (Easy)

Can pupils create a keyboard input that stops all code?

when space key pressed
stop all

Use Hint Cards (p82) to help pupils choose useful blocks if they are struggling

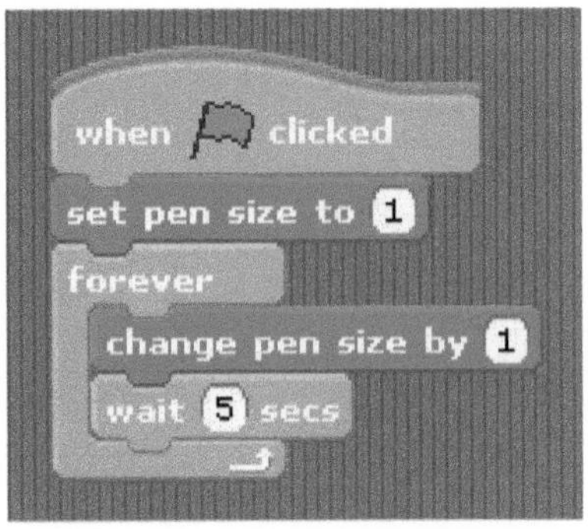
when clicked
set pen size to 1
forever
change pen size by 1
wait 5 secs

Increase pen size solution

Increase Pen Size (Hard)

When decomposing the project some pupils will have noticed the pen size increasing slowly over time. Can they remake this? I often drag the blocks out unconnected as a starting point.

(Hint card available p82.)

Instructions (Middle)

Help cards are available for this.

Create new Sprite called instruction

Text Size 24

Zoom Out

Drag text to top left corner of screen

Type out instructions

Add code to show when game starts or i key is pressed

(Hint card available p83).

inst

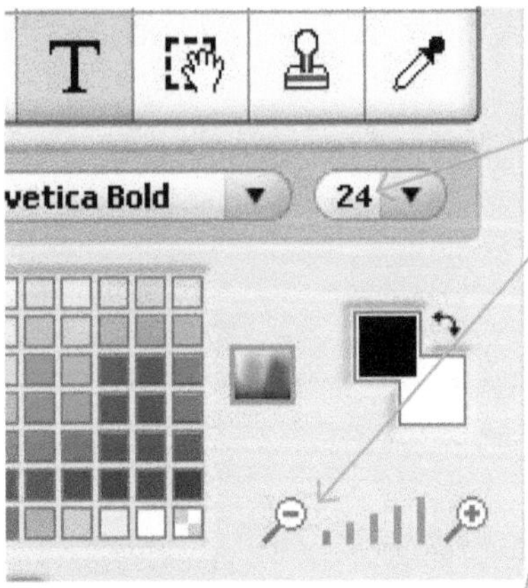
T
vetica Bold
24

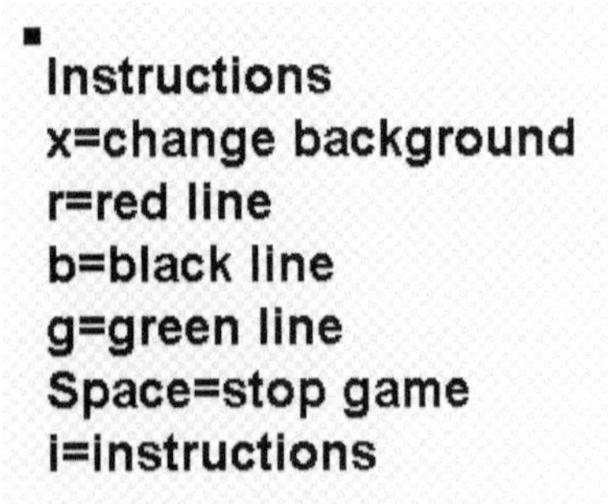
Instructions
x=change background
r=red line
b=black line
g=green line
Space=stop game
i=instructions

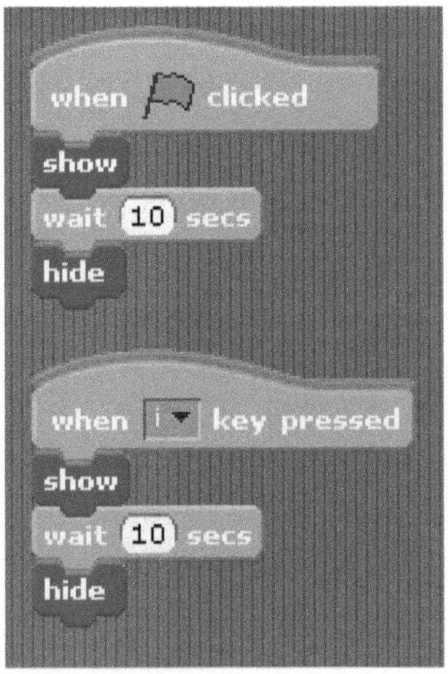
when clicked
show
wait 10 secs
hide
when i key pressed
show
wait 10 secs
hide

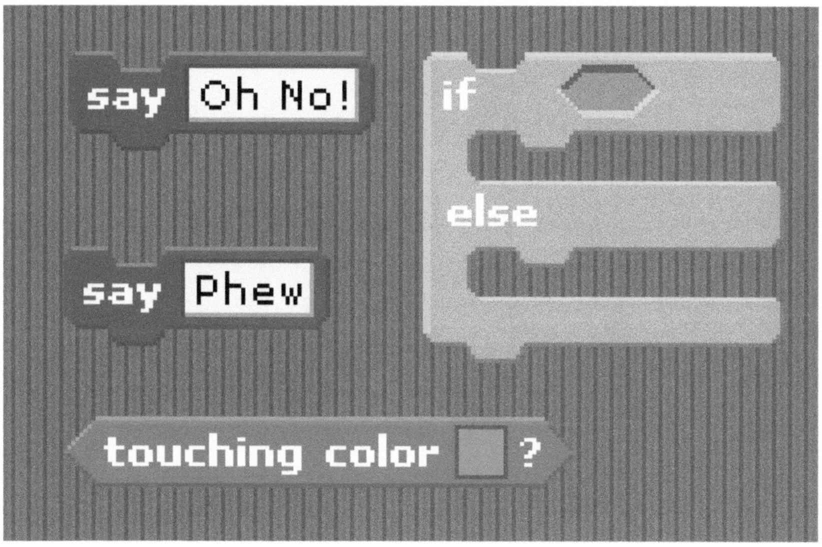
say Oh No!
if
else
say Phew
touching color ?

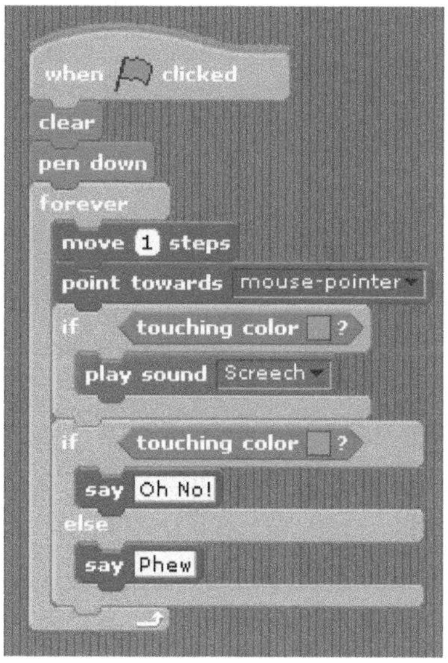
when clicked
clear
pen down
forever
move 1 steps
point towards mouse-pointer
if touching color ?
play sound Screech
if touching color ?
say Oh No!
else
say Phew

Generalising if else within a loop (Middle)

A really nice extension is to ask pupils to program the slug so that it says one thing when touching the road and another if touching the background colour.

You can introduce the blocks above as a hint for anyone who needs them

(Hint card available p82.)

At the end don't forget to go back to your decomposed list. Ask the pupils if they found it helpful to break up all the jobs and solve them separately.

Print extra independent extension activities in the pupil books and send them home

Hint Cards

Photocopy, cut up and use if and when needed.

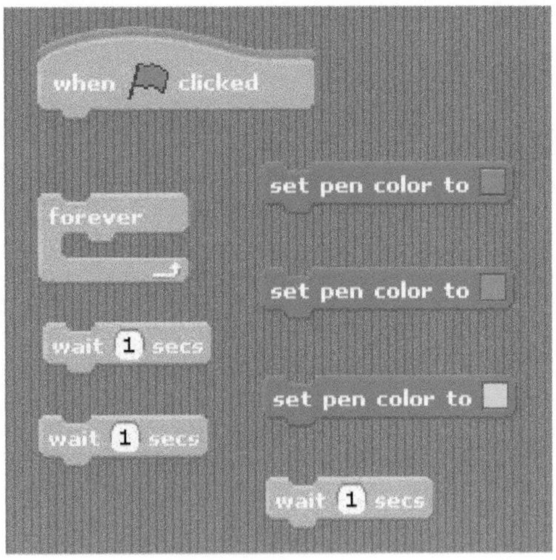
when clicked
forever
wait 1 secs
wait 1 secs
set pen color to
set pen color to
set pen color to
wait 1 secs

Multi-coloured line

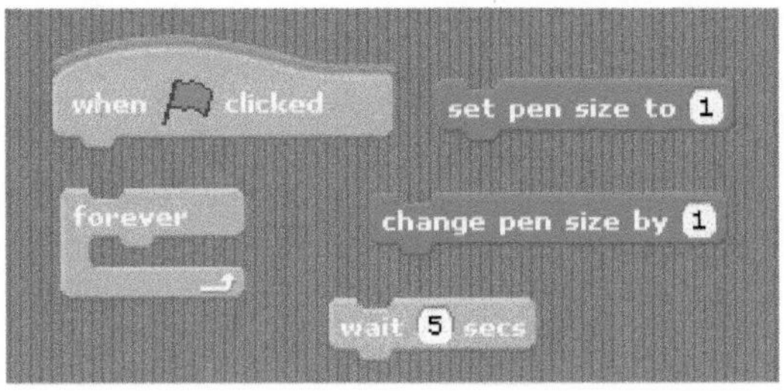
when clicked
set pen size to 1
forever
change pen size by 1
wait 5 secs

Line gets larger

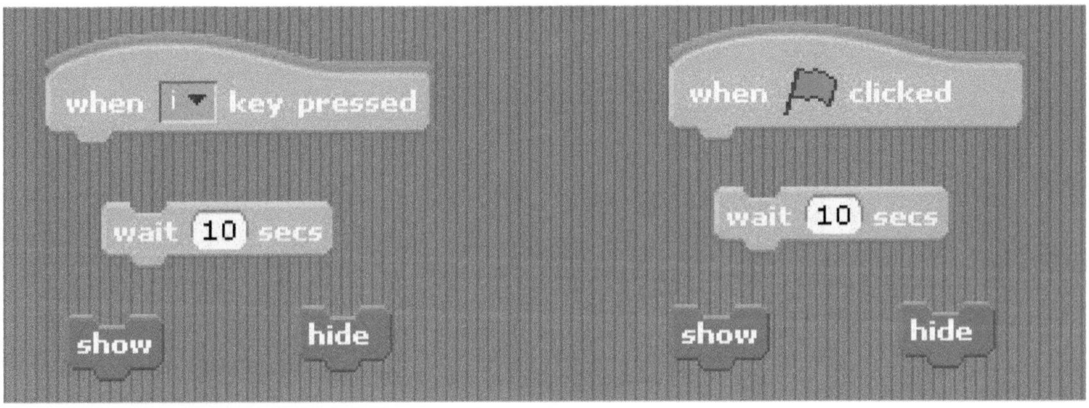
when i key pressed
wait 10 secs
show
hide
when clicked
wait 10 secs
show
hide

Instructions

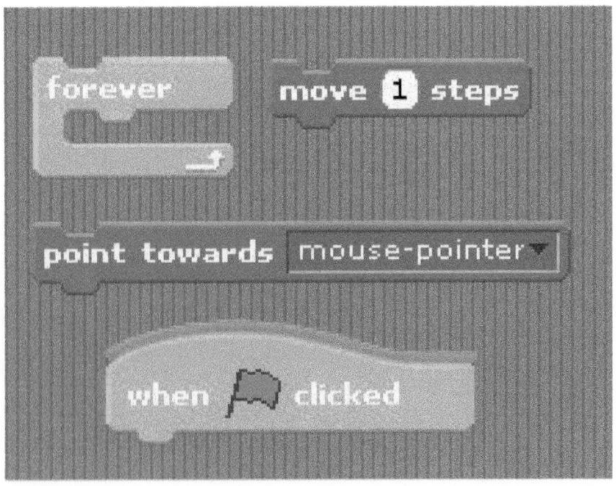
forever
move 1 steps
point towards mouse-pointer
when clicked

Move and follow the mouse

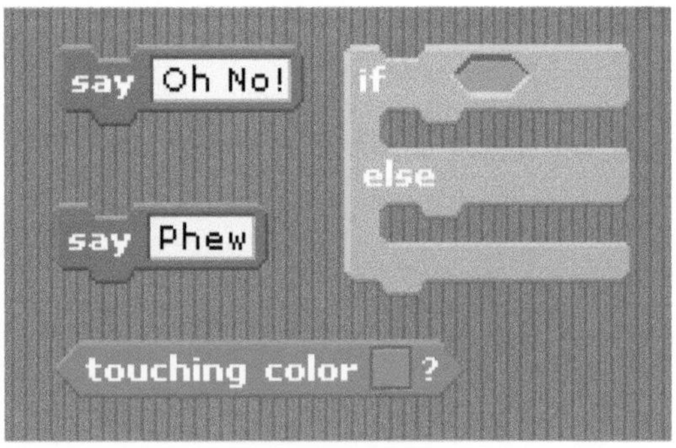
say Oh No!
if
else
say Phew
touching color ?

Say inside the line

Create a list of Instructions

code-it.co.uk

Scratch Slug Trail
Help Card

code-it.co.uk

Paint new sprite

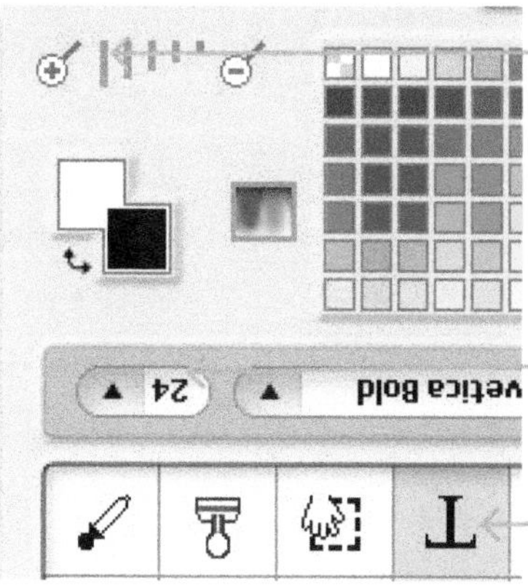

vetica Bold
24

Text Tool

Font Size 24

Zoom Out

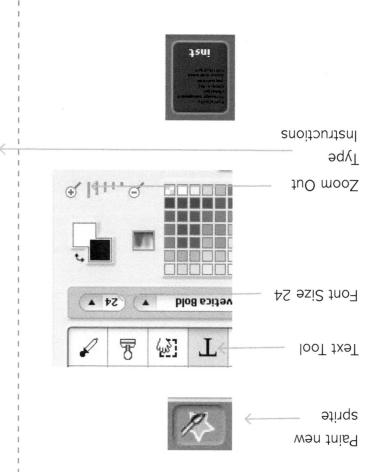

Type Instructions

inst

Instructions
x=change background
r=red line
b=black line
g=green line
Space=stop game
i=instructions

2D. Selection Investigation

Time to complete module

3 hours

Module Aim: Create a sprite and a field of coloured dots. What can your pupils program the sprite to do when it touches the spots?

National Curriculum Programs of Study

Pupils should be taught to:

- ***design, write and debug programs that accomplish specific goals,*** including controlling or simulating physical systems; solve problems by decomposing them into smaller parts
- ***use sequence, selection, and repetition in programs; work with variables and various forms of input and output***
- ***use logical reasoning to*** explain how some simple algorithms work and to ***detect and correct errors in algorithms and programs***

Debugging Hints

Read code aloud. If code blocks don't have a yellow outline when run, have they remembered to wrap everything in a forever loop so the condition gets checked over and over again.

Module Learning Focus

By the end of the module children will be able to:

- Use simple selection within a loop independently with confidence
- Investigate Scratch blocks to find out which can be triggered by touching a colour
- Investigate a single selection block and an if else choice selection block

Computer Science Concepts

- if else selection
- if selection
- Selection with a loop

Assessment for Learning

At the end of each session direct pupils to page 14 of pupil workbook 2 to help them reflect on what they have learnt. It is often worth working through this line by line to avoid pupils filling in everything with a smiley face. You can also annotate this to record pupils who have needed much more support or have demonstrated greater understanding.

Adult Focus

All adults need to be clear that they are to support using hints only and not solve things for pupils.

Computational Thinking **Generalisation:** adapting a solution that works for one problem to solve others.

There is a video walk through of the programming elements here https://youtu.be/pVaehwvaPhA

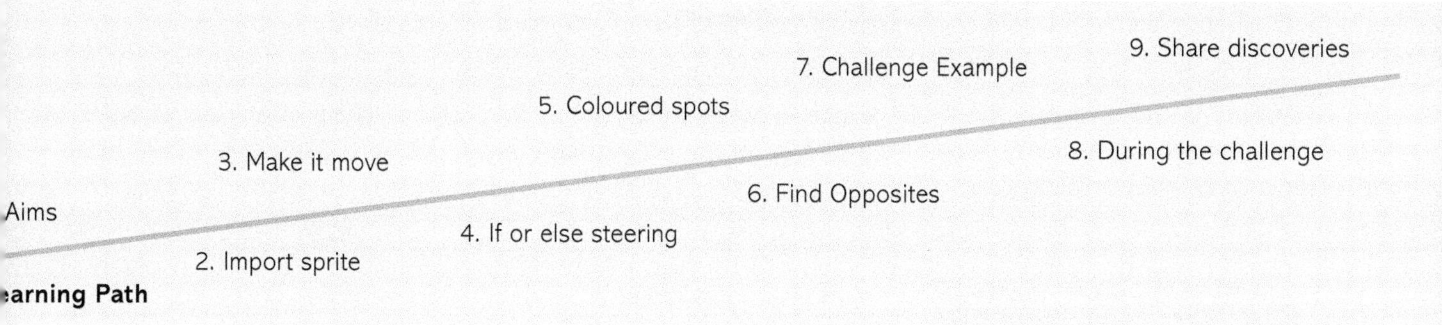
9. Share discoveries
7. Challenge Example
5. Coloured spots
8. During the challenge
3. Make it move
6. Find Opposites
Aims
4. If or else steering
2. Import sprite
arning Path

1. Aims

Introduce the idea of generalisation, adapting a solution that worked for one problem to solve another. Remind pupils of how they used selection within a loop to check if the slug was touching a colour in the slug trail game. You might want to open that planning and draw out where that was. Explain that in this module they are going to adapt this solution to work in a similar but different way.

Precondition

It helps to have used selection in the quiz and the slug trail game before using this module.

2. Import a simple transport sprite

Ask pupils to import a simple transport sprite without attached scripts. Choose new sprite from file, transportation folder.

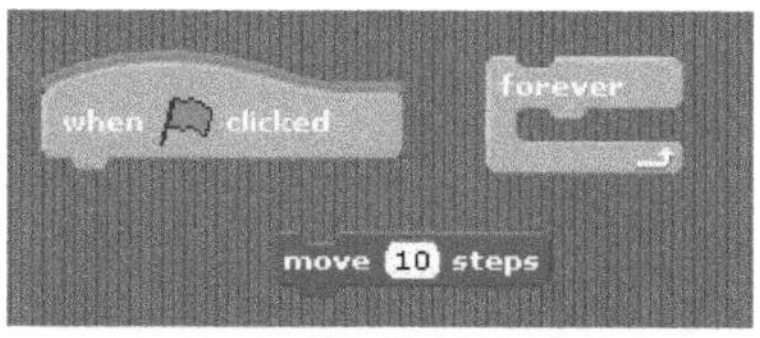
when clicked
forever
move 10 steps

3. Make it move

Drag out these blocks or challenge pupils to make it move themselves if they have completed the slug trail game.

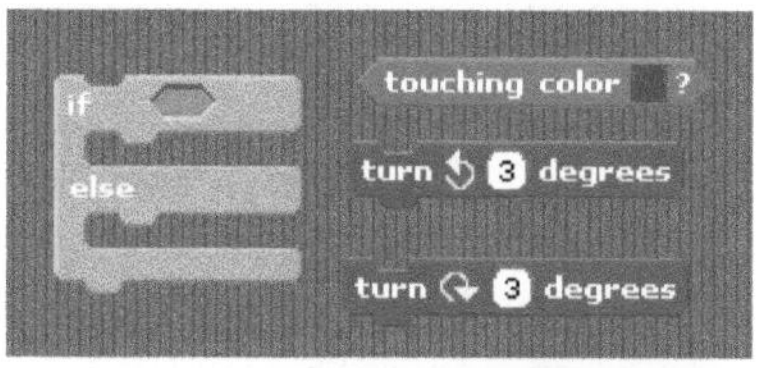
if
else
touching color ?
turn 3 degrees
turn 3 degrees

4. If or else steering

Drag out these blocks and challenge pupils to use the same idea as they did to check if the slug was inside or outside the line to steer the sprite. Suggest that they may want to change the number of degrees turn. After an appropriate period of struggle snap the code together as shown and tell pupils that they are not to add anything else to this block. Can they describe what is happening in the block to a neighbour?

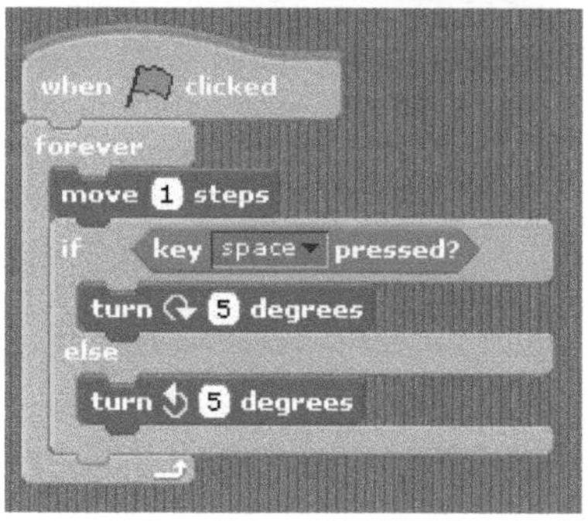
when clicked
forever
move 1 steps
if key space pressed?
turn 5 degrees
else
turn 5 degrees

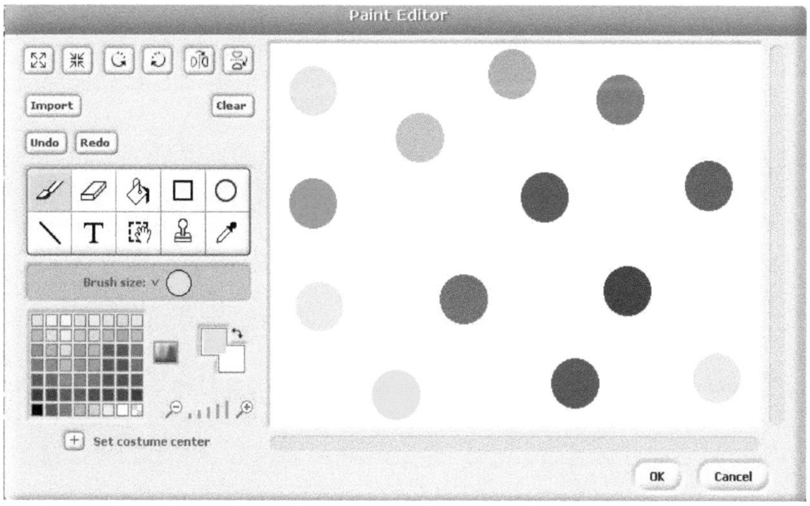
Paint Editor
Import
Clear
Undo
Redo
Brush size:
Set costume center
OK
Cancel

5, Coloured spots background

Show pupils how to create coloured blobs on a plain background. Ask them to leave gaps that the sprite can travel through. Make sure each spot is a different colour. Stage, Background, Edit, rectangle, ellipse tools or paint- brush on next to largest size.

6. Find Opposites

Give pupils lots of time in pairs to find code blocks and blocks which cancel out the code blocks effect. It helps to feed back an early example from code they have used before such as pen up pen and down from the Smoking Car. Get pupils to share these opposite effect blocks with the rest of the class. You could record these for the class to use later.

Left clock inside touching colour block

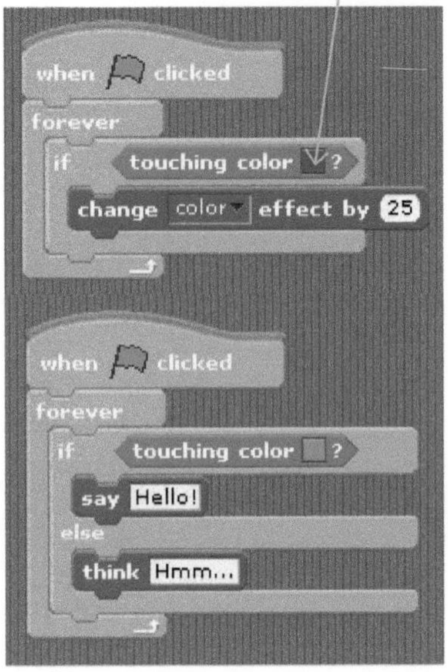
when clicked
forever
if touching color ?
change color effect by 25
when clicked
forever
if touching color ?
say Hello!
else
think Hmm...

NOTE

The clear graphic effects block can cancel out other graphics effects in other blocks. You can check if this is happening by only running the move and steer block and one effects block at a time.

7. Challenge Example

Demonstrate how the sprite can respond to the colour by creating these two example blocks of code. Make sure you draw out changing the colour to match one of the colours on the stage by left clicking inside the touching colour block and then left clicking the colour chooser dropper on one of the colours on the stage. Show pupils how to duplicate code by right clicking on the top block and then left clicking on duplicate - so that they can copy and adapt rather than dragging every block out manually.

8. During the Challenge

Draw out that they are generalising by adapting a solution that worked to solve a similar problem. Remind pupils to build each new selection block in its own code - not adding it in to the move and steer loop. This way if it doesn't work as they want they haven't stopped the base program working. Wait commands can halt programs very easily. You may want to use the help sheet provided for Special Education Needs (SEN) pupils or latecomers. If you haven't got headphones I advise limiting sound blocks as a reward for great ideas elsewhere as these can be distracting for others. It is very easy to get stuck investigating just one type of blocks. Periodically ask pupils to move on to investigating other types of programming blocks. A few pupils will recreate the same idea to work for lots of colours. Check that they understand that the challenge is to find new ways of using selection within a loop, not just repeat the same way for different colours.

9. Share discoveries

This is a great module for sharing what everyone has learnt through setting screens on presentation mode and trying each others creations.

Assessment

This is a great module to assess as it involves lots of pupils' own ideas.

High Lots of different ideas that use at least three different type of blocks. Or working ideas that change a variable when it touches a colour.

Middle Three or more unique ideas from more than one block type.

Low Less than three unique ideas or ideas, from only one block type.

NOTES Y4 pupils have investigated what happens to variables if they have used them previously in the quiz. I don't mention this but encourage it if they ask.

NOTES Some pupils may come up with game ideas. I have often let them explore these independently as part of this module.

Selection Investigation help

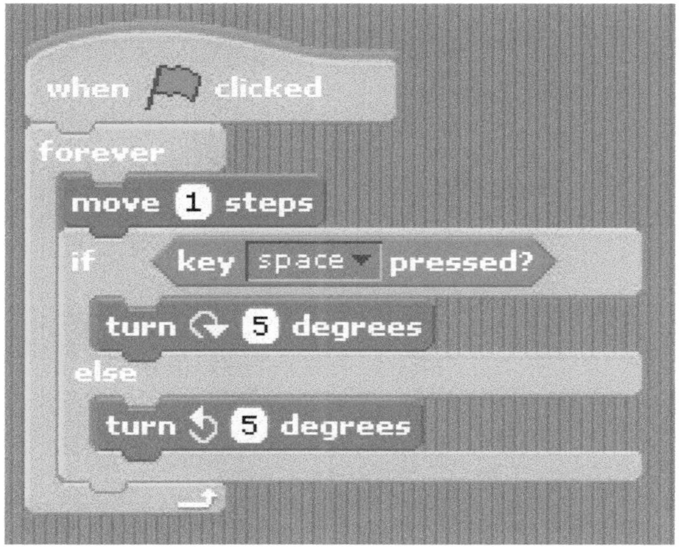
when clicked
forever
move 1 steps
if key space pressed?
turn 5 degrees
else
turn 5 degrees

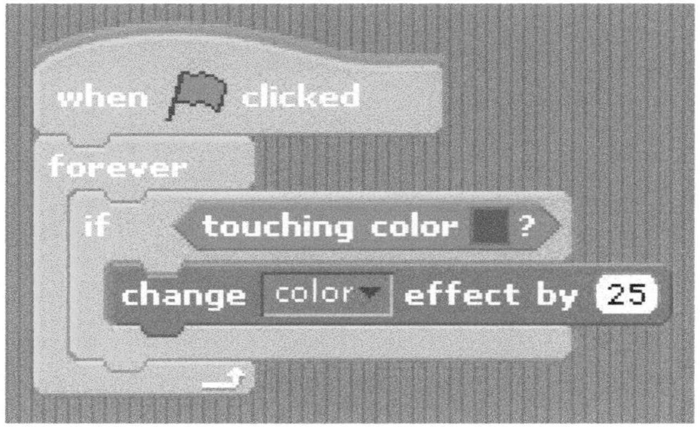
when clicked
forever
if touching color ?
change color effect by 25

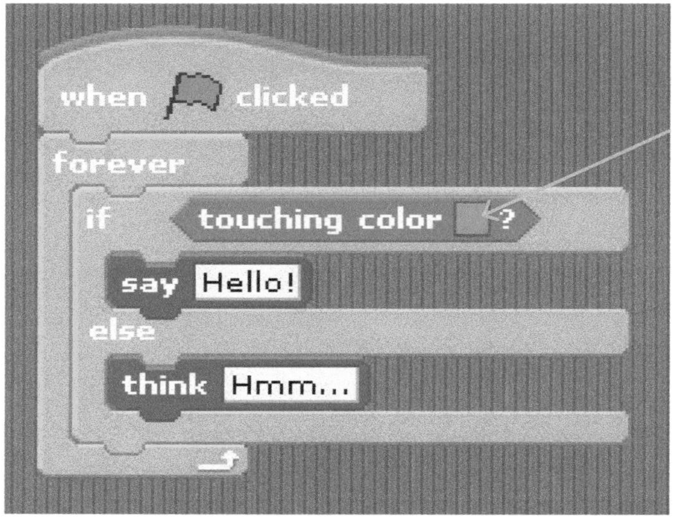
when clicked
forever
if touching color ?
say Hello!
else
think Hmm...

Left click to change colour

Computational Thinking **Generalisation** - adapting a solution that works for one problem to solve others.

Selection Investigation Help Sheet

code-it.co.uk

2E. Train Your Computer To Do Maths

Time to complete module

2 hours

Module Aim: Write algorithms and convert them into programs to solve maths problems.

National Curriculum Programs of Study

Pupils should be taught to:

- ***design, write and debug programs that accomplish specific goals,*** including controlling or simulating physical systems; solve problems by decomposing them into smaller parts
- ***use sequence,*** selection, and repetition ***in programs; work with variables*** and various forms of input and output
- ***use logical reasoning*** to explain how some simple algorithms work and ***to detect and correct errors in algorithms and programs***

Debugging Hints

Go back to your algorithm: does your program mirror your algorithm? Trace your algorithm step by step: does it match your program?

Computational Thinking

Generalisation: adapting a solution that works for one problem to solve others.

Algorithms: precise step by step instructions or rules for achieving something

Module Learning Focus

By the end of the module children will be able to:

- Create and work with variables to store and manipulate numbers
- Convert simple maths problems into algorithms and then into code
- Generalise an algorithm to solve a different type of maths problem
- Use symbols in algorithms

Computer Science Concepts

- Convert user input into a variable
- Write Algorithms
- Convert Algorithms into programs
- -Work with multiple variables

Maths Concepts

- Add
- Subtract
- Divide
- Multiply
- Multi stage problems

Assessment for Learning

At the end of each session direct pupils to page 17 of pupil workbook 2 to help them reflect on what they have learnt. It is often worth working through this line by line to avoid pupils filling in everything with a smiley face. You can also annotate this to record pupils who have needed much more support or have demonstrated greater understanding.

Adult Focus

All adults need to be clear that they are to support using hints only and not solve things for pupils.

Resources

- Class Instructions Slides
  http://code-it.co.uk/wp-content/uploads/2015/08/maths.pdf
- 3 Plastic beakers to demonstrate with
- Pupil workbooks algorithm creation page

4. Pupils write more algorithms and convert to code

3. Convert Addition Algorithm to programming using key

2. Write Addition Algorithm as class

[Sh]are challenge

[Lea]rning Path

1. Share Challenge

Use the slides to explain how we can train our computer to do maths, explaining that computers know nothing unless humans tell them what to do and that all programming is an algorithm turned into code. Stop at slide 10. (Print out of slides on page 92.)

Top Tip

Stick to low amount numbers as it is easier to use with pencils

2. Write Addition Algorithm as a class

Use slide 10 (class instruction slides) to go over the rules

1. All numbers must be in pots (variables)
2. All pots (variables) must have different names
3. Can + (add) - (subtract) / (divide) & * (multiply) pots (variables)
4. Can look into pot (variable) to see what is inside

Notation to create on a class board alongside the pots example

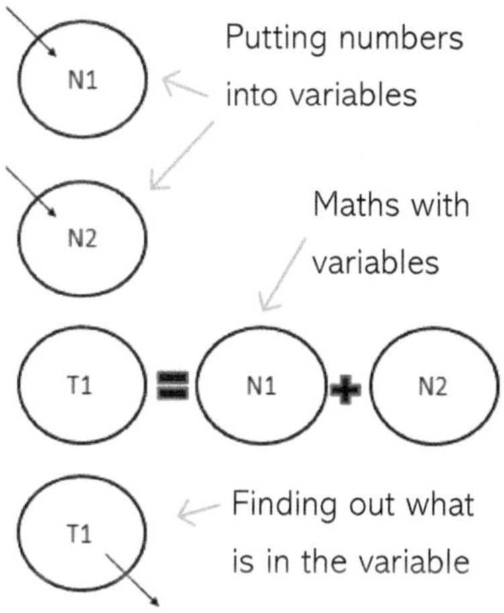
Putting numbers into variables
N1
N2
Maths with variables
T1
N1
N2
T1
Finding out what is in the variable

Number two pots (variables) as N1 and N2 explain that these can hold our numbers to be added. Get two pupils to hold these. On a class board add two circles with an arrow notation to put numbers into variables.

Explain that we need a pot (variable) to hold our total. Label a third beaker T1 short for total1. Create two more notes to say + and = and position them between the pots. Explain that we can now get the computer to add what is in N1 to N2 and put the result in T1.

Check that it meets the rules.

Model this with small amounts of pencils in the pots. Draw out that this algorithm can add any two numbers. On the board add the sum as notation T1 = N1 + N2.

Now explain that we need to look into the T1 pot variable to see what is inside and add the final circle with the arrow pointing out as shown. Give pupils time to copy this into their pupil workbooks page 9 It helps to allow lower ability maths pupils time to model this with pots and pencils.

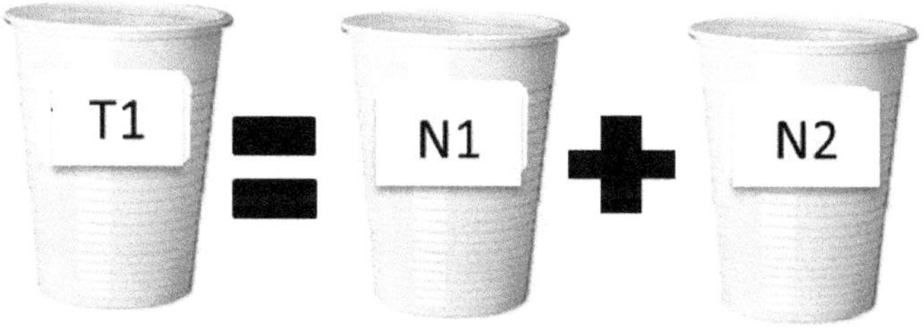
T1
N1
N2

Physical model with pots

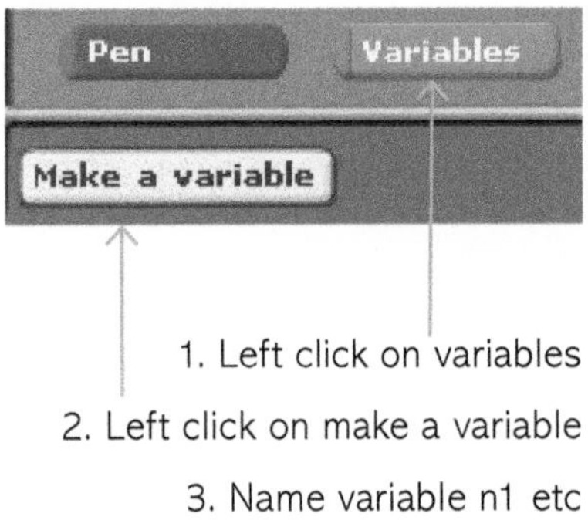
Pen
Variables
Make a variable
1. Left click on variables
2. Left click on make a variable
3. Name variable n1 etc

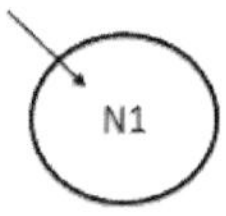
N1

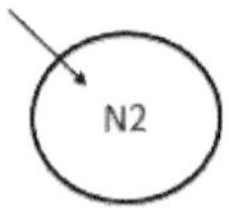
N2

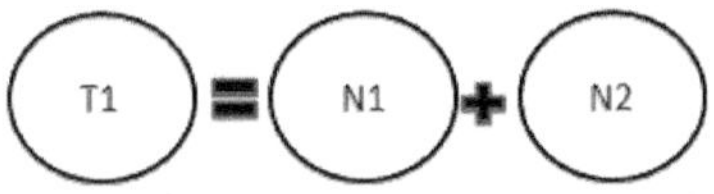
T1
N1
N2

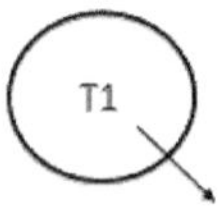
T1

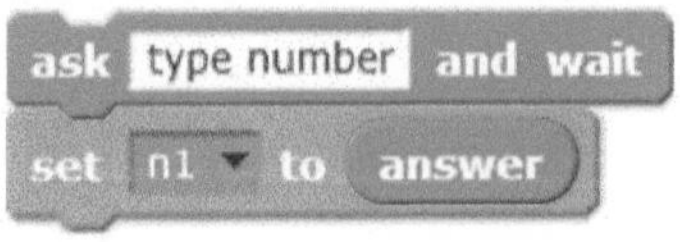
ask type number and wait
set n1 to answer

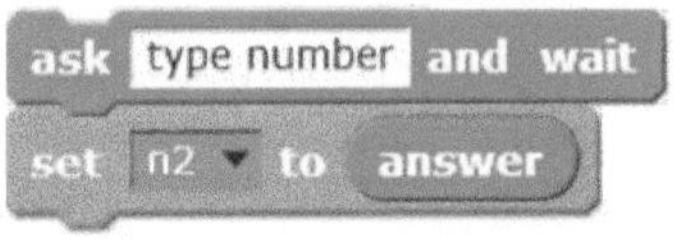
ask type number and wait
set n2 to answer

set t1 to n1 + n2

say t1 for 2 secs

3. Convert Addition Algorithm using Key

Load Slide 11 which shows the key to converting the algorithm into Scratch programming code. As pupils are logging on and loading a blank copy of Scratch explain that they now need to convert their algorithms into a computer program. Warn pupils that the computer language could be very different from our written algorithm.

Common Bugs

Pupils only create one number into variable input block. Refer them back to their algorithm in the first place and ask them to point out which code goes with which part of the algorithm, it can help to hold their algorithm up alongside the code. Pupils use change the variable instead of set the variable.

Get them to compare their code with example on the board.

Remind pupils how to create variables. Give pupils time to convert their algorithm into Scratch code and test it. Remind them that the order of their algorithm should stay the same in their Scratch code.

4. Pupils write more algorithms and convert to code

Once they have written and tested their code to add two numbers challenge them to write an algorithm to subtract, multiply or divide one number from another. They must write their algorithm in their pupil work books first and show it to you before converting it into code. It can be a good idea to force a move away from the computers to do this. When they have finished this move on to adding three numbers before adding two numbers and multiplying by a third. With multi stage number challenges insist that they only do one calculation or input on each line as Scratch doesn't have brackets* and the order can change the outcome. Save each sub total in a new variable (t1, t2 etc) You may wish to find simple two stage problems in their maths text books and challenge them to solve these. Make sure they always write an algorithm first.

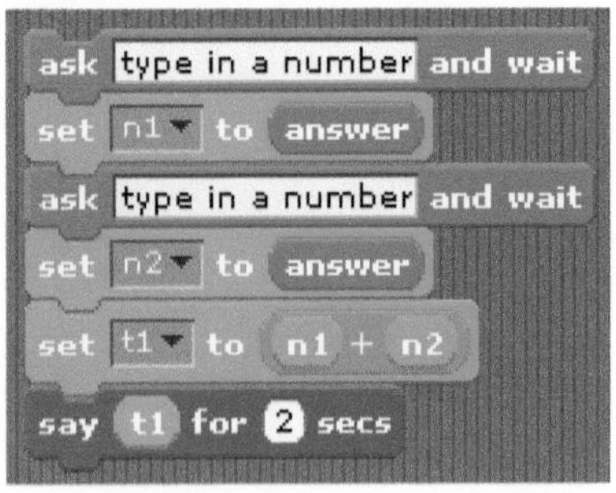
ask type in a number and wait
set n1 to answer
ask type in a number and wait
set n2 to answer
set t1 to n1 + n2
say t1 for 2 secs

Correct add two numbers code

* there is an order but I wouldn't get into this at this stage

Programming as a Maths Testing Tool

```
ask [type in a number] and wait
set [n1] to (answer)
ask [type in a number] and wait
set [n2] to (answer)
ask [type in a number to multiply by] and wait
set [n2] to (answer)
set [t1] to ((n1) + (n2))
set [t2] to ((t1) * (n3))
say (t2) for (2) secs
```

```
ask [type in a number] and wait
set [n1] to (answer)
ask [type in a number] and wait
set [n2] to (answer)
set [t1] to ((n1) + (n2))
ask [type in a number to multiply by] and wait
set [n2] to (answer)
set [t2] to ((t1) * (n3))
say (t2) for (2) secs
```

These solutions both add two numbers and then multiply a third from the total of the first two numbers. Both solutions are correct and equally efficient as they use the same amount of code.

Because Scratch can cope with other mathematical operations such as greater than or less than this can be used as a form of digital literacy where pupils prove that they understand the stages of a problem by writing a program to solve them. For some children this might be the practical hook that they need to see that Maths is useful beyond their text books.

> **Computational Thinking**
>
> Generalisation: Adapting a solution that works for one problem to solve others

Ask them which computational thinking skill they are using when they adapt an addition algorithm to work with multiple stages.

Answer: Generalisation

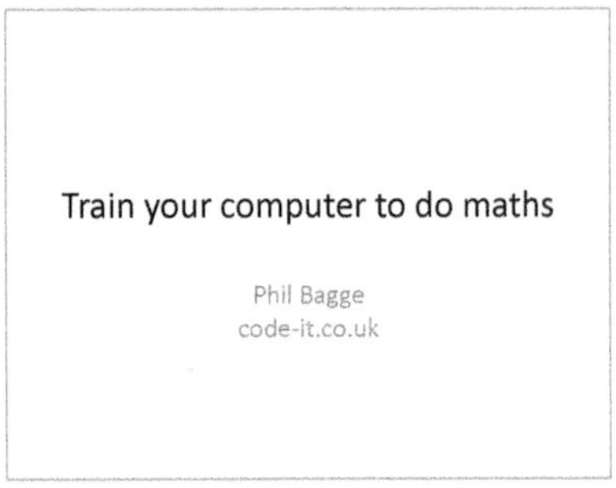
Train your computer to do maths
Phil Bagge
code-it.co.uk

Computers know nothing
DOH!

They don't even know how to speak
....

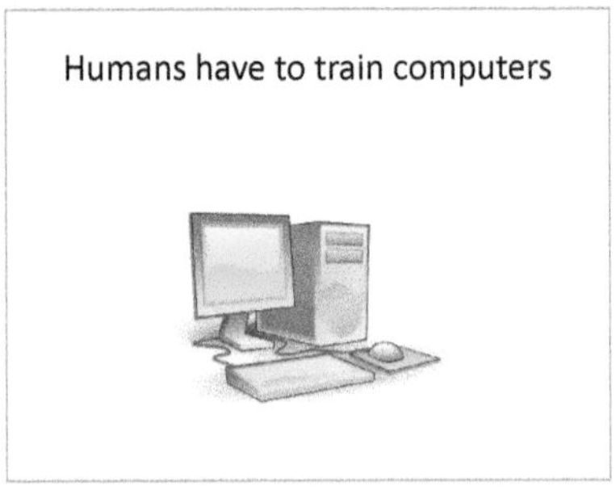
Humans have to train computers

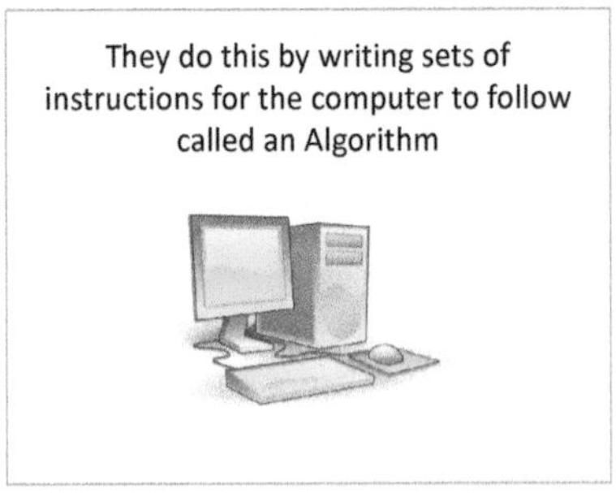
They do this by writing sets of instructions for the computer to follow called an Algorithm

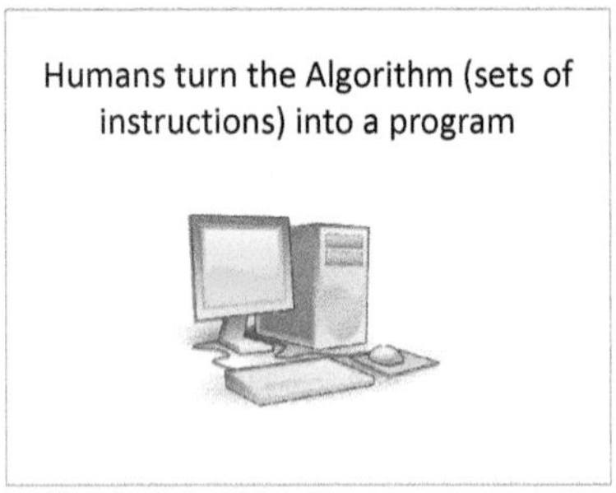
Humans turn the Algorithm (sets of instructions) into a program

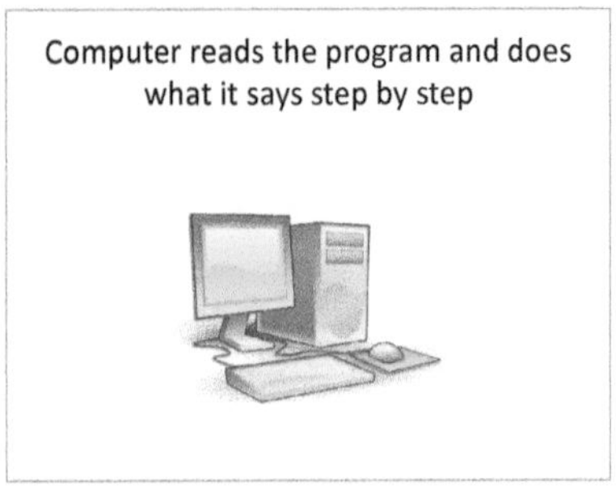
Computer reads the program and does what it says step by step

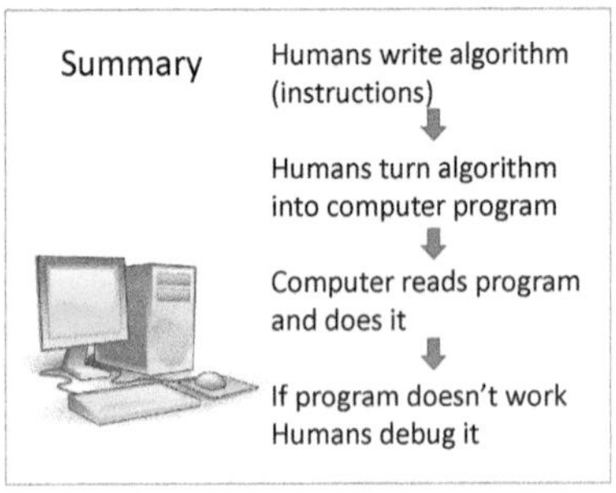
Summary
Humans write algorithm (instructions)
Humans turn algorithm into computer program
Computer reads program and does it
If program doesn't work Humans debug it

Shhh... We are going to train our computer to do maths sums for us

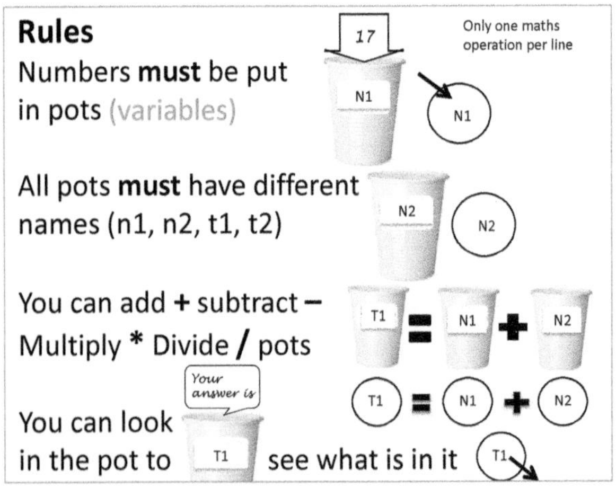
Rules
Numbers must be put in pots (variables)
17
N1
Only one maths operation per line
All pots must have different names (n1, n2, t1, t2)
N2
You can add + subtract – Multiply * Divide / pots
T1 = N1 + N2
Your answer is
You can look in the pot to see what is in it
T1

Slide 10

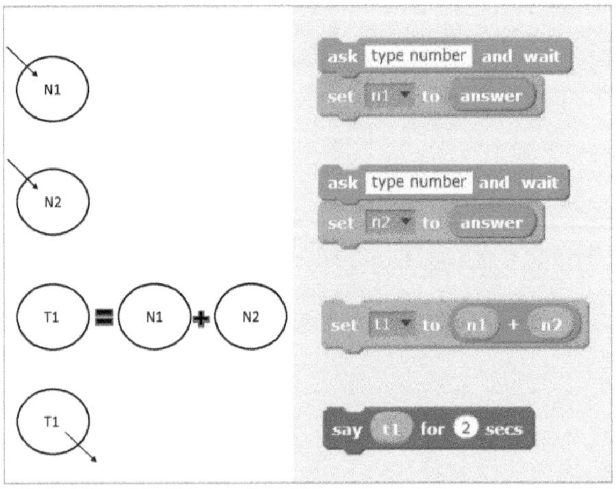
N1
ask type number and wait
set n1 to answer
N2
ask type number and wait
set n2 to answer
T1 = N1 + N2
set t1 to n1 + n2
T1
say t1 for 2 secs

Slides can be found online at http://code-it.co.uk/wp-content/uploads/2015/08/maths.pdf

Chapter 3

3A. Counting Machine

Module Aim: Create and adapt a counting machine.

Time to complete module

3 hours

Module Learning Focus

By the end of the module children will be able to:

- Solve simple maths problems using Scratch code
- Understand the benefit of changing a variable within a loop
- Investigate and modify a simple program that changes a variable
- Begin to look for ways to generalise this idea elsewhere

Computer Science Concepts:

- Repeat x times loops
- Variables in a loop
- Reporting a variable by using it within a say command

Maths Concepts

- Counting in multiples, counting backwards, counting in halves, counting in tenths, counting in hundredths, counting from a different starting number

Assessment for Learning

At the end of each session direct pupils to page 8 of pupil workbook 3 to help them reflect on what they have learnt. It is often worth working through this line by line to avoid pupils filling in everything with a smiley face. You can also annotate this to record pupils who have needed much more support or have demonstrated greater understanding.

Adult Focus

All adults need to be clear that they are to support using hints only and not solve things for pupils.

Computational Thinking - Evaluation is how we look at algorithms and determine how useful they are, how adaptable, how efficient, how correct. There may be many algorithmic solutions to a problem, evaluation asks which one was best and why?

National Curriculum Programs of Study

Pupils should be taught to:

- ***design, write and debug programs that accomplish specific goals,*** including controlling or simulating physical systems; solve problems by decomposing them into smaller parts
- ***use sequence,*** selection, and ***repetition in programs; work with variables and various forms of input and output***
- ***use logical reasoning to*** explain how some simple algorithms work and to ***detect and correct errors in algorithms and programs***

Useful Hints

Help pupils understand counting down as repeated subtraction as counting up is repeated addition https://youtu.be/Kdg41Tr6ZaQhtml. Pupils trace step by step what is happening to the number in the loop.

Resources Pot or mug Lots of pencils Post-it note

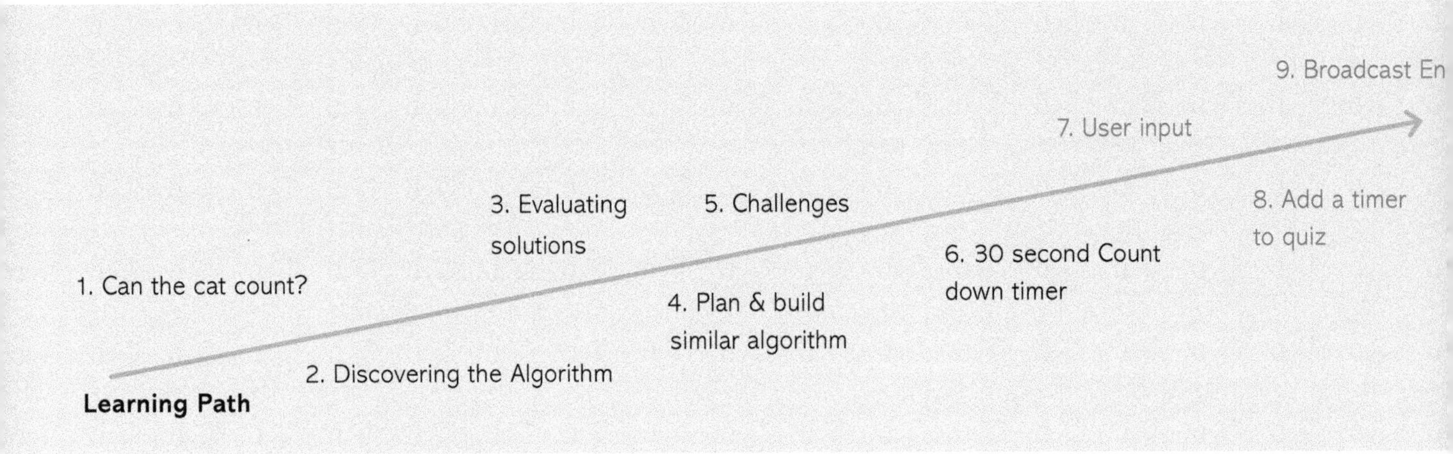
1. Can the cat count?
2. Discovering the Algorithm
3. Evaluating solutions
4. Plan & build similar algorithm
5. Challenges
6. 30 second Count down timer
7. User input
8. Add a timer to quiz
9. Broadcast En
Learning Path

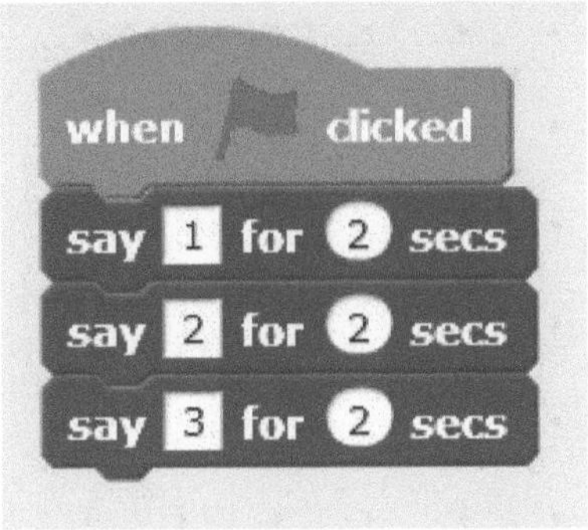
when clicked
say 1 for 2 secs
say 2 for 2 secs
say 3 for 2 secs

1. Can the cat count?

Ask pupils if they can work out a way to make the cat count. They will often come up with lots of say commands strung together. Welcome their efforts and ask them what the draw backs are for this method (very time consuming). If they don't come up with this ask them if they would be happy to make the cat count to 1000 using their method?

2. Discovering the Algorithm

Remind pupils of when they created a variable to hold the score in the maths quiz. Bring back to mind the two useful variable blocks, set variable and change variable. Model emptying the pot and filling it with 0 or a set number of pencils as you set the variable to whatever the number is. Ask them where they set the variable to 0 in the quiz. Answer at the start, so each quiz was fair and the score wasn't carried over if you attempted the quiz a second time. Now model changing the variable by 1 inside a repeat loop. Give the pupil helper the variable pot, label its count using the post-it note. Set the variable to zero by removing all pencils. Now model changing the variable by 1 by putting a pencil in the pot. After each change get the student to look into the pot/variable and report the number of pencils. Ask pupils what this repeated process of changing the variable by 1 and saying the variable could be inside. Most groups will come up with a loop. Now give pupils more time to see if they can come up with a better way to count using what you have just modelled.

There are videos video illustrating this at http://youtu.be/VsHmGgkYQK4 and http://youtu.be/_26bc5twFRg

You may need to remind pupils how to create a variable in Scratch 2.0 Data

Make a variable

Variable name: Count

For all sprites

OK

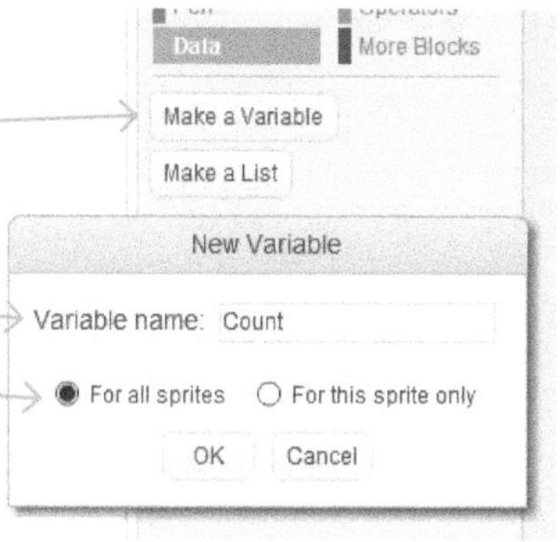
Data
More Blocks
Make a Variable
Make a List
New Variable
Variable name: Count
For all sprites
For this sprite only
OK
Cancel

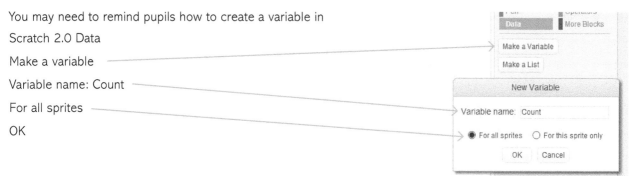

3. Evaluating Solutions

Typical pupil solutions may look like this. This is a really good opportunity to **evaluate** both the sequence of say commands and this changed variable inside a loop. Which is most efficient? Which uses the least code to count to 1000?

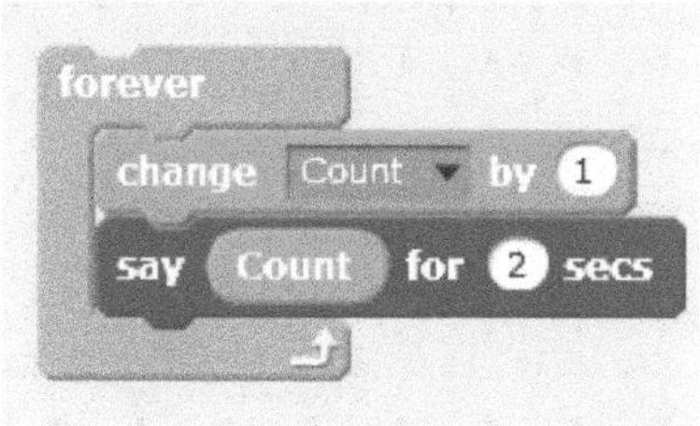
forever
change Count by 1
say Count for 2 secs

4. Plan and Build Similar Algorithm

Explain that a computer scientist has come up with a similar version of their counting algorithm. Ask them to turn to page 9 where they will need to match the Scratch blocks with the algorithm flow chart. The correct matching blocks are on page 99. Once they have completed this they can build the new counting machine in the scripts area of a new sprite. It can be tempting to let them use their old solutions but these often have flaws, such as using a forever loop, that make them less useful for counting and it is a useful skill to read and interpret a flowchart algorithm.

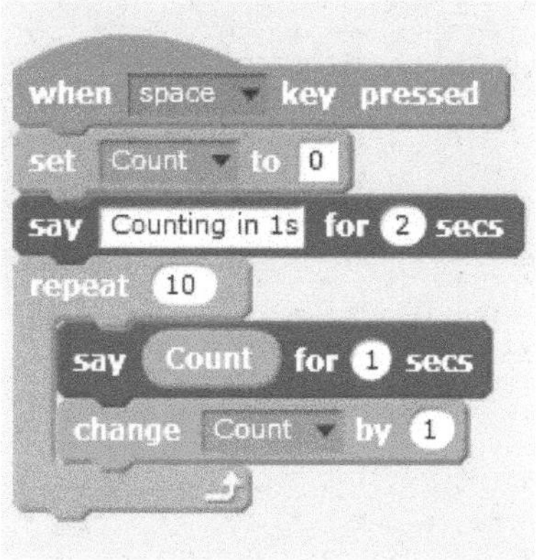
when space key pressed
set Count to 0
say Counting in 1s for 2 secs
repeat 10
say Count for 1 secs
change Count by 1

5. Challenges

As pupils finish building and testing their counting machine encourage them to work their way through the challenges found on page 10 of the pupil workbook and come and point out what they changed to solve this on the challenges sheet (page 99) of the teacher workbook.

Challenges Count faster, count in 2s, count in 7s, count backwards, count in halves, count in tenths, count in hundredths, start from 30, start from -60. Combine previous challenges: for example start from 100 count backwards in 7s.

Counting Challenges Answers

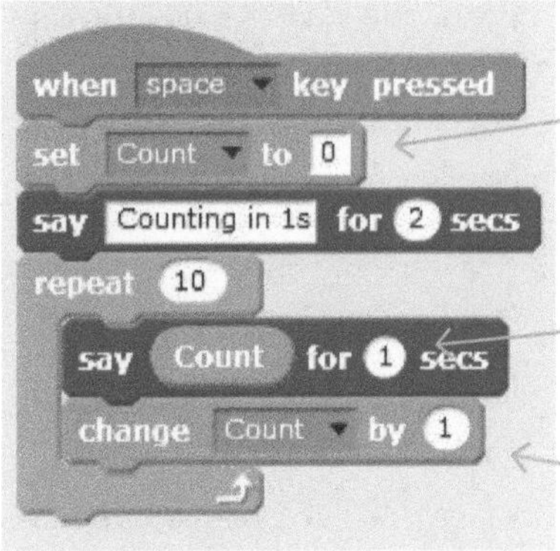
when space key pressed
set Count to 0
say Counting in 1s for 2 secs
repeat 10
say Count for 1 secs
change Count by 1

Start counting from 30 change set variable to 30, start counting from -60 set variable to -60

Count faster change seconds to decimal fraction such as 0.5

Count in 2s change variable to 2, count in 7s change variable to 7, count backwards change variable to negative number, count in halves change variable to 0.5, count in tenths change variable to 0.1, count in hundredths change variable to 0.01,

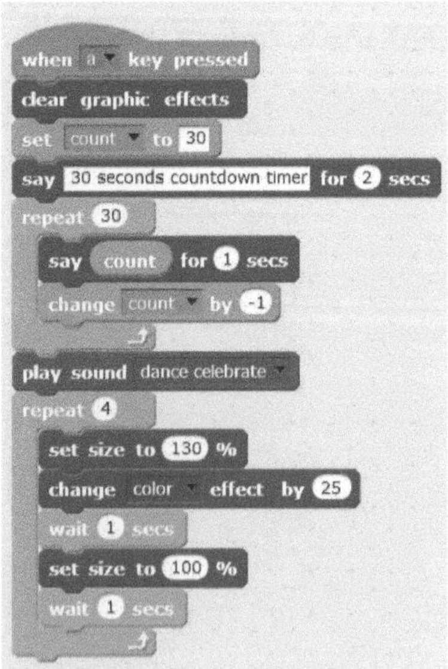
when a key pressed
clear graphic effects
set count to 30
say 30 seconds countdown timer for 2 secs
repeat 30
say count for 1 secs
change count by -1
play sound dance celebrate
repeat 4
set size to 130 %
change color effect by 25
wait 1 secs
set size to 100 %
wait 1 secs

6. Countdown timer

As pupils finish the challenges explain that you would like them to program a 30 seconds count down timer that you can use in class for mental maths. Can they adapt their counting machine to do this? Can they make sure that it alerts everyone when it finishes?

This is one possibility but there are many variations on the ending.

7. User Input

Explain that the teacher would like to be able to set the timer so that they can determine how many seconds it runs for. Ask if they can remember a way of inputting user information into a programme while it is running. If you covered the quiz someone should remember the ask command. Drag out an ask command and ask where the user input goes. Draw out that it goes into the answer block. Can we use this to set the time? Very few pupils will solve this without hinting that ask can input into more than one answer block. I recommend dragging out another answer block after a period of struggle.

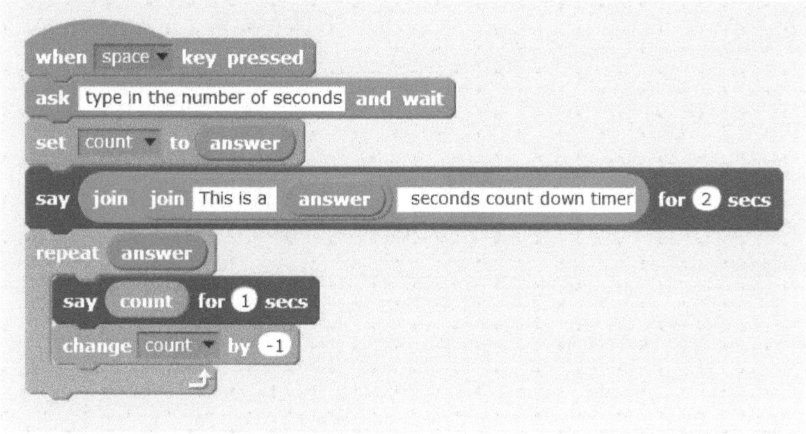

when space key pressed
ask type in the number of seconds and wait
set count to answer
say join join This is a answer seconds count down timer for 2 secs
repeat answer
say count for 1 secs
change count by -1

The use of the say command is an optional extra and can be suggested as an extension if pupils don't arrive at it independently.

8. Add a timer to the Maths Quiz

If your pupils previously created the Maths quiz an interesting extension is to require them to add a timer to their quiz.

9. Broadcast End

An enjoyable extension to this is to recap how broadcasts can be made to trigger multiple events elsewhere in the program and then suggest they use this in as many ways as they can to indicate that the timer has finished.

https://youtu.be/BwFT6dYAUzO

Match the Scratch blocks to the flow chart by drawing lines to them

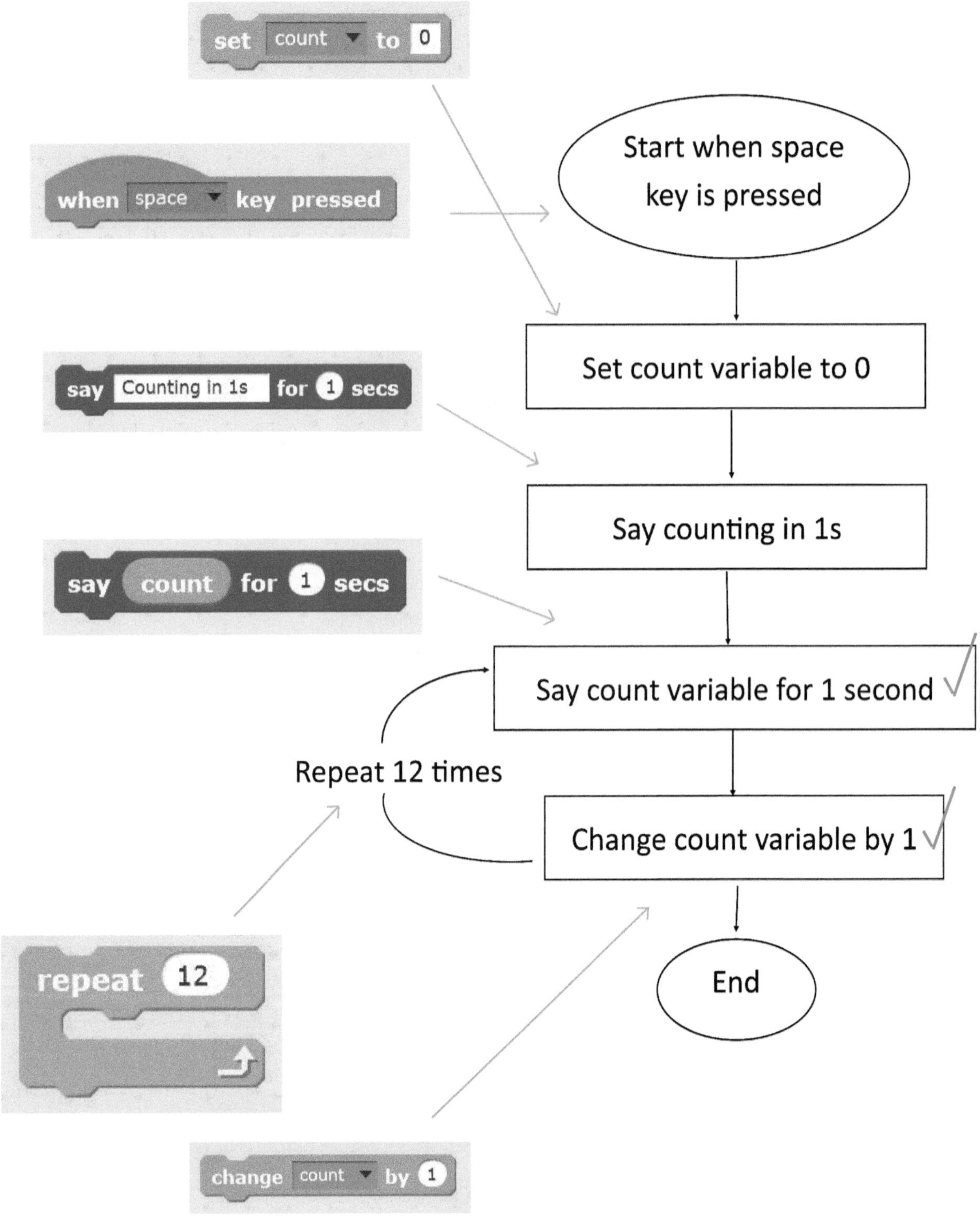
set count to 0
when space key pressed
say Counting in 1s for 1 secs
say count for 1 secs
repeat 12
change count by 1
Start when space key is pressed
Set count variable to 0
Say counting in 1s
Say count variable for 1 second
Repeat 12 times
Change count variable by 1
End

Tick the two blocks that get repeated 12 times

Point to what you changed

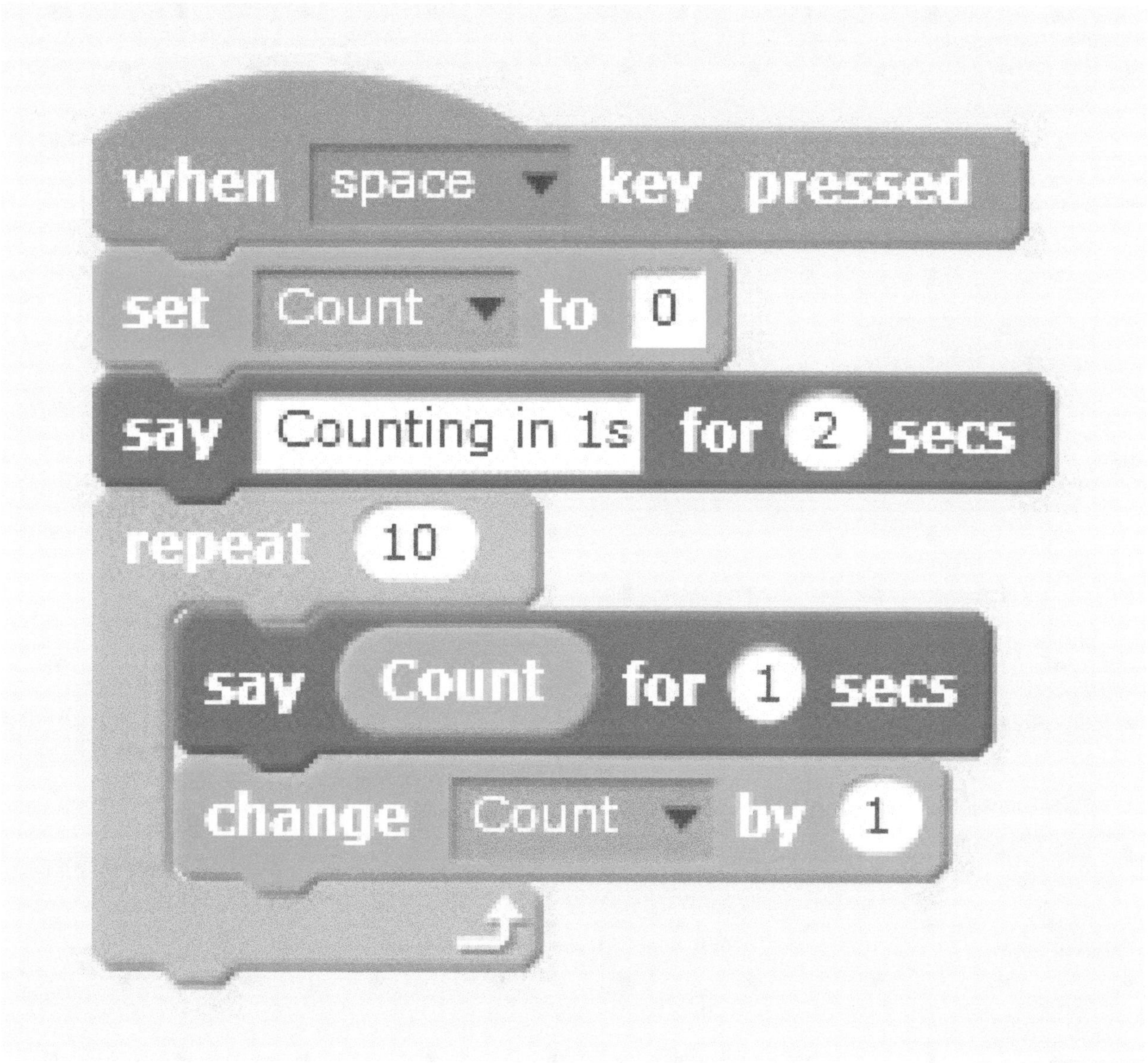
when space key pressed
set Count to 0
say Counting in 1s for 2 secs
repeat 10
say Count for 1 secs
change Count by 1

3B. Music Abstraction

Time to complete module

1 hours

Module Aim: Convert a music track into code using abstraction to help.

National Curriculum Programs of Study

Pupils should be taught to:

- ***design, write and debug programs that accomplish specific goals,*** including controlling or simulating physical systems; solve problems by decomposing them into smaller parts
- ***use sequence,*** selection, and repetition ***in programs;*** work with variables and various forms of input and output
- ***use logical reasoning to*** explain how some simple algorithms work and to ***detect and correct errors in algorithms and programs***

Useful Hints

Divide and conquer is a good strategy here as it can help to divide up the program into sections and listen to every selection to find bugs. When a bug is spotted the user can move to tracing code.

Pupils trace step by step what is happening to the sound blocks as they play to spot ones that don't sound right.

Module Learning Focus

By the end of the module children will be able to:

- Explain how they used abstraction to reduce the complexity of a task
- Look for the most important aspects of something and discard aspects that are not important
- Create a musical algorithm by listening to a musical track and creating symbols to record pitch
- Convert their musical algorithm to code and test for closeness to the original sound track

Computer Science Concepts

- Sequence
- Repeat loops
- Creating algorithm
- Abstraction
- Generalisation

Assessment for Learning

At the end of each session direct pupils to page 12 of pupil workbook 3 to help them reflect on what they have learnt. It is often worth working through this line by line to avoid pupils filling in everything with a smiley face. You can also annotate this to record pupils who have needed much more support or have demonstrated greater understanding.

Adult Focus

All adults need to be clear that they are to support using hints only and not solve things for pupils

Computational Thinking **Abstraction:** is the skill of reducing complexity by hiding irrelevant detail and focussing on the most important element.

Precondition: It is advisable that all pupils have completed the Music Machine first to familiarise themselves with the music blocks

5. Convert algorithm to code
4. Convert sound track to algorithm
3. Abstract the song
2. Identify elements
1. Explain Task
arning Path

1. Explain Task

Your baby brother or sister will only sleep if they can listen to Baa Baa Black Sheep. You have a plan to program a simple notes only chip, similar to those you find in greetings cards, to play them to sleep.

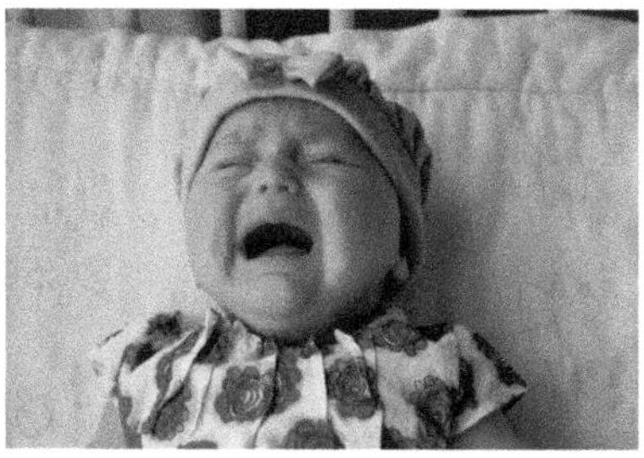

2. Identify elements

Play this sound track either on You Tube https://www.youtube.com/watch?v=P6n0Y2RyeWE or on the web. http://www.wordsforlife.org.uk/songs/baa-baa-black-sheep The video is preferable as it has more elements for pupils to identify. Ask pupils to work in pairs, recording in their pupil workbooks page 13 to identify all the elements on the track. Collect and list all the elements that they identify (accept visual elements as well).

3. Abstract the song

Remind them of the main task **music** to **algorithm** to **code**
Explain that we can use abstraction to help us do this.
Point out the **Abstraction Definition** in the pupil workbook.
Can they work in pairs to **identify all the elements that won't help them program this as musical notes in Scratch, and which elements are the most important?** They can put a cross by them in the pupil workbook page 13

You are looking for high and low notes as important (pitch) and how long the notes last for. Most classes will get the pitch but not all will get the length of notes.
The rest - video, words, percussion etc is irrelevant

Abstraction

Reduce complexity by hiding irrelevant detail and focussing on the most important element.

Irrelevant detail not helpful to program this as notes in Scratch	Most Important elements that will help us program this as notes in Scratch

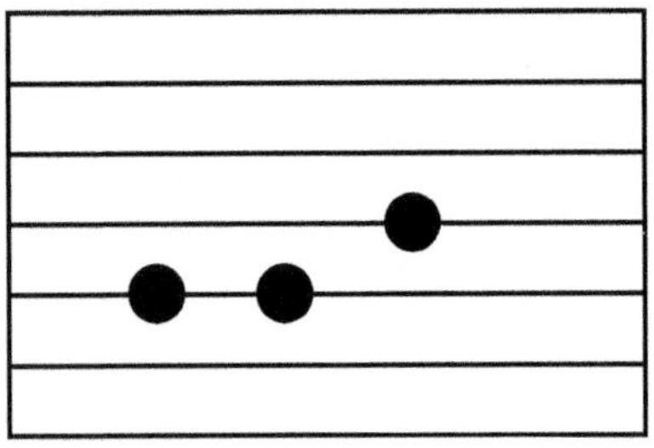

Shazam
An app like Shazam, which seeks to identify music, looks at pitch changes and length of notes before comparing it against its existing database of tracks to find the music.

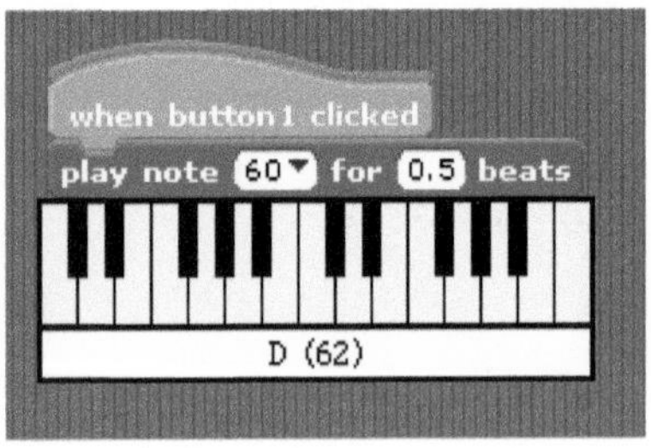
when button1 clicked
play note 60 for 0.5 beats
D (62)

4. Convert sound track to algorithm

Explain that it would be really useful to have a sound track that hasn't got all this irrelevant detail. Play this basic Baa Baa Black Sheep Midi file here http://ingeb.org/songs/baabaabl.mid. You will need quick time installed to play it.

Ask pupils to turn to the pupil workbook page 14 where there is a page of staves that they can use to record with dots how the pitch changes.

Encourage pupils to play the sound track lots of times to help them create the right notation algorithm. Are any notes quicker or slower than others? How can they represent those? How will they code them in Scratch?

5. Convert Algorithm to Code

You may need to remind pupils of the keyboard on the Scratch note. Sticking to the white notes is also best. Tell pupils that the first note is C 60 as this really helps.

A great incentive is to have a table competition to see who can code the most accurate track.

You could also generalise using this method to code other songs.

Print extra independent extension activities in the pupil books and send them home.

3c. Random Word or Sentence Generator

Module Aim: Create a program that uses lists to generate random words or phrases

Time to complete module

1-2 hours

Module Learning Focus

By the end of the module children will be able to:

- Create a list
- Randomly access items in lists
- Combine lists and text to produce meaning
- Begin to think of ways this might be used elsewhere

Computer Science Concepts

- Creating a list to store information
- Accessing random items from a list

Assessment for Learning

At the end of each session direct pupils to page 16 of pupil workbook 3 to help them reflect on what they have learnt. It is often worth working through this line by line to avoid pupils filling in everything with a smiley face. You can also annotate this to record pupils who have needed much more support or have demonstrated greater understanding.

Adult Focus

All adults need to be clear that they are to support using hints only and not solve things for pupils.

Generalisation: Adapting a solution to accomplish something else

National Curriculum Programs of Study

KS2

Pupils should be taught to:

- ***design, write and debug programs that accomplish specific goals,*** including controlling or simulating physical systems; solve problems by decomposing them into smaller parts
- ***use sequence,*** selection, and repetition ***in programs***; work with variables and various forms of input and output
- ***use logical reasoning to*** explain how some simple algorithms work and to ***detect and correct errors in algorithms and programs***

KS3

- ***make appropriate use of data structures (for example, lists, tables or arrays)***

Useful Hints

Bugs tend to be simple in this module and mainly confined to pupils not reading the settings they have chosen on the lists.

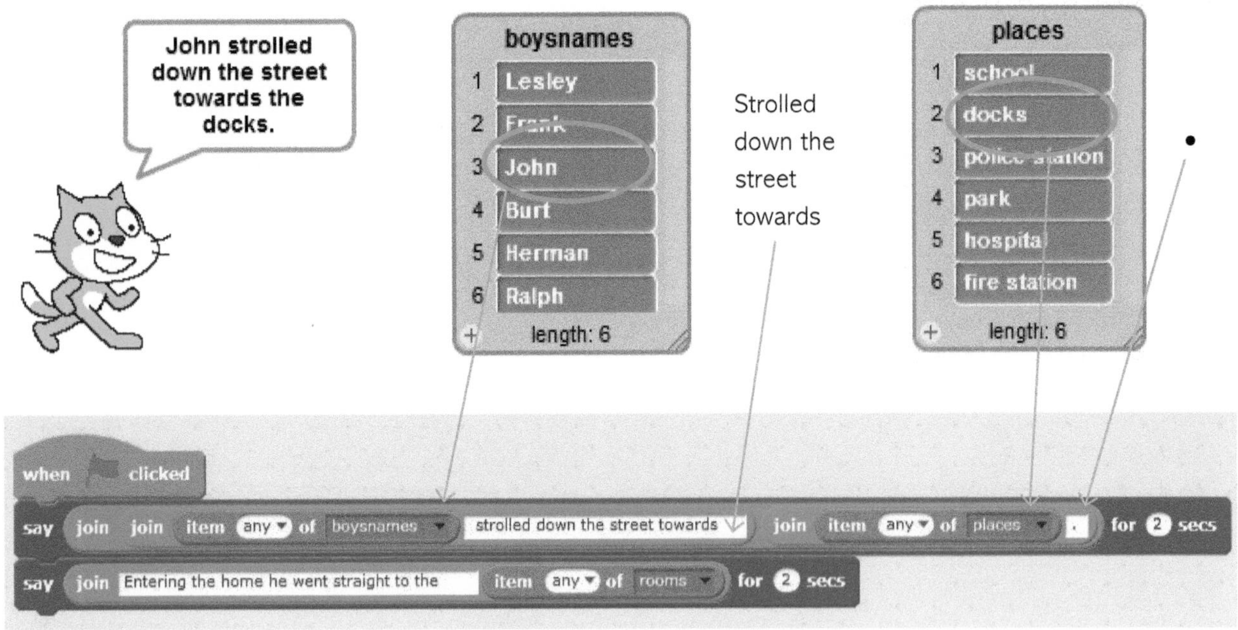
John strolled down the street towards the docks.
boysnames
1 Lesley
3 John
4 Burt
5 Herman
6 Ralph
length: 6
Strolled down the street towards
places
1 school
2 docks
4 park
6 fire station
length: 6
when clicked
say join join item any of boysnames strolled down the street towards join item any of places . for 2 secs
say join Entering the home he went straight to the item any of rooms for 2 secs

Context

There are so many literacy or humorous things you can do with this idea. Pupils could create random words for KS1 pupils to read by combining a word starter list and a word ending list. You could generate a random story start by combining random places and random feelings. You could show pupils the basics and let them decide what to do with it. Watch out for the random romance generator, list of names loves list of names.

Introduction

Write a list on a board at the front of the class with six class names on it. Roll a dice to choose a child. Use the list to ask question, admonish children, choose who to praise, who to compliment etc. Explain that programmers can use lists as well. Show the class how to make an identical list called names using Scratch. Use a join to add some text to the name. Test the program and give pupils time to create it. If your class has used Scratch a lot why not drag the blocks out and let them puzzle out how they fit together. After pupils have tested this basic idea move onto your theme.

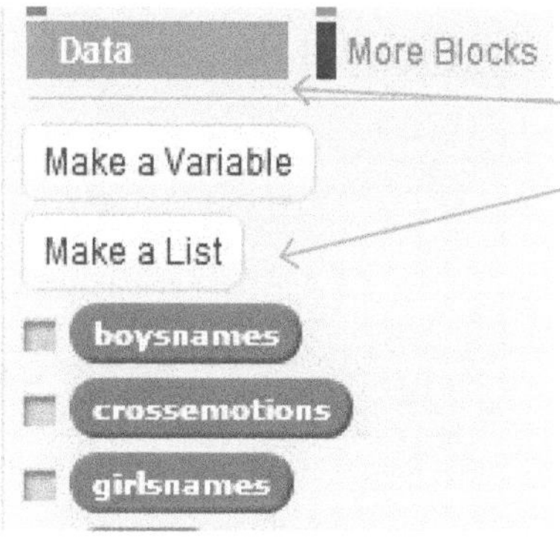
Data
More Blocks
Make a Variable
Make a List
boysnames
crossemotions
girlsnames

Create a list

Click Data then

Make a list

Limited Screen Space If you are using netbooks or your computers have very limited screen space encourage pupils to build short say commands and build vertically rather than horizontally.

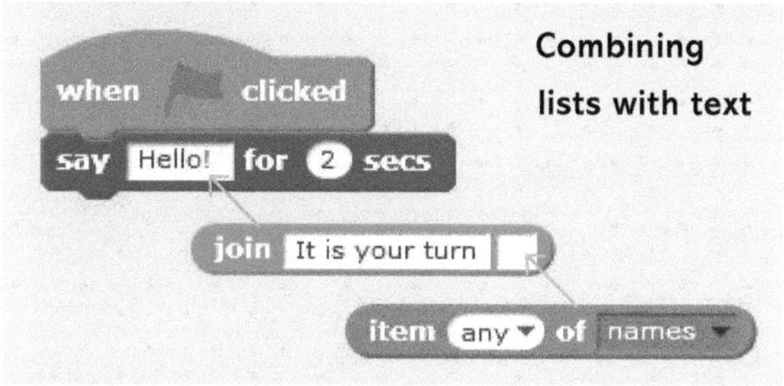
when clicked
say Hello! for 2 secs
join It is your turn
item any of names

Combining lists with text

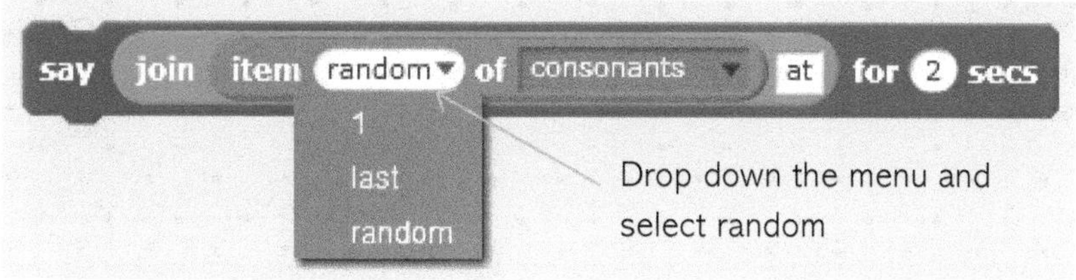
say join item random of consonants at for 2 secs
1
last
random

Drop down the menu and select random

Selecting Items From a List

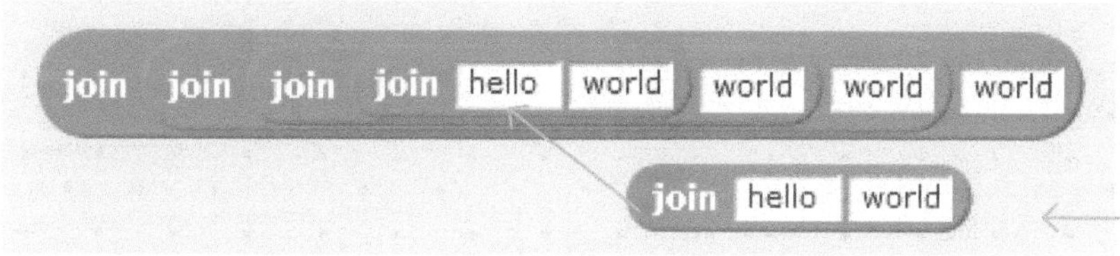
join join join join hello world world world world
join hello world

Working with Joins

Don't forget to leave extra spaces in the joins if you need spaces between words. Combine joins inside joins if you need to join multiple lists or text sections.

Add to a List

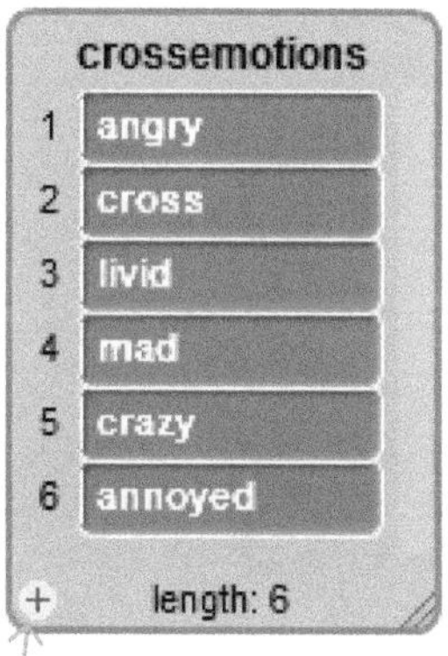
crossemotions
1 angry
2 cross
3 livid
4 mad
5 crazy
6 annoyed
+
length: 6

Click the + symbol to add things to the list

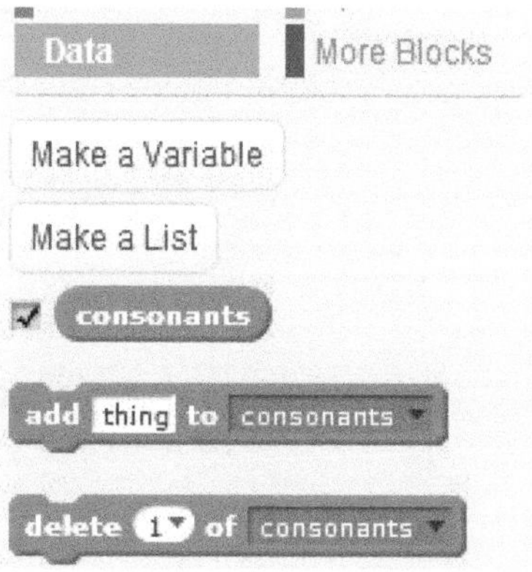
Data
More Blocks
Make a Variable
Make a List
consonants
add thing to consonants
delete 1 of consonants

Tick the list to show the words and untick it to hide the words. The list can be used whether hidden or shown.

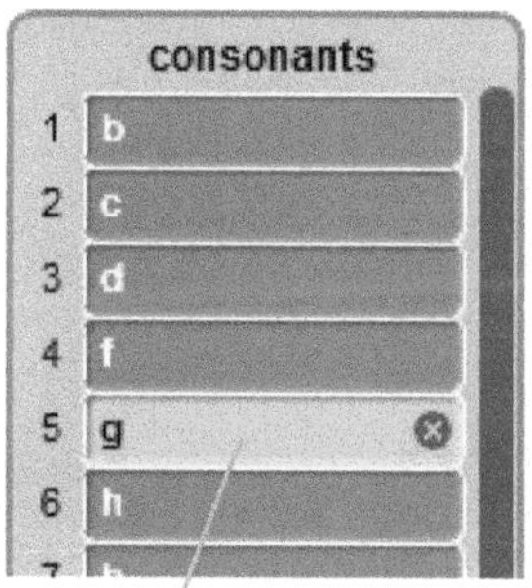
consonants
1 b
2 c
3 d
4 f
5 g
6 h

Edit

Click on an item in a list and click x to delete that item

Earlier versions of Scratch 2.0 don't have this feature.

Create a list

Click Data then

Make a List

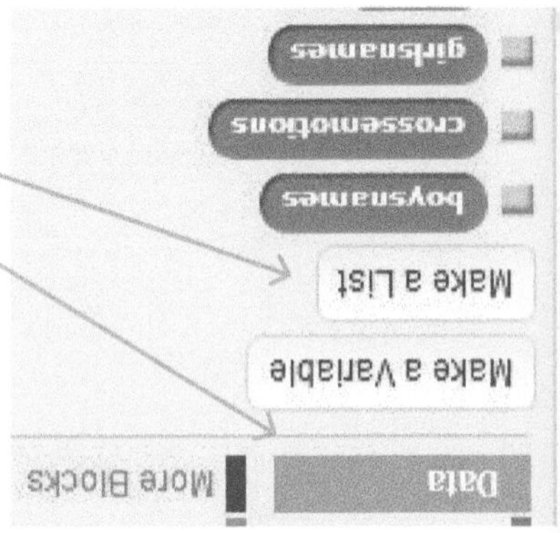
Data
More Blocks
Make a Variable
Make a List
boysnames
crossemotions
girlsnames

Add to a List

crossemotions
1 angry
2 cross
3 livid
4 mad
5 crazy
6 annoyed
+
length: 6

Click the + symbol to
add things to the list

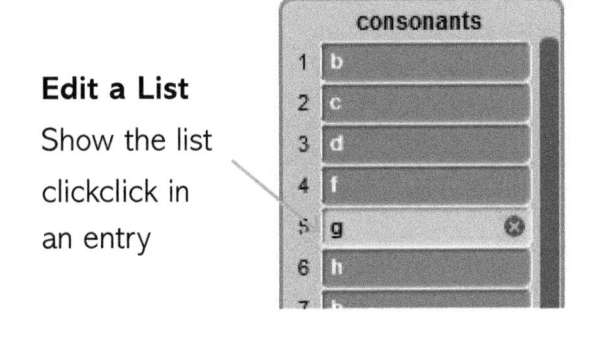

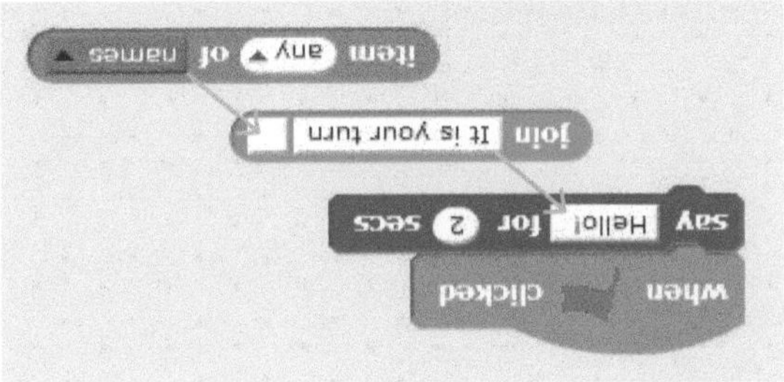
when clicked
say Hello! for 2 secs
join It is your turn
item any of names

Combining lists with text

Edit a List

Show the list

clickclick in

an entry

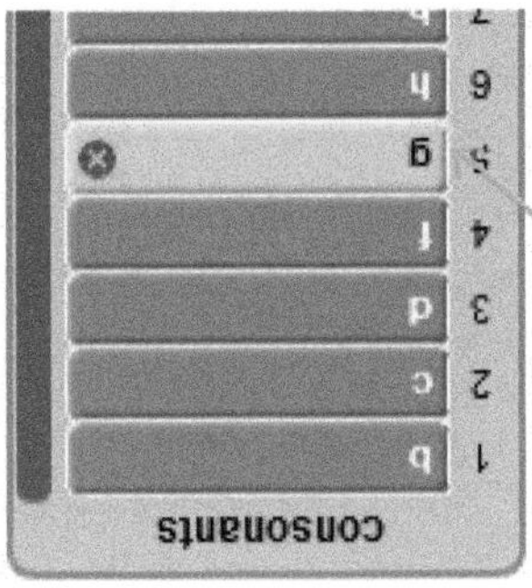
consonants
1 b
2 c
3 d
4 f
5 g
6 h

Scratch
Random Word
Help

code-it.co.uk

Random
Word
Help
Card

code-it.co.uk

3D. Coins

Module Aim: Create a program that calculates and records how many coins there are in a given number of pence

Time to complete module

2 hours

Module Learning Focus

By the end of the module children will be able to:

- Use greater than and less than when comparing numbers
- Spot the pattern in the part completed algorithm
- Convert algorithm to code
- Use the algorithm to help identify bugs

Computer Science Concepts

- Converting algorithm into code
- Reading a flow chart
- Converting user input into a variable
- Repeat until loop
- Creating, inputting and deleting from a list
- Subtracting from a variable
- Pattern recognition which is a part of generalisation

Maths Concepts

- Less than
- Greater than
- Subtracting multiples

Assessment for Learning

At the end of each session direct pupils to page 18 of pupil workbook 3 to help them reflect on what they have learnt. It is often worth working through this line by line to avoid pupils filling in everything with a smiley face. You can also annotate this to record pupils who have needed much more support or have demonstrated greater understanding.

Adult Focus

All adults need to be clear that they are to support using hints only and not solve things for pupils.

Computational Thinking- Pattern recognition is part of generalisation, adapting a solution that solved one problem to solve another

National Curriculum Programs of Study

Pupils should be taught to:

- design, *write and debug programs that accomplish specific goals,* including controlling or simulating physical systems; solve problems by decomposing them into smaller parts
- *use sequence, selection, and repetition in programs; work with variables and various forms of input and output*
- *use logical reasoning to explain how some simple algorithms work and to detect and correct errors in algorithms and programs*

Useful Hints

Refer pupils to the algorithm to see if they have converted it properly.

Refer pupils to working blocks of code above or below the section that doesn't work. What is different in that block?

Feed imaginary amount through the code to trace what would happen to it.

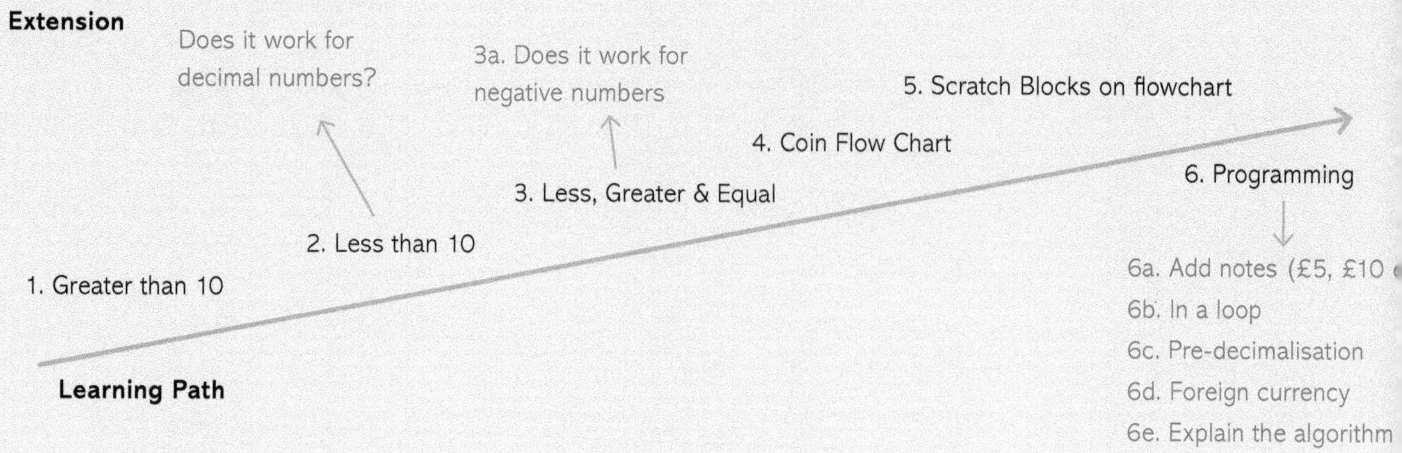
Extension
Does it work for decimal numbers?
3a. Does it work for negative numbers
5. Scratch Blocks on flowchart
4. Coin Flow Chart
6. Programming
3. Less, Greater & Equal
2. Less than 10
1. Greater than 10
6a. Add notes (£5, £10
6b. In a loop
6c. Pre-decimalisation
6d. Foreign currency
6e. Explain the algorithm
Learning Path

> If your pupils are secure in understanding < and > you can skip 1-3 and go straight onto section 4. You could do section 1-3 in Y4 if it fitted with your Maths curriculum.

1. Greater than 10

Before you start explore < & > with numbers on the board. Then model this basic code below or write what this code does (Text in bold) and challenge pupils to try and make it independently.

If the amount typed in is greater than 10 say greater than 10 else say is less than 10.

Refer pupils back to the quiz where they used an if else conditional selection block before.

Test it out with a range of whole numbers by left clicking on the block.

Left clicking on a block runs the block without having to include a start block.

> Note use of say without timings which will remain until another say command is used.

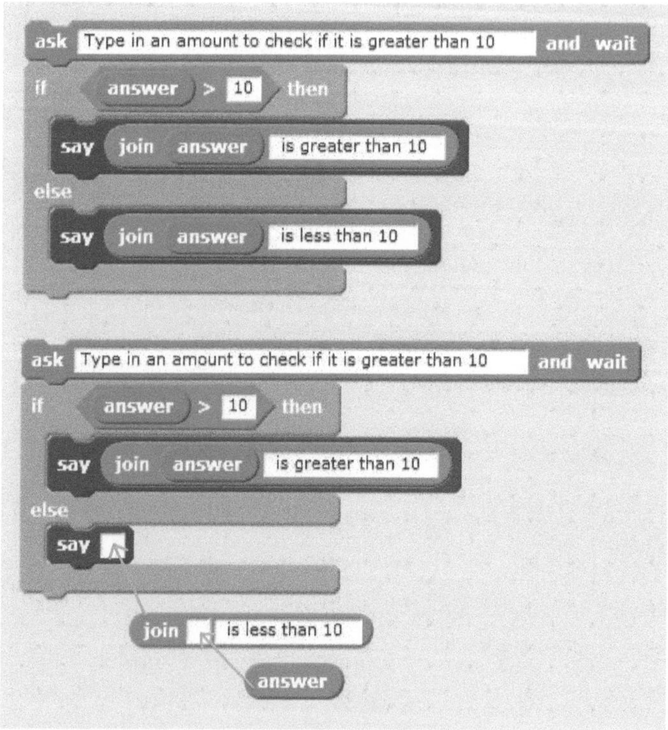
ask Type in an amount to check if it is greater than 10 and wait
if answer > 10 then
say join answer is greater than 10
else
say join answer is less than 10
ask Type in an amount to check if it is greater than 10 and wait
if answer > 10 then
say join answer is greater than 10
else
say
join is less than 10
answer

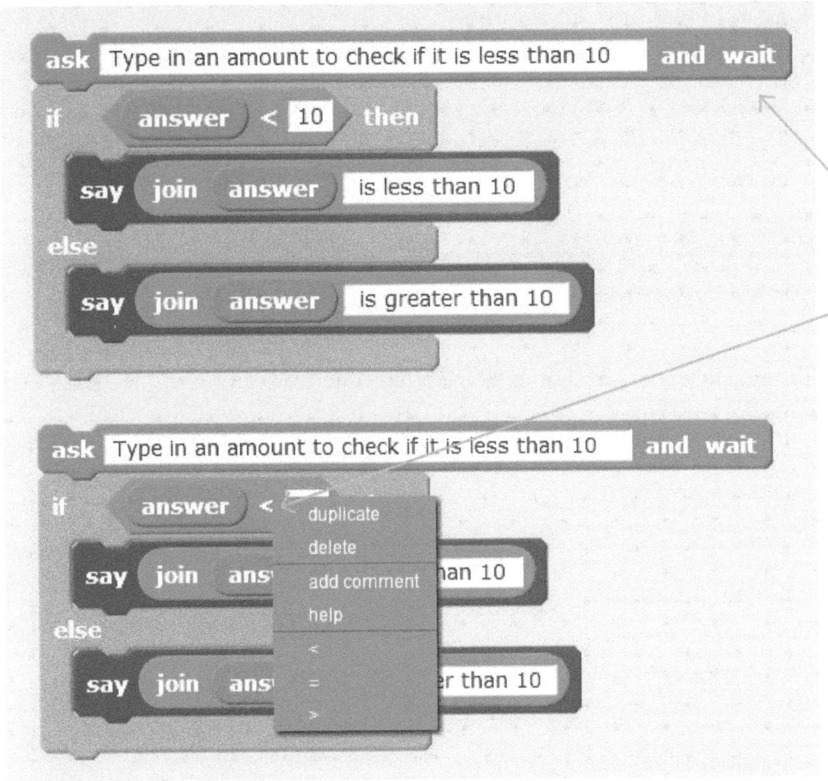
ask Type in an amount to check if it is less than 10 and wait
if answer < 10 then
say join answer is less than 10
else
say join answer is greater than 10
ask Type in an amount to check if it is less than 10 and wait
if answer <
say join ans
an 10
else
say join ans
r than 10
duplicate
delete
add comment
help
<
=
>

2. Less than 10

Can they adapt the code to investigate less than?

You may wish to show them how to duplicate the block by right clicking on the top block and left clicking duplicate.

They can also right click on the symbol to change its meaning.

Test this with other numbers.

2a. Does it work if you input decimal numbers or make your test number a decimal?

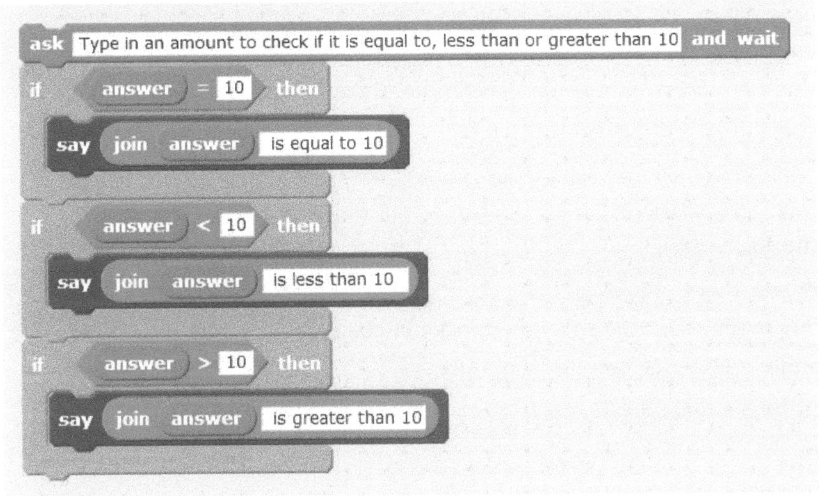
ask Type in an amount to check if it is equal to, less than or greater than 10 and wait
if answer = 10 then
say join answer is equal to 10
if answer < 10 then
say join answer is less than 10
if answer > 10 then
say join answer is greater than 10

3. Less, Greater & Equal

See if pupils can tell you what is wrong with our less than and greater than machines. Often they don't check to see if something is equal to. Demonstrate typing in a number equal to the number. Challenge pupils to adapt their code to check for < > and =.

3a. Does it work for negative numbers?

4. Coin Flow Chart

Explain that we are now going to create a machine that chooses the largest coins possible to make from the pence inputted by the user. So if 15p was inputted it would work out that the best way to turn this into change would be a 10p and a 5p. Draw a very basic input and output machine on the board. Feed 450 into the machine and explain that the machine checks to see if it can take 200 away from 450. It can so it does. Draw a £2 coin next to the machine and explain that this was the 200 it took away which is the same as a £2 coin. Repeat this to subtract another 200 (£2 coin) when it can't take away another 200.

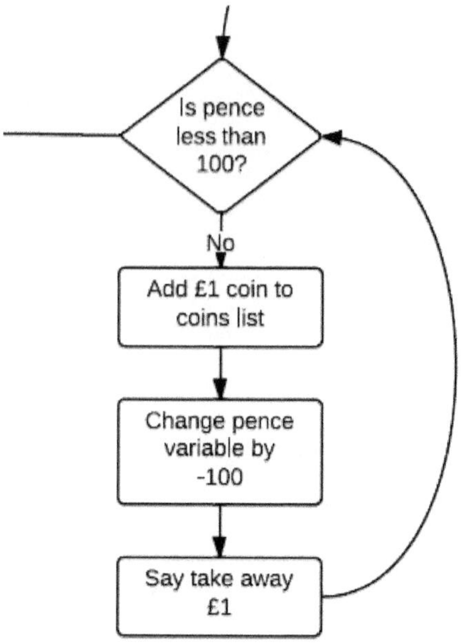
Is pence less than 100?
No
Add £1 coin to coins list
Change pence variable by -100
Say take away £1

4. Coin Flow Chart Continued

It tries to take away 100 (£1 coin). When it can't do this it tries to take away 50 (50p). It can do this so draw another coin. The machine has worked out the largest coins into which you could change 450. You may need to work some more examples if pupils don't get this.

Sort pupils in to mixed ability pairs. Hand out the part completed coin flow chart in pupil workbooks. Explain that this flow chart describes the coin sorting program.

Can pupils work out what to fill in for the three blank blocks? They are trying to spot the pattern.

Check pupils answers and ask them to explain what the next pattern would be.

Answer

Add 50p to coins list

Change pence variable by -50

Say take away 50p

5. Scratch Blocks to Flow Chart

Now ask pupils to draw lines to connect the Scratch blocks with the flowchart algorithm. Warn pupils that the language may be different but there are clues. Alert pupils that more than one coding block may go with a flow chart block.

Use the flowchart to code answer sheet later in the chapter to check their solutions.

You might wish to display the blocks in colour on the interactive whiteboard. This can be found at:
http://code-it.co.uk/wp-content/uploads/2015/05/coinsblocks.pdf

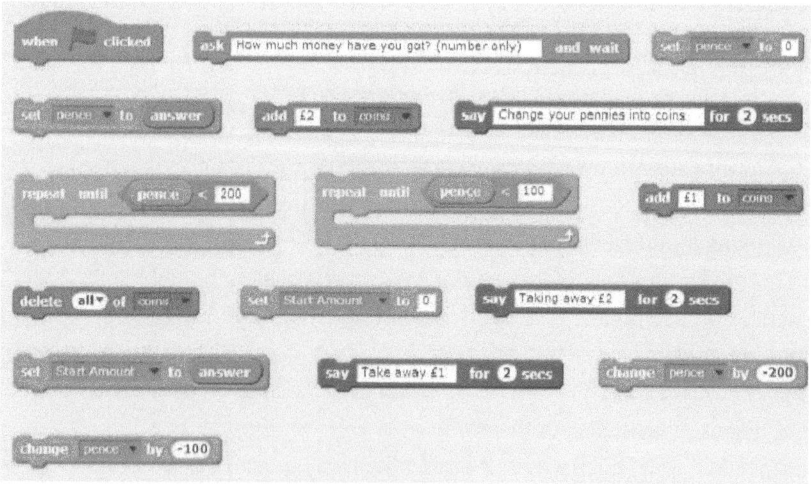
when clicked
ask How much money have you got? (number only) and wait
set pence to 0
set pence to answer
add £2 to coins
say Change your pennies into coins for 2 secs
repeat until pence < 200
repeat until pence < 100
add £1 to coins
delete all of coins
set Start Amount to 0
say Taking away £2 for 2 secs
set Start Amount to answer
say Take away £1 for 2 secs
change pence by -200
change pence by -100

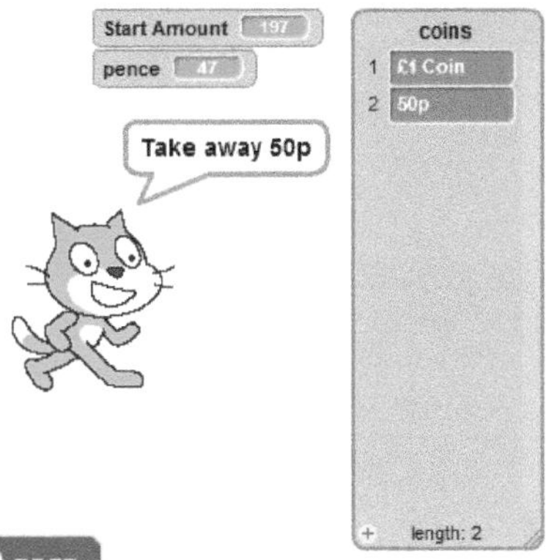
Start Amount 197
pence 47
Take away 50p
coins
1 £1 Coin
2 50p
length: 2

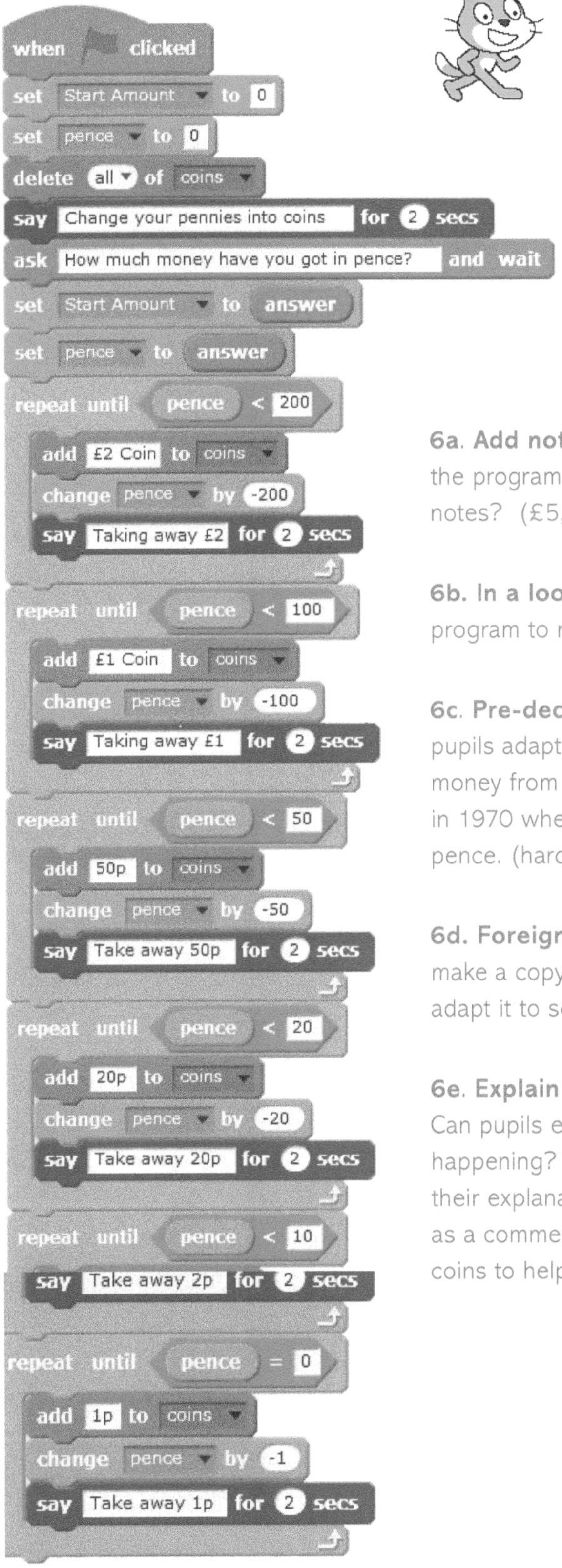
when clicked
set Start Amount to 0
set pence to 0
delete all of coins
say Change your pennies into coins for 2 secs
ask How much money have you got in pence? and wait
set Start Amount to answer
set pence to answer
repeat until pence < 200
add £2 Coin to coins
change pence by -200
say Taking away £2 for 2 secs
repeat until pence < 100
add £1 Coin to coins
change pence by -100
say Taking away £1 for 2 secs
repeat until pence < 50
add 50p to coins
change pence by -50
say Take away 50p for 2 secs
repeat until pence < 20
add 20p to coins
change pence by -20
say Take away 20p for 2 secs
repeat until pence < 10
say Take away 2p for 2 secs
repeat until pence = 0
add 1p to coins
change pence by -1
say Take away 1p for 2 secs

6. Programming

The finished program will look similar to this. If pupils make mistakes (bugs) get them to check their annotated algorithms and see if it matches their programming. Get them to go through line by line with their partner.

If pupils haven't created and used a list in the random word module on page 103 then they will need instruction on how this works. There are good ideas on introducing a list in that module.

6a. Add notes Can pupils adapt the program independently to add notes? (£5, £10 etc)

6b. In a loop Can pupils get the program to run continuously?

6c. Pre-decimalisation Can pupils adapt the program to sort money from before decimalisation in 1970 when the pound had 240 pence. (hard challenege)

6d. Foreign currency Can pupils make a copy of their program and adapt it to sort foreign currency?

6e. Explain the algorithm
Can pupils explain what is happening? They could video their explanations or record them as a comment. They could use coins to help them.

Print extra independent extension activities in the pupil books and send them home.

Pre-Decimal

Here are two useful pre-decimal websites

- http://resources.woodlands-junior.kent.sch.uk/
- customs/questions/moneyold.htm http://gwydir.demon.co.uk/jo/units/money.htm

Flowchart to Code Answers

Coin Sorter Write in what should go in the empty flow chart shapes Draw lines to connect the flow chart algorithm with the code blocks

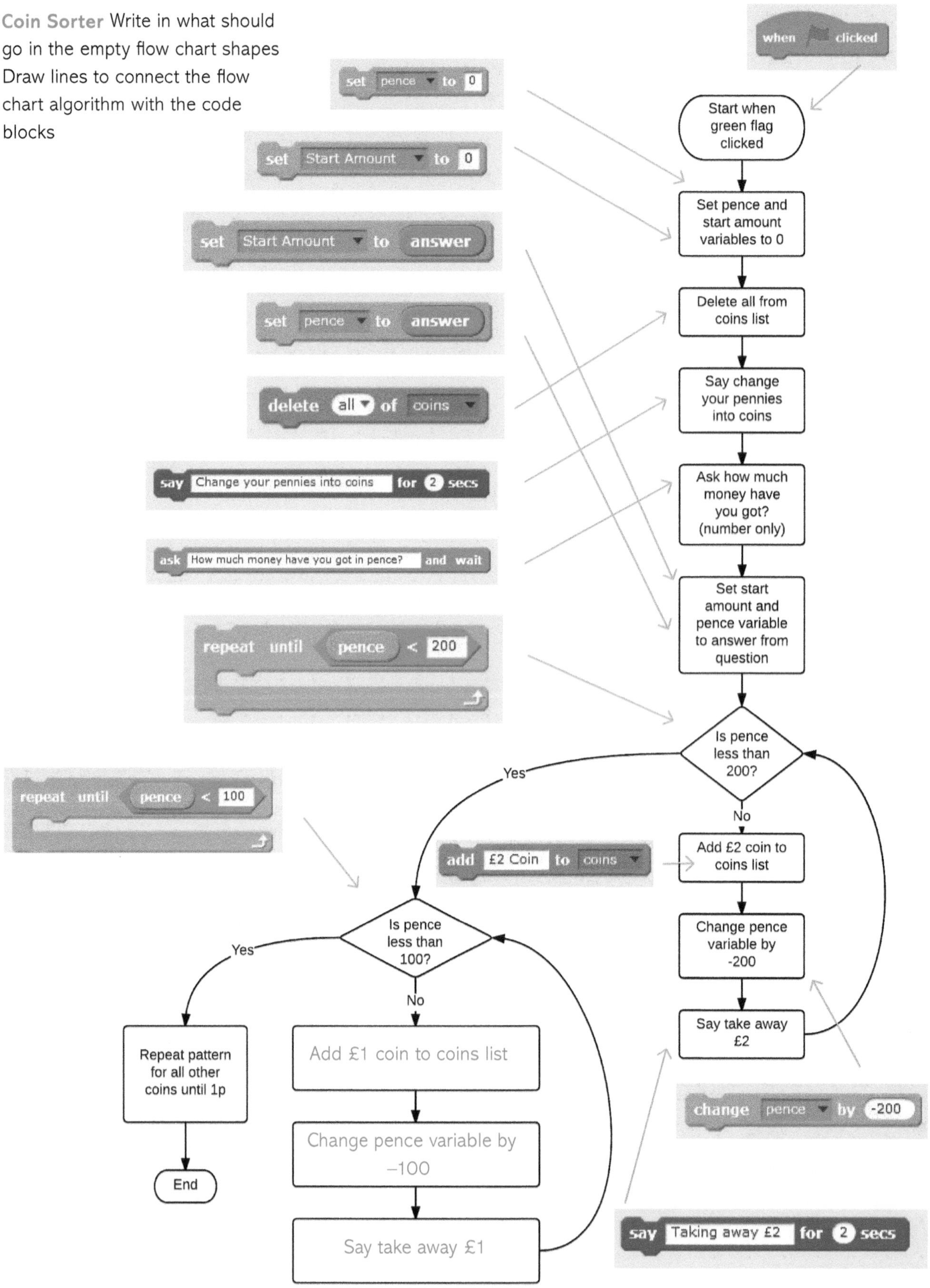
when clicked
set pence to 0
set Start Amount to 0
set Start Amount to answer
set pence to answer
delete all of coins
say Change your pennies into coins for 2 secs
ask How much money have you got in pence? and wait
repeat until pence < 200
repeat until pence < 100
add £2 Coin to coins
change pence by -200
say Taking away £2 for 2 secs
Start when green flag clicked
Set pence and start amount variables to 0
Delete all from coins list
Say change your pennies into coins
Ask how much money have you got? (number only)
Set start amount and pence variable to answer from question
Is pence less than 200?
Yes
No
Add £2 coin to coins list
Change pence variable by -200
Say take away £2
Is pence less than 100?
Yes
No
Repeat pattern for all other coins until 1p
End
Add £1 coin to coins list
Change pence variable by –100
Say take away £1

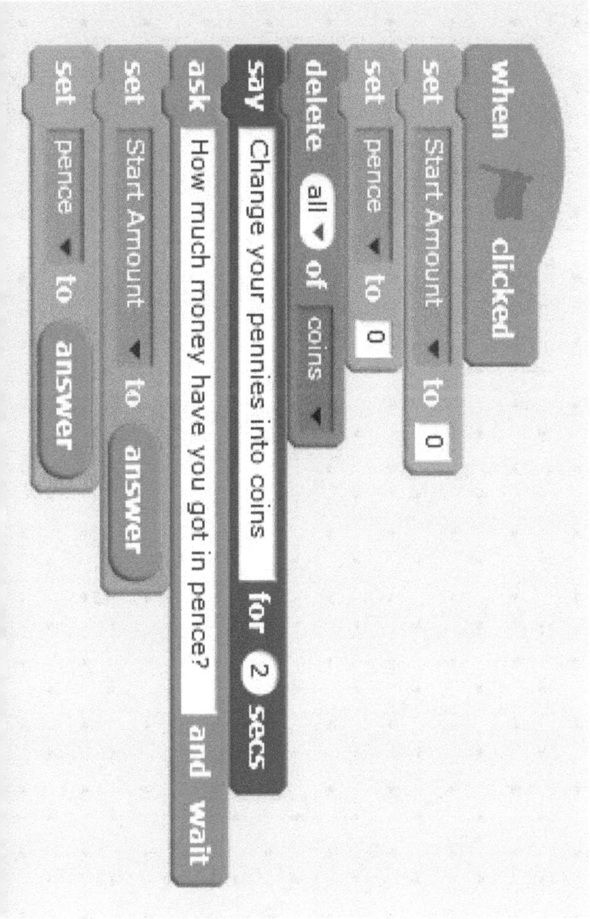
when clicked
set Start Amount to 0
set pence to 0
delete all of coins
say Change your pennies into coins for 2 secs
ask How much money have you got in pence? and wait
set Start Amount to answer
set pence to answer

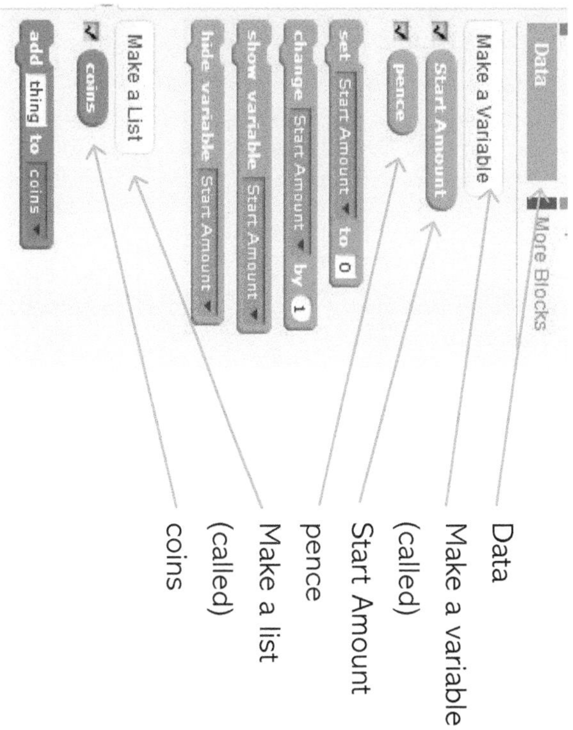
Data
More Blocks
Make a Variable
Start Amount
pence
set Start Amount to 0
change Start Amount by 1
show variable Start Amount
hide variable Start Amount
Make a List
coins
add thing to coins
Data
Make a variable
(called)
Start Amount
pence
Make a list
(called)
coins

Scratch coins

Help &

Debugging Card

code-it.co.uk

Create

Variables

&

List

code-it.co.uk

3E. Crab Maze

Time to complete module

4 hours

Module Aim: Create a maze game where the crab sprite steers through a maze, collecting coins and score until it reaches the maze end which takes it to another level. If it hits the wall the game ends

National Curriculum Programs of Study

Pupils should be taught to:

- ***design, write and debug programs that accomplish specific goals,*** including controlling or simulating physical systems; ***solve problems by decomposing them into smaller parts***
- ***use sequence, selection, and repetition in programs; work with variables and various forms of input and output***
- ***use logical reasoning to*** explain how some simple algorithms work and ***to detect and correct errors in algorithms and programs***

Useful Hints

Referring back to their decomposition planner to determine what they wanted the game to do and then comparing this with the code they have created to see if they are the same

Reading code aloud

Explaining code to a neighbour

Testing code one section at a time (left click on the section)

Module Learning Focus

By the end of the module children will be able to:

- Decompose the game
- Program a working multilevel game
- Debug errors that might occur
- Use coordinates to move sprites when needed

Computer Science Concepts

- Decomposition
- Variable to collect score
- Loops
- Conditional selection

Maths Concepts

- Decimal fractions
- Angles
- X & Y Coordinates

Assessment for Learning

At the end of each session direct pupils to page 21 of pupil workbook 3 to help them reflect on what they have learnt. It is often worth working through this line by line to avoid pupils filling in everything with a smiley face. You can also annotate this to record pupils who have needed much more support or have demonstrated greater understanding.

Adult Focus

All adults need to be clear that they are to support using hints only and not solve things for pupils.

Computational Thinking: Decomposition - Breaking a problem up into smaller chunks and solving these separately.

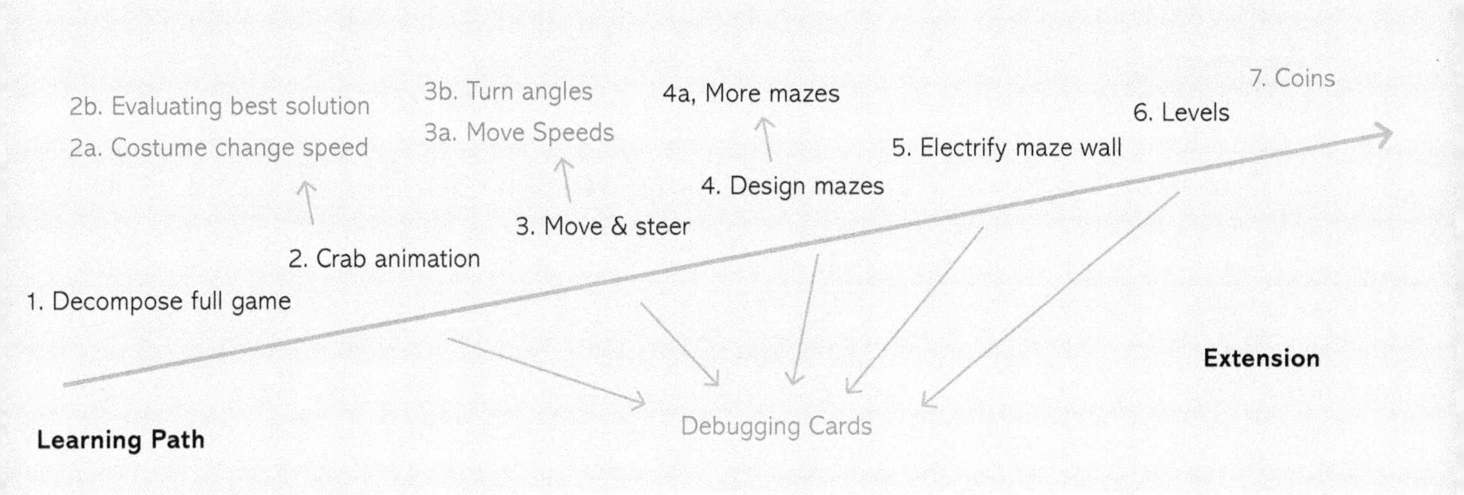

7. Coins
2b. Evaluating best solution
3b. Turn angles
4a, More mazes
6. Levels
2a. Costume change speed
3a. Move Speeds
5. Electrify maze wall
4. Design mazes
3. Move & steer
2. Crab animation
1. Decompose full game
Extension
Debugging Cards
Learning Path

1, Decompose the full game

Open a modern web browser and encourage pupils to navigate to http://scratch.mit.edu/projects/22804830/. Let them play the game but **don't let them look at the code.** Ask them to work in pairs to list all the things that they will need to make, and all the things they will need to make it do, recording these individually in their pupil's workbooks on page 22. Go through this with the class using the teacher version on page 122 to make sure they have decomposed all the elements. They are decomposing the game, breaking it up into smaller chunks to help them solve how to create parts of this separately. You may wish to explain that this is something programmers do to help make problem solving manageable, and sometimes so that large groups of programmers can work on the same project at the same time. They will need to refer to their decomposition planner as they attempt to recreate the game later.

New sprite:

2, Crab Animation

Open Scratch, right click on the cat and delete the cat. Click on the choose new sprite from file button and navigate to the animals folder. Inside select the crab. Click between the two pictures inside the crab sprite. Ask pupils what they can see. (Crab claws open and close). Explain that we would like to automate that process so that the crab opens and closes its claws as it moves.

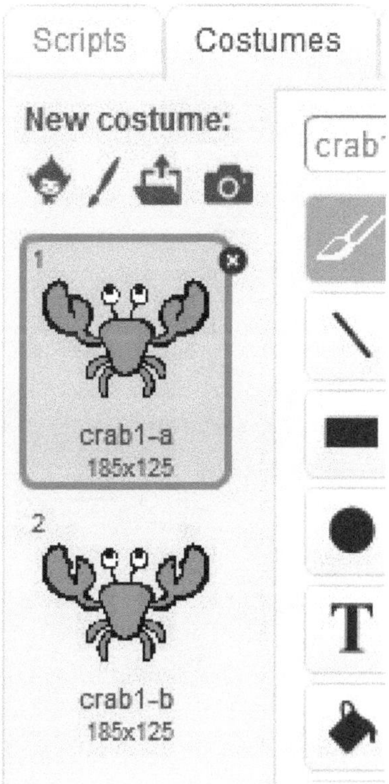

Scripts
Costumes
New costume:
crab
1
crab1-a
185x125
2
crab1-b
185x125
T

Lesson pace

If pupils have worked their way through the earlier gaming strand many will be confident to attempt much of this independently using hint cards. I look out for areas that are very new such as X and X coordinates and changing levels to offer teaching support. Small groups may need teaching support with other areas and every class is different.

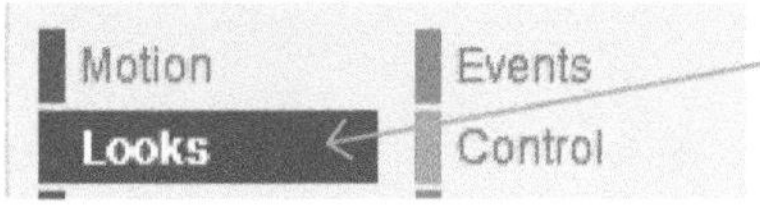
Motion
Events
Looks
Control

Can pupils work out a way to automatically change from one costume to another? You may wish to remind them where the costume blocks are.

If pupils need a hint provide them with the **crab animation hint card [teachers book page 124]**. This has these blocks on but no indication of order.

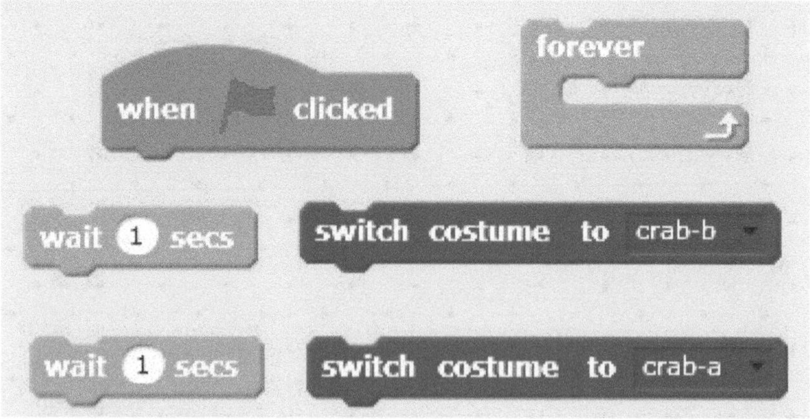
forever
when clicked
wait 1 secs
switch costume to crab-b
wait 1 secs
switch costume to crab-a

2a. Costume change speed

Challenge pupils to make the claw costumes change faster without using a 0. They can then investigate how using a decimal fraction will speed the change up.

2b. Evaluating Best Solution

Which solution is best? The one with the least code is most efficient but the two costume blocks allows us to use another costume for something else.

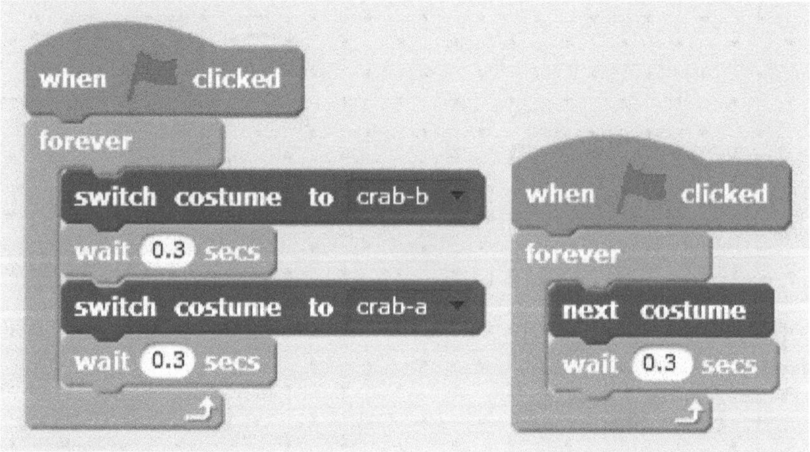
when clicked
forever
switch costume to crab-b
wait 0.3 secs
switch costume to crab-a
wait 0.3 secs
when clicked
forever
next costume
wait 0.3 secs

Possible Solutions

The forever block could start with a wait

3. Move and Steer

Can pupils work out a way to make the crab move for ever? You may wish to show them the **crab move hint card 123 of teachers book** if they get stuck.

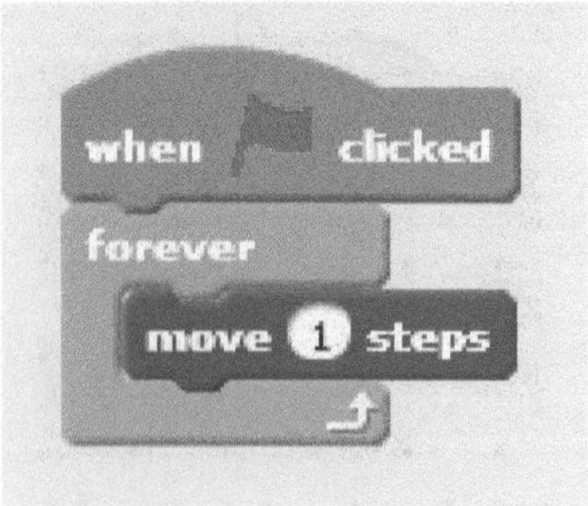
when clicked
forever
move 1 steps

Move solution

3a. Challenge them to slow the crab down

They can do this by reducing the move to less than 1 without using 0.

3 Move and steer continued

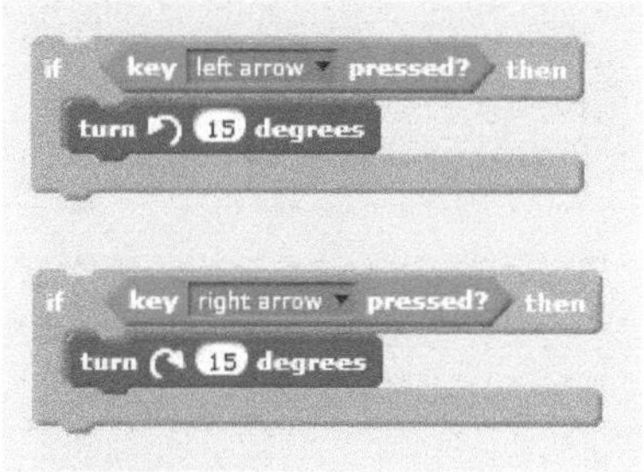
if key left arrow pressed? then
turn 15 degrees
if key right arrow pressed? then
turn 15 degrees

Explain that we now want the computer to turn right if the right arrow keyboard input is pressed and left if the keyboard left arrow key is pressed. Some children might suggest the when space key is pressed block. Explain that this is quite slow to use within games as it is not constantly checked inside a loop.

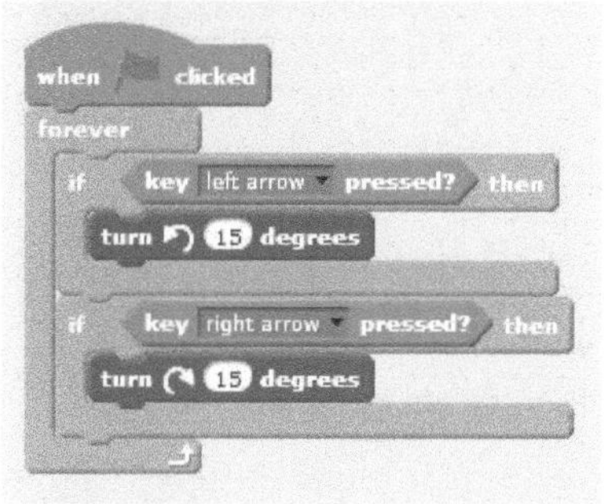
when clicked
forever
if key left arrow pressed? then
turn 15 degrees
if key right arrow pressed? then
turn 15 degrees

Introduce the idea of conditional selection if you haven't introduced this idea before in the Quiz, Slug Trail game or selection investigation. You can use these real examples before using the coding ones.
http://code-it.co.uk/wp-content/uploads/2015/05/ConditionalSelection.pdf
Now demonstrate how to make two steering blocks, but before pupils go and make these themselves ask them how we can get the program to check if the condition is met over and over again. If you have emphasised the forever loop repetitive aspect enough before, pupils will suggest using a forever loop. Drag the blocks into the forever loop with the move block. You can ask why we wouldn't place these blocks inside the costume change forever loop. (Answer: the time wait block will slow all the blocks down).

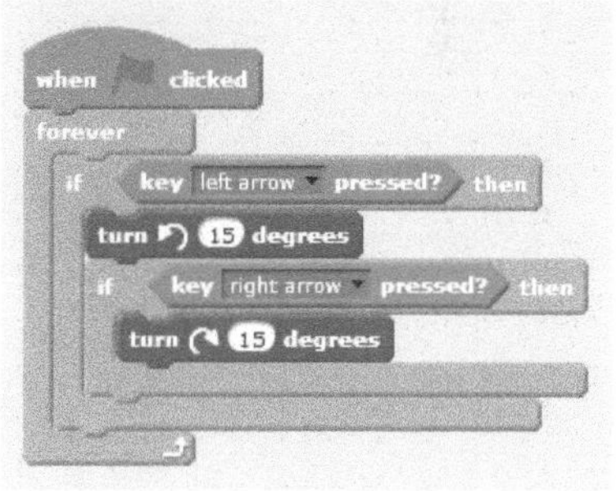
when clicked
forever
if key left arrow pressed? then
turn 15 degrees
if key right arrow pressed? then
turn 15 degrees

Common Errors

The most likely error is to drag an if block inside another one.
Ask pupils to check to see if their if blocks are lined up underneath each other. In this example the right arrow condition will only be checked if the left arrow has been pressed.

3b. Investigate angles other than 15 degrees

Ask pupils if 15 degrees is the best turn amount. Get them to investigate other turn angles.

4. Design Mazes

Click on **Stage** and **backdrops** and demonstrate creating a Maze background using **only** one colour for the walls. Either use a different colour for the start place and another for the end of the Maze or use text for the start and end but make sure the text is a different colour from the walls and each other. Make sure you include a border all round the edges so the Crab cannot leave the Maze.

4. Design Mazes Continued

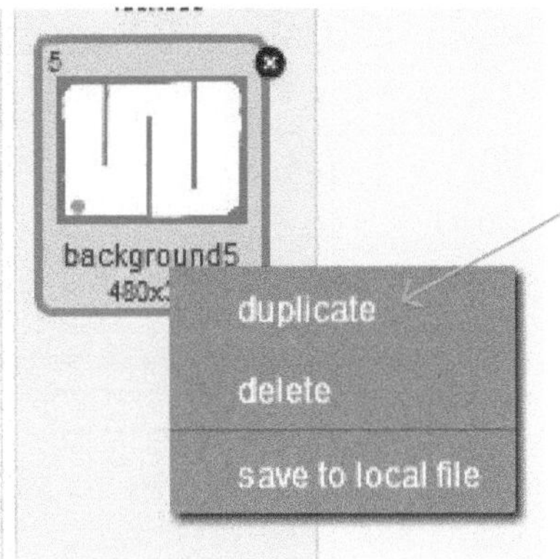
5
background5
480x3
duplicate
delete
save to local file

Once pupils have created a maze show them how they can right click and duplicate. Now edit the maze rubbing out the inner walls but leaving the outer walls and start and finish place the same.

Eyedropper

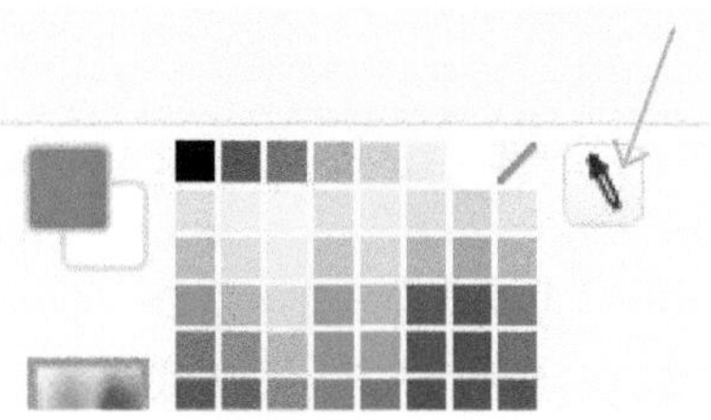

Check that they use the same colour walls, start and finish blocks on every maze or the stop all when the crab touches the wall will not work.

Use the eraser tool to rub out inner walls and the eyedropper tool to select the same wall colour

T

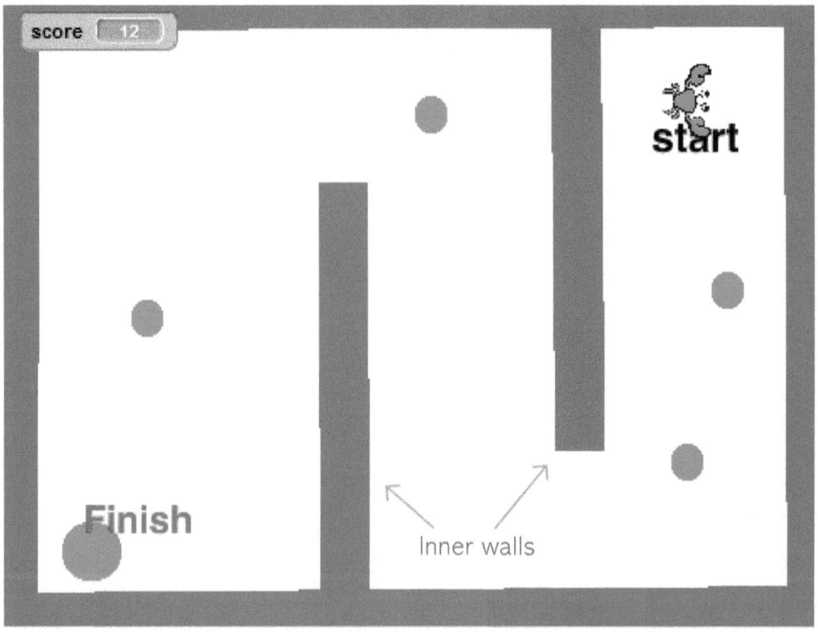
score 12
start
Finish
Inner walls

Do their mazes get progressively harder?

5. Electrify Wall Maze

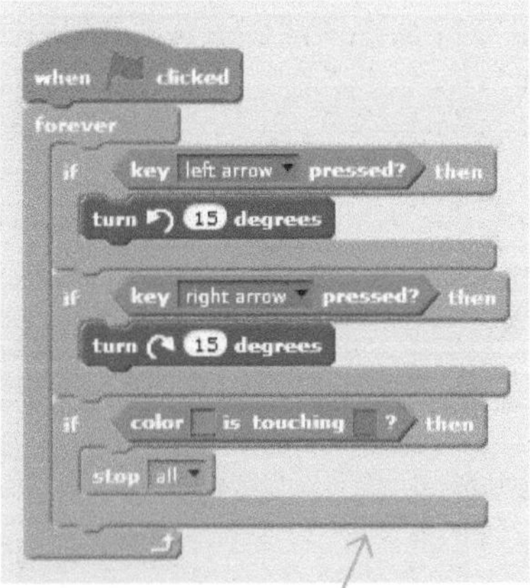
when clicked
forever
if key left arrow pressed? then
turn 15 degrees
if key right arrow pressed? then
turn 15 degrees
if color is touching ? then
stop all

Remind pupils of their decomposed task to end the game when the crab touches the walls. Write **if the colour red of the crab is touching the colour of their maze then stop all.** You may want to provide hints using the electrify wall help card page 125 of the teacher book.

You may want to demonstrate this for those that don't work it out from the help card. Drag out an if block and talk pupils through creating the code as shown. Make sure you show them how to change the colour by clicking in the squares and the selecting the colours using a colour eyedropper tool. The first colour is the crabs followed by the colour of the wall. Finally ask pupils where we can place this so it will be checked over and over again? Incidentally this could be its own forever loop but we use less code placing it in the main loop.

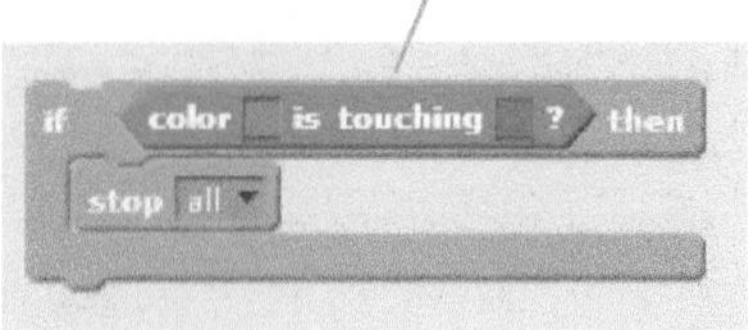
if color is touching ? then
stop all

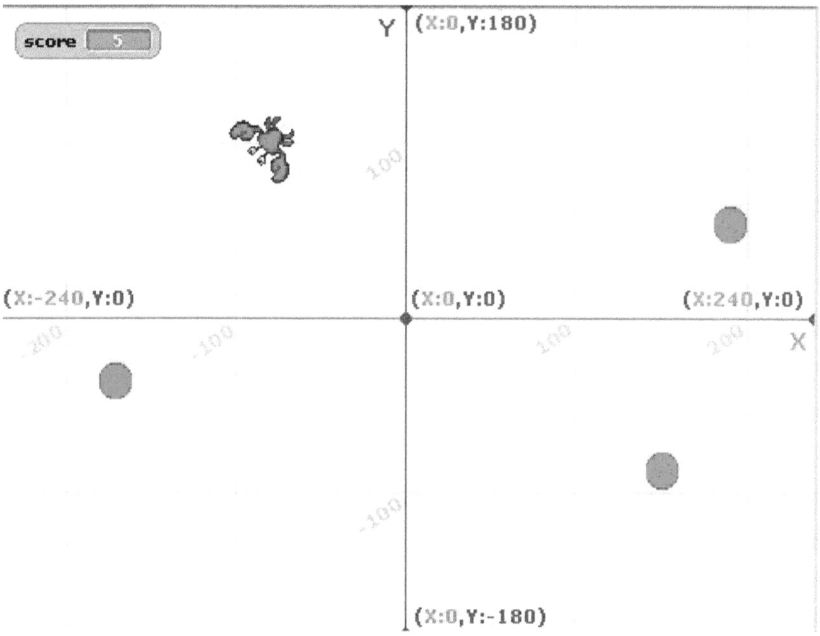
score 5
Y
(X:0,Y:180)
(X:-240,Y:0)
(X:0,Y:0)
(X:240,Y:0)
X
(X:0,Y:-180)

Click on Stage, then backdrops: choose backdrop from library, last one is the xy-grid

Point out that everywhere we position the cursor on the background it has a grid reference. Point out the changes on the x and y indicator just to the bottom right of the screen. Start in the centre of the screen and move up, asking pupils to note what is happening to the Y axis. Now go back to 0 in the middle and ask them to predict what will happen if we go down. Y becomes negative, relate to other negative numbers like temperature. Repeat with the X axis, moving right first. Explain that this is good to know but that there is an easier way to find the X and Y position of everything on the screen. Open the motion blocks and ask them to watch the **go to x and y** block. Now move the crab to a new position. The go to x and y block will change. Do this lots of times until every child has seen this change. Challenge them to use the go to x and y block and a point in direction block to create a start spawn point.

6. Levels Spawn Point

Start by asking pupils what is the problem with ending our game by touching the walls at the moment? Pupils should identify that the crab is left touching the wall so when the game is restarted it ends straight away. Explain that we can create a spawn point so that the crab will always start the game from the same place.

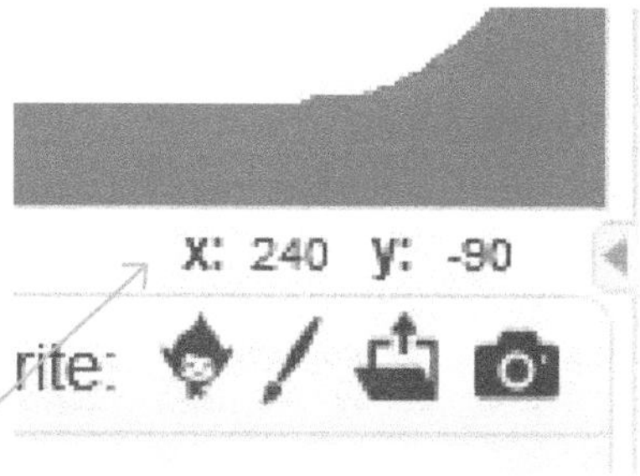
x: 240 y: -90
rite:

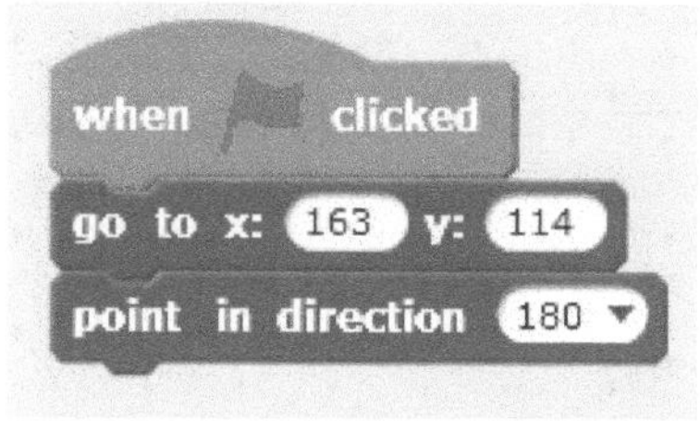
when clicked
go to x: 163 y: 114
point in direction 180

6. Levels

Explain that we can now use the X and Y and the if colour is touching to change levels. Gather all those ready to move on and whisper to two children that when you say **change level** they must wave their hands in the air. Explain to all the pupils that we are going to use a broadcast signal to change the level. Make sure you include the word **change level** lots of times so pupils with the code have to wave their hands. Explain that they are picking up your broadcast of change level where as everyone else can hear it but they don't have any code to tell them what to do.

This video explains how broadcasts works and it may be useful for the teacher to watch before the lesson https://youtu.be/BwFT6dYAUzO

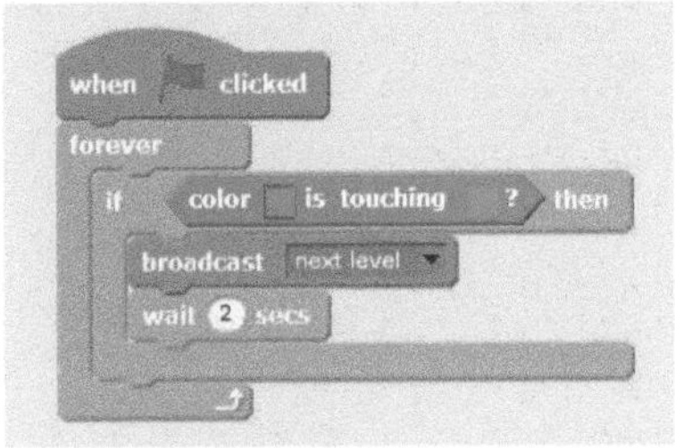
when clicked
forever
if color is touching ? then
broadcast next level
wait 2 secs

Code to create a starting background

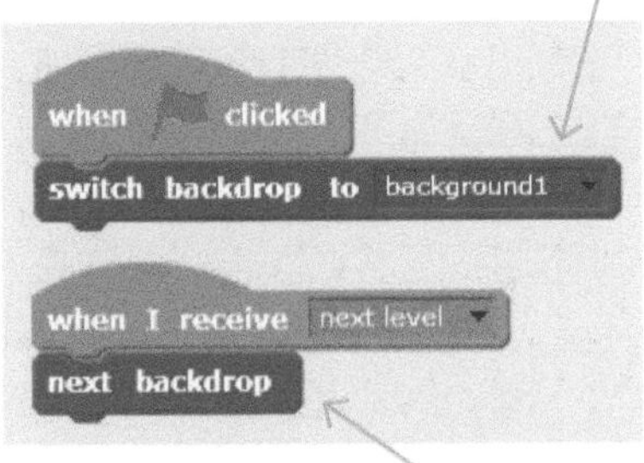
when clicked
switch backdrop to background1
when I receive next level
next backdrop

Code in the stage scripts area to change backdrops

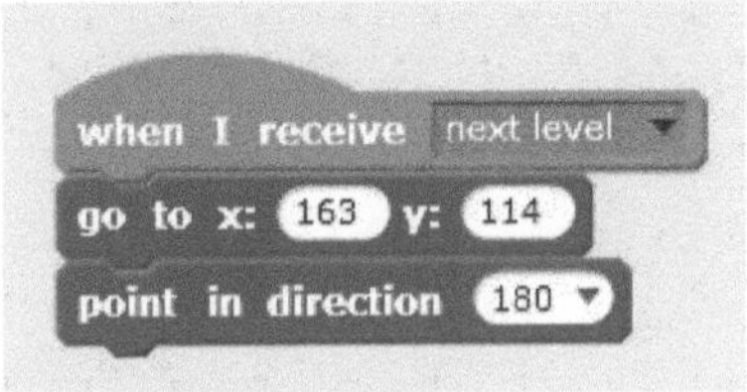
when I receive next level
go to x: 163 y: 114
point in direction 180

Code in the crab scripts area to return the crab to start position

6. Levels Continued

Create code that says if colour red of crab touches colour of end of level then broadcast. Show them that this doesn't do anything. Explain that this is like them at the moment: they can receive the change level broadcast but they don't have any code to know what to do with it. The two children who you whispered to by contrast will have been programmed to wave when we broadcast change level.

Now show the pupils how they can pick up the broadcast in the stage area to change the background. Then show them how we can also use the X and Y code to receive the broadcast and pick up the change level and return the crab to the start position.

Broadcasts can be very tricky, so encouraging pupils to view your example on the computer and click between Stage and Crab helps them to see code that works in action.

7. Coin Scoring

Ask pupils to refer back to their decomposed planner. What do they want the coins to do?

Answer

- Reappear when game starts
- Disappear when touched by the crab
- Reappear when a new level starts
- Increase the score by one when touched by the crab

What blocks would be useful for these things?

Reappear when game starts	Show, green flag
Disappear when touched by the crab	If touching crab, hide
Reappear when a new level starts	Broadcast next level, show
Increase the score by one when touched by the crab	Change variable by 1, touching crab

Can pupils work independently to try and solve these issues one at a time? A solution can be found next but it is by no means the only one.

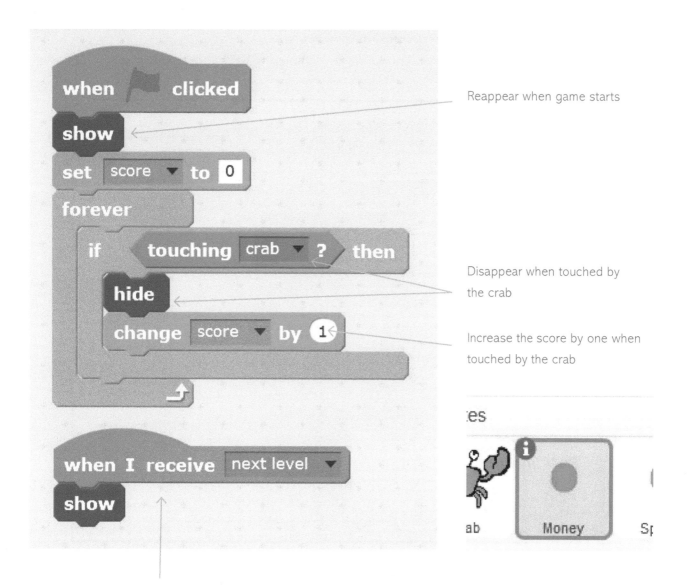

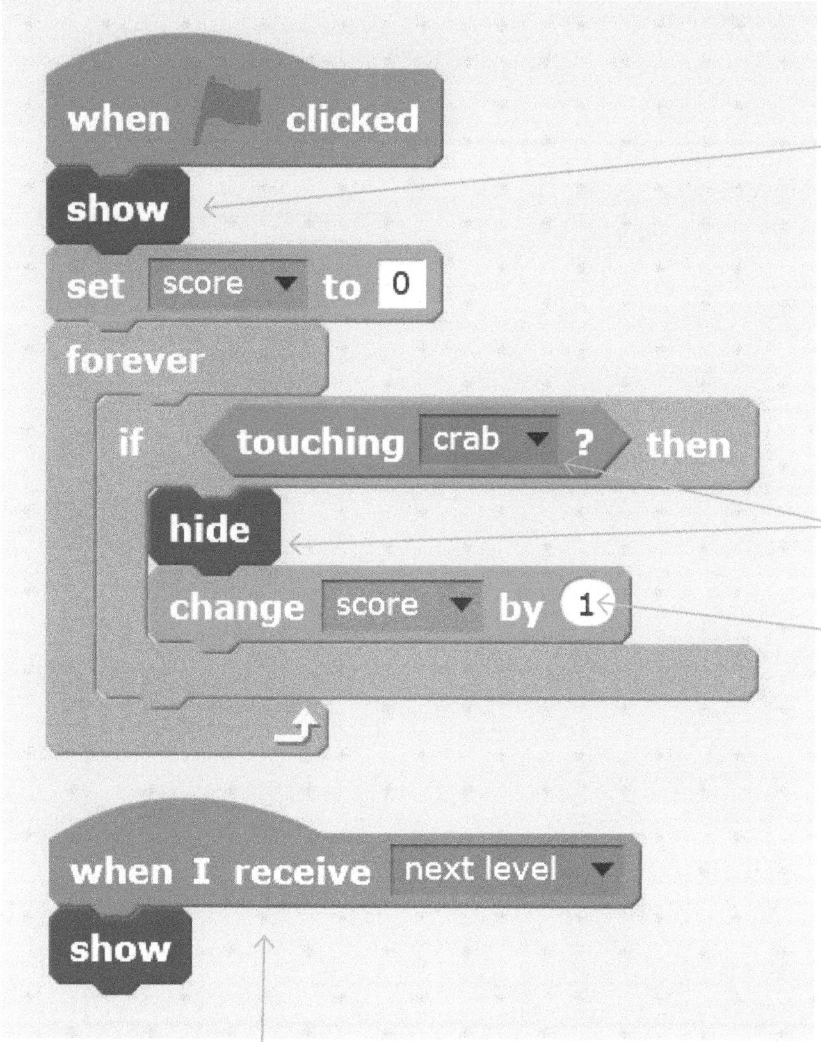
when clicked
show
set score to 0
forever
if touching crab ? then
hide
change score by 1
when I receive next level
show
Reappear when game starts
Disappear when touched by the crab
Increase the score by one when touched by the crab
Reappear when a new level starts

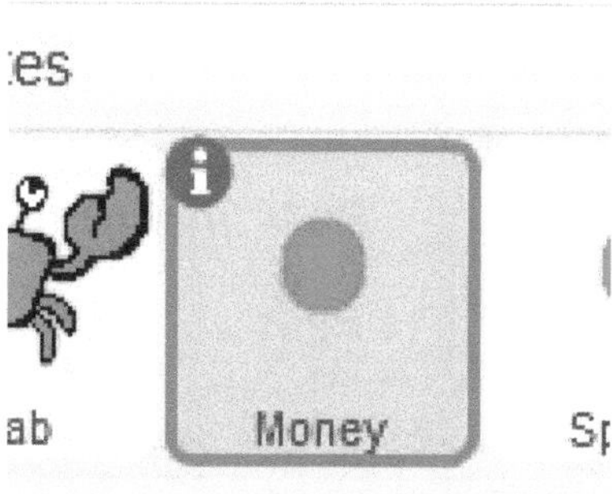
Money

Pupils can be challenged to come up with their own refinements to adapt the game.

Crab Maze Answers

What objects do you need to make?

Crab, Score Board, Mazes, Coins (red dots) start and finish point

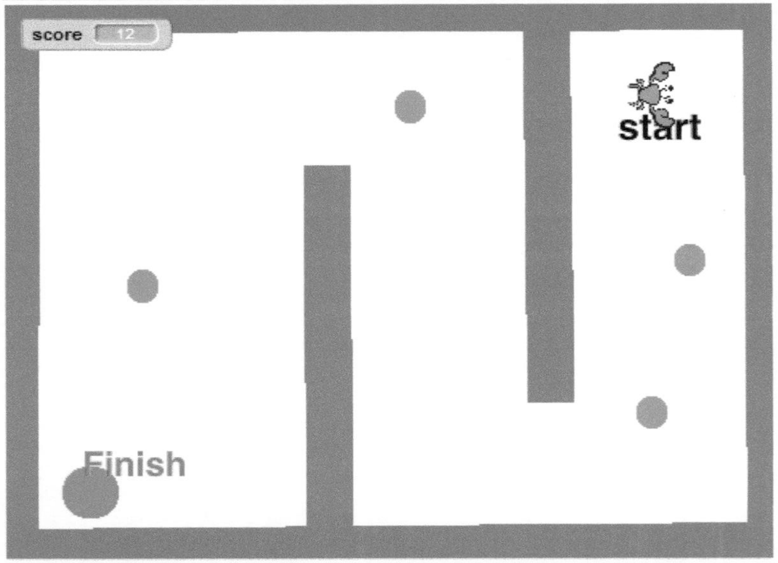
score 12
start
Finish

What would you add to make the games even better?

Decompose Crab Game

What do you need to make the crab do?

Move continuously

Turn right when right arrow pressed

Turn left when left arrow pressed

Animate claws

End game/stop when crab hits the wall

What do you need to make the coins do?

Appear when game starts

Disappear when crab hits them

Increase score when crab hits them

Reappear for each level

What do you need to make the crab do when it reaches the finish?

Go back to start

Change the maze

NOTE

Pupils don't always attach the effects to the correct object which is perfetly understanable but the most important thing is that they have decomposed most of the effects.

Useful moving blocks

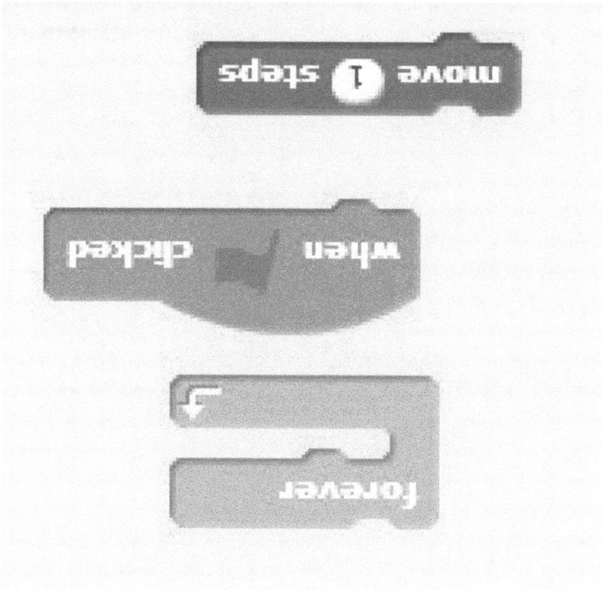
move 1 steps
when clicked
forever

Scratch Crab Maze Help Card

Crab Move Hint Card

code-it.co.uk

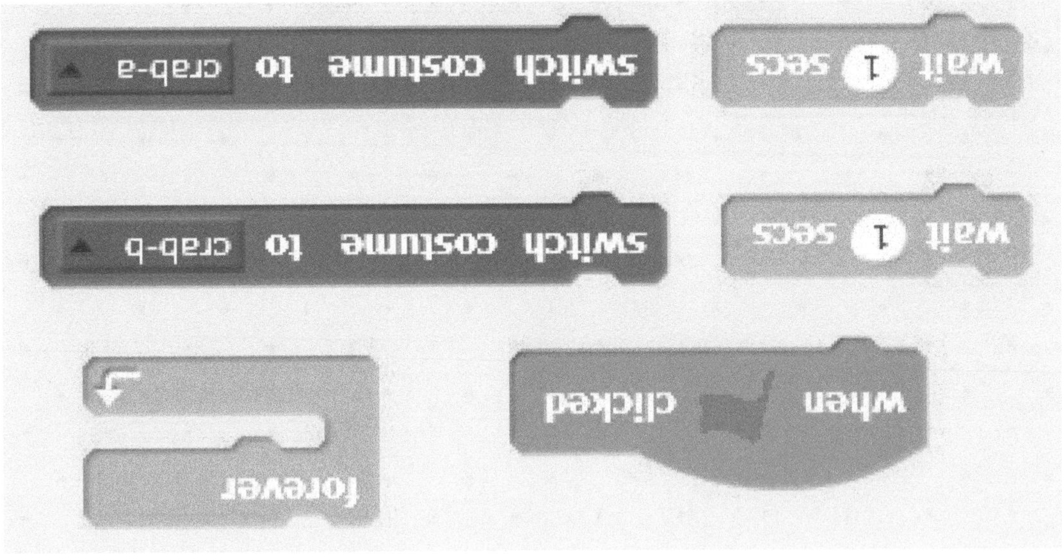
switch costume to crab-a
wait 1 secs
switch costume to crab-b
wait 1 secs
forever
when clicked

Scratch Crab Maze

Help Card

Crab Animation Hint Card

code-it.co.uk

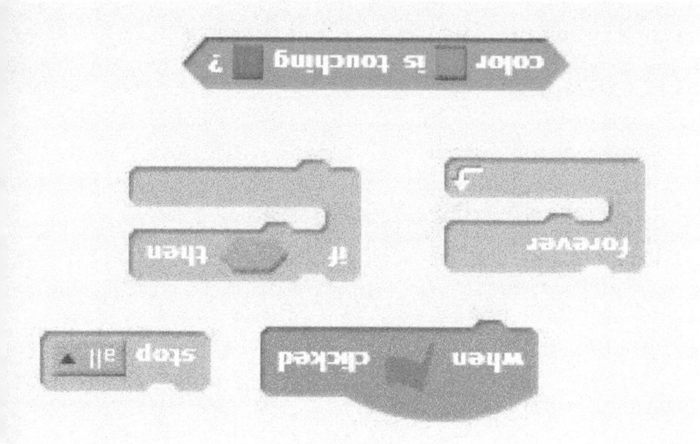
when clicked
stop all
if then
forever
color is touching ?

Useful blocks

Scratch Crab Maze

Help Card

Crab Electrify Maze Help Card

code-it.co.uk

3F. Toilet Fan

Time to complete module

1.5 – 2 hours

Module Aim: Build a simple fan out of **Lego WeDo** and then program it in **Scratch 1.4.**

National Curriculum Programs of Study

KS2 Computing

Pupils should be taught to:

- *design, write and debug programs that accomplish specific goals, including controlling or simulating physical systems;* solve problems by decomposing them into smaller parts
- *use sequence, selection, and repetition in programs; work with variables and various forms of input and output*
- *use logical reasoning to explain how some simple algorithms work and to detect and correct errors in algorithms and programs*

KS2 Design & Technology Programs of Study Technical Knowledge

- *apply their understanding of computing to program, monitor and control their products.*

Module Learning Focus

By the end of the module children will be able to:

- Design and create a lego fan attending to key safety factors
- Program the fan to do increasingly difficult tasks

Computer Science Concepts

- Sequence
- Conditional Selection
- Variables

Maths Concepts

- Greater than and less than

Assessment for Learning

At the end of each session direct pupils to page 24 of pupil workbook 3 to help them reflect on what they have learnt. It is often worth working through this line by line to avoid pupils filling in everything with a smiley face. You can also annotate this to record pupils who have needed much more support or have demonstrated greater understanding.

Adult Focus

All adults need to be clear that they are to support using hints only and not solve things for pupils.

Useful Hints

It can take a while for drivers to load so pupils need to be prepared for this. A reminder that the blocks appear in the bottom of the motion sensor section is helpful.

Pointing pupils to the support card available is useful. For an extra challenge staple up the edges of the increase speed using variable card and challenge them to use the hints rather than the solution inside.

Computational Thinking - Evaluation is how we look at an algorithm or code and determine how useful they are, how adaptable, how efficient, how correct. There may be many algorithmic solutions to a problem, evaluation asks which one was best and why?

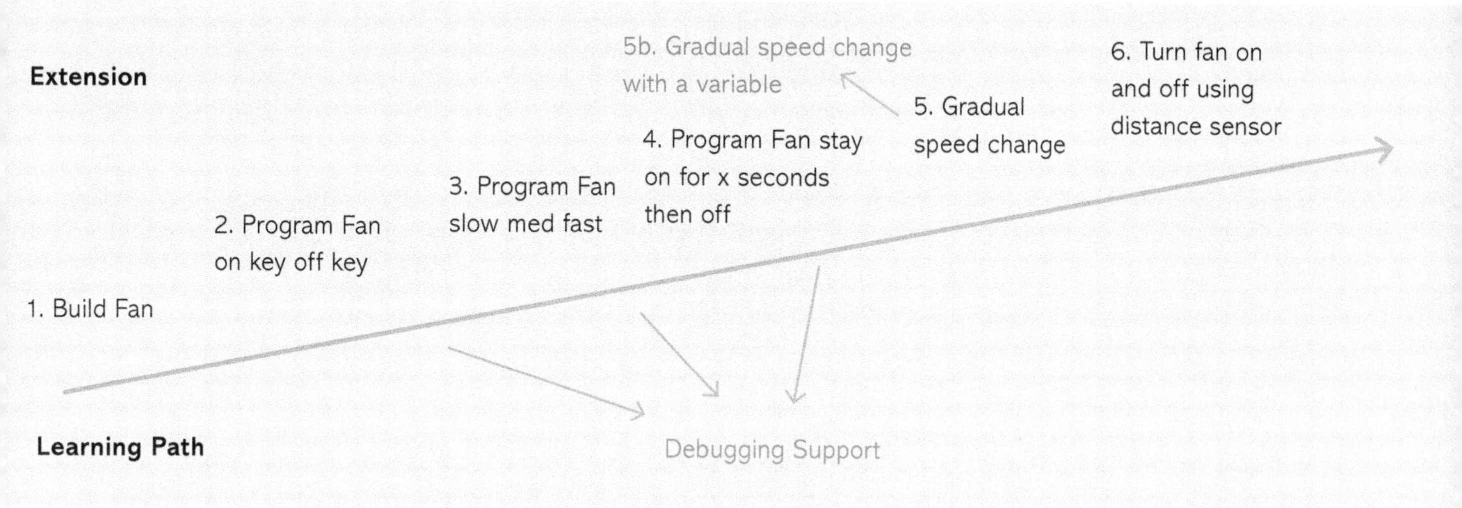
Extension
5b. Gradual speed change with a variable
6. Turn fan on and off using distance sensor
5. Gradual speed change
4. Program Fan stay on for x seconds then off
3. Program Fan slow med fast
2. Program Fan on key off key
1. Build Fan
Learning Path
Debugging Support

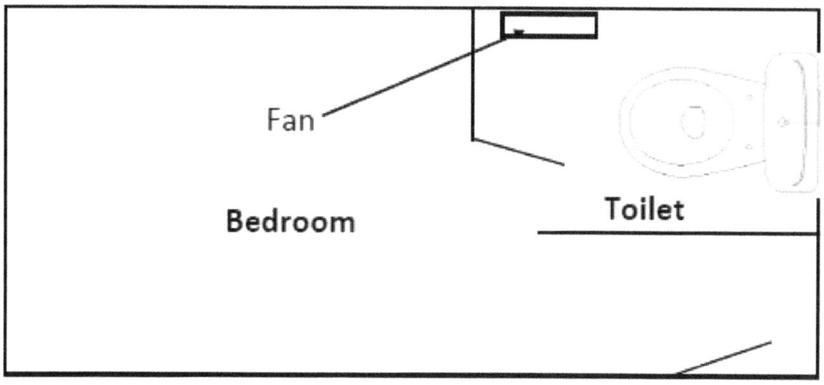
Fan
Bedroom
Toilet

Scenario

An upstairs bedroom has been converted into a flat with built in bathroom and toilet. The new owner doesn't want nasty smells in their bedroom so has installed a fan. The fan extracts (removes) stale air but is too noisy to remain on all the time.

1. Build Fan

Give pupils boxes of **Lego WeDo.** One between two is ideal but one between three will work. Explain the scenario and add restrictions about not swapping Lego between boxes. Show pupils how the USB block, motor and distance sensor blocks fix together. Explain that the fan must be mounted and should not fall off. The fan does not have to have curved blades to draw air as it is a proto-type to sort out the programming aspects. Give pupils time to build. Some will need help in seeing that the fan needs to be fixed and not loose or the motor will not drive it. Allow them to move on in groups when you have checked their models are safe.

Note

Don't make a fan yourself or pupils will copy it taking away the building and design part of the challenge.

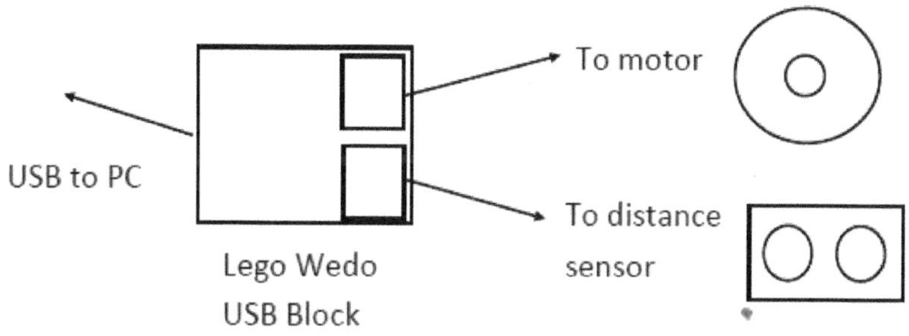
To motor
USB to PC
To distance sensor
Lego Wedo USB Block

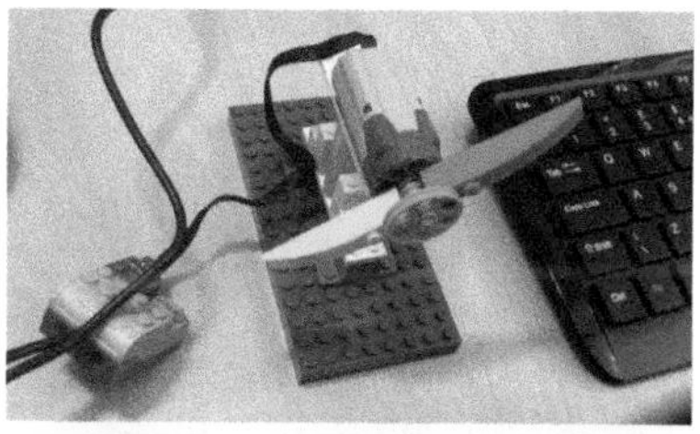

Fan examples

Plug a pupils finished model into USB port show them the extra blocks that appear in the motion section at the bottom once the USB has initiated (often takes 2 minutes). Stress that they must follow the programming challenges found on their Success Criteria sheets and that you will be checking these. Don't show them what to do!

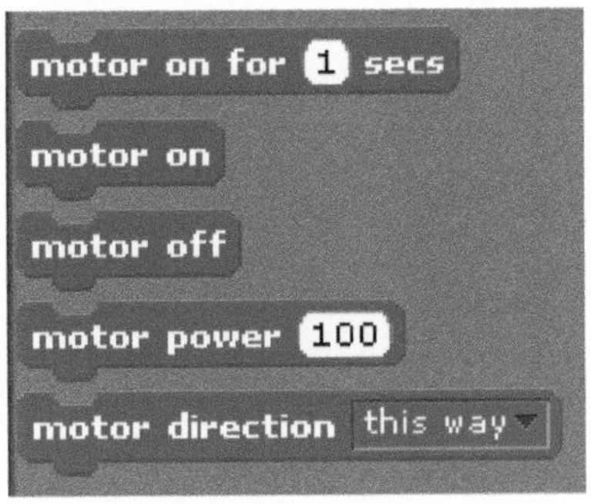
motor on for 1 secs
motor on
motor off
motor power 100
motor direction this way

Extra control blocks

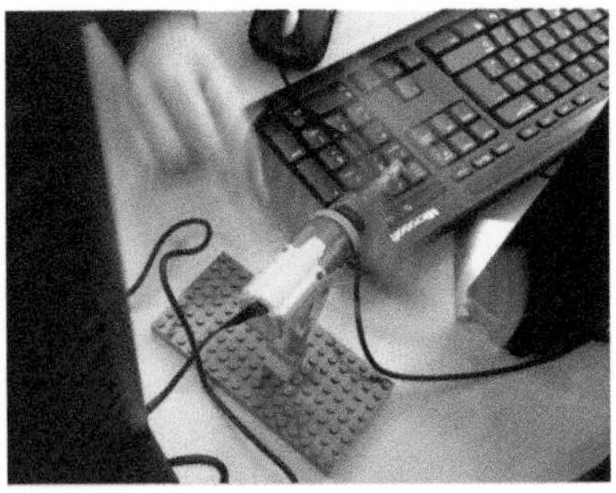

2. Program fan on key (o) and off key (x)

The solution to the far right is quicker to respond as it is constantly checking the condition inside a loop.

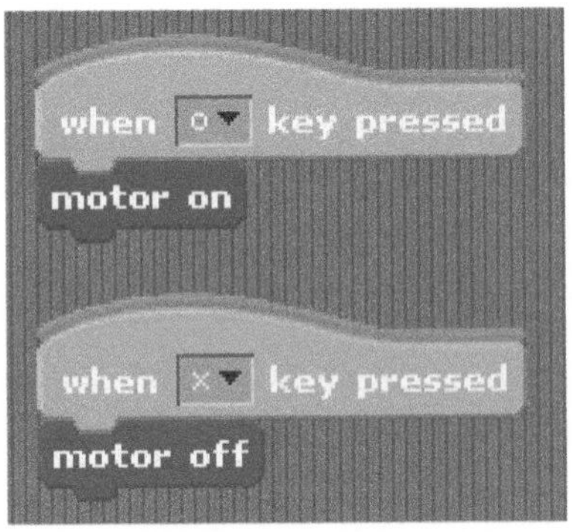
when o key pressed
motor on
when x key pressed
motor off

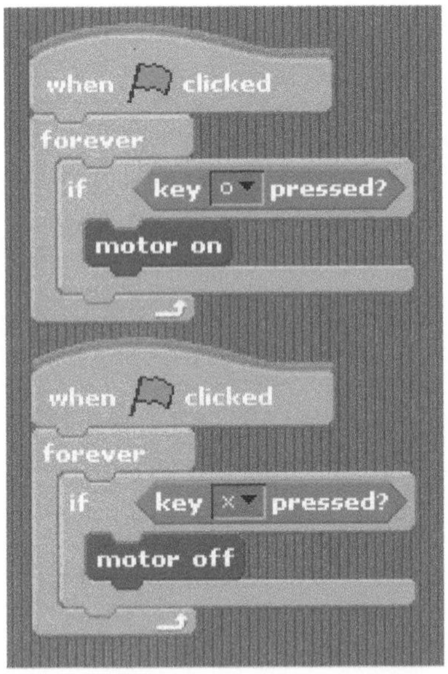
when clicked
forever
if key o pressed?
motor on
when clicked
forever
if key x pressed?
motor off

3. Program fast (f) slow (s) and medium (m) keys

Motor power works on a percentage so numbers above 100 just default to 100%.

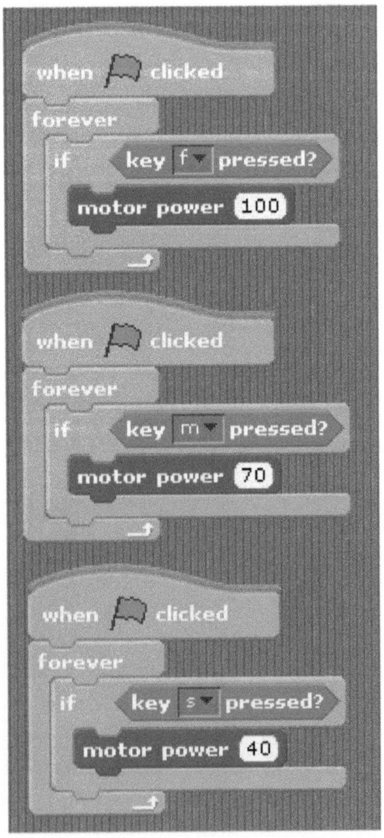
when clicked
forever
if key f pressed?
motor power 100
when clicked
forever
if key m pressed?
motor power 70
when clicked
forever
if key s pressed?
motor power 40

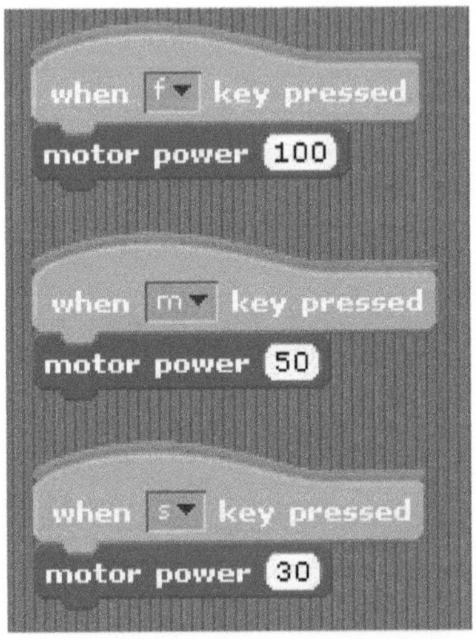
when f key pressed
motor power 100
when m key pressed
motor power 50
when s key pressed
motor power 30

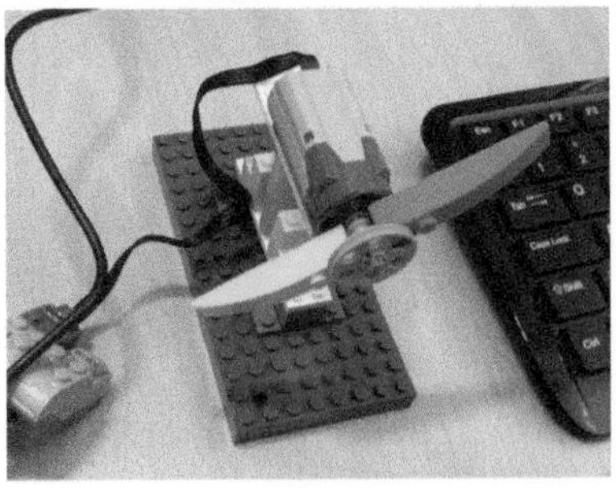

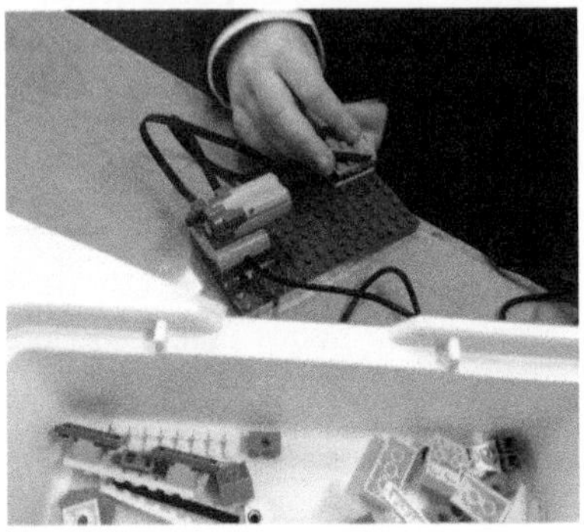

4. Program the fan to start from one key, stay on for 5 seconds then turn off

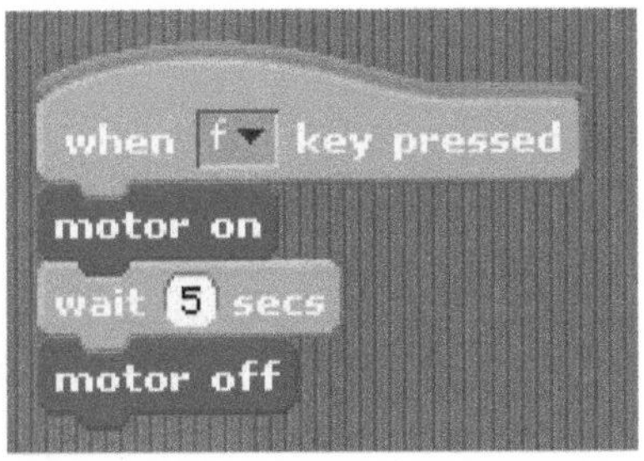
when f key pressed
motor on
wait 5 secs
motor off

5. Program the fan to start slow. Move to medium speed before spinning at maximum speed before slowing back down to slow again - all within a 10-20 second time frame and all triggered by (r) key

5a. Gradual speed change with a variable

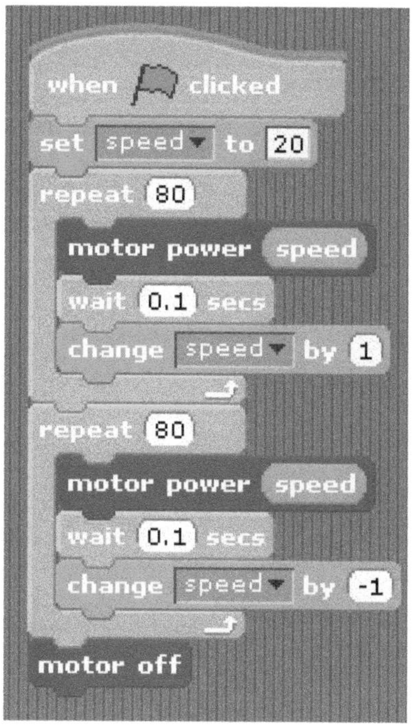
when clicked
set speed to 20
repeat 80
motor power speed
wait 0.1 secs
change speed by 1
repeat 80
motor power speed
wait 0.1 secs
change speed by -1
motor off

Speed change with a variable

HINT 1

Remind pupils of the counting machine where the variable was changed inside the loop.

Ask them what number they could replace with a variable?

Answer motor power

HINT 2

Give one pupil a pot and write motor power speed variable on it. Pretend to be the motor and as you loop through, add another pencil into the pot (change speed by 1) and make louder motor noises and faster moves of your arm, as the speed increases. Draw out that you are in a loop.

There is a support card for this, but fold it and staple it shut before handing it out and challenge pupils to solve it without looking inside at the solution.

Evaluation

If pupils create the speed change with and without a variable there is an excellent opportunity to discuss both solutions in the context of evaluation.

The solution with a variable is clearly more efficient as it uses less code and can easily be adapted by changing just a few things.

6. Turn fan on and off using distance sensor

There is a support card for this activity which asks pupils to convert a flowchart algorithm into code.

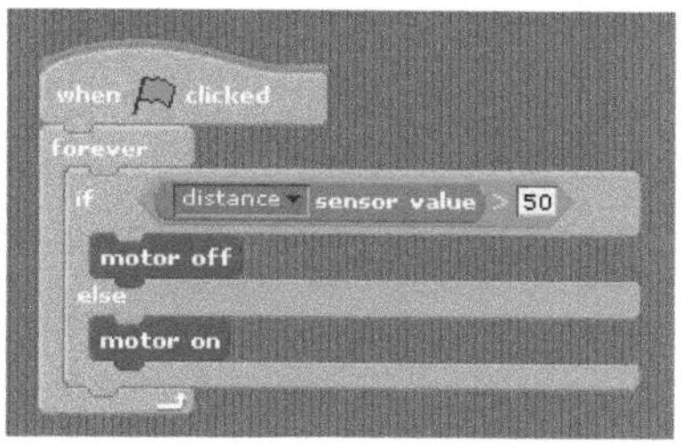
when clicked
forever
if distance sensor value > 50
motor off
else
motor on

Print extra independent extension activities in the pupil books and send them home

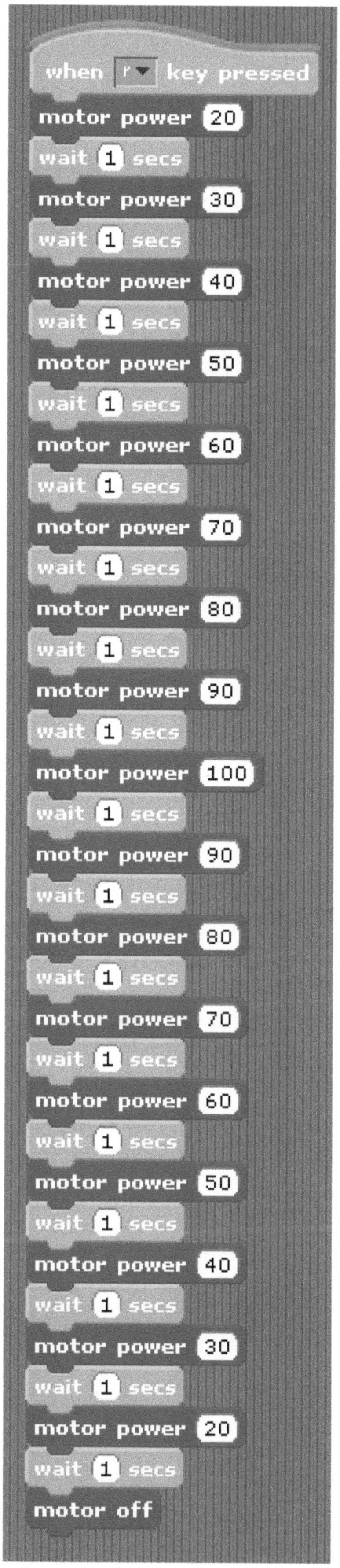
when r key pressed
motor power 20
wait 1 secs
motor power 30
wait 1 secs
motor power 40
wait 1 secs
motor power 50
wait 1 secs
motor power 60
wait 1 secs
motor power 70
wait 1 secs
motor power 80
wait 1 secs
motor power 90
wait 1 secs
motor power 100
wait 1 secs
motor power 90
wait 1 secs
motor power 80
wait 1 secs
motor power 70
wait 1 secs
motor power 60
wait 1 secs
motor power 50
wait 1 secs
motor power 40
wait 1 secs
motor power 30
wait 1 secs
motor power 20
wait 1 secs
motor off

Speed change without a variable

Flow chart algorithm solution

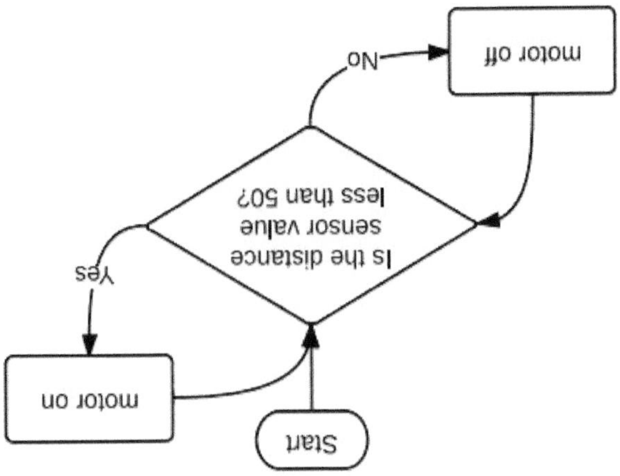

Start
Is the distance sensor value less than 50?
Yes
No
motor on
motor off

Scratch Blocks

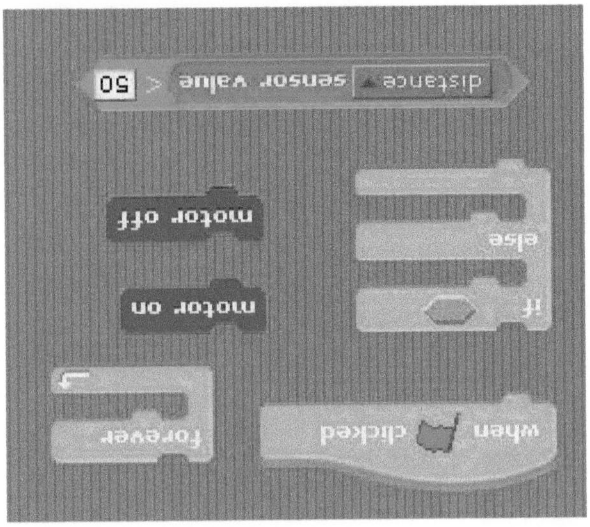

when clicked
forever
if
else
motor on
motor off
distance sensor value
50

Toilet Fan

Help

Card

code-it.co.uk

Turn the fan on when within 50 mm of the distance sensor and off when further than 50 mm

code-it.co.uk

Teacher Note Staple card shut and challenge pupil to solve without looking at the solution

Solution

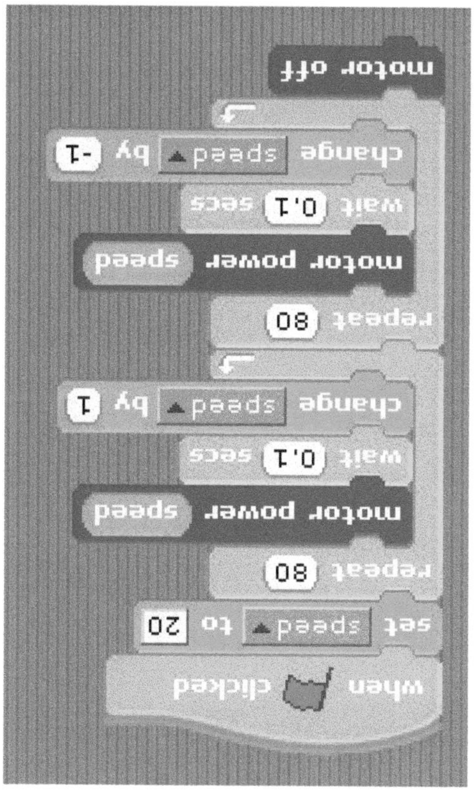

when clicked
set speed to 20
repeat 80
motor power speed
wait 0.1 secs
change speed by 1
repeat 80
motor power speed
wait 0.1 secs
change speed by -1
motor off

Speed up

Speed down

code-it.co.uk

Toilet Fan

Debugging

Support

code-it.co.uk

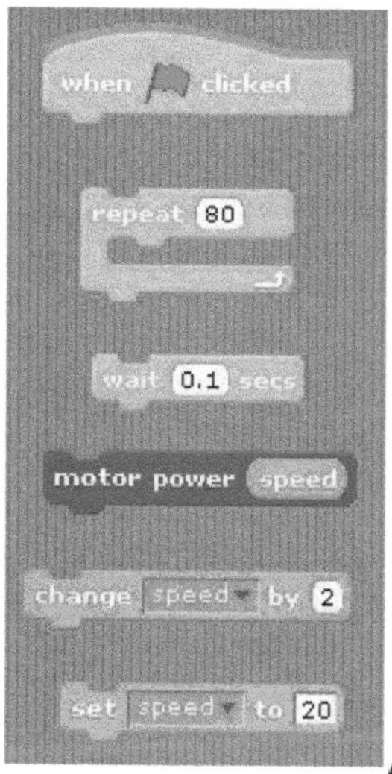

when clicked
repeat 80
wait 0.1 secs
motor power speed
change speed by 2
set speed to 20

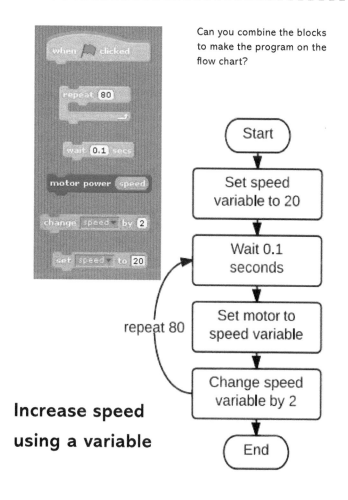

Can you combine the blocks to make the program on the flow chart?

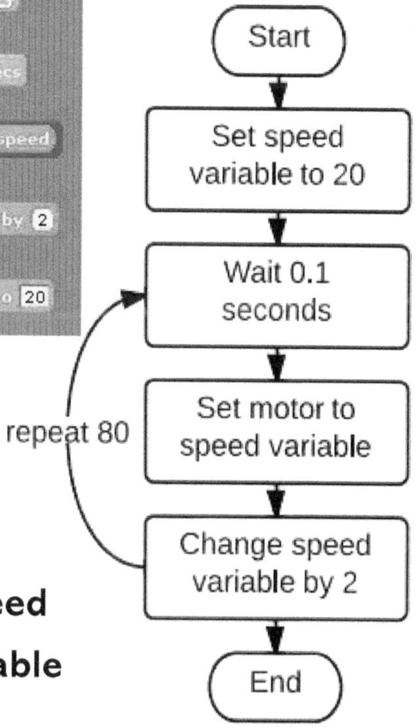

Start
Set speed variable to 20
Wait 0.1 seconds
Set motor to speed variable
Change speed variable by 2
repeat 80
End

Increase speed using a variable

3G. Car Park Barrier

Time to complete module

1.5 –2 hours

Module Aim: Build a simple car park barrier out of **Lego, WeDo** and then program it in **Scratch 1.4**

National Curriculum Programs of Study

KS2 Computing

Pupils should be taught to:

- *design, write and debug programs that accomplish specific goals, including controlling or simulating physical systems;* solve problems by decomposing them into smaller parts
- *use sequence, selection, and repetition in programs; work with variables and various forms of input and output*
- *use logical reasoning to explain how some simple algorithms work and to detect and correct errors in algorithms and programs*

KS2 Design & Technology Programs of Study Technical Knowledge

- *apply their understanding of computing to program, monitor and control their products.*

Module Learning Focus

By the end of the module children will be able to:

- Design and create a car park barrier attending to key safety factors
- Program the barrier to do increasingly difficult tasks

Computer Science Concepts

- Sequence
- Conditional Selection
- Variables

Maths Concepts

- Greater than and less than

Assessment for Learning

At the end of each session direct pupils to page 26 of pupil workbook 3 to help them reflect on what they have learnt. It is often worth working through this line by line to avoid pupils filling in everything with a smiley face. You can also annotate this to record pupils who have needed much more support or have demonstrated greater understanding.

Adult Focus

All adults need to be clear that they are to support using hints only and not solve things for pupils.

Useful Hints It can take a while for drivers to load so pupils need to be prepared for this.
A reminder that the blocks appear in the bottom of the motion section is helpful.
Pointing pupils to the support card available is useful.

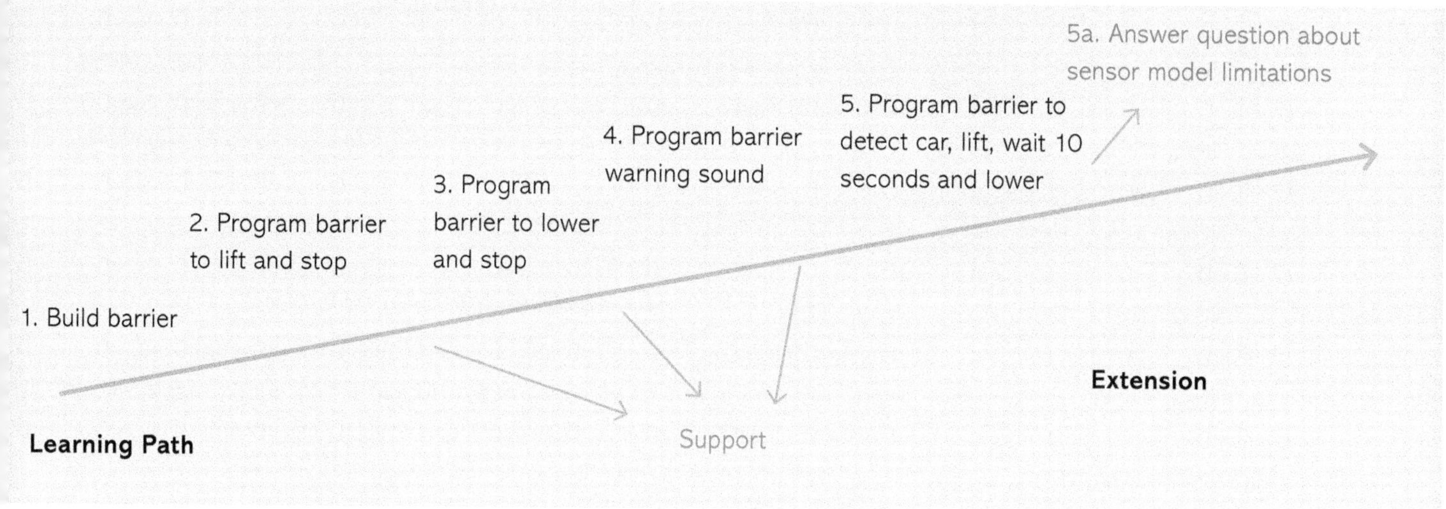
5a. Answer question about sensor model limitations
5. Program barrier to detect car, lift, wait 10 seconds and lower
4. Program barrier warning sound
3. Program barrier to lower and stop
2. Program barrier to lift and stop
1. Build barrier
Extension
Support
Learning Path

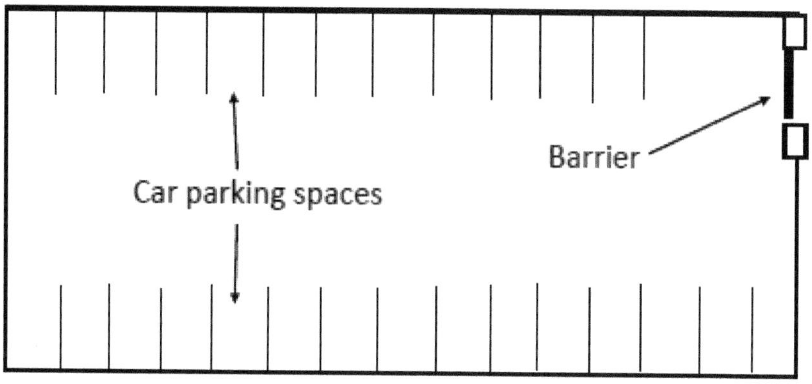
Car parking spaces
Barrier

Scenario

A local supermarket has a car park that is increasingly being used by local businesses for employer parking. This has meant that some supermarket customers are unable to park. The supermarket is investigating various forms of barrier control.

1. Build Barrier

Give pupils boxes of **Lego WeDo.** One between two is ideal but one between three will work. Explain the scenario, you may wish to find a picture of a car park barrier or focus pupils on a barrier near them. Add restrictions about not swapping **Lego** between boxes. Show pupils how the USB block, motor and distance sensor blocks fix together. Explain that the barrier will need to be light enough for the motor to lift. Ideally the barrier arm should rest on a pillar when not in use. They may also wish to find ways to limit its upwards movement so that the barrier points up but cannot travel a full 180 degrees to hit anyone behind the barrier. Give pupils time to build. Allow them to move on in groups when you have checked their models are safe and fulfil the design criteria.

> Don't make a barrier yourself or pupils will copy it taking away the building and design part of the challenge.

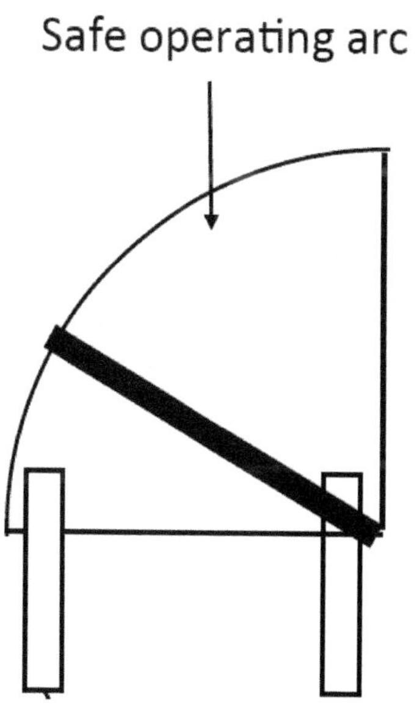
Safe operating arc

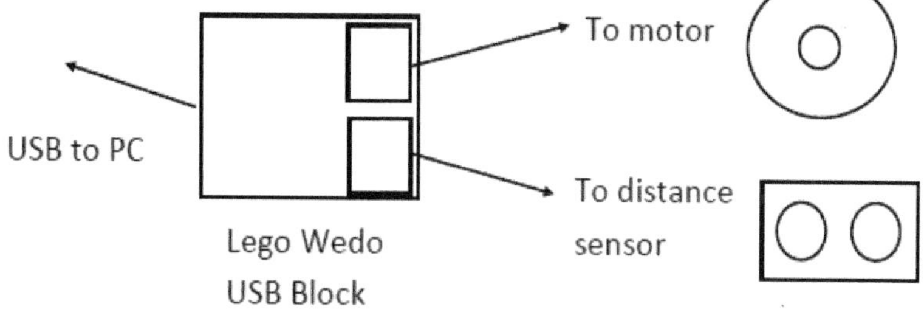
USB to PC
Lego Wedo
USB Block
To motor
To distance
sensor

USB block, motor and distance sensor blocks fix together

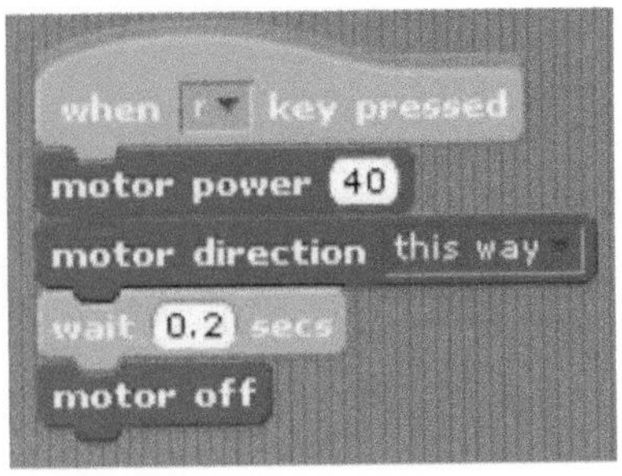
when r key pressed
motor power 40
motor direction this way
wait 0.2 secs
motor off

2. Program the barrier to rise and then stop

If pupils have completed the fan they won't find this activity totally new to them. However making it rise smoothly to the right position is not easy. If they have created a stop at the top so that the barrier can only move in a 90 degree arc the power settings are less crucial. The correct code will depend on the weight of the barrier.

3. Program the barrier to lower and then stop

Programming the barrier to lower smoothly to the right position is not easy. If they have created a stop at the bottom so that the barrier won't hit the ground the power settings are less crucial. The correct code will depend on the weight of the barrier and the speed you program it to lower.

> **Note**
>
> Sometimes pupils will use very different programming techniques and different blocks. As long as the code does what it needs to do then, celebrate their creativity.

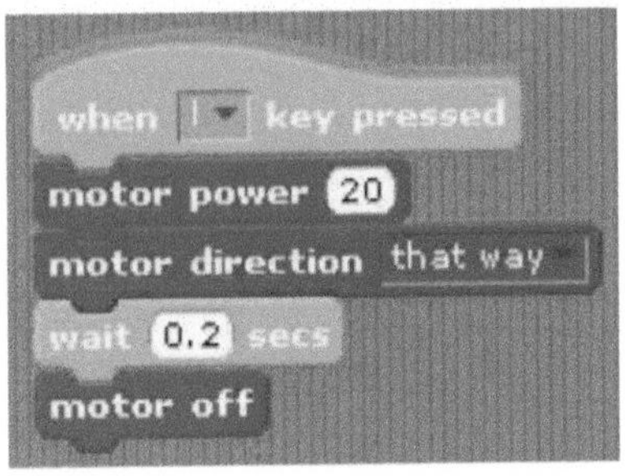
when l key pressed
motor power 20
motor direction that way
wait 0.2 secs
motor off

4. Program barrier warning sound

Adding a sound block before the barrier rises or lowers can be done in many ways. Pupils could even record their own sounds if you have microphones.

5. Program the barrier to detect the car, lift the barrier, wait 10 seconds and lower barrier

The lifting and lowering of the barrier programming can be duplicated from challenge 2 and 3. Give pupils a while to struggle without help first as some will remember solutions to this type of issue with the fan. If they are still struggling after a suitable period of time give them the sensor help card p136. Explain that this is the working program as a flowchart. They will need to match the blocks on the sheet to the chart as well as reuse rise and lower blocks created earlier.

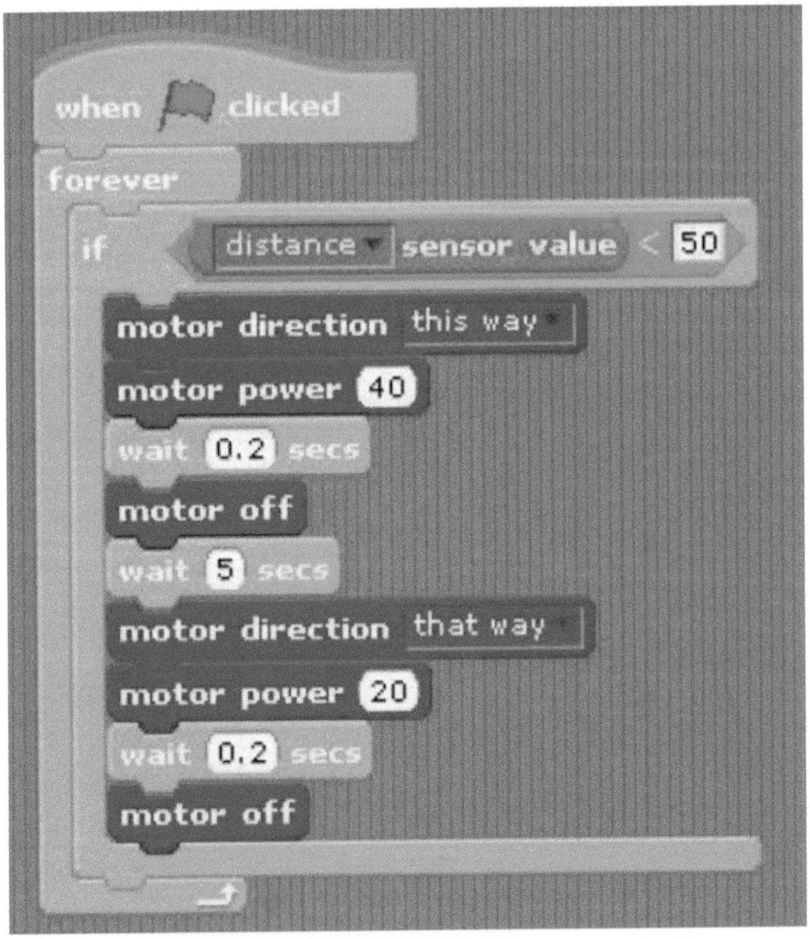
when clicked
forever
if distance sensor value < 50
motor direction this way
motor power 40
wait 0.2 secs
motor off
wait 5 secs
motor direction that way
motor power 20
wait 0.2 secs
motor off

6. Program the barrier to detect the car, lift the barrier, wait 5 seconds and lower barrier continued

On the learning intentions page in the pupil workbooks there is a question about the design faults of the sensor model.

The design fault is that if a car takes longer than 5 seconds to move through then the barrier it will come crashing down on it. This could be fixed by a second sensor to detect when the car has left. Unfortunately you can't do this with **Lego WeDo** at the moment.

Computational Thinking: **Decomposition** - Breaking up a complex problem into manageable chunks and solving these separately before recomposing them into a final solution.

Although the focus has not been on decomposition in this module the solution to programming the car barrier to rise and fall can be built using decomposition. Drawing pupils' attention to this will enable them to spot these opportunities in the future.

Print extra independent extension activities in the pupil books and send them home

Match the code blocks to the flow chart to help you program the distance sensor to raise the barrier

when clicked

forever

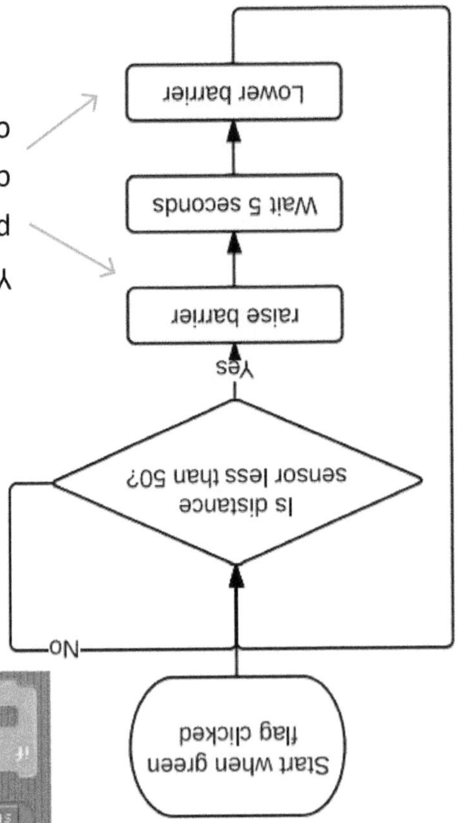
Start when green flag clicked
Is distance sensor less than 50?
Yes
No
raise barrier
Wait 5 seconds
Lower barrier

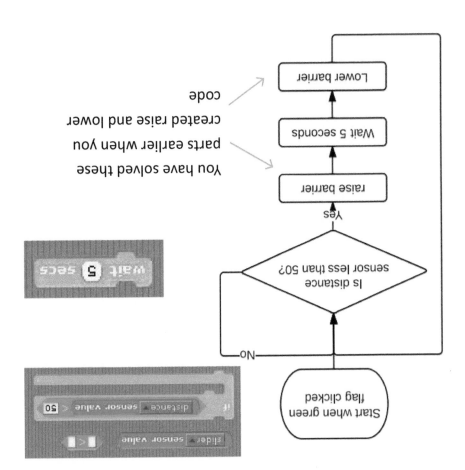

You have solved these parts earlier when you created raise and lower code

wait 5 secs

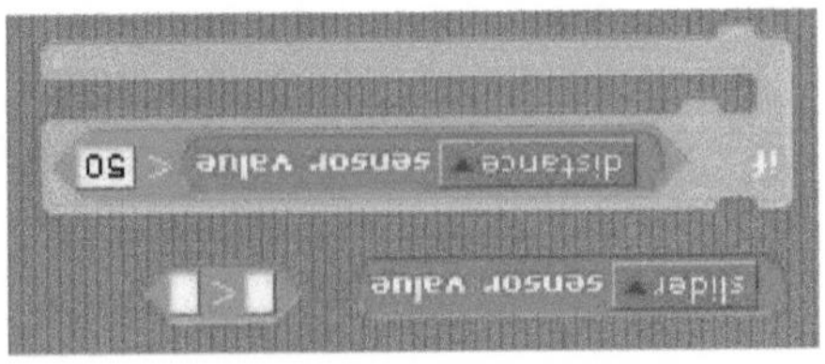
if
distance sensor value < 50
slider sensor value

Car Park Barrier

Support

Card

code-it.co.uk

Program the barrier to detect the car if less than 50mm away, lift the barrier, wait 5 seconds and lower the barrier

code-it.co.uk

3H. Angle Sorter

Module Aim: Create a program that determines which type of angle you are using once you have inputted it in degrees.

Time to complete module

2-3 hours

National Curriculum Programs of Study

KS2

Pupils should be taught to:

- design, *write and debug programs that accomplish specific goals,* including controlling or simulating physical systems; solve problems by decomposing them into smaller parts
- *use sequence, selection,* and repetition in pro-grams; work with variables and *various forms of input and output*

KS3

- *understand simple Boolean logic* [for example, *AND,* OR and NOT] *and some of its uses in* circuits and *programming*

Module Learning Focus

By the end of the module children will be able to:

- Examine a basic menu system that uses multiple conditions inside selection to determine people's age.
- Prove that they understand this by adding the next ages to the program.
- Re-purpose (generalise) this by examining different types of angles and producing a program that tells the user what type of angle they are using from the degree turn typed in.
- Begin to understand importance of ordering information

Computer Science Concepts

- Conditional Selection
- And Or statements

Maths Skills

- Using greater than and less than
- Understanding that equals means the same as
- Reading, revising, understanding and ordering the names of different types of angles

Differentiation and Assessment for Learning

At the beginning of each session the learning intention sheet of pupil workbook 3 page 28 is shared and the learning journey expanded through success criteria. Pupils feed their progress back to the teacher through annotating this sheet with faces either during or at the end of the lesson. Teachers can also annotate the sheet to indicate those who need more or less help in future lessons.

Adult Focus

All adults need to be clear that they are to support using hints only and not solve things for pupils.

Computational Thinking **Algorithm:** a precise step by step guide to achieving a specific outcome.

Generalisation: adapting a solution that solved one solution to solve another

Useful Hints

Read the code aloud tracing it with your finger. Does it make sense? Have you read the greater than or less than symbol correctly? Explain what the code is doing at every stage

5. Draw the angle
4. Code Angles Menu
3. Angles Algorithm
2. Complete menu
1. Examine menu

Learning Path

1. Examine Menu

Show pupils the simple age menu as set out below. Where have we used something similar? Answer - the Maths Quiz. Can anyone think of a quicker way of doing this if we needed to cover up to age 100? Answer we need to cover ranges of numbers from say 2 to 4.

Now open up or create the complex age menu, look at the two selection statements and point out the AND statement that joins them. Ask pupils what they think it means? Answer - both conditions must be fulfilled. Look at the selection block with OR separating the conditions. What does this mean? Answer - one of the conditions must be met.

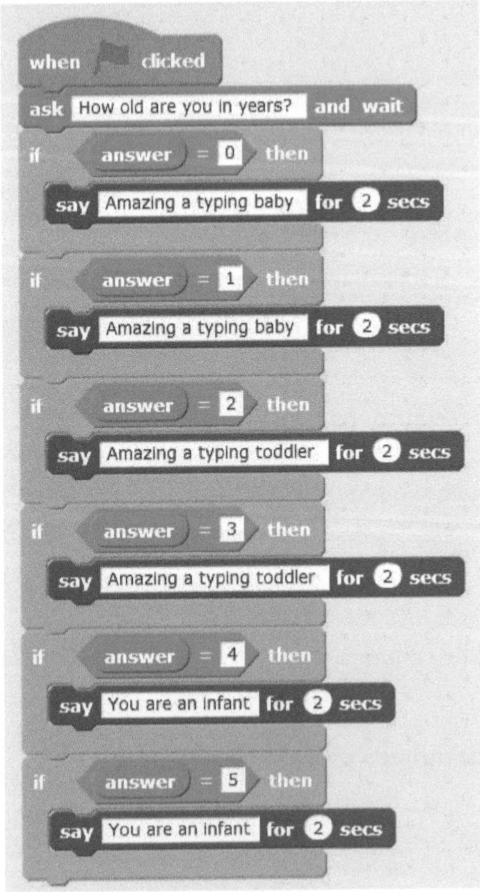
when clicked
ask How old are you in years? and wait
if answer = 0 then
say Amazing a typing baby for 2 secs
if answer = 1 then
say Amazing a typing baby for 2 secs
if answer = 2 then
say Amazing a typing toddler for 2 secs
if answer = 3 then
say Amazing a typing toddler for 2 secs
if answer = 4 then
say You are an infant for 2 secs
if answer = 5 then
say You are an infant for 2 secs
Simple age menu

Code Resources

You can find this code online at https://scratch.mit.edu/projects/55754510/.
The simpler code to use first is connected inside the Dog Sprite. The more complex Code Example to use next is inside the cat sprite. Make sure you detach the green flag from the dog code and attach it to the code inside the cat.

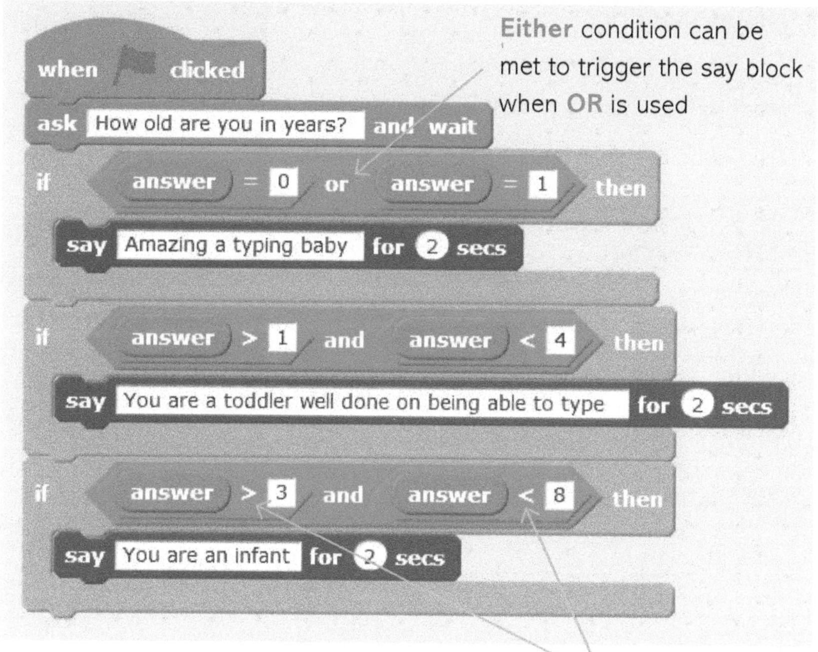
Either condition can be met to trigger the say block when OR is used
when clicked
ask How old are you in years? and wait
if answer = 0 or answer = 1 then
say Amazing a typing baby for 2 secs
if answer > 1 and answer < 4 then
say You are a toddler well done on being able to type for 2 secs
if answer > 3 and answer < 8 then
say You are an infant for 2 secs

Both conditions must be met when AND is used

Complex age menu

Some pupils find meeting the < and > outside of a simple maths context daunting and may need help reading the statements in context.

If answer typed in is **greater than 1 AND less than 4** then say you are a toddler well done on being able to type.

2. Complete the menu

Can pupils use their new knowledge of **AND** and **OR** to add the next two stages of age, Junior School (7-11) and Secondary (12-18) school.

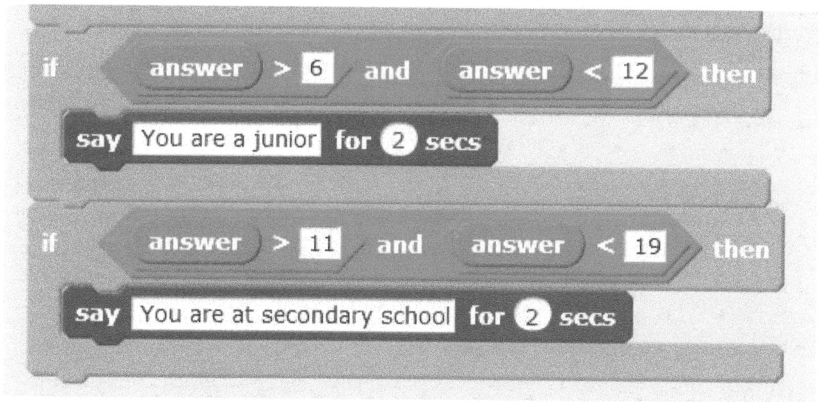
if answer > 6 and answer < 12 then
say You are a junior for 2 secs
if answer > 11 and answer < 19 then
say You are at secondary school for 2 secs

A solution to this puzzle is here

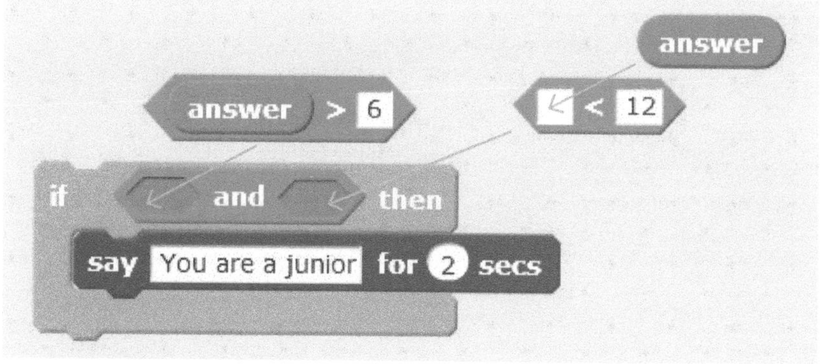
answer
answer > 6
< 12
if and then
say You are a junior for 2 secs

Note

Find how the code is snapped together. It doesn't matter which condition is on the right but it does matter that the answer block is on the left hand side in this case.

3. Angles Algorithm

As pupils complete the last task point them to page 29 of the pupil's workbook. Their task is to sort out the different angle types into size order from smallest to largest on the table.

Name of Angle	Properties of Angle
Acute Angle	Greater than 0 degrees less than 90 degrees
Right Angle	Equal to 90 degrees
Obtuse Angle	Greater than 90 degrees less than 180 degrees
Straight Angle	Equal to 180 degrees
Reflex Angle	Greater than 180 degrees less than 360 degrees
Full Rotation	Equal to 360 degrees

Check pupils' Angle Types Algorithm Answers before allowing them to code

4. Code Angles Menu

Once they have had their angle algorithm checked they can independantly turn it into Scratch code that tells the user what an angle is when they type in the size in degrees.

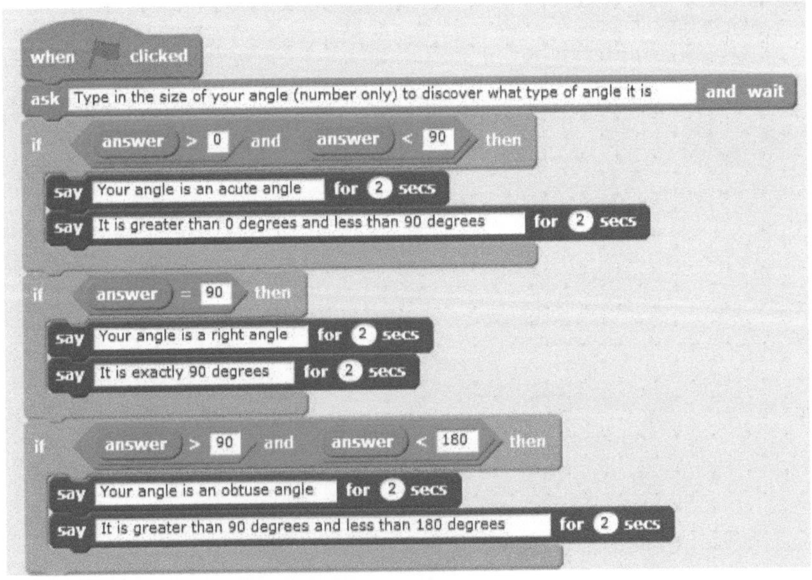
when clicked
ask Type in the size of your angle (number only) to discover what type of angle it is and wait
if answer > 0 and answer < 90 then
say Your angle is an acute angle for 2 secs
say It is greater than 0 degrees and less than 90 degrees for 2 secs
if answer = 90 then
say Your angle is a right angle for 2 secs
say It is exactly 90 degrees for 2 secs
if answer > 90 and answer < 180 then
say Your angle is an obtuse angle for 2 secs
say It is greater than 90 degrees and less than 180 degrees for 2 secs

5. Draw the angle inputted by the user

Can the program automatically draw the angle inputted by the user?

There are lots of ways of doing this.

Previous lines are removed

The sprite is centred

The sprite direction is reset

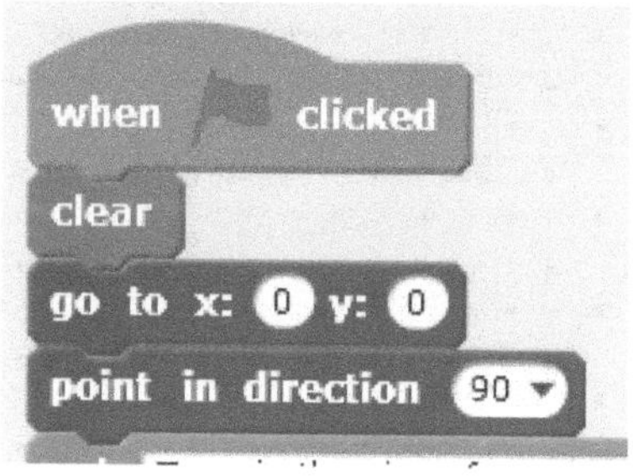
when clicked
clear
go to x: 0 y: 0
point in direction 90

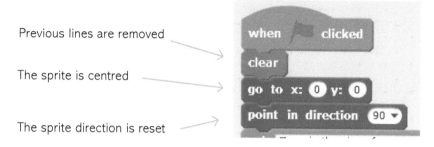

Main program is here

The turn in degrees is inputted using the answer block. It could also be put into a variable before being used

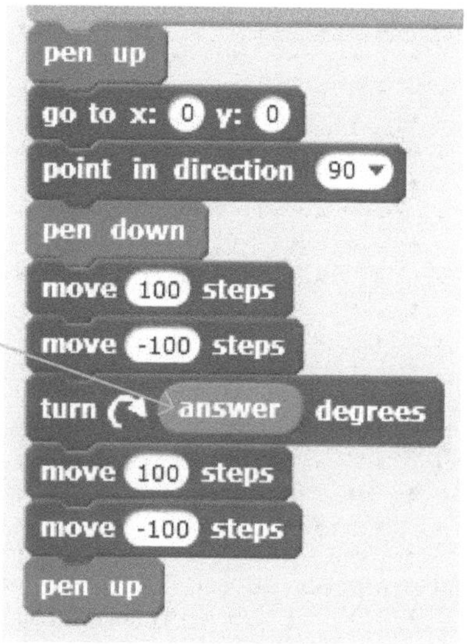
pen up
go to x: 0 y: 0
point in direction 90
pen down
move 100 steps
move -100 steps
turn answer degrees
move 100 steps
move -100 steps
pen up

Last Thought

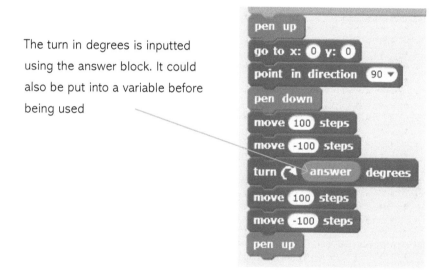

Can pupils come up with any other way of using this?

Learning Intentions model answer

Using two conditions can save time and use less code because a range of numbers can be covered rather than just one.

I can explain the difference between AND OR

Both conditions have to be met if AND is used

Only one condition has to be met if OR is used

Print extra independent extension activities in the pupil books and send them home

4A. Times Tables Game

Time to complete module

3-4 hours

Module Aim: decompose a times tables game individually and then build their own version useful to their maths group or class.

National Curriculum Programs of Study

KS2

Pupils should be taught to:

- *design, write and debug programs that accomplish specific goals,* including controlling or simulating physical systems; *solve problems by decomposing them into smaller parts*
- *use sequence, selection, and repetition in programs; work with variables and* various forms of input and output
- *use logical reasoning to explain how some simple algorithms work and to detect and correct errors in algorithms and programs*

Useful Hints

Don't hand out hint cards unless pupils can tell you what they are trying to create or can refer to their decomposition planner. Modelling physically what they are trying to do helps with moving and randomly setting a direction challenges.

Module Learning Focus

By the end of the module children will be able to:

- Decompose a game independently
- Use the decomposed planner to build their own version
- Find solutions independently to each programming challenge
- Begin to evaluate code efficiency

Computer Science Concepts

- Decomposing
- Forever loops
- Variables

Maths Concepts

- Multiplication tables
- Degrees

Assessment for Learning

At the end of each session direct pupils to page 4 of pupil workbook 4 to help them reflect on what they have learnt. You can also annotate this to record pupils who have needed much more support or have demonstrated greater understanding.

Adult Focus

All adults need to be clear that they are to support using hints only and not solve things for pupils.

Computational Thinking

Decomposition: break up a problem into sections and solve each section separately

Evaluation: looking at the most efficient or best code

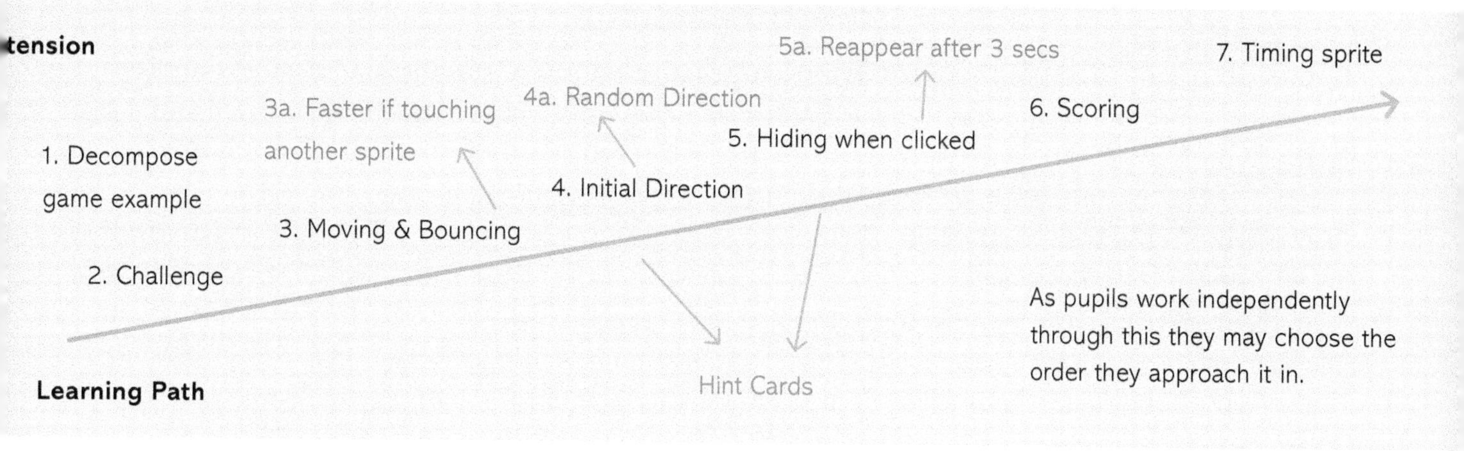

Extension
5a. Reappear after 3 secs
7. Timing sprite
3a. Faster if touching another sprite
4a. Random Direction
6. Scoring
5. Hiding when clicked
1. Decompose game example
4. Initial Direction
3. Moving & Bouncing
2. Challenge
As pupils work independently through this they may choose the order they approach it in.
Learning Path
Hint Cards

1. Decomposing Game Example

Show pupils a variant of the game in presentation mode. You play the game whilst they decompose its elements http://scratch.mit.edu/projects/16084505/. Don't let them look at the code. The decomposed planner is in workbook.

If you don't have a lot of time there is a 100 sprite templates on http://code-it.co.uk/bookmedia.

Pupils can delete the sprites they don't need.

2. Challenge

Pupils choose a table to create. Ask them to recreate the game they decomposed earlier. If they finish that successfully they can think of ways to adapt and modify it to add their own twist or flavour to the project. Give pupils time to create the right and wrong answer number discs as sprites. Pupils need approximately 20 sprites, 10 correct answers and 10 incorrect answers. Allow pupils to work independently supporting with hint cards that show the blocks they could use if they have attempted a solution independently and are still stuck.

It is worth encouraging pupils to create working code in one correct sprite and one incorrect one before dragging the code on top of other sprites to duplicate it.

> **Useful Hints**
>
> Don't hand out hint cards unless pupils can tell you what they are trying to create or can refer to their decomposed planner.

Programming Evaluation

The following are possible solutions. However as in all programming there are many right answers. Look for two different solutions to the same problem. If one uses much more code than the other you have a perfect opportunity to talk about the computational thinking skill of evaluation. The solution with less code being more efficient.

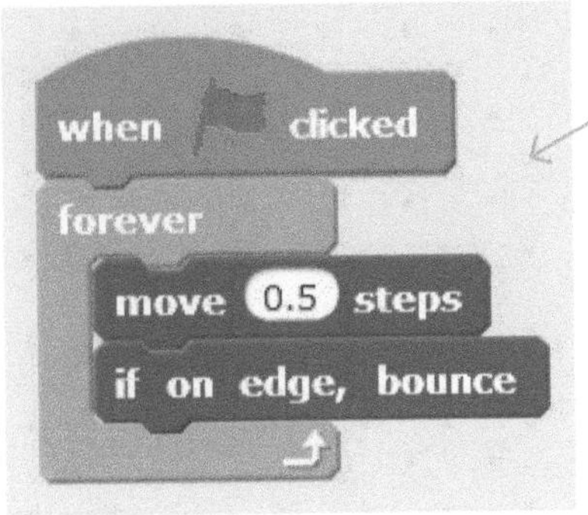
when clicked
forever
move 0.5 steps
if on edge, bounce

3. Moving & Bouncing

One very likely solution will be this. The number of steps may change once pupils start to play test the game. Support card available p151.

3a. Faster if touching another sprite

These are two possible solutions. A reminder of the selection investigation is often enough of a hint without the support card. Support card available.

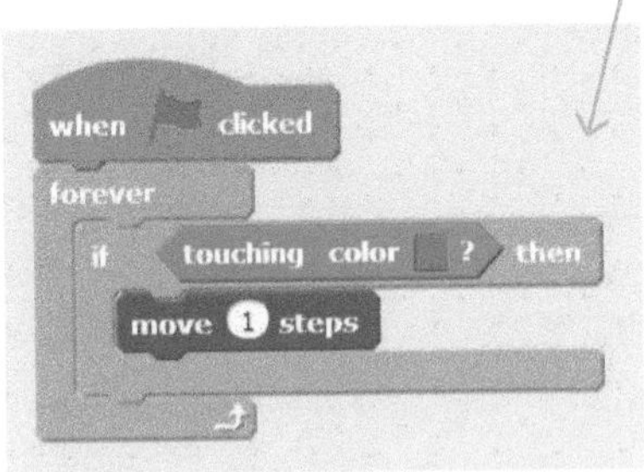
when clicked
forever
if touching color ? then
move 1 steps

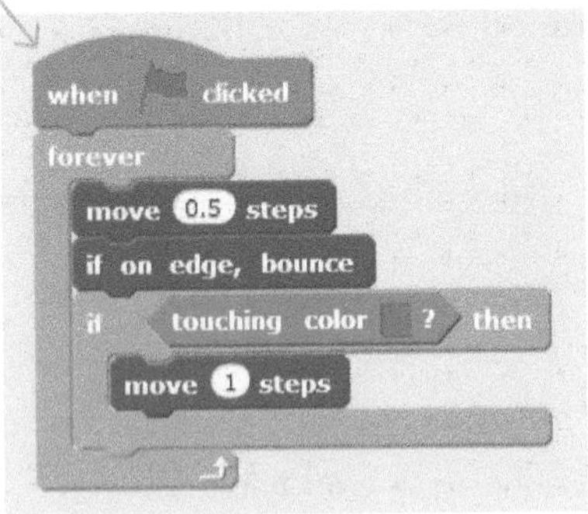
when clicked
forever
move 0.5 steps
if on edge, bounce
if touching color ? then
move 1 steps

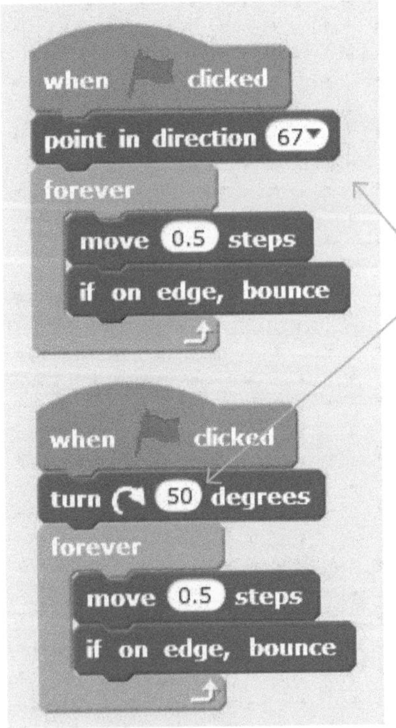
when clicked
point in direction 67
forever
move 0.5 steps
if on edge, bounce
when clicked
turn 50 degrees
forever
move 0.5 steps
if on edge, bounce

4. Set initial direction of sprite so that they all bounce in different directions

Point in Direction hint card page 156

These will work as long as a different direction has been manually typed into each box. A better solution is to randomly choose direction. Depending on their maths ability pupils may need a little help visualising what random and 360 means.

Get them to pretend they are the sprite. Get them to turn 90 degrees, 180, 270 360 etc. Then tell them to spin slowly.

Get a friend to call out stop before they get all the way round. Do this a couple of times. Do they know where they will be pointing? Relate this to the random block.

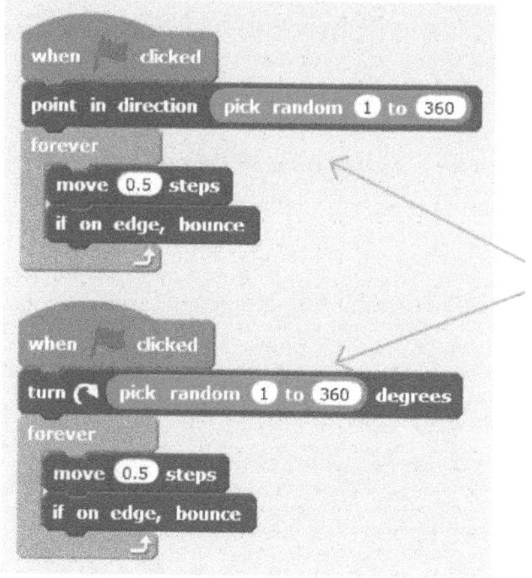
when clicked
point in direction pick random 1 to 360
forever
move 0.5 steps
if on edge, bounce
when clicked
turn pick random 1 to 360 degrees
forever
move 0.5 steps
if on edge, bounce

These are a better solution as the sprites move in a different random direction every time the game starts.

Direction could be in its own block

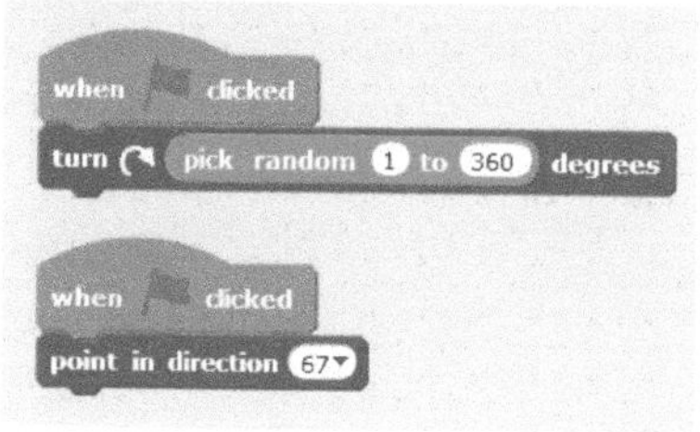
when clicked
turn pick random 1 to 360 degrees
when clicked
point in direction 67

5. Hiding a correct number sprite when it is clicked and making it reappear when the game starts

Possible solutions are:

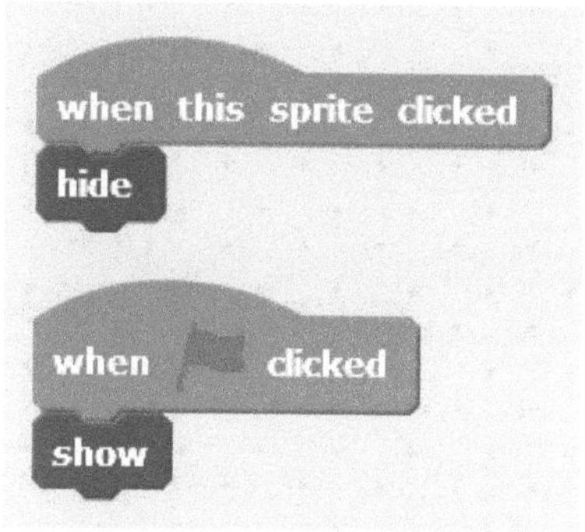
when this sprite clicked
hide
when clicked
show

5a. Making a sprite reappear after x seconds

when this sprite clicked
hide
wait 3 secs
show
when clicked
show

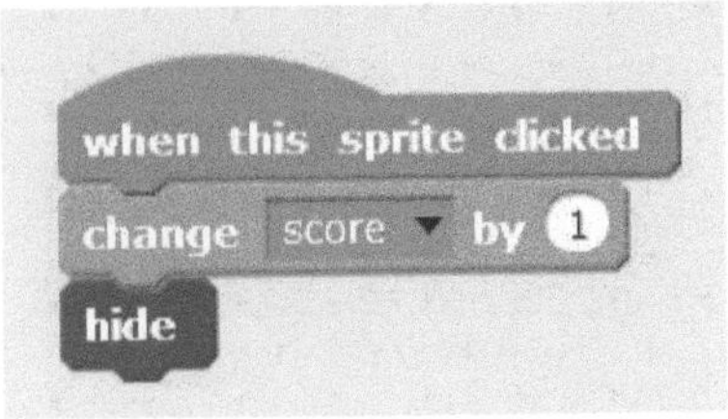
when this sprite clicked
change score by 1
hide

Increasing score by one when clicked

6. Provide scoring where a correct choice will increase the score and an incorrect choice will decrease the score

Before you hand out a hint card remind pupils of variables they have used in the past.

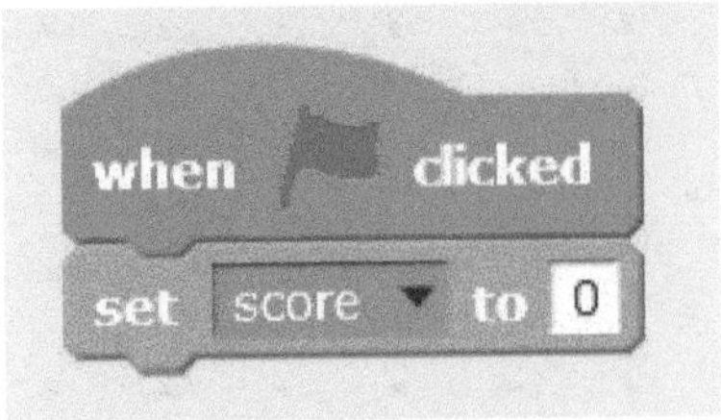
when clicked
set score to 0

Set score to 0 when game starts
Only needed on one sprite

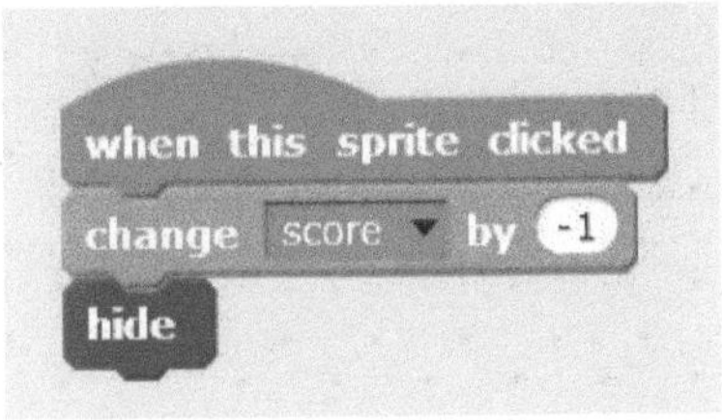
when this sprite clicked
change score by -1
hide

Decrease score by one when clicked

7. Create a timer

Decrease score by one when clicked.

The timer needs to start the game/scoring, give instructions. hide itself while the game is going on, report the final score and end the game. There is a hint card available.

One possible solution is this:

Instructions

Count down to start

Set score to 0

Hiding sprite while game goes on

Timing the game

Revealing itself

Reporting the score inside the variable

End the game

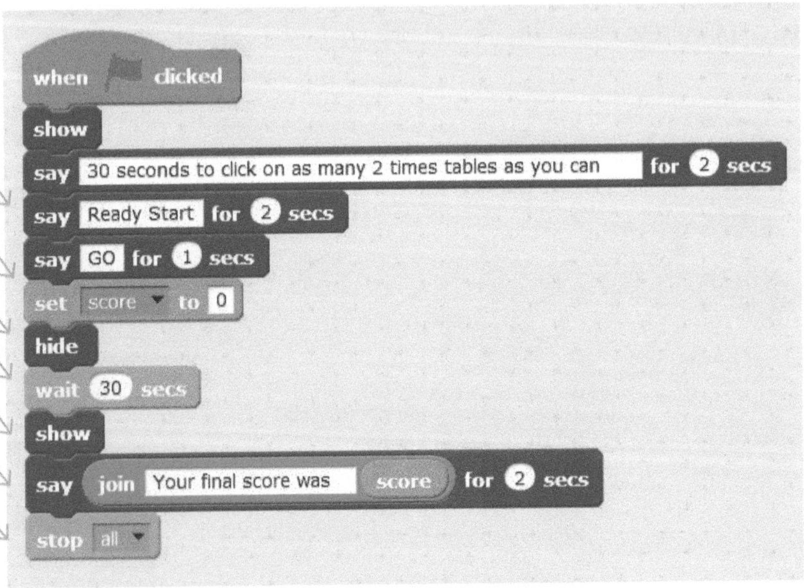
when clicked
show
say 30 seconds to click on as many 2 times tables as you can for 2 secs
say Ready Start for 2 secs
say GO for 1 secs
set score to 0
hide
wait 30 secs
show
say join Your final score was score for 2 secs
stop all

Further Extensions

Change background when wrong sprite is clicked

Pupils could use a broadcast to trigger a background change in the stage area.

Ask the user to set how long the game lasts

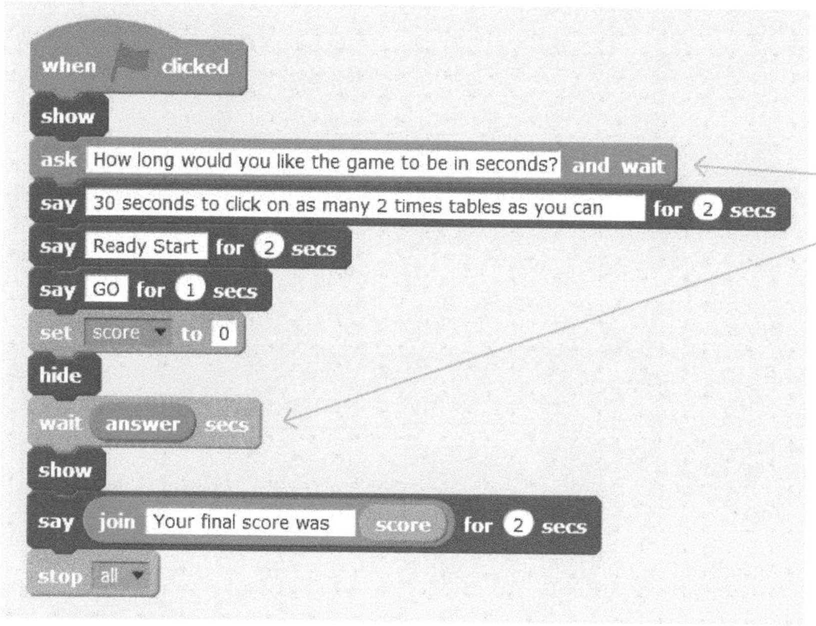
when clicked
show
ask How long would you like the game to be in seconds? and wait
say 30 seconds to click on as many 2 times tables as you can for 2 secs
say Ready Start for 2 secs
say GO for 1 secs
set score to 0
hide
wait answer secs
show
say join Your final score was score for 2 secs
stop all

The question is asked and the answer sets the timer length

Q. Which block is redundant in this code?

A. Say 30 seconds block has been replaced by the ask block.

Adapt the game

The best extension is to ask pupils to adapt the idea to give it their own twist or flavour. They may want to use the adapt the idea page in their pupil workbooks page 6 to help them think through and reflect on what was learnt. Working with someone else who has finished helps with this.

Sometimes it helps to see examples of pupils' work

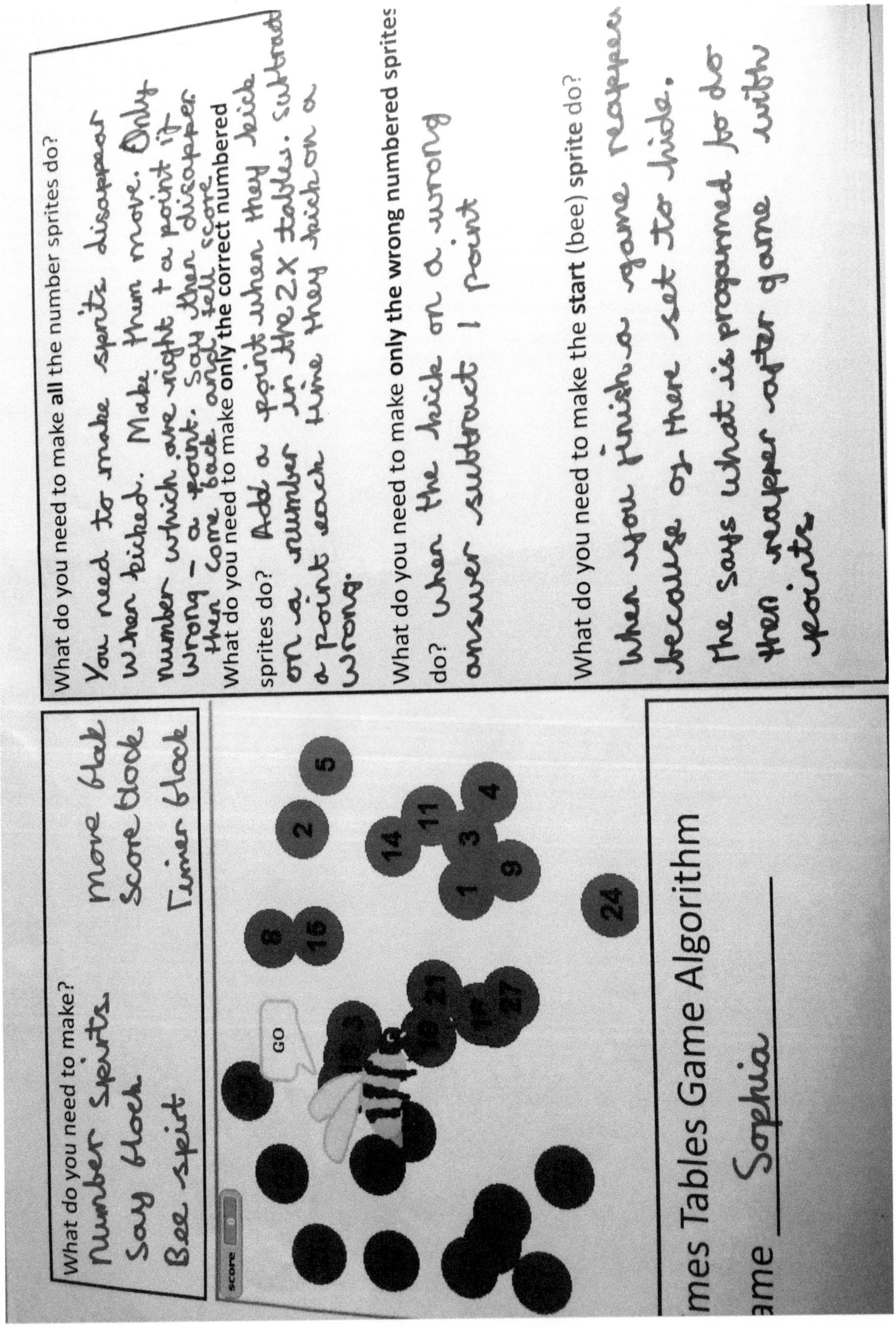
mes Tables Game Algorithm
ame Sophia
What do you need to make?
Number Sprits
Say block
Bee spirt
More block
Score block
Timer block
SCORE
GO
What do you need to make all the number sprites do?
You need to make sprits disappear when kicked. Make them move. Only number which are right + a point if wrong - a point. Say then disappear then come back and tell score.
What do you need to make only the correct numbered sprites do?
Add a point when they kick on a number in the 2X tables. subtract a point each time they kick on a wrong.
What do you need to make only the wrong numbered sprites do?
when the kick on a wrong answer subtract 1 point
What do you need to make the start (bee) sprite do?
When you finish a game reappear because of there set to hide. The says what is programed to do then reapper after game with points.

Pupil decompose game work samples

Pupil decompose game work samples

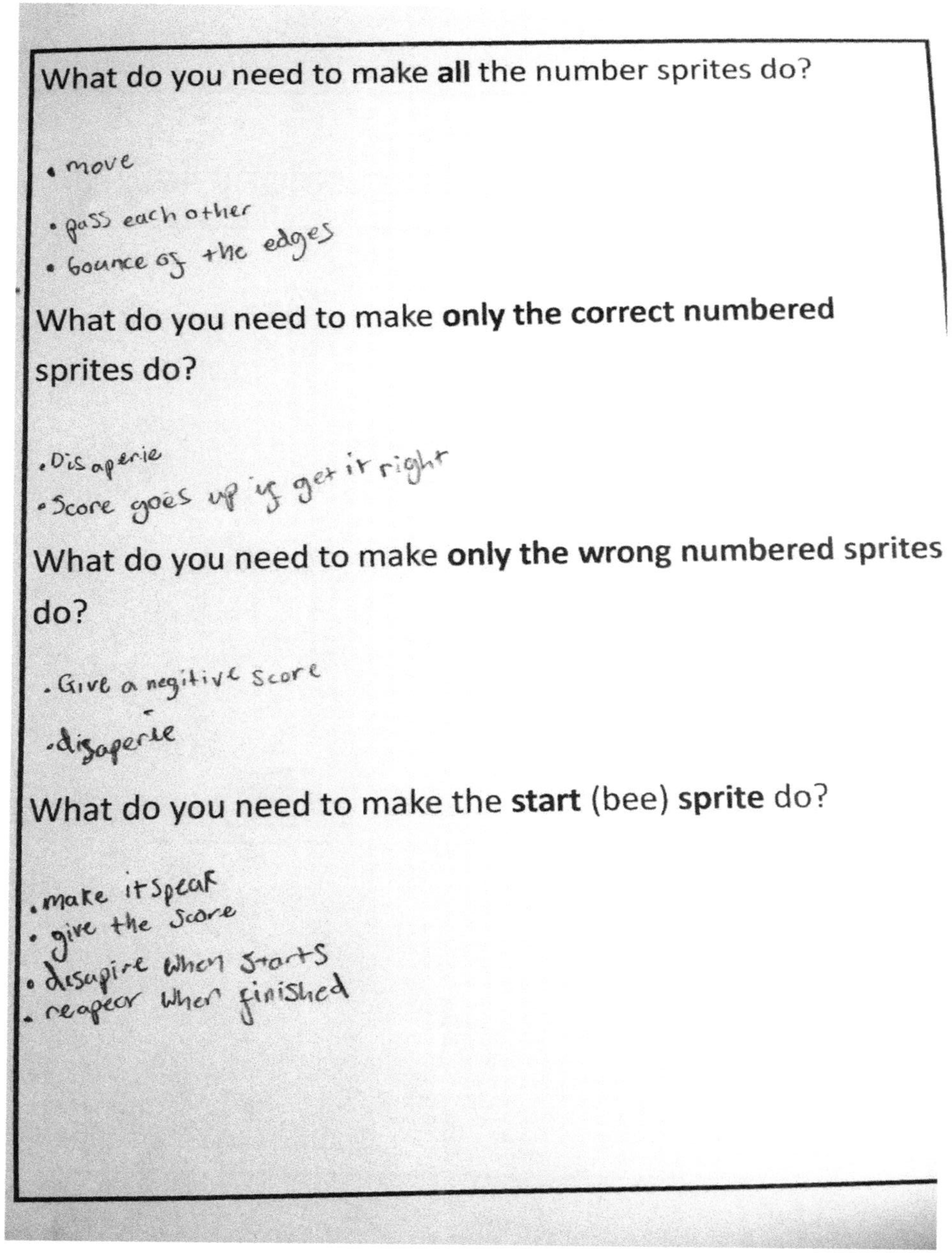

What do you need to make **all** the number sprites do?

- move
- pass each other
- bounce of the edges

What do you need to make **only the correct numbered** sprites do?

- Dis aperie
- Score goes up if get it right

What do you need to make **only the wrong numbered sprites** do?

- Give a negitive Score
- disaperie

What do you need to make the **start** (bee) **sprite** do?

- make it speak
- give the Score
- disapire when starts
- reapear when finished

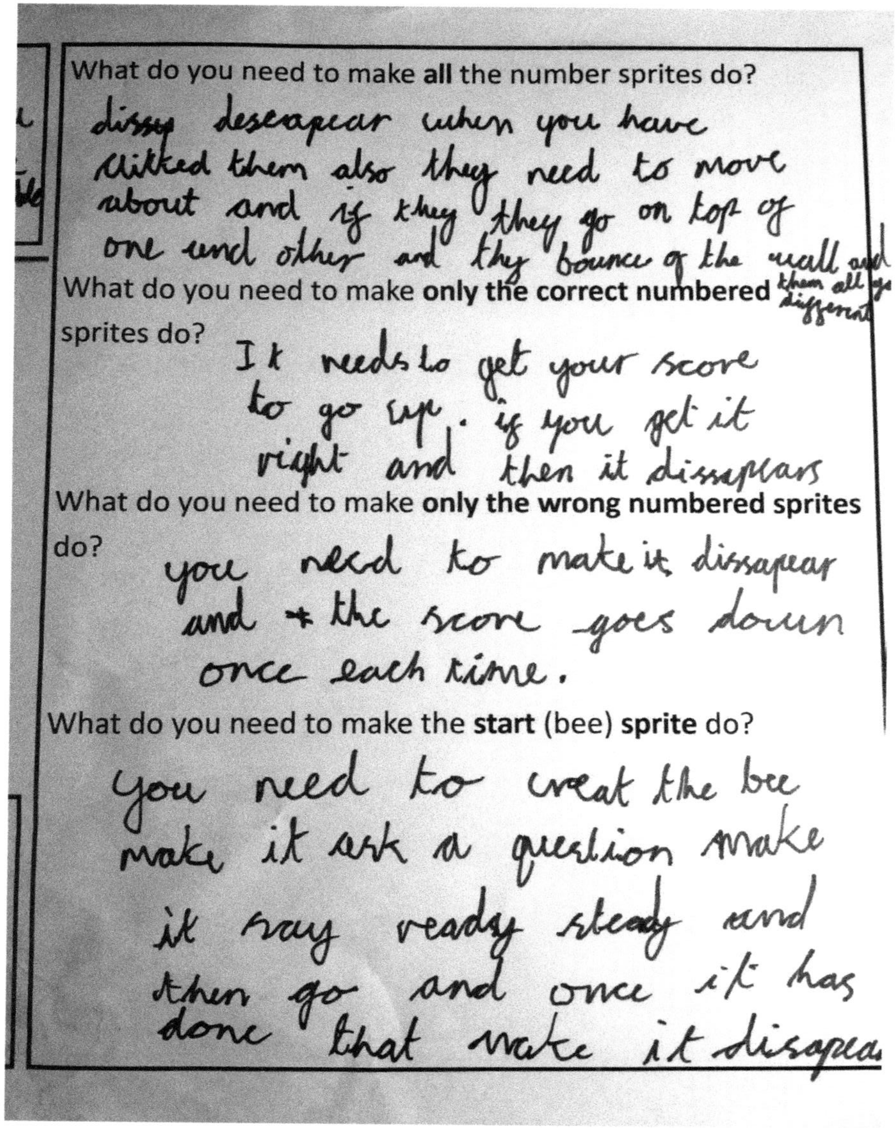

What do you need to make **all** the number sprites do?

dissy desecapear when you have clikked them also they need to move about and if they they go on top of one and other and they bounce of the wall and them all go diffrent

What do you need to make **only the correct numbered** sprites do?

It needs to get your score to go up. if you get it right and then it dissapears

What do you need to make **only the wrong numbered sprites** do?

you need to make it dissapear and + the score goes down once each time.

What do you need to make the **start** (bee) **sprite** do?

you need to creat the bee make it ask a question make it say ready steady and then go and once it has done that make it disapear

Decompose Tables Game

What do you need to make?

Score

Numbers

Start sprite (bee)

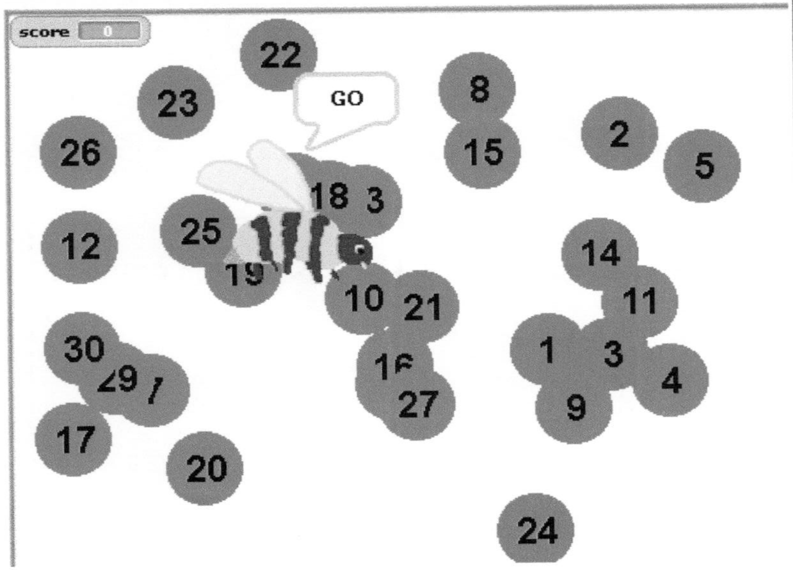
score
GO

Times Tables Game Algorithm

What do you need to make **all** the number sprites do?

move slowly
bounce off walls
start in different (random) direction
hide when clicked
not rotate

What do you need to make **only the correct numbered** sprites do?

Increase score by 1 when clicked on

What do you need to make **only the wrong numbered sprites** do?

decrease score by 1 when clicked on

What do you need to make the **start** (bee) **sprite** do?

give game instructions
hide while game has started
time the game
reappear after 30 seconds
report the score
end the game

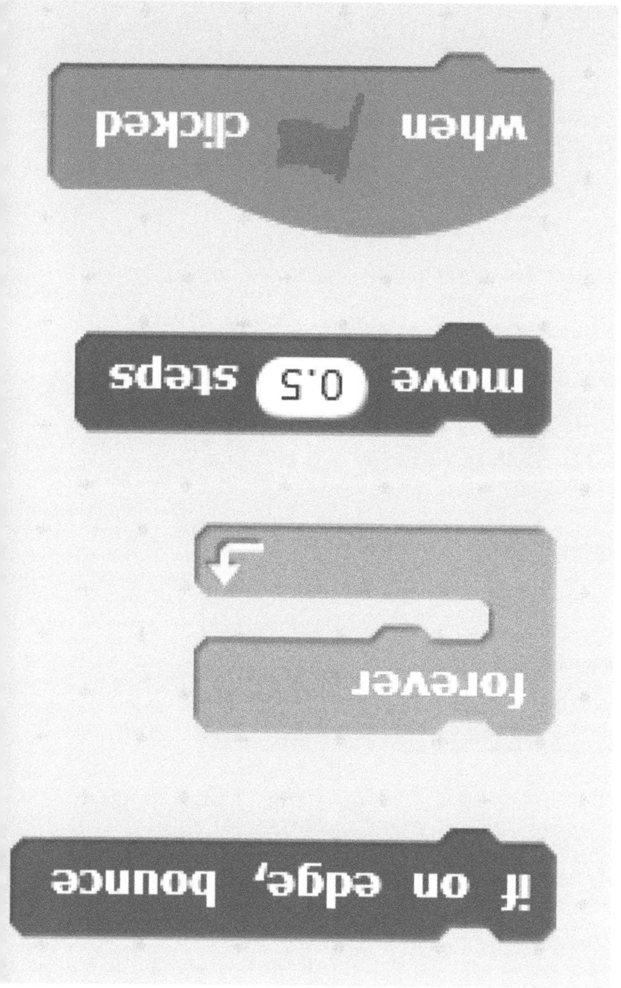
when clicked
move 0.5 steps
forever
if on edge, bounce

code-it.co.uk

Table Game
Hint Card

Move and bounce
off the edges

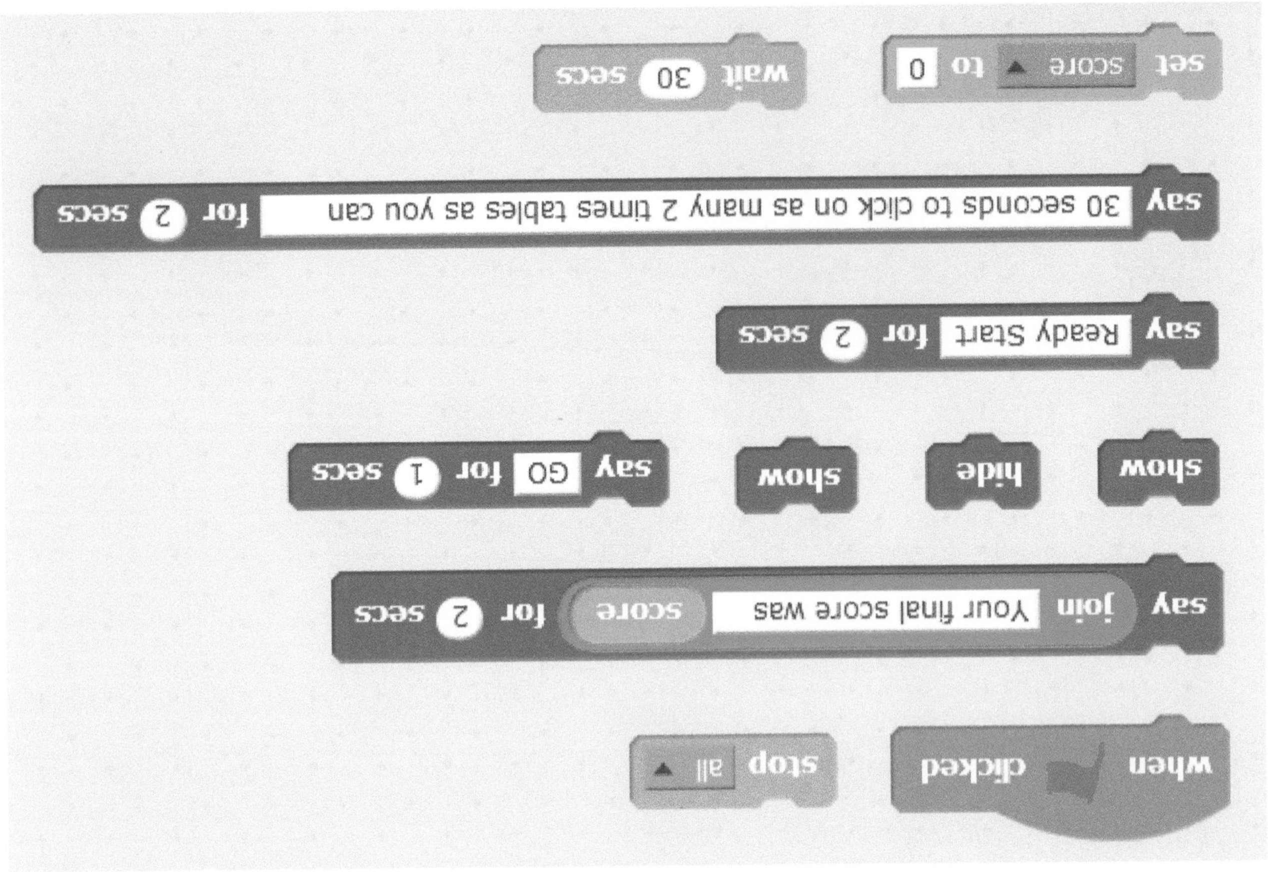
set score to 0
wait 30 secs
say 30 seconds to click on as many 2 times tables as you can for 2 secs
say Ready Start for 2 secs
show
hide
show
say GO for 1 secs
say join Your final score was score for 2 secs
when clicked
stop all

Table Game

Hint Card

Control sprite

Commands

Instructions

Hide for game

Time game length

Report score

End game

when clicked
touching color ?
move 2 steps
if then
forever

code-it.co.uk

Table Game Hint Card

Move faster if touching another sprite

You may not need all of these blocks

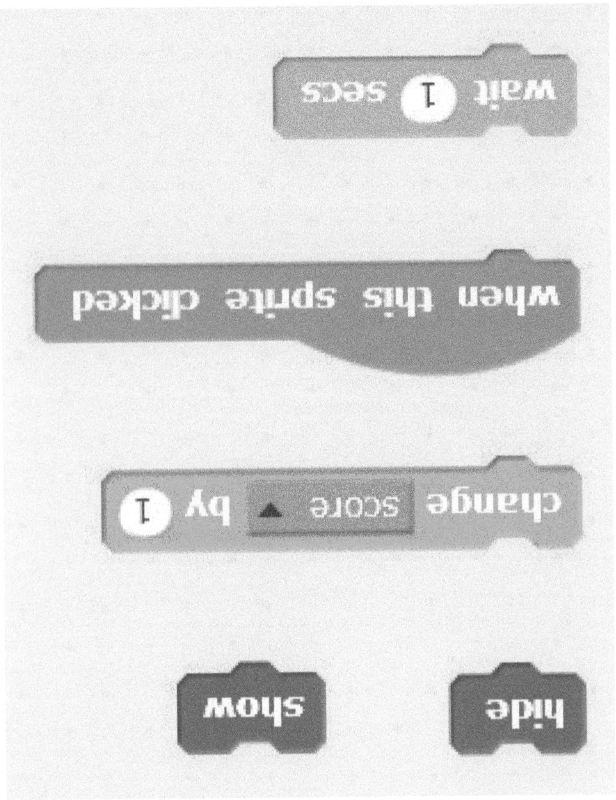
wait 1 secs
when this sprite clicked
change score by 1
show
hide

Table Game

Extension Card

code-it.co.uk

When the number is clicked increase the score by 1 and hide the sprite

code-it.co.uk

Table Game Hint Card

Sprite Rotation

Click on the i to set sprite information

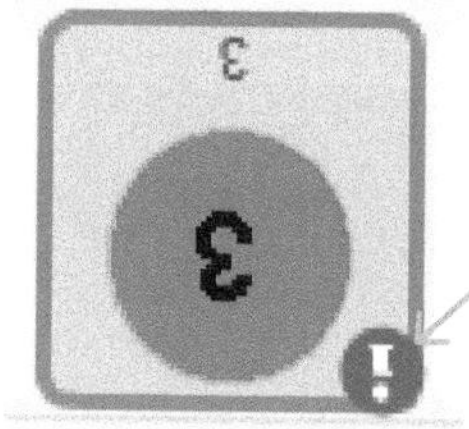
3

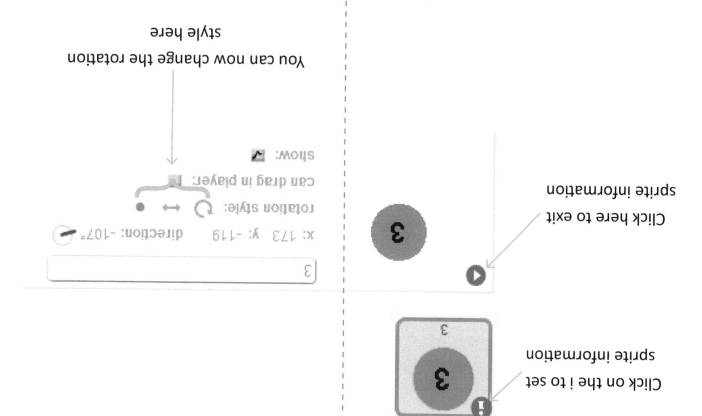

Click here to exit sprite information

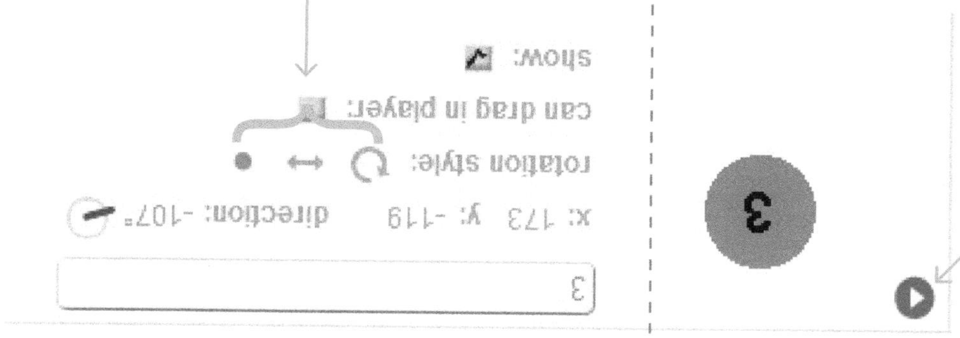
3
x: 173 y: -119 direction: -107°
rotation style:
can drag in player:
show:

You can now change the rotation style here

code-it.co.uk

point in direction 10
pick random 1 to 360
turn 15 degrees
turn 15 degrees

You won't need all of these blocks

Table Game
Hint Card

code-it.co.uk

Sprite points in random direction when starting

code-it.co.uk

4B. Perimeter

Module Aim: Create a program that asks the user for the length of the side and then works out the length of the perimeter of regular 2D shapes.

Time to complete module

3 hours

Module Learning Focus

By the end of the module children will be able to:

- Create a perimeter formula
- Convert this perimeter formula into Scratch code
- Generalise this idea to use with other shapes
- Test and find weak points in the code

Computer Science Concepts

- Convert user input into a variable
- Multiplying or adding variables
- Using one variable to set the amount in another variable
- Using conditional selection blocks to make a menu

Maths Skills

- Perimeter of regular 2D shapes can be calculated by multiplying length of side by number of sides
- Use an asterisk (*) to denote multiply on a computer

Assessment for Learning

At the end of each session direct pupils to page 8 of pupil workbook 4 to help them reflect on what they have learnt. You can also annotate this to record pupils who have needed much more support or have demonstrated greater understanding.

Adult Focus

All adults need to be clear that they are to support using hints only and not solve things for pupils.

Computational Thinking

Algorithm formula algorithm for calculating perimeter

Generalisation: adapting a solution for an equilateral triangle to work for other 2D shapes

National Curriculum Programs of Study

KS2

Pupils should be taught to:

- *design, write and debug programs that accomplish specific goals,* including controlling or simulating physical systems; *solve problems by decomposing them into smaller parts*
- *use sequence, selection, and repetition in programs; work with variables and various forms of input and output*

KS3

- *design and develop modular programs that use procedures or functions*

Useful Hints

Tell pupils what blocks you would use but not how you would snap them together. Can they tell their peers what would happen at each stage in the program?

Learning Path

1. Share idea
2. Find the formula (algorithm) for calculating perimeter of a triangle
3. Converting algorithm into Scratch code
4. Generalising triangle idea to work for other shapes
4a. Perimeter of a rectangle
5. Creating a menu system
6. Even more efficient code
6a. Procedures
6b. Units of measure
6c. Harder maths challenges
7. Testing ar evaluating

Resources: Helpful polygon resource to print http://www.greatlittleminds.com/pages/maths/polygons/regular-polygons.html

Overview

This module is all about moving from algorithm into code. The algorithm is a maths perimeter formula for regular 2d shapes. Pupils create a formula for an equilateral triangle before converting this into Scratch code. They then use the computational thinking skill of generalisation to adapt their idea for use with other regular 2d shapes. It is essential to tie this into Maths perimeter work. The best sessions have occurred alongside or after pupils have refreshed their understanding of perimeter.

1. Share idea

Explain to your class that they are going to make a program that works out the perimeter of regular 2D shapes (where all the sides are the same length). The machine will take the length of one side inputted by the user and calculate the whole perimeter of the regular 2D shape by doing a calculation. However they are going to start by inventing a formula algorithm that will calculate the perimeter of any equilateral triangle.

2. Find the formula (algorithm) for calculating the perimeter of a triangle

Recap how they have used variables in the past (Maths Quiz, Counting Machine, training computer to do maths etc) and explain how variables can work together to add, multiply, divide or subtract any two numbers together.

Using the pupil workbook page 9 how would they plan an algorithm to work out the perimeter of a triangle if the length of one side has been input by the user? Give the pupils variable names of **length of one side and perimeter.** Pupils work on whiteboards. What formula can they discover? (Perimeter = length x 3, perimeter = length + length + length, length x 3 = perimeter or length + length + length = perimeter)

Alternatively you may choose to use the PowerPoint resource **perimeter with variable** found at http://code-it.co.uk/wp-content/uploads/2015/08/perimeterwithvariables.pptx this also leads to the pupil workbook page 9

Hint Remind pupils of Quiz input methods using ask and answer blocks. It is also useful to remind pupils that we are just setting the variables in this module.

3. Converting algorithm into Scratch code

Remind pupils how to create two variables called length and perimeter. Can they find a way to get the user to input the length of one side into the length variable?

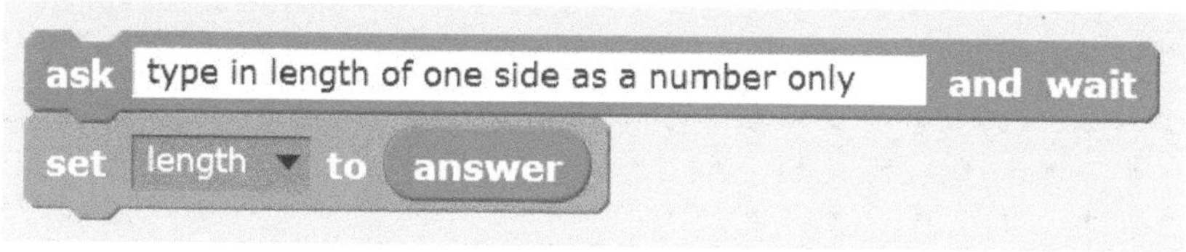
ask type in length of one side as a number only and wait
set length to answer

Can they then work with both variables to turn their formula into Scratch code? See examples below.

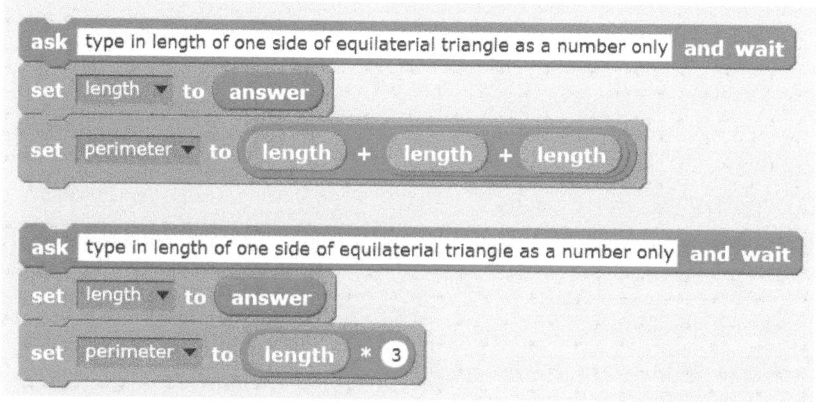
ask type in length of one side of equilateral triangle as a number only and wait
set length to answer
set perimeter to length + length + length
ask type in length of one side of equilateral triangle as a number only and wait
set length to answer
set perimeter to length * 3

Can they report the answer through the sprite say command?

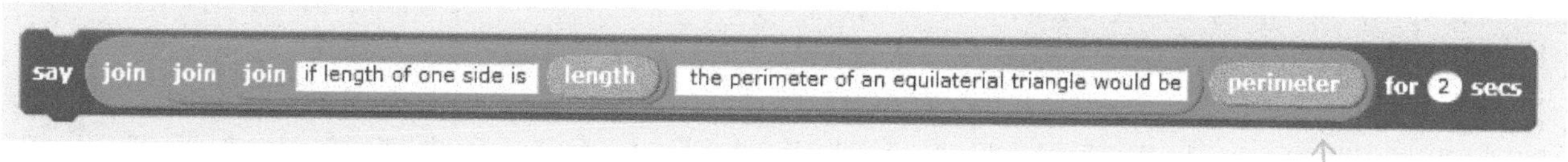
say join join join if length of one side is length the perimeter of an equilateral triangle would be perimeter for 2 secs

Reporting method via say command

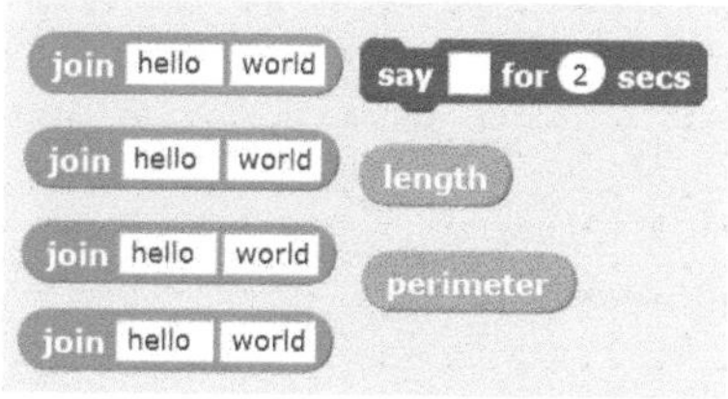
join hello world
join hello world
join hello world
join hello world
say for 2 secs
length
perimeter

Hint Drag out the Scratch blocks they could use.

4. Generalising triangle code to work for other shapes

Can they use skill of generalisation to adapt their solution to work with other regular 2D shapes? A reminder of how to duplicate (right click on top code block you wish to duplicate and select copy) and that they won't need a starting block can be useful.

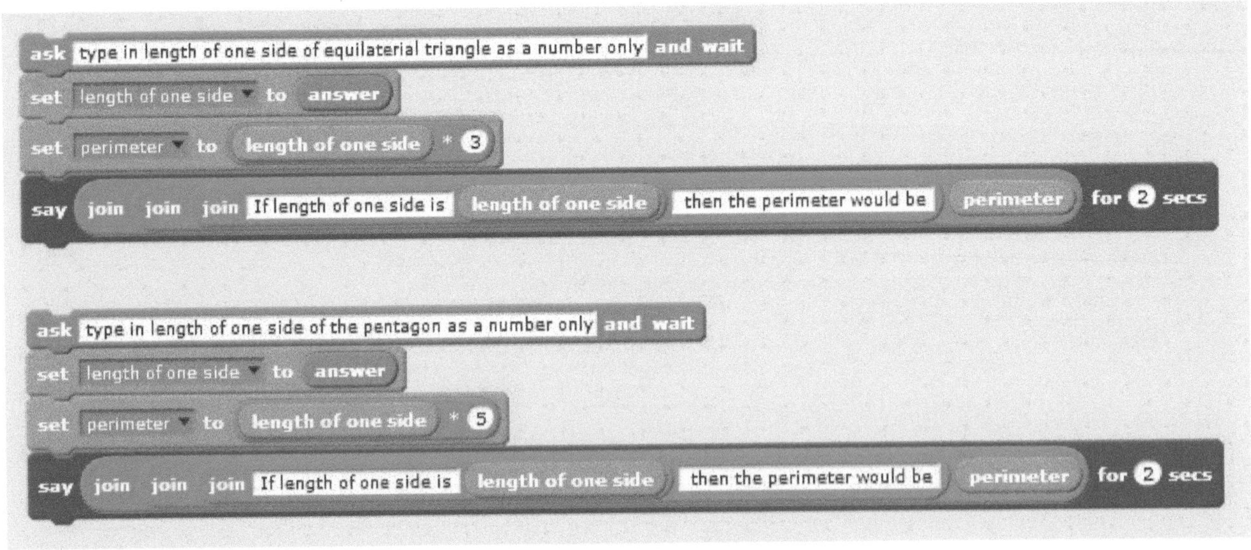
ask type in length of one side of equilaterial triangle as a number only and wait
set length of one side to answer
set perimeter to length of one side * 3
say join join join If length of one side is length of one side then the perimeter would be perimeter for 2 secs
ask type in length of one side of the pentagon as a number only and wait
set length of one side to answer
set perimeter to length of one side * 5
say join join join If length of one side is length of one side then the perimeter would be perimeter for 2 secs

4a. Perimeter of a rectangle

A good extension challenge here is to calculate the perimeter of a rectangle which will need the addition of breadth as only two sides are the same.

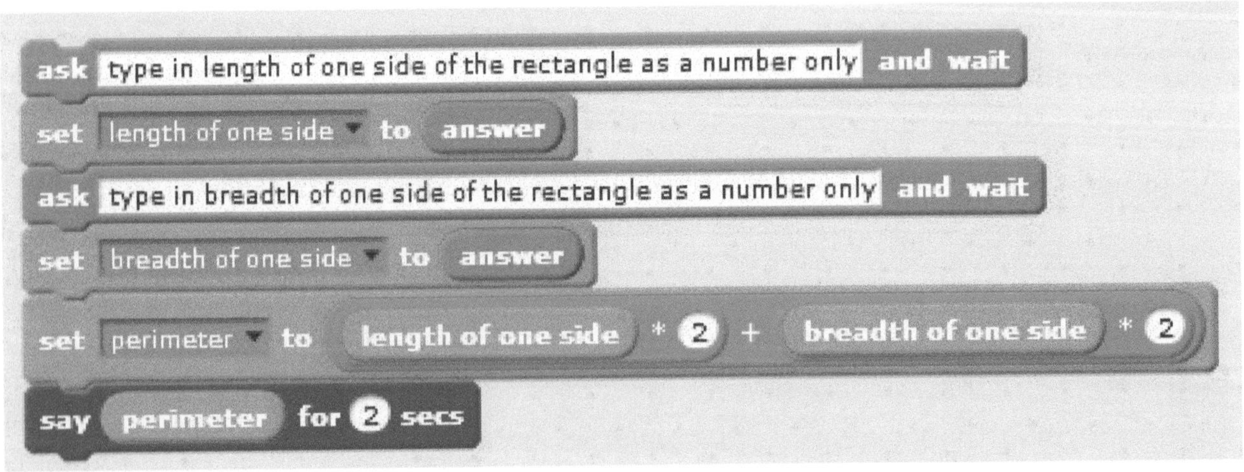
ask type in length of one side of the rectangle as a number only and wait
set length of one side to answer
ask type in breadth of one side of the rectangle as a number only and wait
set breadth of one side to answer
set perimeter to length of one side * 2 + breadth of one side * 2
say perimeter for 2 secs

This is one possible solution to the perimeter rectangle.

5. Creating a menu system

Create this simple menu system. Where would their blocks of generalised code go?

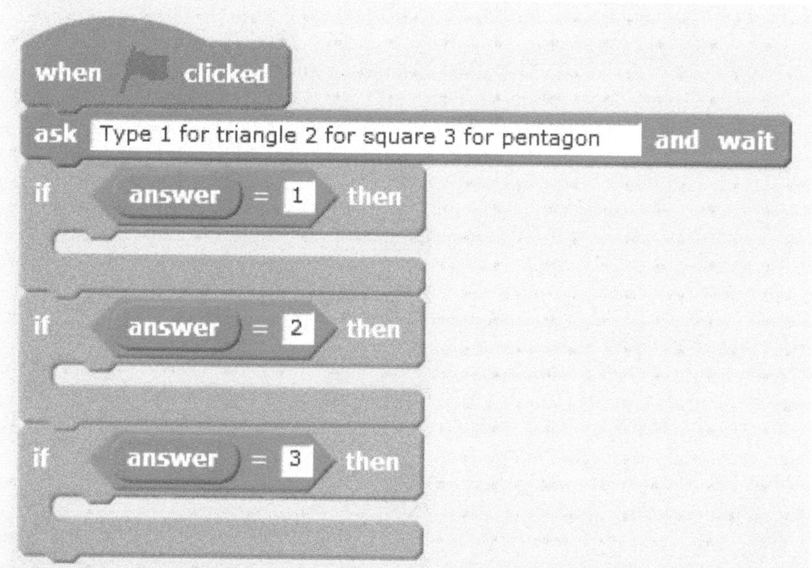
when clicked
ask Type 1 for triangle 2 for square 3 for pentagon and wait
if answer = 1 then
if answer = 2 then
if answer = 3 then

Menu with formulas included

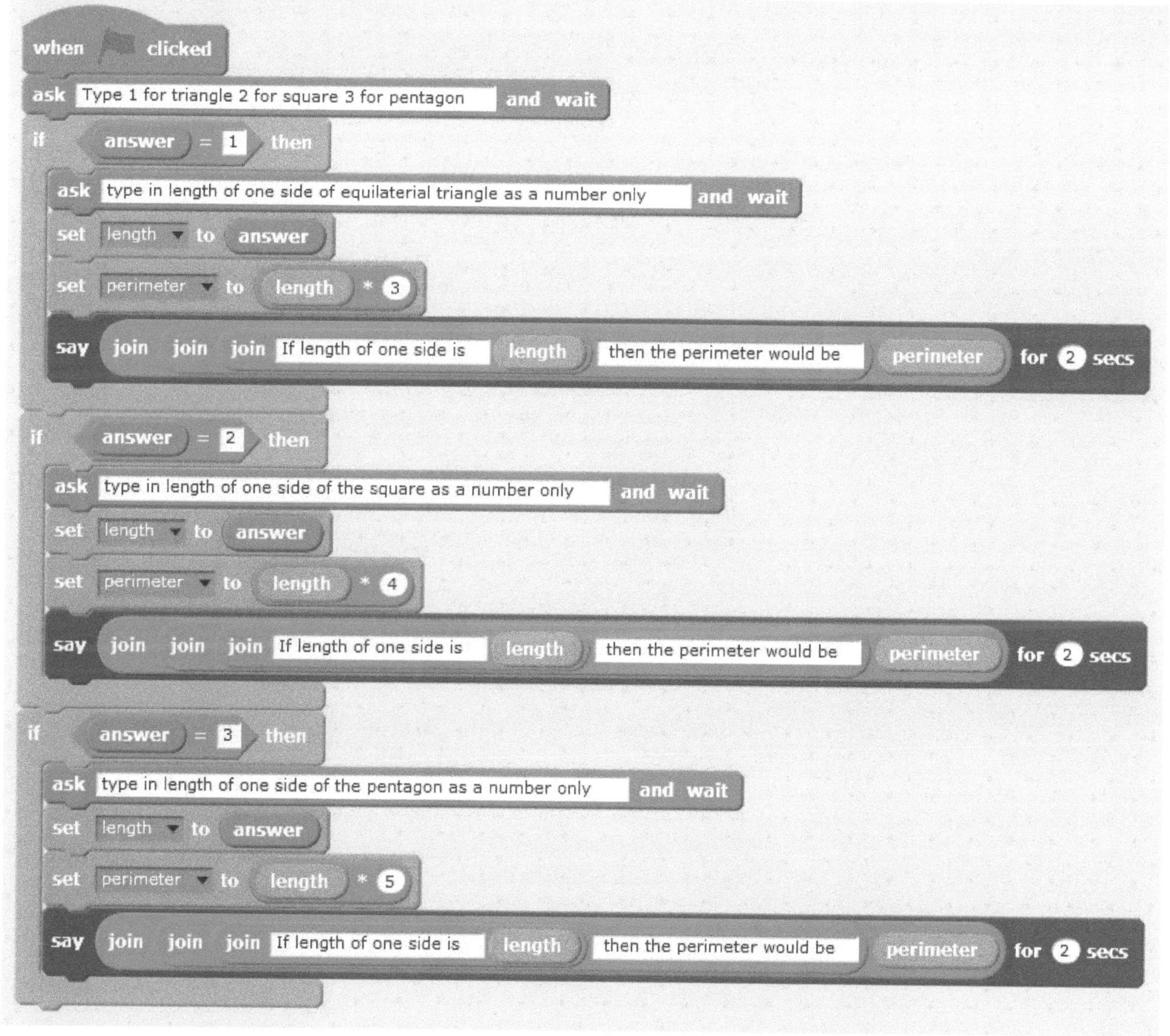
when clicked
ask Type 1 for triangle 2 for square 3 for pentagon and wait
if answer = 1 then
ask type in length of one side of equilaterial triangle as a number only and wait
set length to answer
set perimeter to length * 3
say join join join If length of one side is length then the perimeter would be perimeter for 2 secs
if answer = 2 then
ask type in length of one side of the square as a number only and wait
set length to answer
set perimeter to length * 4
say join join join If length of one side is length then the perimeter would be perimeter for 2 secs
if answer = 3 then
ask type in length of one side of the pentagon as a number only and wait
set length to answer
set perimeter to length * 5
say join join join If length of one side is length then the perimeter would be perimeter for 2 secs

6. Even more efficient code

In computing your first algorithm is not always your most efficient. Looking at all the code blocks inside the menu system - is there another element that could be made into a variable? Answer - the number of sides. Can students come up with a more efficient way of calculating the perimeter of regular 2d shapes that uses that information and less coding blocks?

Explanation

Technically the ask answer blocks are a single fixed variable but I don't find it helpful to explain this to pupils. By converting the ask user input into a variable it is saved for future use rather than being lost when the ask answer block is used for something else.

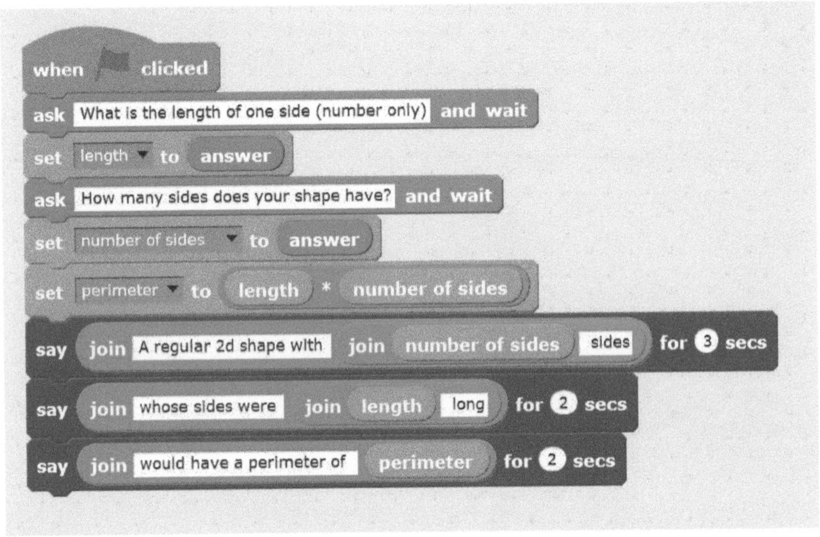

when clicked
ask What is the length of one side (number only) and wait
set length to answer
ask How many sides does your shape have? and wait
set number of sides to answer
set perimeter to length * number of sides
say join A regular 2d shape with join number of sides sides for 3 secs
say join whose sides were join length long for 2 secs
say join would have a perimeter of perimeter for 2 secs

Whilst it is better to turn the number of sides into a variable (as shown above) where it can be reused, in many contexts it is entirely possible just to use the ask answer combination directly as shown below.

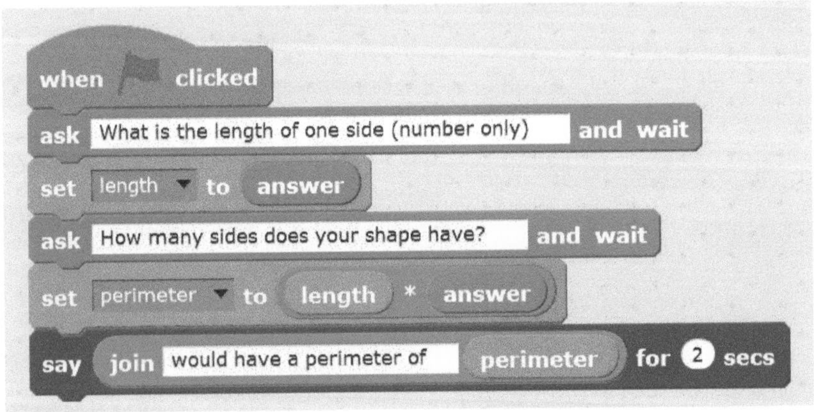

when clicked
ask What is the length of one side (number only) and wait
set length to answer
ask How many sides does your shape have? and wait
set perimeter to length * answer
say join would have a perimeter of perimeter for 2 secs

Although not as useful for the user some pupils' programs may just contain the answer.

say perimeter for 2 secs

6a. Procedures

The same effect can also be produced by building their own procedure only available in Scratch 2.0.

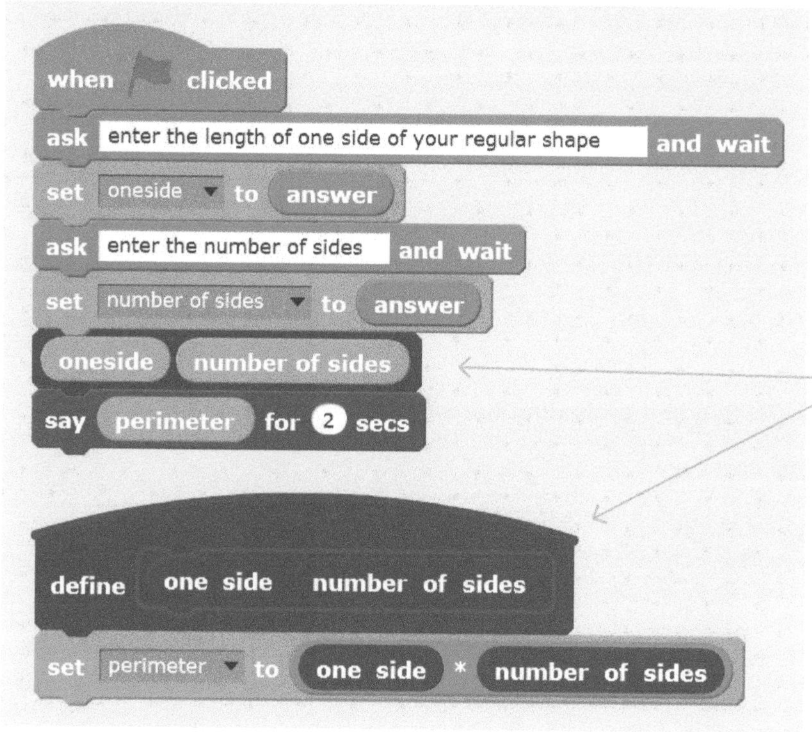
when clicked
ask enter the length of one side of your regular shape and wait
set oneside to answer
ask enter the number of sides and wait
set number of sides to answer
oneside number of sides
say perimeter for 2 secs
define one side number of sides
set perimeter to one side * number of sides

This block runs this block

Although procedures are not mentioned until KS3 your more able will appreciate using these in upper KS2.

A procedure is a way of designing a separate block of code that can be used many times. Information is fed into the procedure from the main block. If the procedure feeds information directly back into the main code this is called a function. Scratch 2.0 does procedures but not functions.

6b. Units of measure

If we type in cm, mm or m at the end of the number in the ask block, the computer won't understand that we are dealing with numbers so we have to deal with units separately.

Can pupils create code that allows the user to use units?

Units could be put inside another variable as variables can hold words as well as numbers.

6c. Harder Maths Challenges

Can pupils adapt this idea to write an algorithm to calculate the perimeter of a circle from its radius, circumference of a circle from its diameter - or many other maths challenges? What would they like to calculate?

7. Testing and evaluating the algorithm/programming

Does it work?

Can you break it in presentation mode? Are there any circumstances where it won't work?

The menu system won't work if you type any number other than 1, 2 or 3.

How easy is it for other users to use your program? Have you asked them? Have they tried it? Can they break your program in presentation mode?

SEN Adapting for pupils with very low Maths skills.

You could easily adapt this to have the input number add 10, 100, 1000 etc or multiplied by 2, 3, 4 etc. The computational thinking and programming is the same.

Perimeter Powerpoint

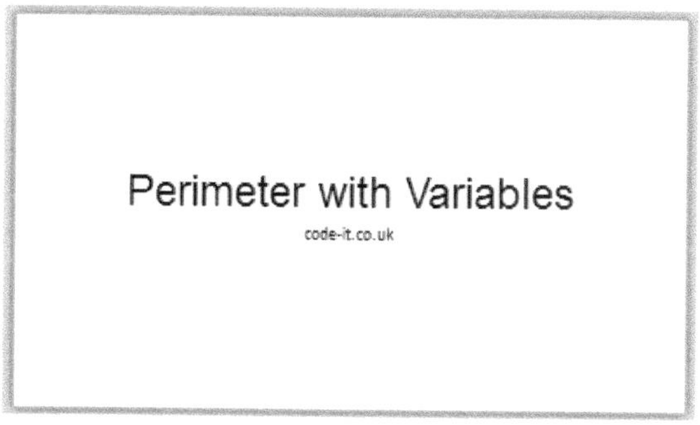
Perimeter with Variables
code-it.co.uk

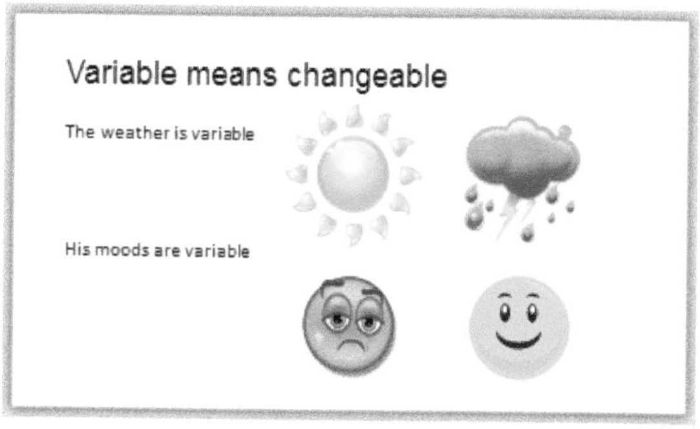
Variable means changeable
The weather is variable
His moods are variable

If we said the weather is variable what do we mean? If we said someone's moods are variable what do we mean?

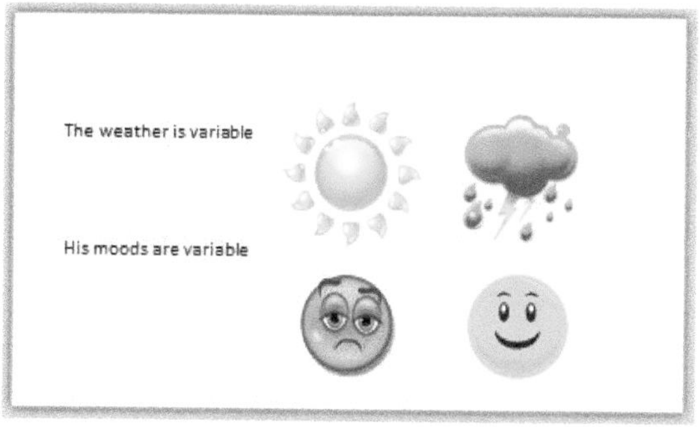
The weather is variable
His moods are variable

Correct variable means changeable. NOTE: Variables in programming can also be used to hold constant un-changing numbers or text but this knowledge can be added at a later date when the idea of storing changeable data is clearly understood.

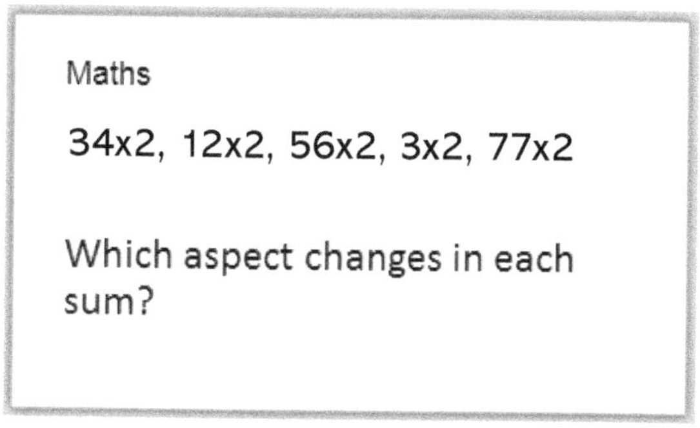
Maths
34x2, 12x2, 56x2, 3x2, 77x2
Which aspect changes in each sum?

Which aspects is changeable or variable in these sums?

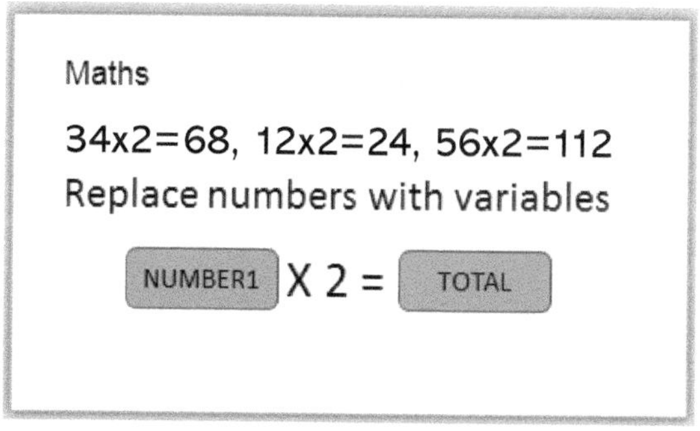
Maths
34x2=68, 12x2=24, 56x2=112
Replace numbers with variables
NUMBER1
X 2 =
TOTAL

All of the first numbers have been changed for the variable number1 and all of the totals have been changed for the total variable at the end. But this formula algorithm is still unworkable on a computer. What still needs to change? Allow thinking/discussion time.

You can find a copy of the slides online at http://code-it.co.uk/wp-content/uploads/2015/08/perimeterwithvariables.pptx

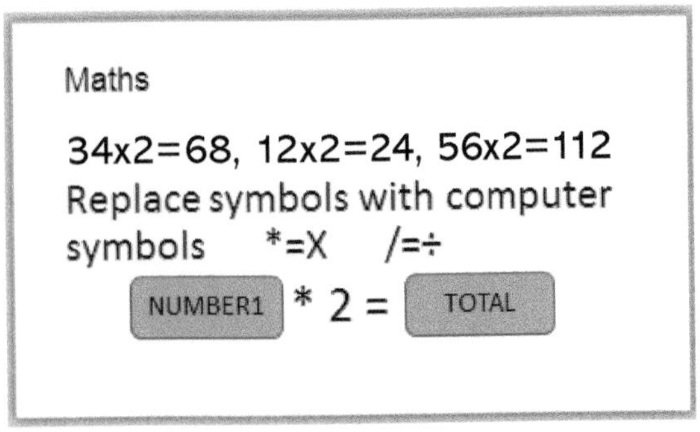
Maths
34x2=68, 12x2=24, 56x2=112
Replace symbols with computer symbols *=X /=÷
NUMBER1 * 2 = TOTAL

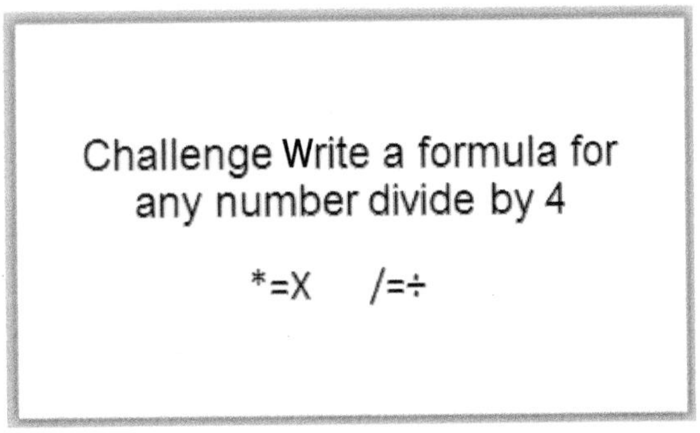
Challenge Write a formula for any number divide by 4
*=X /=÷

Well spotted

A computer can't read x as it is the letter x as in box so on a computer we need a new symbol to represent multiply and we use the asterix * symbol found above the number 8 on the keyboard.

There is also no obelus ÷ symbol on the keyboard so we use the forward slash / instead.

Write a formula with variables to divide any number by 4.

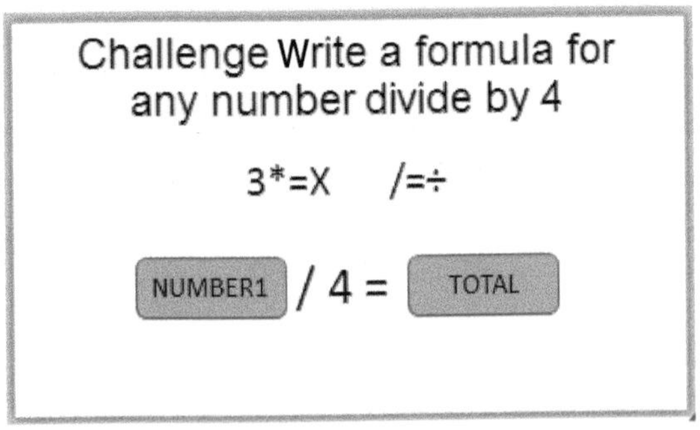
Challenge Write a formula for any number divide by 4
3*=X /=÷
NUMBER1 / 4 = TOTAL

You could also reverse the order and have Total = number1 /4.

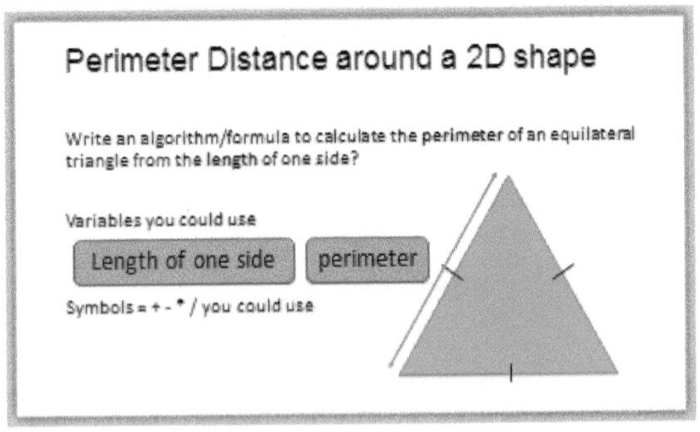
Perimeter Distance around a 2D shape
Write an algorithm/formula to calculate the perimeter of an equilateral triangle from the length of one side?
Variables you could use
Length of one side
perimeter
Symbols = + - * / you could use

Write an algorithm formula to calculate the perimeter of an equilateral triangle (where all the sides are the same length.)

You could use length of one side and perimeter variables with the correct computerised maths symbols.

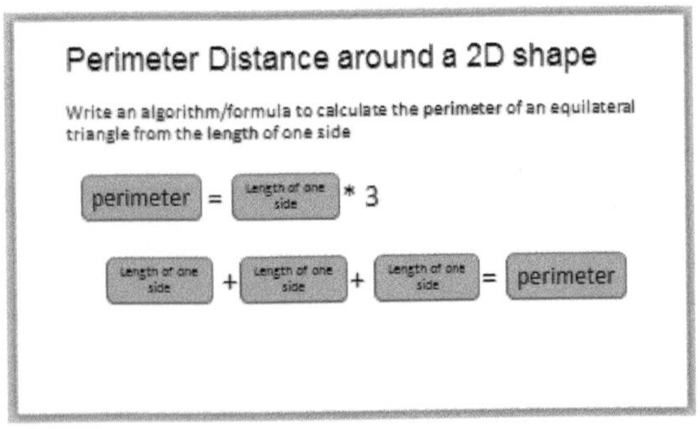
Perimeter Distance around a 2D shape
Write an algorithm/formula to calculate the perimeter of an equilateral triangle from the length of one side
perimeter = Length of one side * 3
Length of one side + Length of one side + Length of one side = perimeter

Which one did you write?

Remember the formula can go the other way round as well.

4c. Clock

Module Aim: Program a working clock from a part-complete flowchart algorithm.

Time to complete module

3 hours

Module Learning Focus

By the end of the module children will be able to:

- Interpret a flow chart algorithm
- Finish the flowchart pattern (generalisation)
- Convert the flowchart into Scratch code

Computer Science Concepts

- Repeat x times loops
- Variables in a loop
- Read and amend a flowchart algorithm
- Inputs & broadcasts
- Use a variable within a say command

Maths Concepts

- 60 seconds in a minute
- 360 degrees in circle
- 60 minutes in an hour
- Divide by 360
- 24 hours in a day

Assessment for Learning

At the end of each session direct pupils to page 11 of pupil workbook 4 to help them reflect on what they have learnt. You can also annotate this to record pupils who have needed much more support or have demonstrated greater understanding.

Adult Focus

All adults need to be clear that they are to support using hints only and not solve things for pupils.

National Curriculum Programs of Study

KS2

Pupils should be taught to:

- *design, write and debug programs that accomplish specific goals,* including controlling or simulating physical systems;
- *solve problems by decomposing them into smaller parts use sequence, selection, and repetition in programs; work with variables and various forms of input and output*
- *Use logical reasoning to explain how some simple algorithms work and to detect and correct errors in algorithms and programs*

Computational Thinking

Algorithm: a precise step by step guide to achieving a specific outcome

Generalisation: spotting the pattern where one part of the algorithm has been adapted and re-used in a similar but different way

Debugging Hints

Direct pupils back to the flowchart: have they followed the same pattern? They may need to check this step by step.

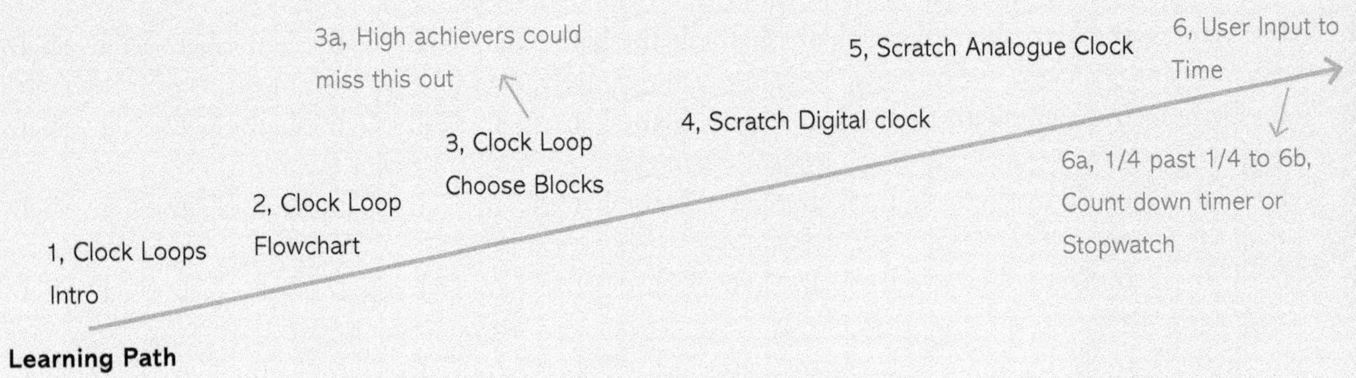
3a, High achievers could miss this out
5, Scratch Analogue Clock
6, User Input to Time
4, Scratch Digital clock
3, Clock Loop Choose Blocks
6a, 1/4 past 1/4 to 6b, Count down timer or Stopwatch
2, Clock Loop Flowchart
1, Clock Loops Intro
Learning Path

1, Clock Loops Intro

Explain to the class that today they are going to design and program a clock.
Show them this online digital clock http://www.online-stopwatch.com/large-digital-clock/ or the time on a digital watch get them to work in pairs to record what is happening to the seconds and minutes over three minutes in their pupil workbooks page 12.
Go through their answers and draw out that they are similar to the ones to the right.

Unplugged Dependency

I recommend you teach Playground Games Flow Charts before attempting this module. This can be found at http://code-it.co.uk/unplugged/ playgroundgames/playgroundoverview.html.

Thinking through the clock algorithm

Record the step by step actions that happen on a digital clock over three minutes

Every second the seconds increase by 1
This happens until the seconds reach 60
The minutes are then increased by 1
The seconds are set back to 0

What do you think will happen when the minutes reach 60?

The hours are increased by 1
The minutes are set back to 0
The seconds are set back to 0

What do you think will happen when the hours reach 24?

Seconds, minutes and hours all set back to 0

If you were coding a clock in Scratch what variables would you need to create to hold changing numbers?

Seconds
Minutes
Hours
Larger units are also correct such as
Days
Months
Years

2. Clock Loop Flowchart

Ask pupils to open the unfinished flowchart on page 13 of the pupil work book and ask them to work in pairs to fill in the missing blocks. Explain that there is a pattern where an idea has been generalised, adapted and used again. They can look back to finished parts of the flowchart or to their understanding of how a clock works to help them.

Don't explain how a flowchart works apart from to say start at start. Can they work in pairs to identify the connection between their algorithm ideas for the clock and the flow chart?

Teacher Support: You may wish to see a working copy of the code yourself to see how it works. http://scratch.mit.edu/ projects/20995628/

Correct flow chart pattern

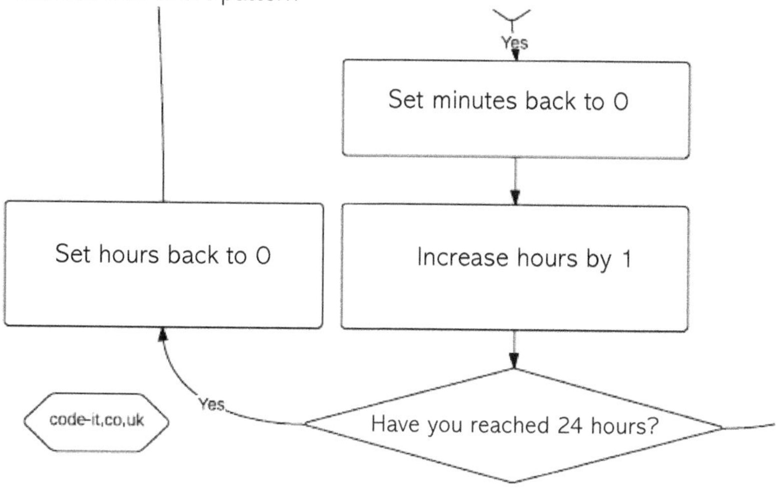
Yes
Set minutes back to 0
Set hours back to 0
Increase hours by 1
Yes
code-it,co,uk
Have you reached 24 hours?

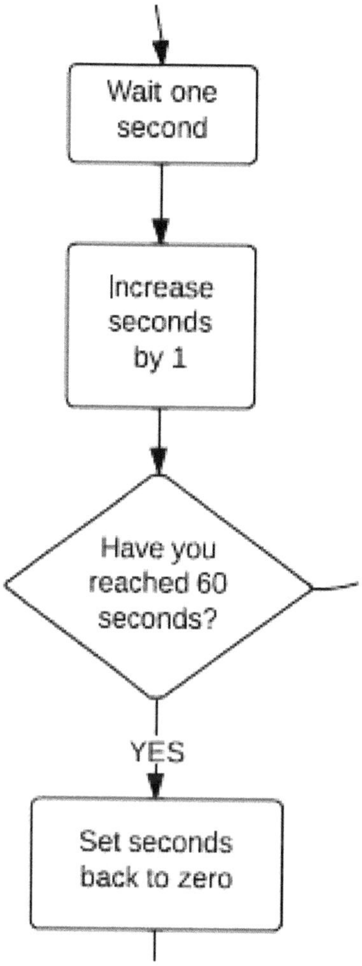
Wait one second
Increase seconds by 1
Have you reached 60 seconds?
YES
Set seconds back to zero

You may need to step through what happens with seconds with some pupils. Start from 55 seconds and work down the flowchart crossing the 60 seconds.

3, Clock Loop Match Scratch Blocks to Flow Chart

Hand out the printed Scratch blocks from page 173 of the teacher's work book and briefly remind pupils of where they may have used some of these before. Explain that their job is to match the Scratch blocks to where they would fit on the flowchart in their pupil work book. Don't place them over the flow chart shapes.

You can use the blocks match sheet to check if they have got these correct before they can start coding.

It helps if pupils work individually but discuss in pairs.

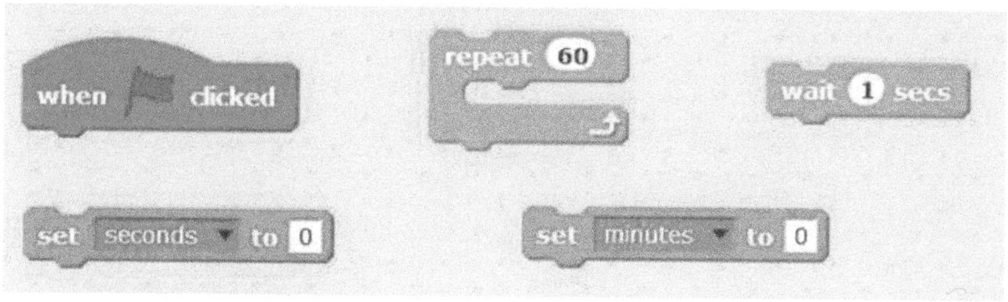
when clicked
repeat 60
wait 1 secs
set seconds to 0
set minutes to 0

4. From Flowchart algorithm to Scratch Digital Clock

Allow pupils plenty of time to work in pairs but code individually. Explain that they are not allowed to start coding the analogue hands until they have a fully functioning tested digital clock.

You may want to explain during the session that setting the **wait until less than** 1 second will speed the clock up for testing purposes.

Here are two of the most common solutions:

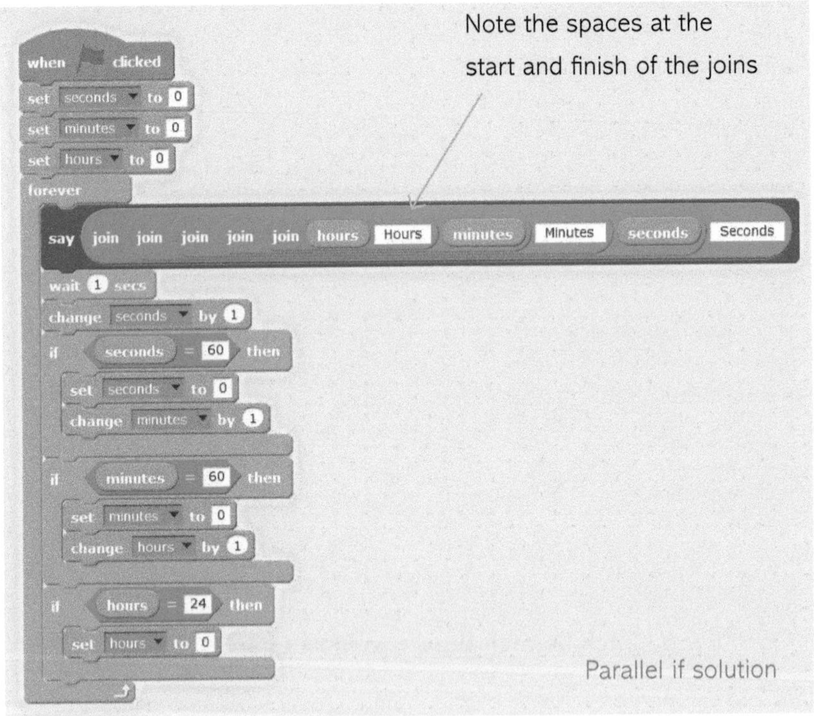
Note the spaces at the start and finish of the joins
when clicked
set seconds to 0
set minutes to 0
set hours to 0
forever
say join join join join join hours Hours minutes Minutes seconds Seconds
wait 1 secs
change seconds by 1
if seconds = 60 then
set seconds to 0
change minutes by 1
if minutes = 60 then
set minutes to 0
change hours by 1
if hours = 24 then
set hours to 0

Parallel if solution

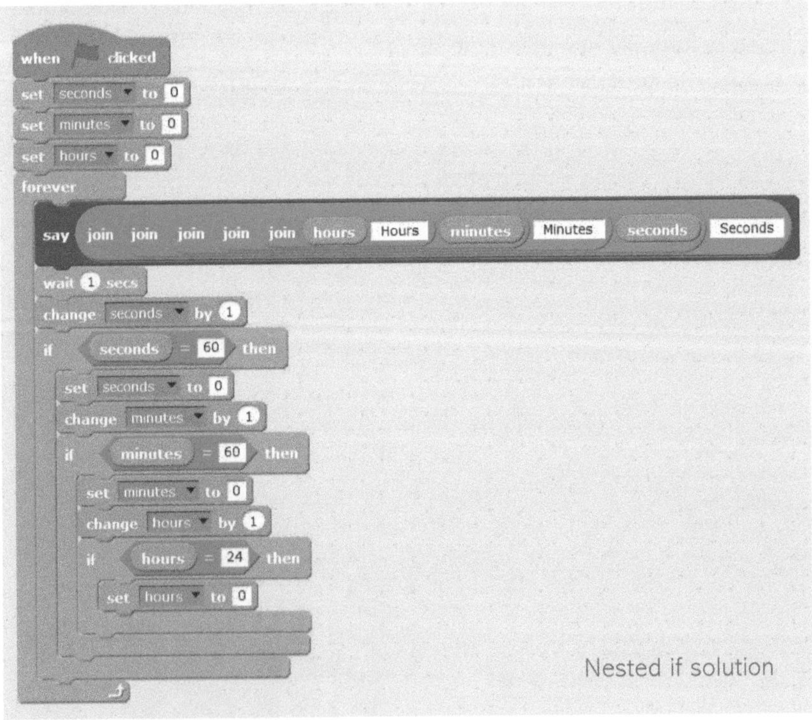
when clicked
set seconds to 0
set minutes to 0
set hours to 0
forever
say join join join join join hours Hours minutes Minutes seconds Seconds
wait 1 secs
change seconds by 1
if seconds = 60 then
set seconds to 0
change minutes by 1
if minutes = 60 then
set minutes to 0
change hours by 1
if hours = 24 then
set hours to 0

Nested if solution

Programming Efficiency

Both these solutions work well but one is slightly more efficient than the other. The nested if solutions on the right only checks minutes if seconds are equal to 60 and only checks hours if minutes are equal to 24. It runs less code each loop making it more efficient. The parallel if selection blocks checks seconds, minutes and hours every forever loop.

5. Scratch Analogue Clock

You may wish to show pupils how to create hands that will easily rotate.

Create a new sprite and name it **seconds.**

Draw a thin straight line for the second hand making sure it is drawn facing right.

Use the centre tool to set the centre on the far left end of the line.

Do the same for the minutes and hours.

Arrange them all so the left hand ends all line up.

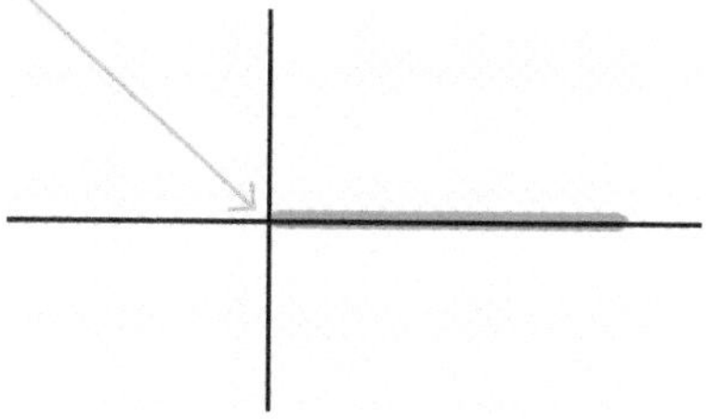

Don't help with the coding of these other than to remind pupils that there are 360 degrees in a circle. You may need to help pupils with Maths SEN.

They will need to divide 360 by 60 for the seconds and minutes.

They will need to divide 360 by 12 for the hours.

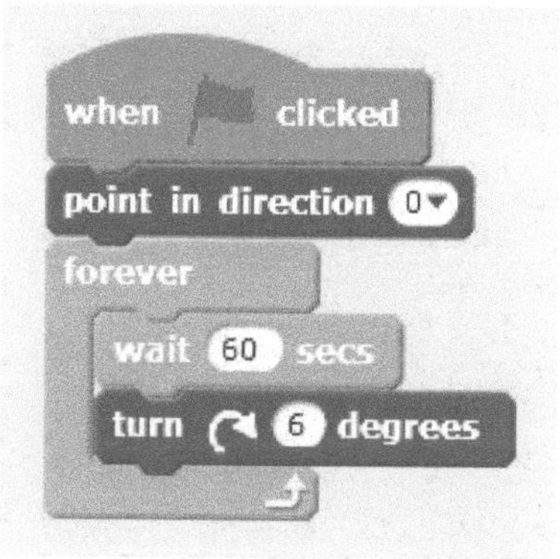
when clicked
point in direction 0
forever
wait 60 secs
turn 6 degrees

Minutes example

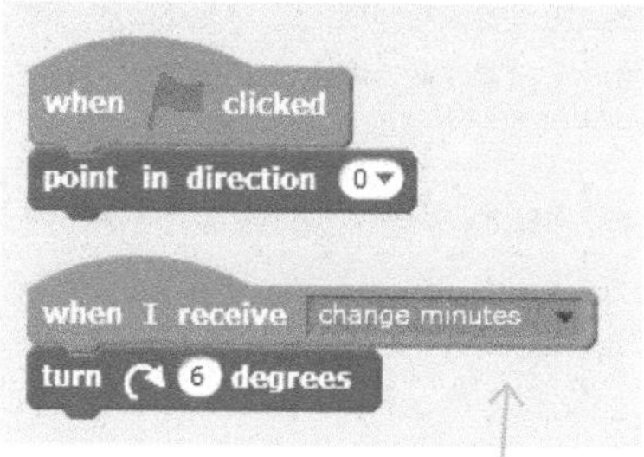
when clicked
point in direction 0
when I receive change minutes
turn 6 degrees

This minutes example uses a broadcast command triggered within the main clock code.

You can watch a video explaining how broadcasts work here https://youtu.be/BwFT6dYAUzO

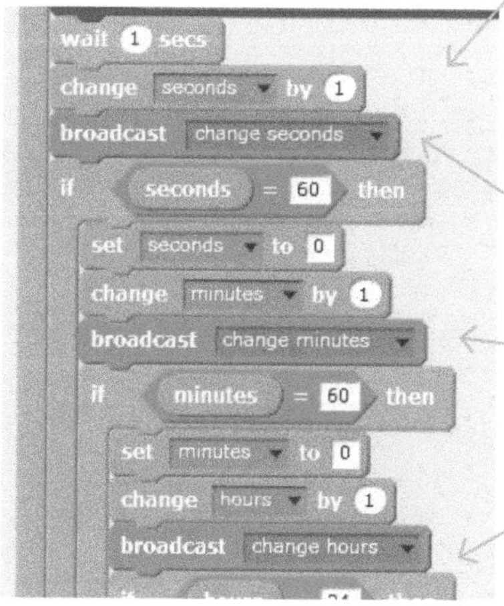
wait 1 secs
change seconds by 1
broadcast change seconds
if seconds = 60 then
set seconds to 0
change minutes by 1
broadcast change minutes
if minutes = 60 then
set minutes to 0
change hours by 1
broadcast change hours

Broadcasts triggered

ask What's your name? and wait

answer

6. User Input to time

Clocks need to be set to the correct time.

Can the pupils think of a way to do this?

Ask input blocks feeding into initial variable setting would be the easiest way.

Can pupils think of a way to stop someone inputting a number that was outside the range of correct possibilities such as 25 hours? There are good opportunities here for initial discussion around error-checking by programs.

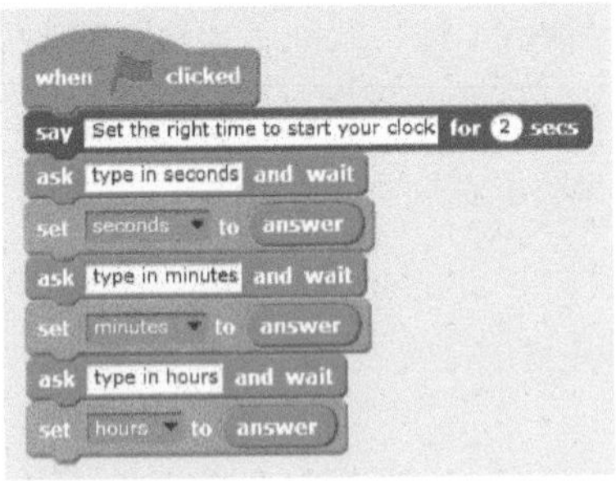
when clicked
say Set the right time to start your clock for 2 secs
ask type in seconds and wait
set seconds to answer
ask type in minutes and wait
set minutes to answer
ask type in hours and wait
set hours to answer

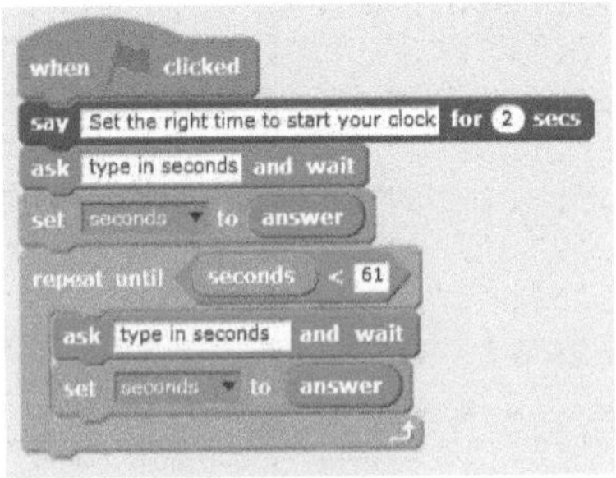
when clicked
say Set the right time to start your clock for 2 secs
ask type in seconds and wait
set seconds to answer
repeat until seconds < 61
ask type in seconds and wait
set seconds to answer

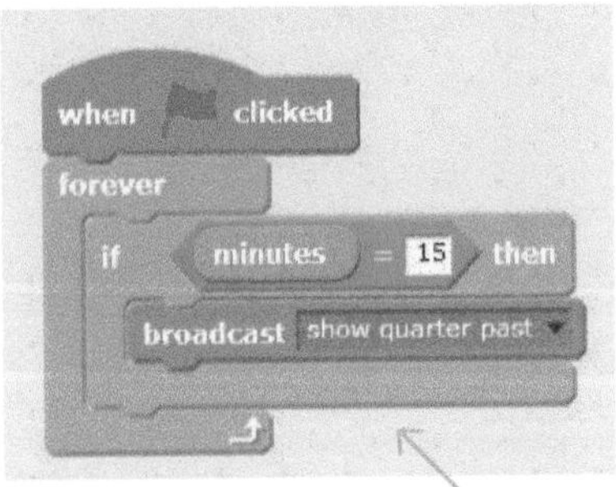
when clicked
forever
if minutes = 15 then
broadcast show quarter past

Quarter Past

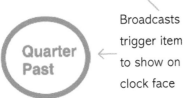

Broadcasts trigger item to show on clock face

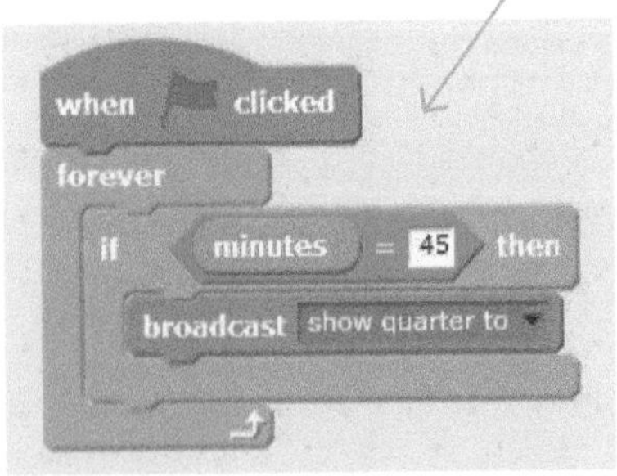
when clicked
forever
if minutes = 45 then
broadcast show quarter to

6a. Clock Face

Can pupils design a clock face to go with their analogue clock which features 1/4 past the hour and 1/4 to the hour when these are being shown by the hands?

6b. Stopwatch or Count Down Timer

Can pupils repurpose this to make either a count down timer or a stopwatch with tenths or hundredth of a second?

Count down will change variables by -1.

Stopwatch will need new tenth and hundredth variable.

Tenth change variable by 0.1.

Hundredth change variable by 0.01.

Thousandth change variable by 0.001.

Print extra independent extension activities in the pupil books and send them home

Clock Code Blocks

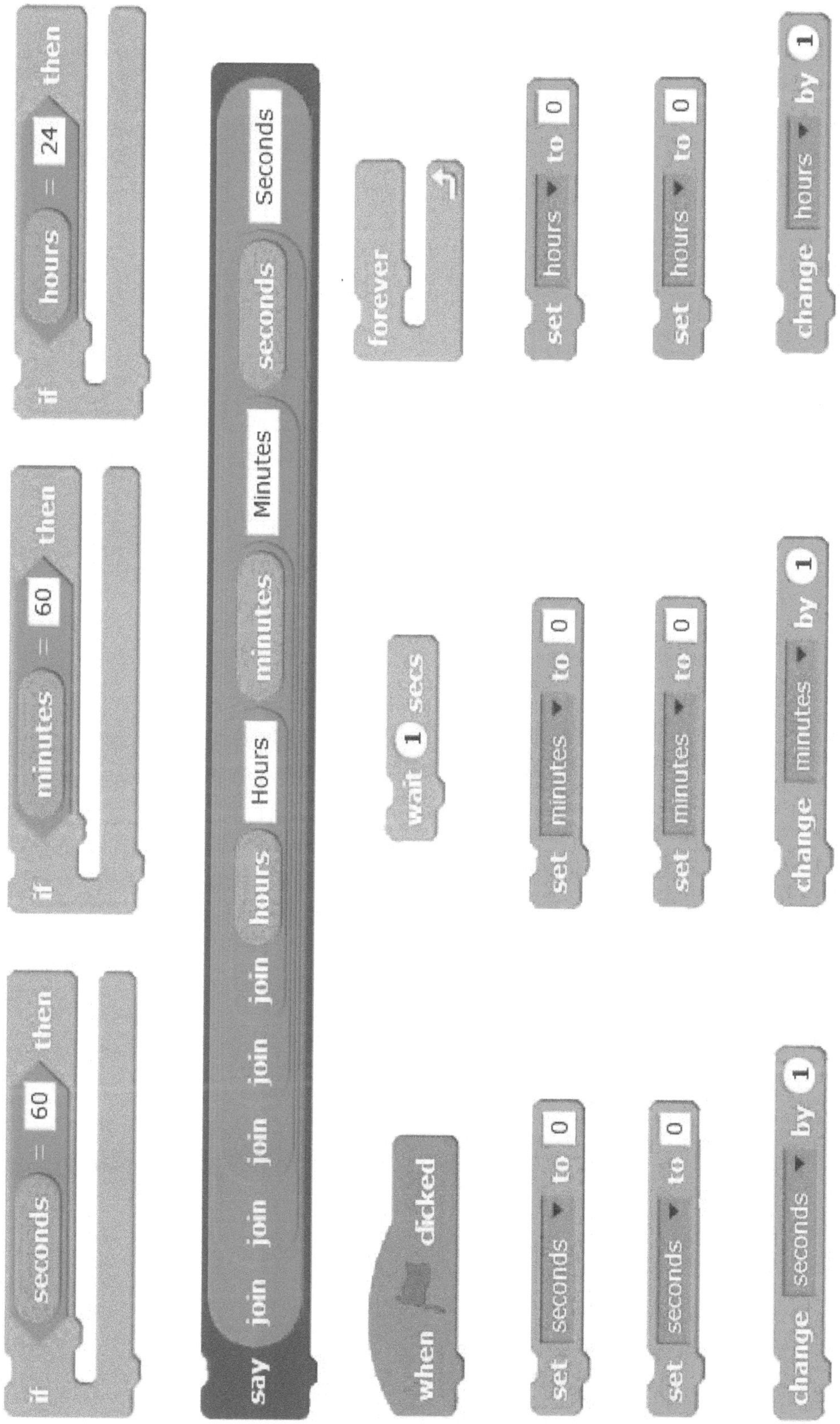
if seconds = 60 then
if minutes = 60 then
if hours = 24 then
say join join join join hours Hours minutes Minutes seconds Seconds
when clicked
wait 1 secs
forever
set seconds to 0
set minutes to 0
set hours to 0
set seconds to 0
set minutes to 0
set hours to 0
change seconds by 1
change minutes by 1
change hours by 1

Blocks Match Sheet

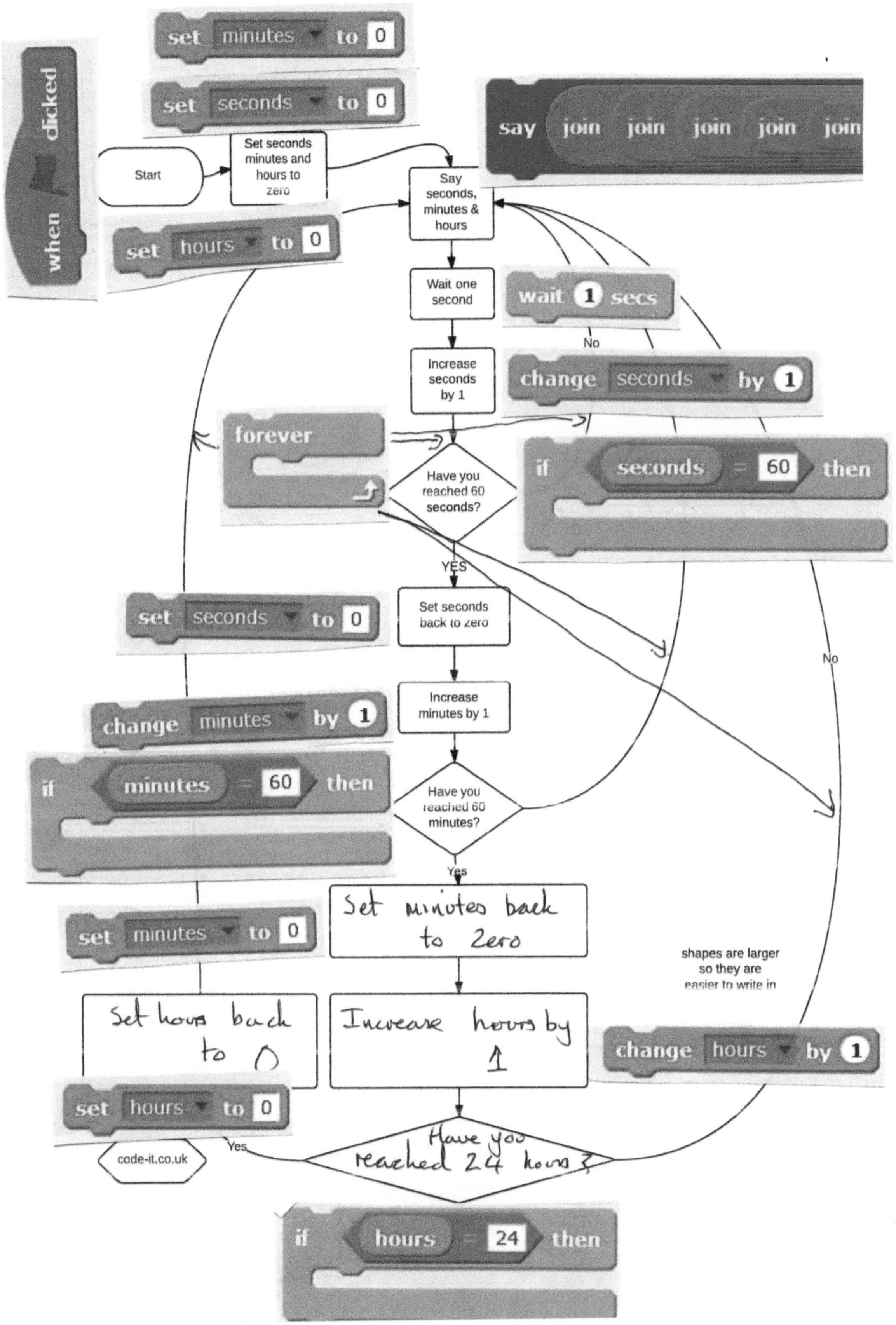
set minutes to 0
set seconds to 0
when clicked
Start
Set seconds minutes and hours to zero
say join join join join join
Say seconds, minutes & hours
set hours to 0
Wait one second
wait 1 secs
No
Increase seconds by 1
change seconds by 1
forever
Have you reached 60 seconds?
if seconds = 60 then
YES
set seconds to 0
Set seconds back to zero
No
change minutes by 1
Increase minutes by 1
if minutes = 60 then
Have you reached 60 minutes?
Yes
Set minutes back to Zero
set minutes to 0
shapes are larger so they are easier to write in
Set hours back to 0
Increase hours by 1
change hours by 1
set hours to 0
code-it.co.uk
Yes
Have you reached 24 hours?
if hours = 24 then

4D. Cartesian Coordinates

Module Aim Expand pupils knowledge of coordinates into all four quadrants

Time to complete module

3 hours

Module Learning Focus

By the end of the module children will be able to:

- Map coordinates in all four quadrants on the planner
- Test their planner algorithm in Scratch code and debug if necessary
- Examine reflection

Computer Science Concepts

- X & Y coordinates to place sprites
- Sequence of code
- Pen blocks (pen up, pen down and clear)

Maths Concepts

- Cartesian Coordinates
- Reflection of shapes into second, third and fourth quadrants

Differentiation and Assessment for Learning

At the beginning of each session the learning intention sheet page 15 is shared and the learning journey expanded through success criteria. Pupils feed their progress back to the teacher through annotating this sheet with smiley faces during or at the end of the lesson. Teachers can also annotate the sheet to indicate those who need more or less help in future lessons.

Adult Focus

All adults need to be clear that they are to support using hints only and not solve things for pupils.

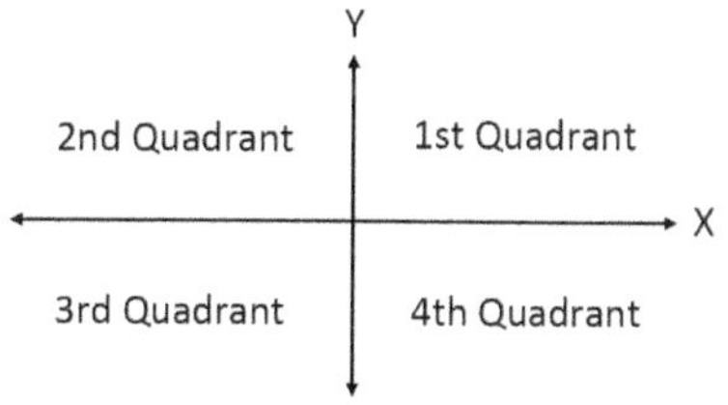
Y
2nd Quadrant
1st Quadrant
X
3rd Quadrant
4th Quadrant

National Curriculum Programs of Study

KS2

Pupils should be taught to:

- ***design, write and debug programs that accomplish specific goals,*** including controlling or simulating physical systems; solve problems by decomposing them into smaller parts
- ***use sequence,*** selection, and repetition ***in programs; work with variables*** and various forms of input and output
- ***use logical reasoning to explain how some simple algorithms work and to detect and correct errors in algorithms and programs***

Debugging Hints

Rarely are bugs difficult in coding problems in this module. They often stem from coordinates written the wrong way round on the planner or pen commands placed in the wrong places. Get pupils to show you how they mapped the coordinates to ascertain if it is a maths bug.

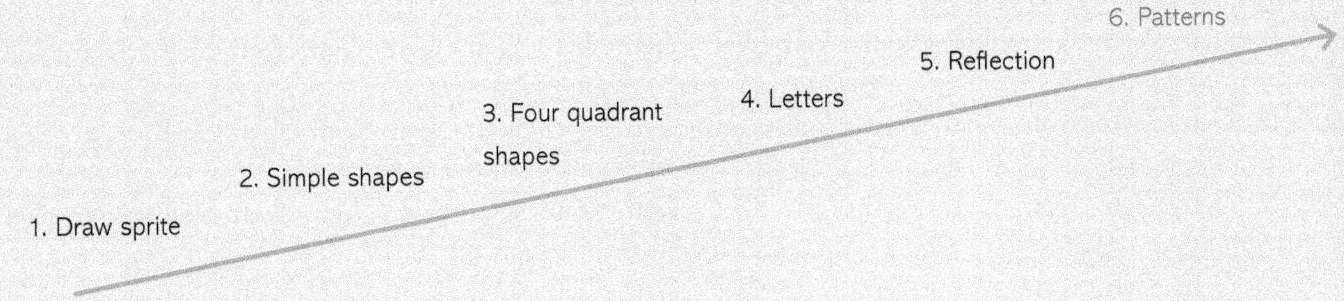
1. Draw sprite
2. Simple shapes
3. Four quadrant shapes
4. Letters
5. Reflection
6. Patterns

Learning Path

Resources

1st Quadrant planner imported into display planner such as Smart notebook or Promethean http://code-it.co.uk/bookmedia

1st Quadrant planner found in pupils workbook 4 page 16.

4 Quadrant planner found in pupil .workbook 4 page 17

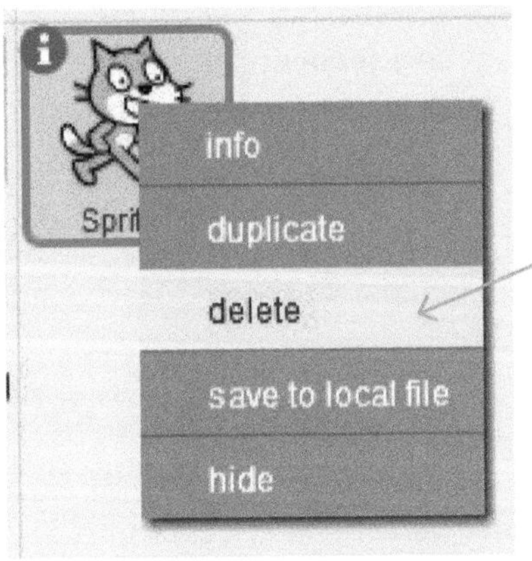
info
duplicate
delete
save to local file
hide

1. Draw Sprite

Open a blank copy of Scratch.

Delete the cat (right click and select delete).

Paint new sprite button.

Drag the line width to about a third.

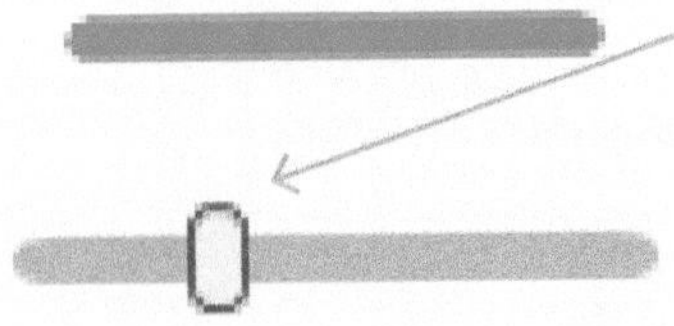

Place one small red dot on the screen.

2. Simple shapes

Show pupils how to open the XY Grid background.

Choose backdrop from library.

The XY Grid is the last one at the bottom.

Stage
1 backdrop
New backdrop:
Choose backdrop from library

Point out the four quadrants and explain that the first quadrant is the one that they have mainly used in Maths in the past. Display the first quadrant resource and demonstrate plotting three points and drawing a simple triangle, recording each coordinate on the planner. Stress how important it is first to plan their algorithm carefully before programming.

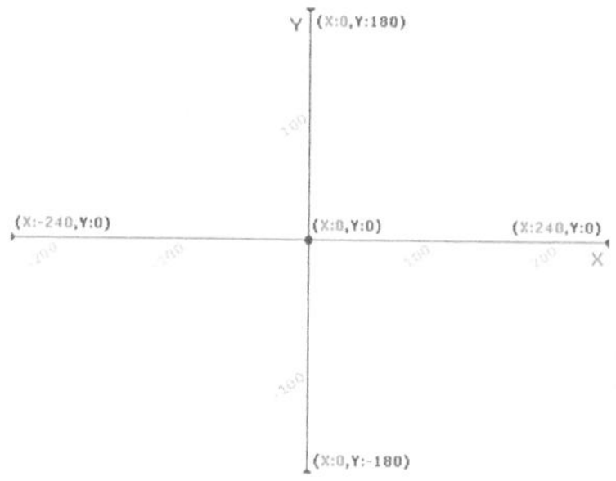
Y
(X:0,Y:180)
(X:-240,Y:0)
(X:0,Y:0)
(X:240,Y:0)
X
(X:0,Y:-180)

I often employ "along the corridor and up and down the stairs/lift" to remind pupils of the correct order and stress recording the coordinates next to each other, not above or below each other.

Check their paper coordinates before allowing them to try and convert this into Scratch code using the glide to X and Y blocks.

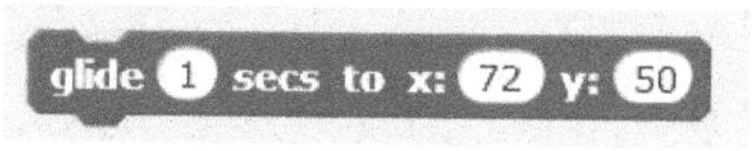
glide 1 secs to x: 72 y: 50

If pupils struggle ask them what they have used to draw lines in the past in the Smoking Car or Slug Trail Game.

pen down
pen up

An example triangle

Pen up stops Scratch drawing a line from the last position.

After you have reached the first coordinate put the pen down to start drawing.

Finally, don't forget to return to your starting position.

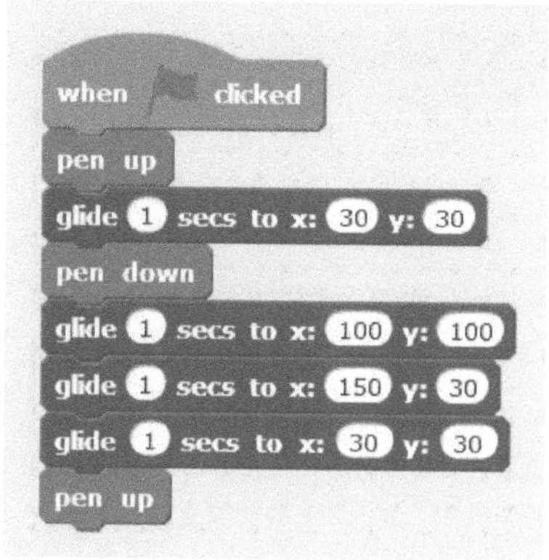
when clicked
pen up
glide 1 secs to x: 30 y: 30
pen down
glide 1 secs to x: 100 y: 100
glide 1 secs to x: 150 y: 30
glide 1 secs to x: 30 y: 30
pen up

2. Simple shapes continued

As pupils finish direct them to plan an algorithm for:

- Steps
- Rectangle
- Irregular pentagon

After they have planned their algorithm on paper they can convert their algorithm into code using Scratch.

Shape management

Allow pupils to choose their own ways of managing their shapes. Some will place each shape in its own block started by a different key board inputs. Some will use new sprites for each shape?

Useful Hint

Look for those who are not recording on the sheet and go over it with them showing them how to do a few coordinates and then leave them to do the rest themselves.

3. Four Quadrant shapes

As pupils finish the first quadrant challenges, show them the four quadrant planner in their pupil workbooks page 17. Demonstrate how this follows the same principles but uses negative numbers. Give them a simple shape that crosses into multiple quadrants. Can they plan those coordinates and show you before coding.

I have a very annoying video that helps some pupils remember the coordinate order:
https://www.youtube.com/watch?v=v_kVJAovOWY&feature=youtu.be

4. Letters

As pupils finish direct them to code 2d letters, using their algorithm planner before coding. You can extend to 3d shapes for the most able.

5. Reflection

Bring all the pupils together who have demonstrated that they understand the tasks so far and explain that you can make your letters reflect in every quadrant and that it take just a few minutes.

http://scratch.mit.edu/projects/17198623/

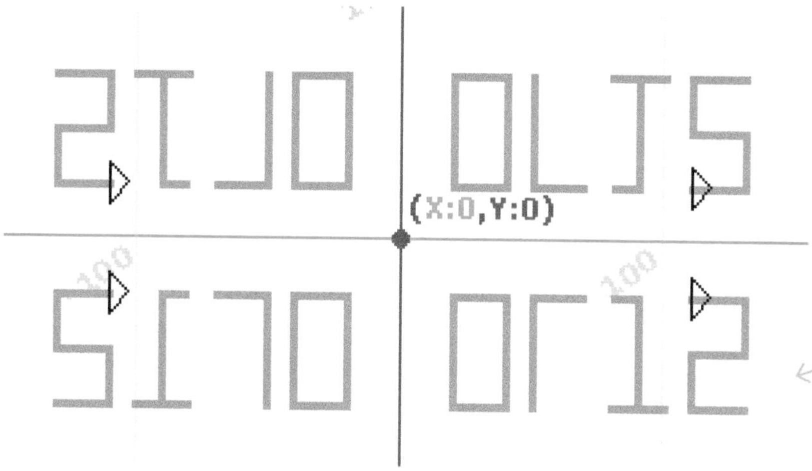
(X:0,Y:0)

Open the example and explain how you just duplicated the code and changed just one thing. Attach the green flag blocks unconnected inside sprites 2, 3 & 4 and run the code.

The finished reflected pattern looks like this.

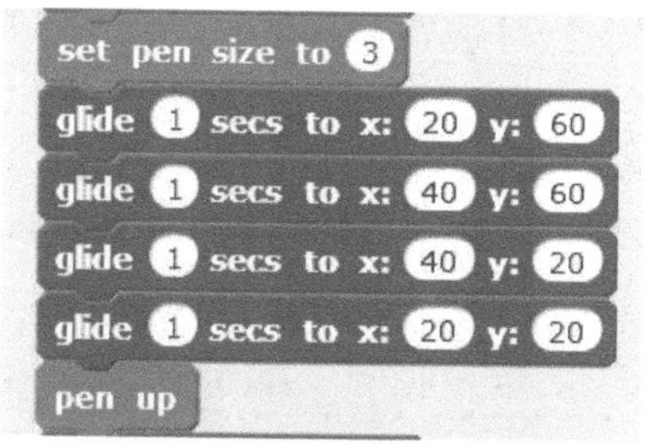
set pen size to 3
glide 1 secs to x: 20 y: 60
glide 1 secs to x: 40 y: 60
glide 1 secs to x: 40 y: 20
glide 1 secs to x: 20 y: 20
pen up

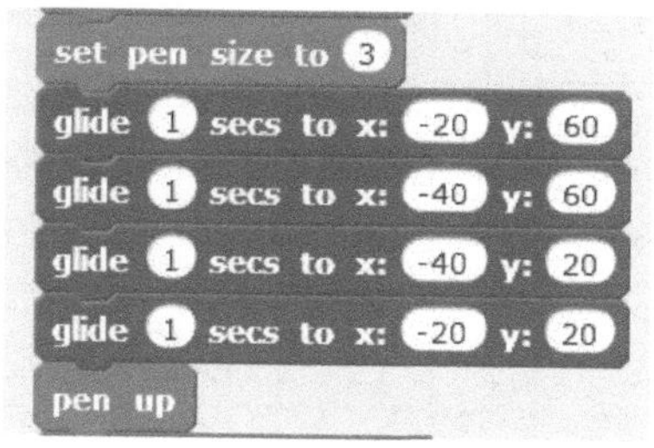
set pen size to 3
glide 1 secs to x: -20 y: 60
glide 1 secs to x: -40 y: 60
glide 1 secs to x: -40 y: 20
glide 1 secs to x: -20 y: 20
pen up

Now show pupils the code in sprite 1 and ask them to look at the first four x and y blocks. Open up the code in sprites 2, 3 and 4 and ask them what is different. They will spot that either X or Y or both has been changed to a negative number. Can they use that knowledge to make their shapes or letters reflect?

6. Patterns

Can they create a reflected pattern using all four quadrants?

This module can be taught alongside the next module extending the more able student to explore other aspects of coordinates such as translation, enlargement and simple rotation.

Print extra independent extension activities in the pupil books and send them home

Four Quadrant Planner

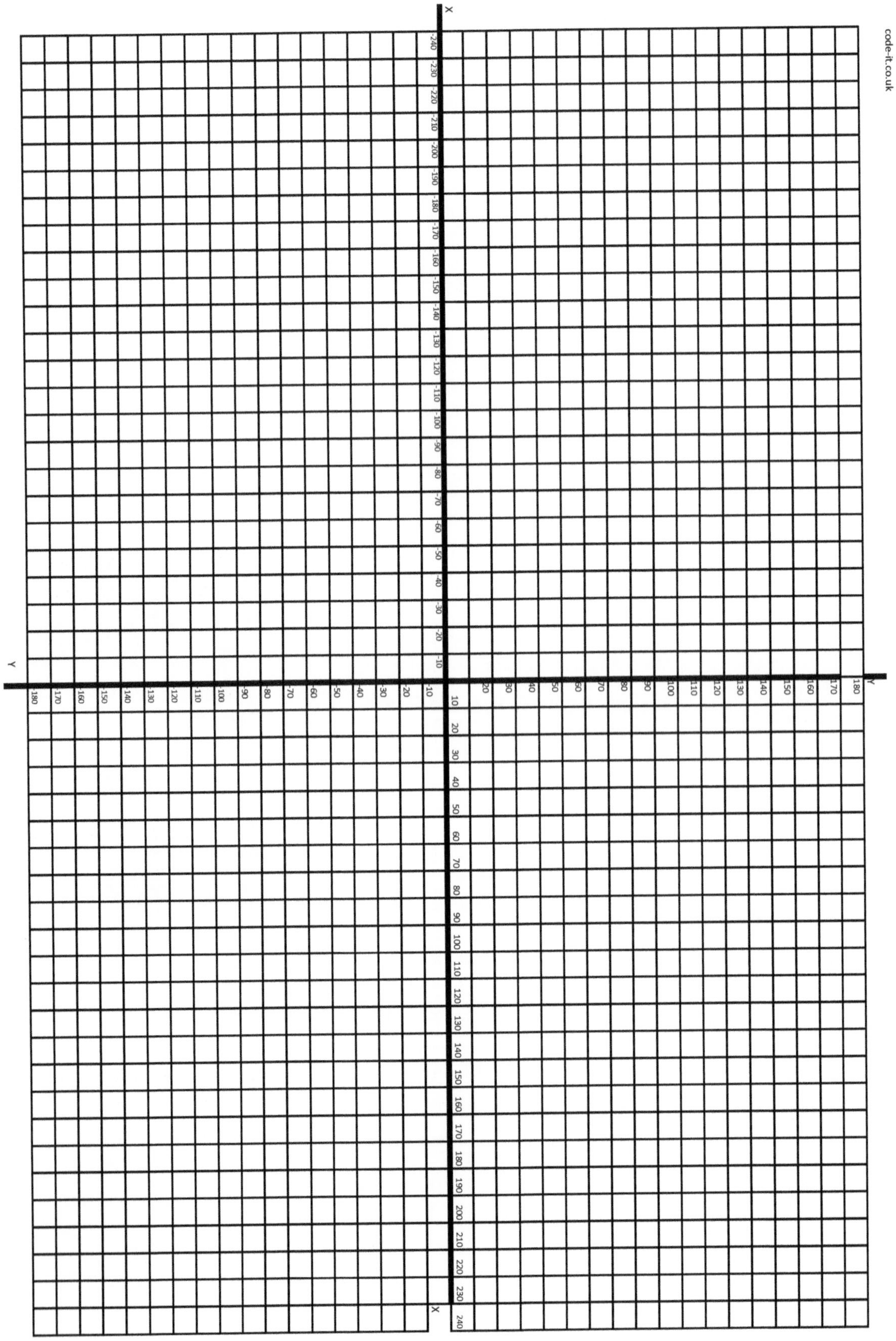
X
Y
code-it.co.uk

4E. Translation, Enlargement & 1/4 Turn Rotation

Module Aim: To explore translation, enlargement and rotation shapes drawn using coordinates

Time to complete module

Variable depending on focus

Module Learning Focus

Learning focus is dependent on how many of these pupils investigate and whether they attempt to create their own version.

Computer Science Concepts

By the end of the module children will be able to:

- Use X & Y coordinates to place sprites
- Report X & Y coordinate positions
- Use variables to adjust X and Y

Maths Concepts

- Cartesian Coordinates
- Reflection of shapes into second third and fourth quadrants
- Translating shapes into other positions (add to X & Y)
- Enlargement of shapes (multiply X & Y)
- Simple rotation of shape through multiples of 90 degrees

Assessment for Learning

At the end of each session direct pupils to page 19 of pupil workbook 4 to help them reflect on what they have learnt. You can also annotate this to record pupils who have needed much more support or have demonstrated greater understanding.

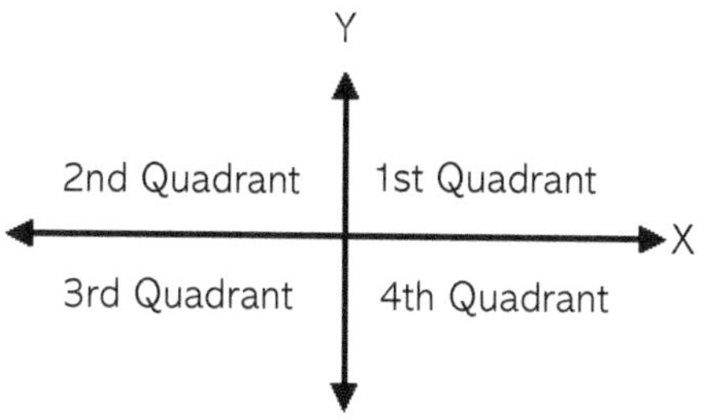
Y
X
2nd Quadrant
1st Quadrant
3rd Quadrant
4th Quadrant

National Curriculum Programs of Study

KS2

Pupils should be taught to:

- *design, write and debug programs that accomplish specific goals,* including controlling or simulating physical systems; *solve problems by decomposing them into smaller parts*
- *use sequence,* selection, and repetition *in programs; work with variables and various forms of input and output*
- *use logical reasoning to explain how some simple algorithms work and to detect and correct errors in algorithms and programs*

Computational Thinking

Decomposition: break up a problem into sections and solve each section separately

Evaluation: looking at the most efficient or best code.

Activities

Exploring translation

This is the simplest activity which involves using the programs to explore what happens to X & Y when positive or negative numbers are added to all the X and Y coordinates. Either Download and load the **triangle translator** from http://code-it.co.uk/bookmedia into either Scratch 1.4 or Scratch 2.0 or view the program online at https://scratch.mit.edu/projects/55592332/.

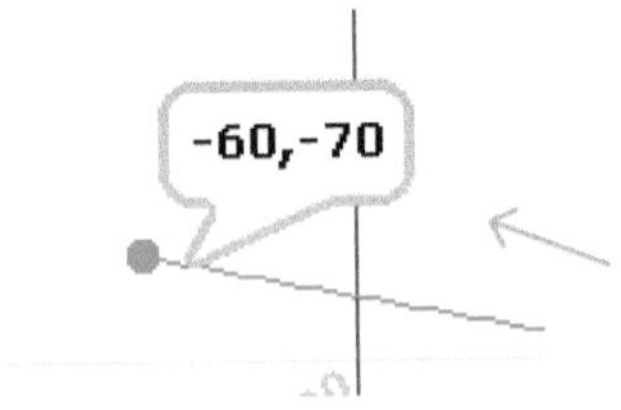
-60,-70

Although the download code was designed in 1.4 it will upload and work perfectly well in Scratch 2.0.

Run the program in presentation mode so that pupils are unable to see the code. Get pupils to note one pair of reported coordinates then add 10 to this number and ask them what has happened to the coordinates when the shape is translated. Repeat with positive Y numbers before moving on to ask what would happen to negative numbers. Can pupils find numbers to add that would place the shapes wholly in a single quadrant? Pupils could mirror this activity off screen adding a fixed amount to all X coordinates and plotting the positions of the shapes. Finally allow pupils to see the code. Can they explain how it works?

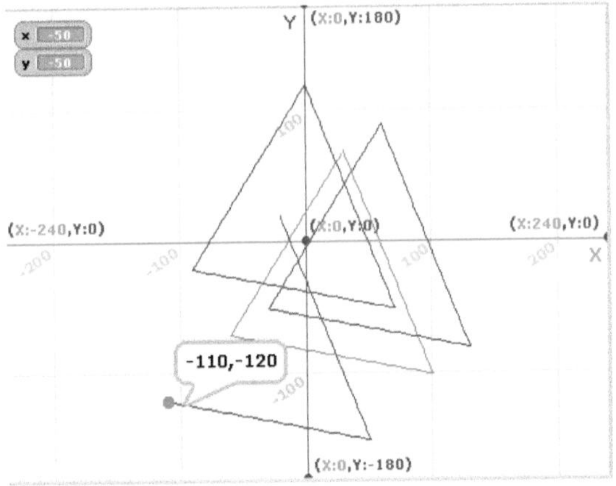
Y
(X:0,Y:180)
(X:-240,Y:0)
(X:0,Y:0)
(X:240,Y:0)
X
-110,-120
(X:0,Y:-180)

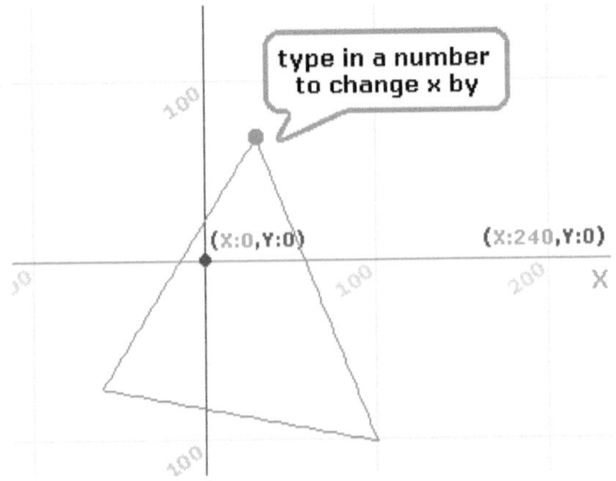
type in a number
to change x by
(X:0,Y:0)
(X:240,Y:0)
X

Exploring Enlargement

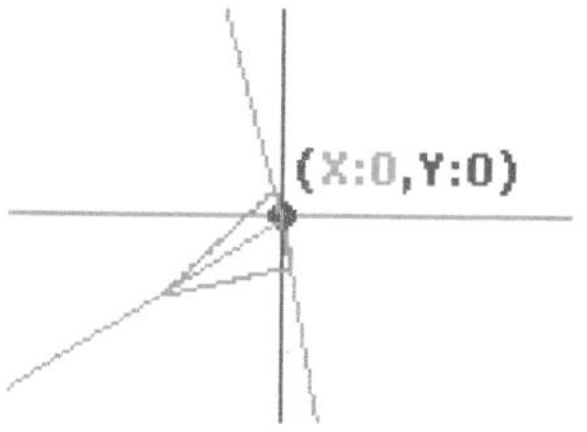
(X:0,Y:0)

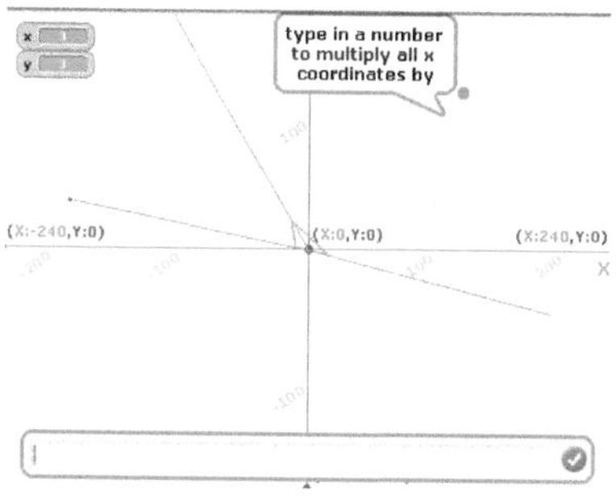
type in a number to multiply all x coordinates by
(X:-240,Y:0)
(X:0,Y:0)
(X:240,Y:0)

This activity involves using the program to explore what happens when the X and Y coordinate values are multiplied. Either download and load the **enlargement1** code from http://code-it.co.uk/bookmedia into either Scratch 1.4 or Scratch 2.0. Or browse to https://scratch.mit.edu/projects/55593716/. Although the download code was designed in 1.4 it will upload and work perfectly well in Scratch 2.0. Ask pupils if adding a number to the coordinate values (moved) translated the shape, then what would you need to do to the X and Y coordinates to enlarge it? (Answer: multiply it). Run the program in presentation mode so that pupils are unable to see the code. Give pupils time to enlarge the shape. They are only limited by the size of the screen. Can they also shrink the shape? (multiply x and y by a decimal fraction less then 1 such as 0.5). Now either download **enlargement2** from http://code-it.co.uk/bookmedia *or view it online at* https://scratch.mit.edu/projects/55594694/. Note with pupils how this draws a line from the centre of enlargement (0,0 in this case) through each pair of coordinates. Give pupils time to explore enlarging shapes: what do they notice about these lines? (If X and Y are enlarged equally the shape coordinates will always lie on these lines). What do pupils think will happen if they multiply by a negative number? Why not explore a negative and a positive number?

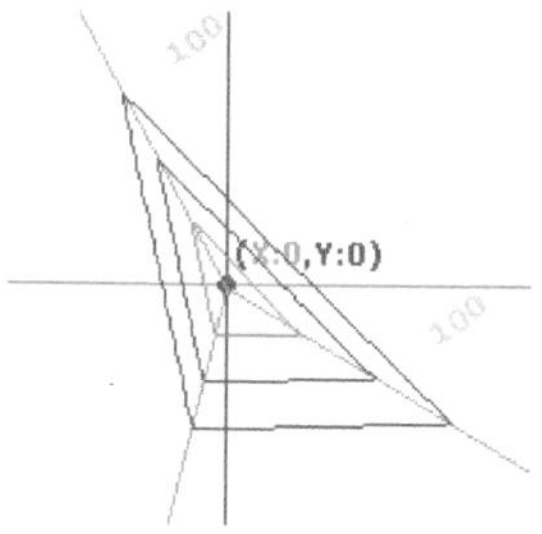

A shape where x and y are enlarged equally in every case

If you wanted your pupils to explore enlargement in just the first quadrant first, then change the range of random generated numbers to positive numbers only.

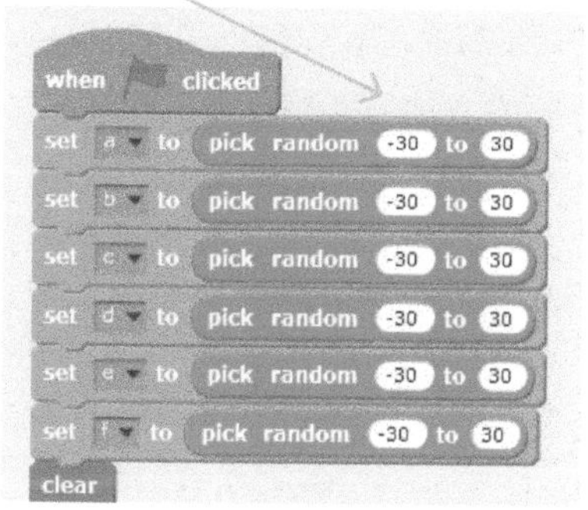
when clicked
set a to pick random -30 to 30
set b to pick random -30 to 30
set c to pick random -30 to 30
set d to pick random -30 to 30
set e to pick random -30 to 30
set f to pick random -30 to 30
clear

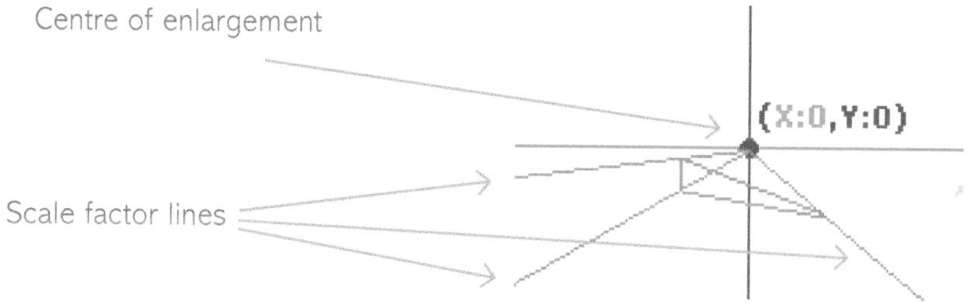
Centre of enlargement
Scale factor lines
(X:0,Y:0)

When exploring multiplying by negative numbers you may wish to use **enlargement3** which has a reverse scale factor line drawn at 180 degrees. You can download this from http://code-it.co.uk/bookmedia. Although this code is written in Scratch 1.4 it will upload and work perfectly in Scratch 2.0. Or you can view the program online at https://scratch.mit.edu/projects/55595646/.

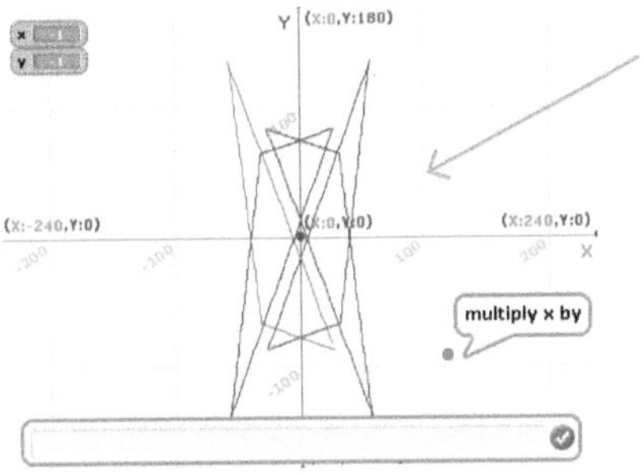
Y (X:0,Y:180)
(X:-240,Y:0)
(X:0,Y:0)
(X:240,Y:0)
X
multiply x by

Exploring ¼ Turn Rotation

Pupils may already have discovered that by multiplying either X or Y or both by a negative 1, then the shape will rotate and mirror for 90° and 270°, but rotate correctly for 180° degrees as shown.

For 90 degrees to truly rotate without mirroring 90° (X, Y) becomes (Y, -X)

180° (X, Y) becomes (-X, -Y) (rotated correctly)

270° (X, Y) becomes (-Y, X) So to rotate a quarter and three quarter turns we need to swap the x and y coordinates as well as make one set of coordinates negative which can be done by multiplying it by -1.

> Please note, mathematicians would assume that the direction of rotation would be anticlockwise as default, where Scratch rotates clockwise by default. A default anticlockwise rotation would lead to the 90° and 270° values identified above being swapped.

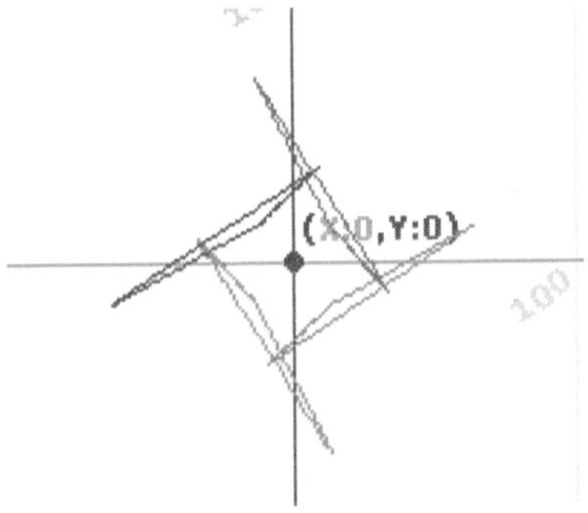
(X:0,Y:0)
100

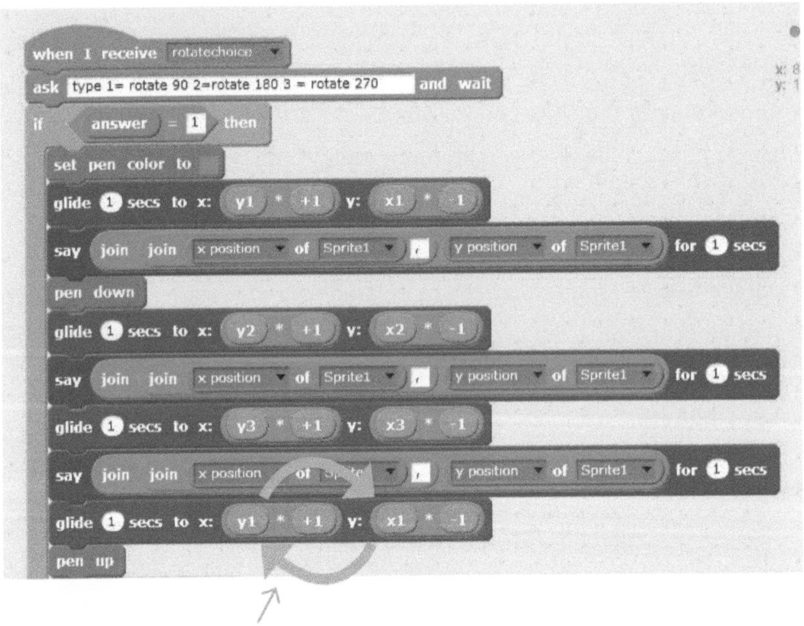
when I receive rotatechoice
ask type 1= rotate 90 2=rotate 180 3 = rotate 270 and wait
if answer = 1 then
set pen color to
glide 1 secs to x: y1 * +1 y: x1 * -1
say join join x position of Sprite1 , y position of Sprite1 for 1 secs
pen down
glide 1 secs to x: y2 * +1 y: x2 * -1
say join join x position of Sprite1 , y position of Sprite1 for 1 secs
glide 1 secs to x: y3 * +1 y: x3 * -1
say join join x position of , y position of Sprite1 for 1 secs
glide 1 secs to x: y1 * +1 y: x1 * -1
pen up

In this code to rotate 90° the X and Y values have been swapped and the Y value has been converted into a negative by multiplying it by -1.

Pupils can explore this using **rotate** which can be downloaded from http://code-it.co.uk/bookmedia and uploaded into either Scratch 1.4 or Scratch 2.0. Or the program can be viewed in a browser at https://scratch.mit.edu/projects/55596168/.

Cartesian Coordinate Translation, Enlargement & Rotation Programming Projects

Decomposing the main elements of the program before building their own version

Use the decomposed planner sheet available on page 20.

There is an answer sheet following this planning.

Once pupils have decomposed the program they can proceed to build their own version.

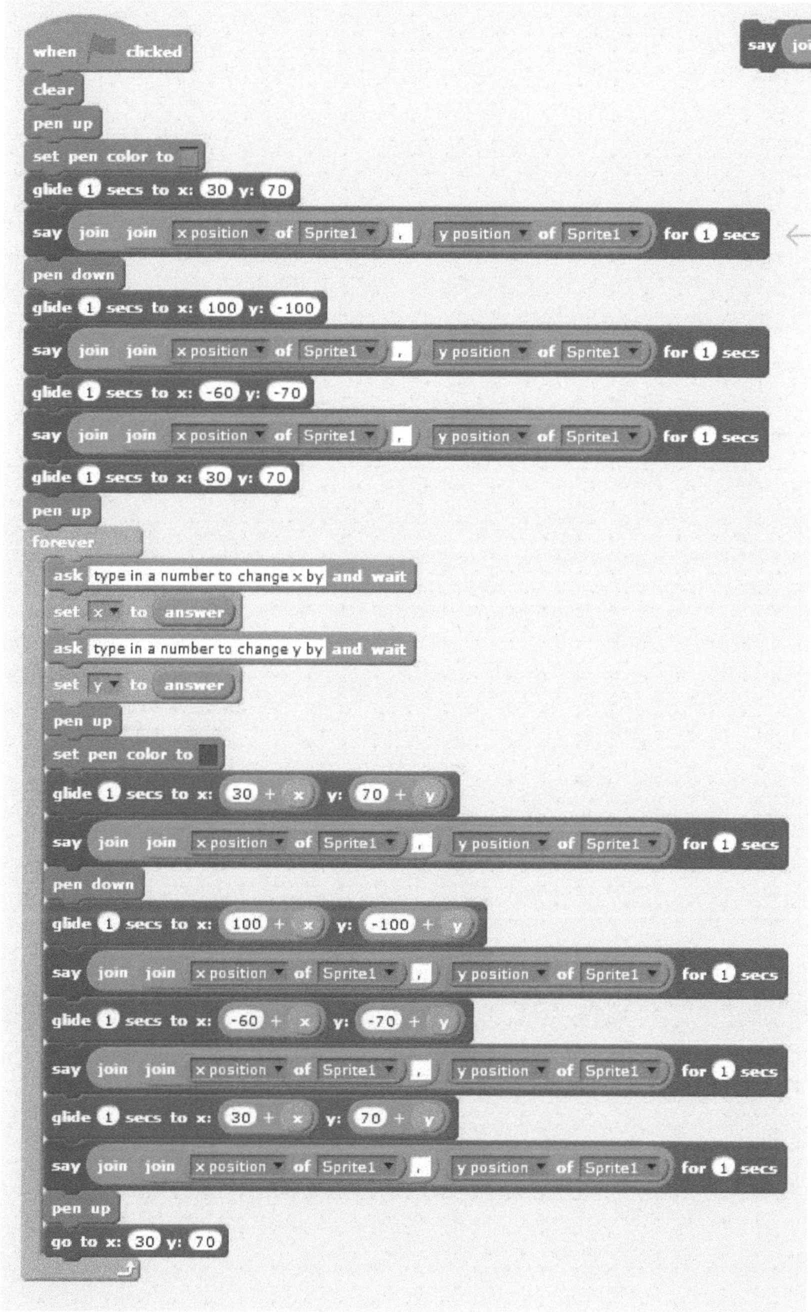
when clicked
clear
pen up
set pen color to
glide 1 secs to x: 30 y: 70
say join join x position of Sprite1 , y position of Sprite1 for 1 secs
pen down
glide 1 secs to x: 100 y: -100
say join join x position of Sprite1 , y position of Sprite1 for 1 secs
glide 1 secs to x: -60 y: -70
say join join x position of Sprite1 , y position of Sprite1 for 1 secs
glide 1 secs to x: 30 y: 70
pen up
forever
ask type in a number to change x by and wait
set x to answer
ask type in a number to change y by and wait
set y to answer
pen up
set pen color to
glide 1 secs to x: 30 + x y: 70 + y
say join join x position of Sprite1 , y position of Sprite1 for 1 secs
pen down
glide 1 secs to x: 100 + x y: -100 + y
say join join x position of Sprite1 , y position of Sprite1 for 1 secs
glide 1 secs to x: -60 + x y: -70 + y
say join join x position of Sprite1 , y position of Sprite1 for 1 secs
glide 1 secs to x: 30 + x y: 70 + y
say join join x position of Sprite1 , y position of Sprite1 for 1 secs
pen up
go to x: 30 y: 70

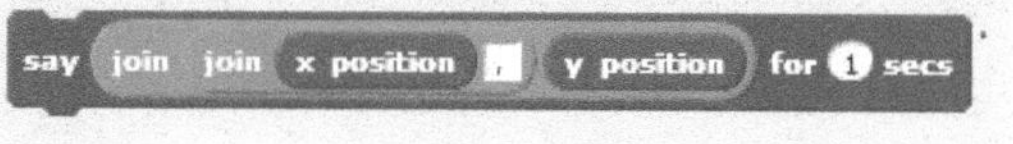
say join join x position , y position for 1 secs

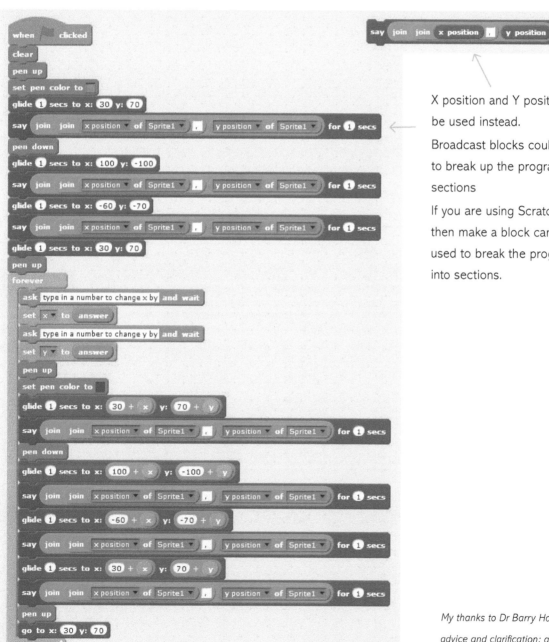

X position and Y position could be used instead.

Broadcast blocks could be used to break up the program into sections

If you are using Scratch 2.0 then make a block can also be used to break the program up into sections.

My thanks to Dr Barry Hobbs for Maths advice and clarification: all errors are of course my own.

Decompose Sheet Answers

Translation Decomposed

What object will you need to make?

Sprite to draw the shape

X and Y variables

X and X background grid

What will you need to make the program do?

Draw a triangle using coordinates

Report the position of the coordinates

Allow the user to add to the X and Y coordinates of the shape

Adjust the X and Y position of the shape by the amount typed in by the user

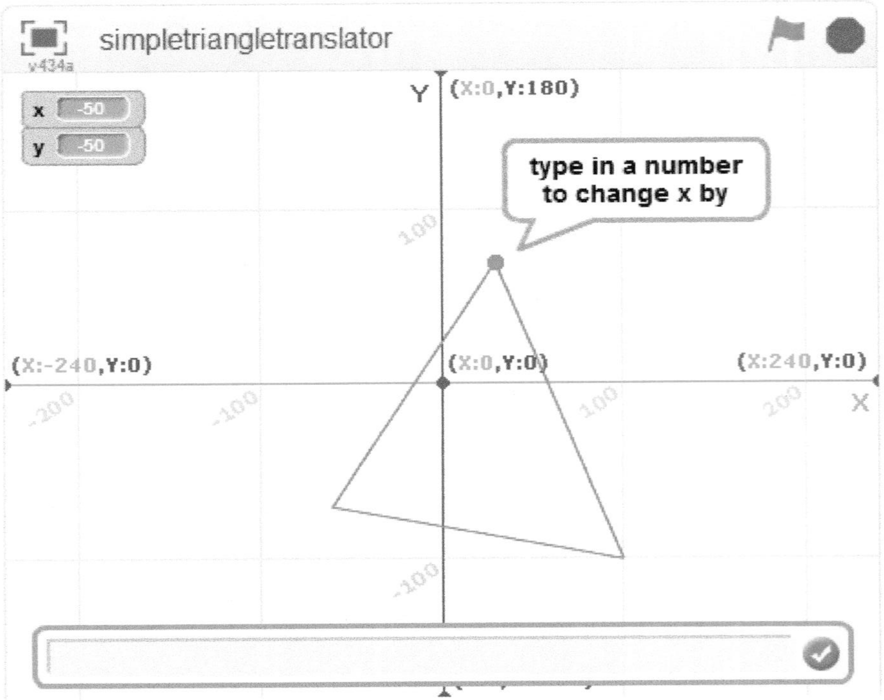
simpletriangletranslator
x -50
y -50
Y
(X:0,Y:180)
type in a number to change x by
(X:-240,Y:0)
(X:0,Y:0)
(X:240,Y:0)
X
100
-100
-200
200

4F. Primary Games Maker

Module Aim Design and create either a platform, trail or moving background game independently.

Time to complete module

1.5 hours to plan and 4.5 hours to create

National Curriculum Programs of Study

KS2

Pupils should be taught to:

- *design, write and debug programs that accomplish specific goals,* including controlling or simulating physical systems; *solve problems by decomposing them into smaller parts*
- *use sequence, selection, and repetition in programs; work with variables and various forms of input and output*
- *use logical reasoning to explain how some simple algorithms work and to detect and correct errors in algorithms and programs*

Learning Overview

Pupils choose which game type to design and create. They work on that game design in groups of 2 or 3 modelling it informally. They then convert these ideas onto a more formal algorithm planner. They look for code that they can reuse from other projects before converting their algorithm into Scratch code. Before the end of the project it is evaluated by their peers before the final improving session. Finally the projects can be published and linked to the school website.

Teachers could allow pupils to use **Lego WeDo** if available and requested.

Computer Science and Maths Concepts

These are dependent on the complexity of the project pupils choose to make.

Adult Focus

All adults need to be clear that they are to support using hints only and not solve things for pupils.

Useful Hints

Adults need to let pupils know that once they have left the planning sessions they will only give hints on code once per pupil in any session. However they will help if there are non coding questions such as how to change the size of a brush in the painting editor.

Pupils can independently access code they have used before or ideas from the Primary Games Maker Help http://code-it.co.uk/wp-content/uploads/2015/05/ScratchPrimaryGamesMaker.pdf.

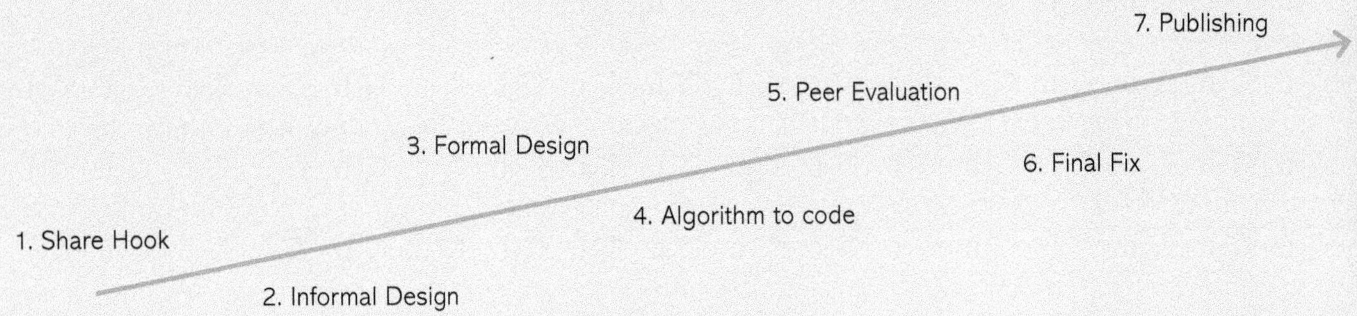
1. Share Hook
2. Informal Design
3. Formal Design
4. Algorithm to code
5. Peer Evaluation
6. Final Fix
7. Publishing

Learning Path

Things to decide before you start

Are you going to give an option of using all genre? Snail Trail is the easiest to adapt as it is a similar start to the Slug Trail in Y4. The Flappy Bat and Platform Game are equally as complex. If this is your first time teaching Scratch you may want to teach one game genre or limit some pupils to designing and creating the snail trail game.

Resources

Unfinished Platform Game for Scratch 1.4 download
http://code-it.co.uk/wp-content/uploads/2015/08/platform.sb

Unfinished Platform Game for Scratch 2.0 download
http://code-it.co.uk/wp-content/uploads/2015/08/platform.zip

Unfinished Snail Trail Game for Scratch 1.4 download
http://code-it.co.uk/wp-content/uploads/2015/08/trail.sb

Unfinished Snail Trail Game for Scratch 2.0 download
http://code-it.co.uk/wp-content/uploads/2015/08/trail.zip

Unfinished Flappy Bat Game for Scratch 1.4 download
http://code-it.co.uk/wp-content/uploads/2015/08/flappybat.sb

Unfinished Flappy Bat Game for Scratch 2.0 download
http://code-it.co.uk/wp-content/uploads/2015/08/flappybat.zip

Support cards are available for some aspects of the planning found at the end of this module.

v434a

Full screen 2.0

Full screen 1.4

1. Share Hook

Explain that a local programmer was developing some games for primary pupils to play but then took a new job and left the projects totally unfinished. Show pupils the games as they are without showing the code (full screen mode) . Explain that their task is to take one of these ideas, design it they way they think it should be made, and then code it in Scratch. Their projects will be tested by their peers to help them improve their programs and spot and fix bugs. Final judgement on the project will come from children in another year group testing their games.

2. Informal Design

Pupils team up in twos or threes to discuss initial ideas.
You can use either of these ideas or choose one that will work better for your class:

- Human modelling, use chalk to draw a stage screen on the playground and then children roleplay the games pretending to be sprites (great for when it is sunny)
- Large sugar paper, scrap paper and unicubes. Pupils model how the game works using blocks and paper.

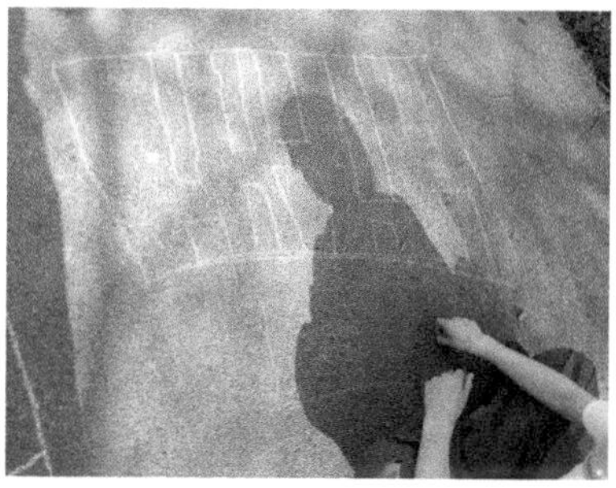

3. Formal Design

After a period of time explain that pupils need to complete a detailed individual planner using the Planner provided in their pupil workbooks. Show them a copy of the example planner in teacher work book page 193 and explain that they need to write, inside the central box, to explain using ordinary non technical language what will happen in their game. After this pupils circle key words and draw lines to the grey boxes where they expand/decompose their ideas on their characters, backgrounds, games features etc in greater detail. There is an online example here http://code-it.co.uk/wp-content/uploads/2015/08/decompose.pdf.

As well as an example in the teachers book page 193.

Finally the white outer boxes are for Scratch code ideas that they can reuse from other projects created in the past. They can open old projects to help themselves but must NOT start coding their projects yet. I often tell pupils that they will have to finish the planner in the next session while everyone else is programming if it is not completed in enough detail, which helps to focus effort.

Note
If you had a pupil whose writing is naturally large print out the A4 planner onto A3

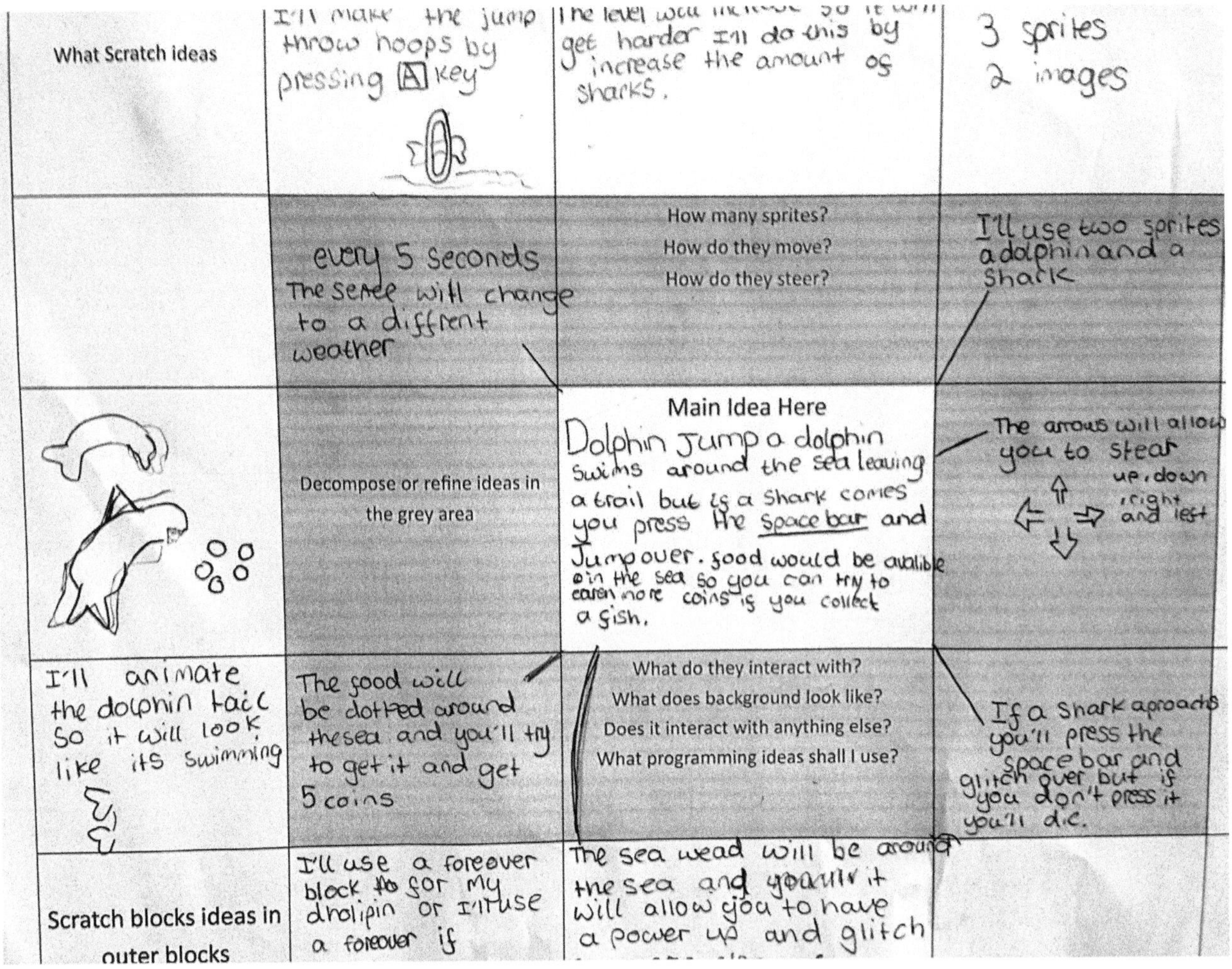
What Scratch ideas
I'll make the jump throw hoops by pressing A key
The level will increase so it will get harder I'll do this by increase the amount of sharks.
3 sprites
2 images
every 5 seconds The scene will change to a diffrent weather
How many sprites?
How do they move?
How do they steer?
I'll use two sprites a dolphin and a shark
Decompose or refine ideas in the grey area
Main Idea Here
Dolphin Jump a dolphin swims around the sea leaving a trail but if a shark comes you press the space bar and Jump over. food would be avalible in the sea so you can try to earn more coins if you collect a fish.
The arrows will allow you to stear up, down right and left
I'll animate the dolphin tail so it will look like its swimming
The food will be dotted around the sea and you'll try to get it and get 5 coins
What do they interact with?
What does background look like?
Does it interact with anything else?
What programming ideas shall I use?
If a shark aproachs you'll press the space bar and glitch over but if you don't press it you'll die.
Scratch blocks ideas in outer blocks
I'll use a forever block for my dholipin or I'll use a forever if
The sea wead will be around the sea and you will it will allow you to have a power up and glitch

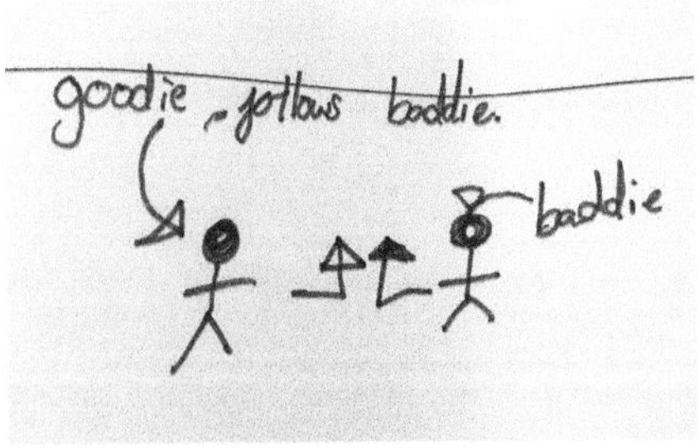
goodie follows baddie.
baddie

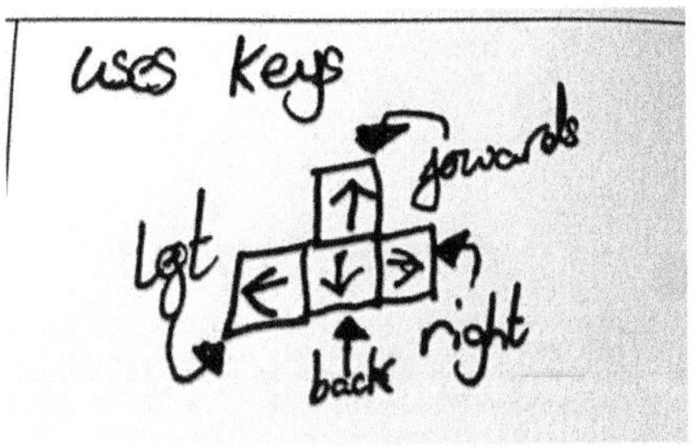
uses keys
forwards
left
back
right

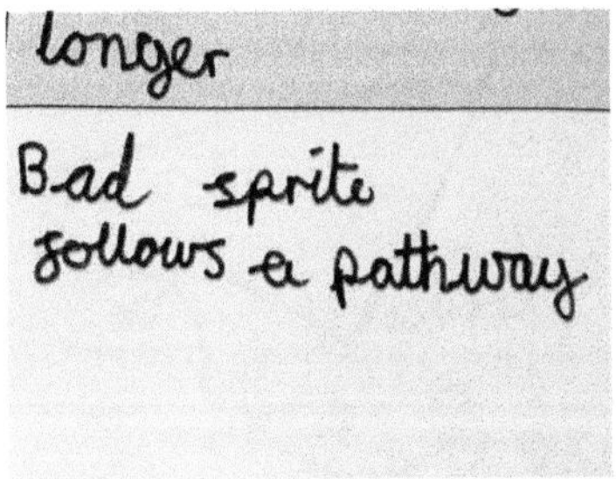
longer
Bad sprite follows a pathway

These decomposed project planners need to be marked before the next session to pick up on any pupils who need more time planning, have attempted a game that is beyond their capabilities (rare at this point) or have not shown enough detail.

Explain ideas in the grey area	When you start the game you will be given the choice of 7 diffrent characters (Baymax, flounder, olaf, stitch, mini, miky, thumper and uh)	How many sprites? How do they move? How do they steer?
When you start the game you will be precented with a starter screen where you get to pick your charater!	Main Idea Here • Disney theme (disney characters). You will choose the disney characters at the starter screens. depending on which charater you choose you will get a different background. You will get points by collecting items that will be dotted over the background. Each Item you collect is 1 points. Beware! The charaters enemy will try and get you! There will always be a grey line and if you touch it you will slow down.	What do they interact with? What does background look like? Does it interact with anything else? To get points Collec the food on the pl each peice of food is 1 point.
Every point you collect gives you more time to collect points and once time has run out it will toatal up and collect your score. (you collect the points by running into them)		A thick grey line lying on the plat form. However I can slow you down and can loose you many lives 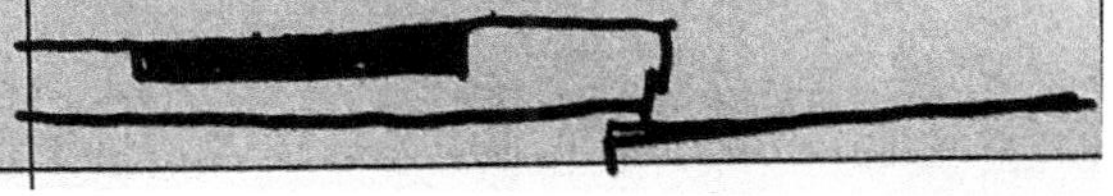

Primary Games Maker Rationale

Most programs are not created from nothing. Programmers adapt other people's ideas and in the process produce something new.

Most pupils need to see working examples of code before creating it themselves.

Planning is important as it forces pupils and teachers to think carefully about what they want to happen. To help pupils to plan we must model some of the steps. It will help most pupils to put their thoughts down on paper but they will need to model the game before doing this.

4. Algorithm to Code

Give pupils plenty of time for this section. I allow one question only from each pupil about their code and once this question has been asked it is gone. This focusses the mind and forces pupils to find solutions for most of their issues. If pupils ask for it you can give them copies of the basic code. (page 194 and page 195)

5. Peer Evaluation

Inside the pupil workbooks there is a peer evaluation sheet for two other pupils to fill in. Remind pupils filling in that they must be neat when writing inside someone else's workbook. Give pupils time to read these and ask questions. There will always be disagreements as it is someone else's opinion and sometimes one person's bug is another person's game feature. The game author can choose to act or not act on the feedback although if the same thing is pointed out by the game testers in another class then marks will be deducted from the project.

6. Final Fix

Allow pupils time to tweak their projects, responding to feedback. There isn't much point asking for feedback if they can't respond to it.

7. Publishing

Finally invite the other class in to try out the games created. Get them to provide oral feedback on the project to the author. A great next step is to publish these on the Scratch 2 website and link or embed on the school website. Just make sure no pupil personal information is included.

Assessing the finished projects

I often talk about this project when writing reports in Year 6. You can look at what hurdles pupils have overcome and how they have designed algorithm and code created to solve problems. Looking through the decomposed planners and their end products will give you a good feel for top, middle and bottom.

Decompose Planner_Example

	Costumes in a forever loop	Forever if key A pressed turn right (S key for left)	Auto right with X & Y to go back to in loop	
	Cop and robber sprites three costumes making them look like they are running from above	Cop and robbers both steer from keys on keyboard. Right, left and forward.	Walls are programmed to go over set distances and then move back after set time	
	Create maze background with lots of different ways to go	Cops and Robbers Cop chases the robber around a maze of roads. Some road maze walls move blocks changing the roadway. Robber is faster for short period of time can accelerate. If cop catches robber he gets a point. For every minute robber stays free he gets a point. If either touch wall they move very slowly.	Spawn point for start of game and if cop catches robber. Same place	Go to X and Y if cop catches robbers
Robber score uses adapted seconds counter	Cop score and robber score held in variables and displayed on screen	Wall slow down movement through colour wall reduces all movement to 1/10th speed	Robber accelerates when another key is pressed	Forever if key 2 pressed move speed 2 10 seconds wait until block can be run again
There is an online version of this to share with pupils at http://code-it.co.uk/wp-content/uploads/2015/08/decompose.pdf				

Flappy Bat Scrolling Background Code Help

code-it.co.uk

Scratch
Flappy Bat Game
Help

code-it.co.uk

Scrolling Background Code

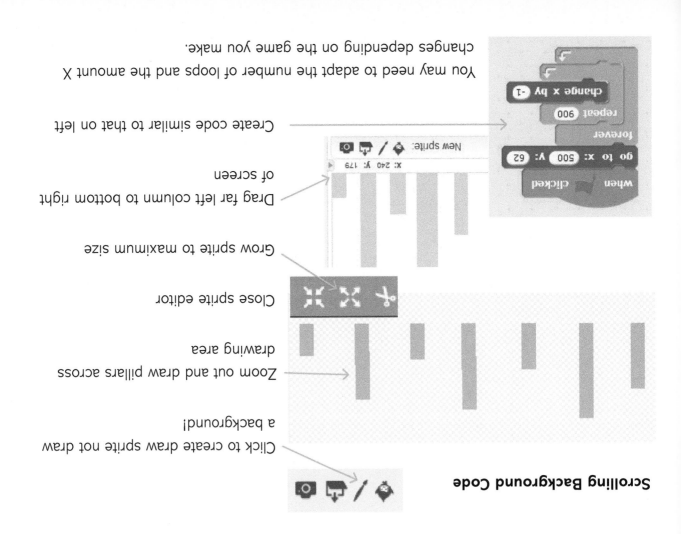

Click to create draw sprite not draw a background!

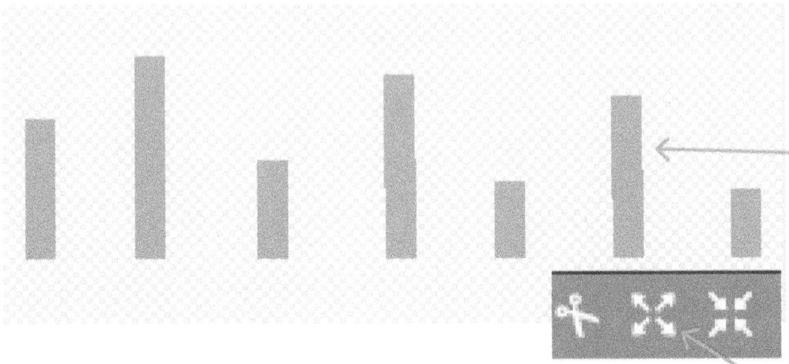

Zoom out and draw pillars across drawing area

Close sprite editor

Grow sprite to maximum size

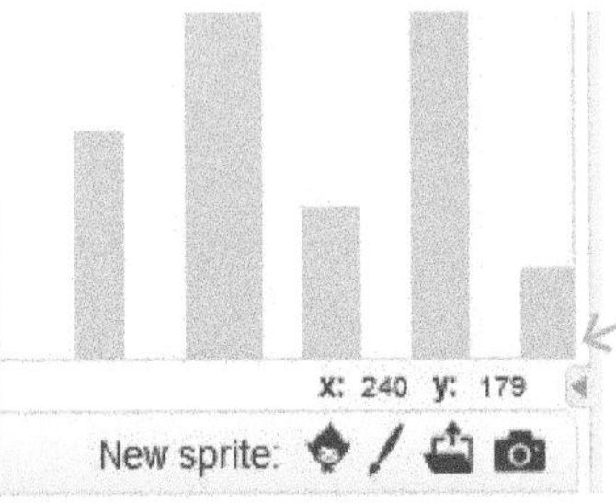
x: 240 y: 179
New sprite:

Drag far left column to bottom right of screen

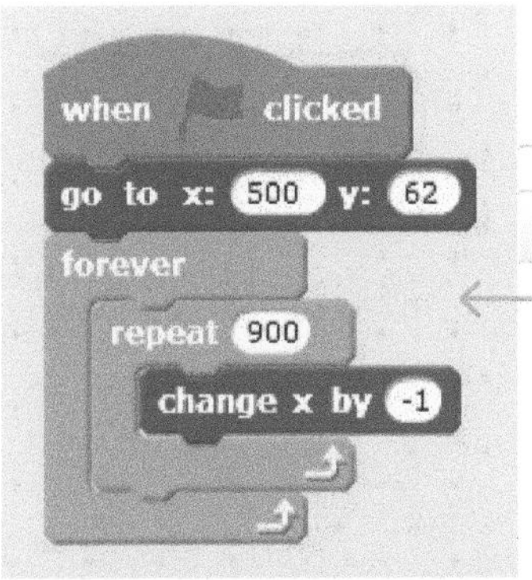
when clicked
go to x: 500 y: 62
forever
repeat 900
change x by -1

Create code similar to that on left

You may need to adapt the number of loops and the amount X changes depending on the game you make.

Scratch

Platform Game

Help

code-it.co.uk

Platform Game Basic Code Help

code-it.co.uk

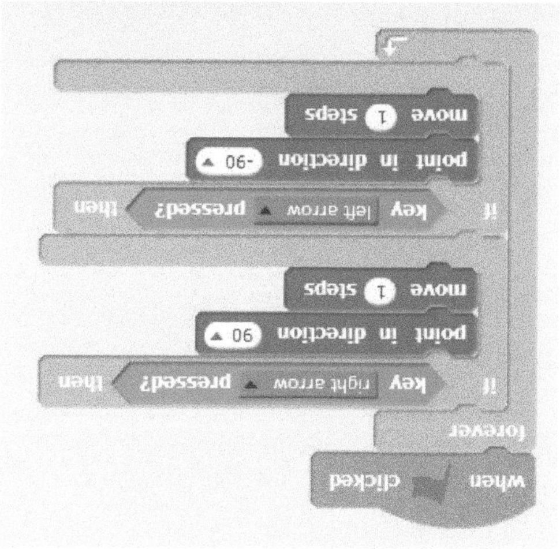
when clicked
forever
if key right arrow pressed? then
point in direction 90
move 1 steps
if key left arrow pressed? then
point in direction -90
move 1 steps

Move right and left when arrow keys pressed

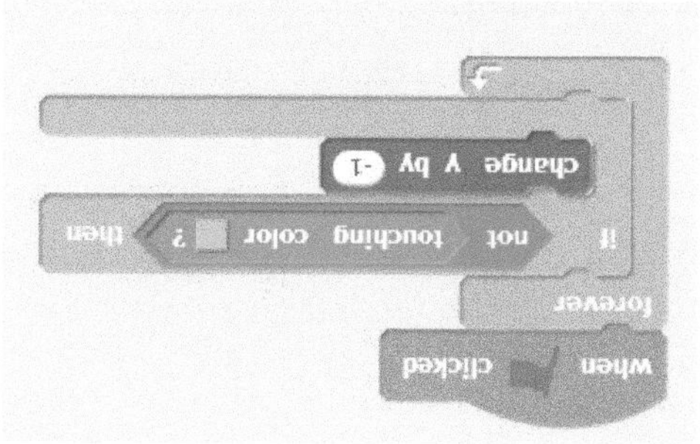
when clicked
forever
if not touching color ? then
change y by -1

Fall unless touching orange

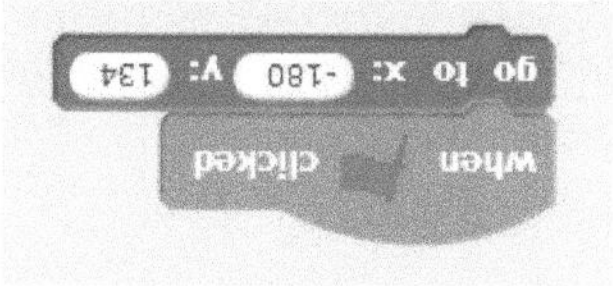
when clicked
go to x: -180 y: 134

Go to start location

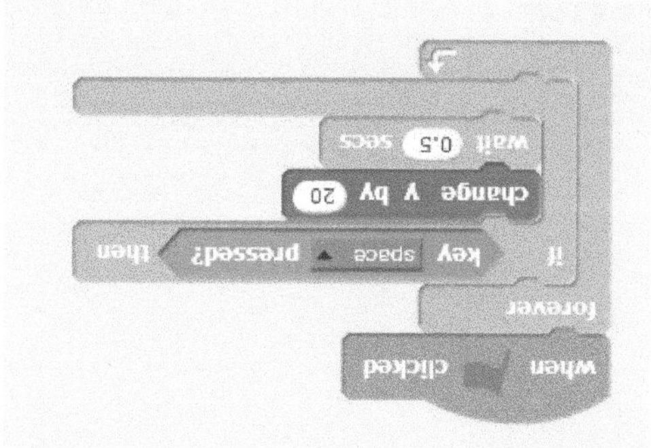
when clicked
forever
if key space pressed? then
change y by 20
wait 0.5 secs

Jump Forever if press space key on keyboard cat moves up

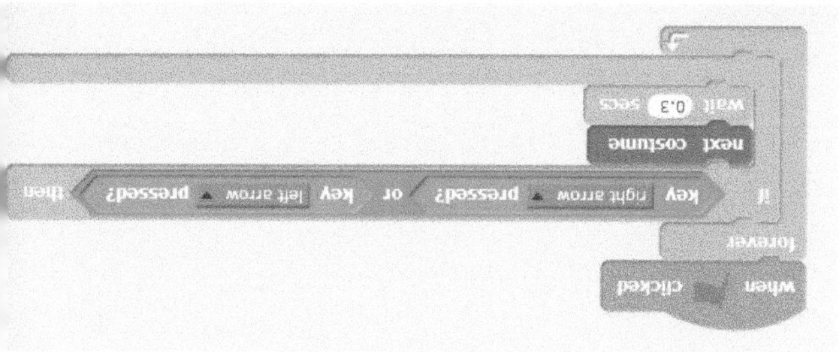
when clicked
forever
if key right arrow pressed? or key left arrow pressed? then
next costume
wait 0.3 secs

Only change costumes when right or left arrow is pressed

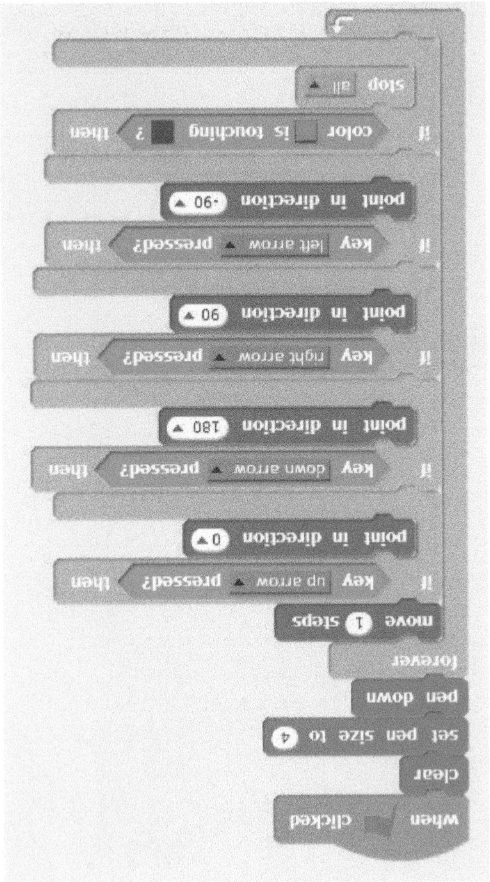

when clicked
clear
set pen size to 4
pen down
forever
move 1 steps
if key up arrow pressed? then
point in direction 0
if key down arrow pressed? then
point in direction 180
if key right arrow pressed? then
point in direction 90
if key left arrow pressed? then
point in direction -90
if color is touching ? then
stop all

Scratch

Snail Trail Game

Help

Snail Trail Game Basic Code Help

4G. Tilt Switch

Module Aim Create or repurpose a scratch program to use the **Lego WeDo** tilt switch.

Module Learning Focus

By the end of the module children will be able to:

- Design, create or adapt a program to be controlled by the Lego tilt switch

Computer Science Concepts

This is very dependent on the projects pupils choose to create or adapt.

Differentiation and Assessment for Learning

At the beginning of each session the learning intention sheet of pupil workbook 4 page 26 is shared and the learning journey expanded through success criteria. Pupils feed their progress back to the teacher by annotating this sheet with smiley faces during, or at the end of, the lesson. Teachers can also annotate the sheet to indicate those who need more or less help in future lessons.

Adult Focus

All adults need to be clear that they are to support using hints only and not solve things for pupils.

Useful Hints

It can take a while for drivers to load so pupils need to be prepared for this.

It is helpful that the blocks appear in the bottom of the motion sensor section.

If a pupil has no idea at all after at least 10 minutes show them how adding a move 1 step inside one of the conditional selection blocks will make the sprite move when tilted that way.

Learning needed before attempting this module

Pupils need to have done lots of basic Scratch programming and have completed at least one open ended gaming module. They also need to have done either the Toilet Fan or the Car Park Barrier modules or both.

Time to complete module

This module is best done in one session of approximately two hours. Lego models left half - built are always liable to lose pieces. This sort of time scale means you can pack it all away securely at the end.

National Curriculum Programs of Study

KS2

Pupils should be taught to:

- *design, write and debug programs that accomplish specific goals, including controlling or simulating physical systems; solve problems by decomposing them into smaller parts*
- *use sequence, selection, and repetition in programs; work with variables and various forms of input and output*
- *use logical reasoning to explain how some simple algorithms work and to detect and correct errors in algorithms and programs*

Computational Thinking
Generalisation: Adapting a solution that solved one thing to solve another. In this case as pupils see that the tilt switch can be made to make the sprite say something, the conditional selection blocks could be used for something different that uses the same idea.

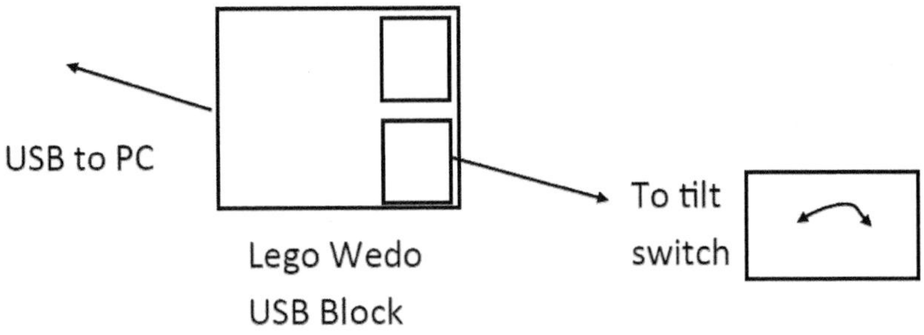
USB to PC
Lego Wedo
USB Block
To tilt
switch

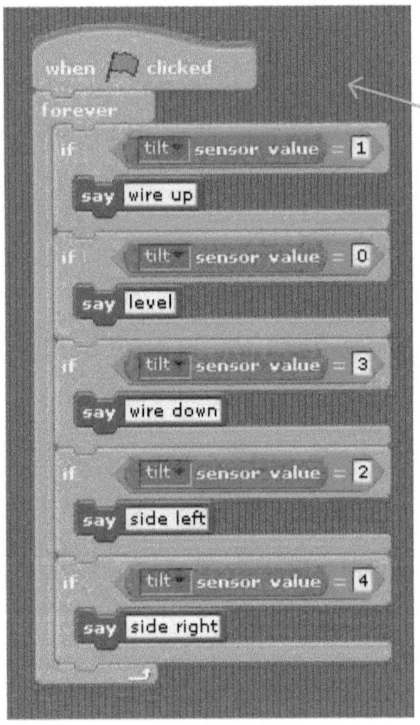
when clicked
forever
if tilt sensor value = 1
say wire up
if tilt sensor value = 0
say level
if tilt sensor value = 3
say wire down
if tilt sensor value = 2
say side left
if tilt sensor value = 4
say side right

1. Planning Ideas Phase

Explain that Lego Wedo comes with a tilt switch that outputs a number when it is tilted in a specific direction. Plug in a single **Lego** tilt switch and demonstrate how it works using this program. I often have the **if** statements all snapped together and ask pupils how I will get this checked continuously. Pupils will tell you to use a forever loop.

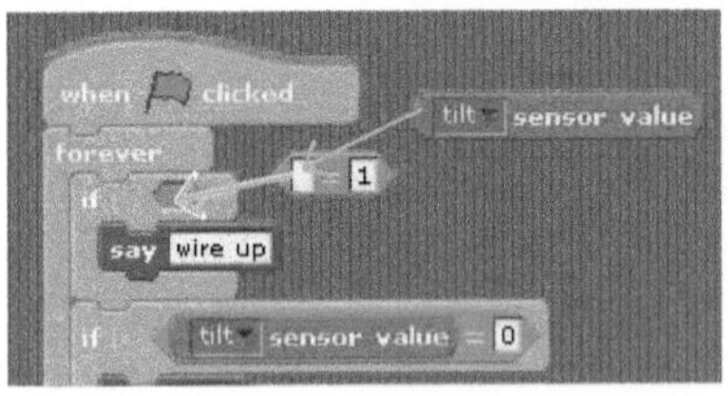
when clicked
forever
tilt sensor value
say wire up
tilt sensor value = 0

Snap the maths operator into the if condition and add a tilt sensor value sensing block

tilt sensor value
sensor button pressed ?

Make sure you tick the tilt sensor value so you can see number value on the screen

Explain that they can use this in any way they like. It could be a way of controlling an on screen program or they could link it with other Wedo and control the motor.

Allow pupils some time to think and discuss what they want to do in small groups or pairs using the questions in the pupil workbook page 27 as an initial impetus.

Give pupils boxes of **Lego WeDo.** One between two is ideal but one between three would work. Add the restrictions about not swapping Lego between boxes.

2. Build Phase

Some pupils will start building things using the WeDo, some will go on to the computer taking the tilt switch with them. Our job as teachers is just to facilitate their creative process.

2. Build Phase Continued

I have never had a group that didn't have an idea but if they didn't I would show them how I could use the tilt switch to control the direction of a sprite. I would then ask them if they had made any games that involved steering or turning.

Some pupil projects will be shorter than others depending on whether they include a lot of Lego building. If someone finishes a short project ask them to briefly document their work using comment blocks and then if they can think of another use for the tilt switch.

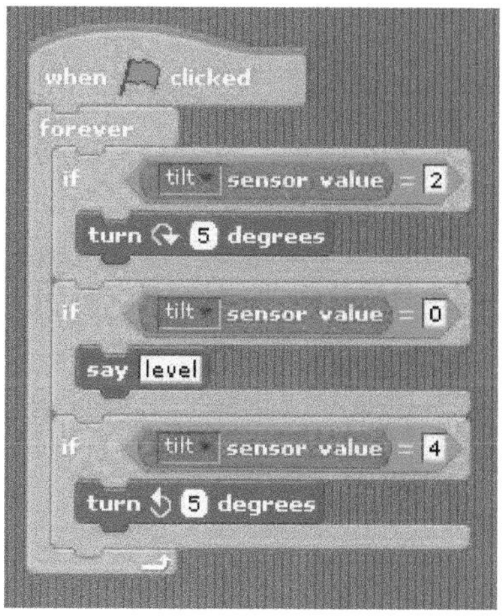
when clicked
forever
if tilt sensor value = 2
turn 5 degrees
if tilt sensor value = 0
say level
if tilt sensor value = 4
turn 5 degrees

3. Evaluating Projects

Two thirds of the way through the build explain that it is useful for other pupils to run their programs and give constructive feedback. Pupils open page 28 of the pupil work-book entitled Giving Helpful Feedback. Give time for two other pupils to test the program and give helpful feedback. You may want to remind pupils to use their best handwriting as they are writing in someone else's workbook.

These are a few of the projects Y6 pupils made at Ringwood Junior School

Peter and Louis program a motor bike handle

http://code-it-cs.blogspot.co.uk/2014/05/peter-and-louis-program-their-game-to.html

Caleb & Sam create a games controller

http://code-it-cs.blogspot.co.uk/2014/05/caleb-sam-create-games-controller-using.html

Callum and Harvey great joystick design

http://code-it-cs.blogspot.co.uk/2014/05/lego-wedo-joystick-great-design-by.html

4H. Chatbot

Time to complete module

3 hours

Module Aim: Pupils code a sprite to talk to the user and make them think the sprite has intelligence

National Curriculum Programs of Study

KS2

Pupils should be taught to:

- ***design, write and debug programs that accomplish specific goals,*** including controlling or simulating physical systems; solve problems by decomposing them into smaller parts
- ***use sequence, selection,*** and repetition in programs; ***work with variables and various forms of input and output***
- ***use logical reasoning to*** explain how some simple algorithms work and to ***detect and correct errors in algorithms and programs***

KS3

make appropriate use of data structures [for example, lists, tables or arrays]

Module Overview

Pupils are introduced to the idea of a chatbot and how difficult this is to do for a computer. Pupils examine teachers version for some possible techniques they could use. Pupils discuss with each other how they might create their own version. Pupils are given time to create their own chatbot which is then evaluated by their peers.

Computer Science Concepts

- Conditional Selection
- Random choice from a list
- Storing data in a variable for reuse

Module Learning Focus

By the end of the module children will be able to:

- identify where variables can be used to store information
- use the ask input to collect information
- respond to a user's specific answer
- develop a style that mimics a human

Differentiation and Assessment for Learning

At the beginning of each session the learning intention sheet of pupil workbook 4 page 30 is shared and the learning journey expanded through success criteria. Pupils feed their progress back to the teacher by annotating this sheet with smiley faces during, or at the end of, the lesson. Teachers can also annotate the sheet to indicate those who need more or less help in future lessons.

Computational Thinking

Generalisation:

Adapting a solution that solved one problem to solve another.

Algorithm Evaluation: Which solution was best?

Learning Path

1. Chat Bot Idea
2. Teacher Version
3. How to adapt and improve
4. Chatbot coding
5. Chatbot evaluation

1. ChatBot Idea

Tell children that someone told you that humans are very different to computers. They explained that computers always respond in the same way to the same inputs. Humans don't always respond in the same way. Explain that if you pushed a pupil the first time they might ignore you but if you pushed them a second or third time you are likely to get a different response. A computer would always respond in the same way.

2. Teacher Version

Humans have been trying to program computers to behave like humans and last night you had a go.

Open Chatbot from http://code-it.co.uk/wp-content/uploads/2015/08/chatbot.sb. Although this is a Scratch 1.4 resource it will open perfectly in Scratch 2.0. Run the first section of code and explain that you got the idea from the Quiz in Year 4.

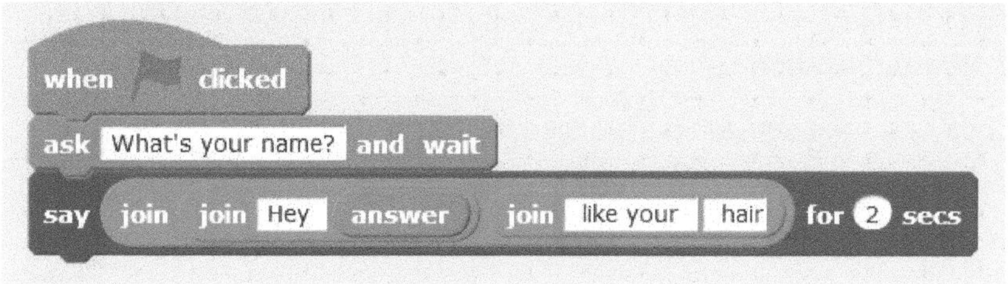
when clicked
ask What's your name? and wait
say join join Hey answer join like your hair for 2 secs

Explain that this was fine but you wanted to use the name they typed in later in the program.

Where would be a good place to store it?

Answer: in a variable.

Create a name variable and adapt the code like this:

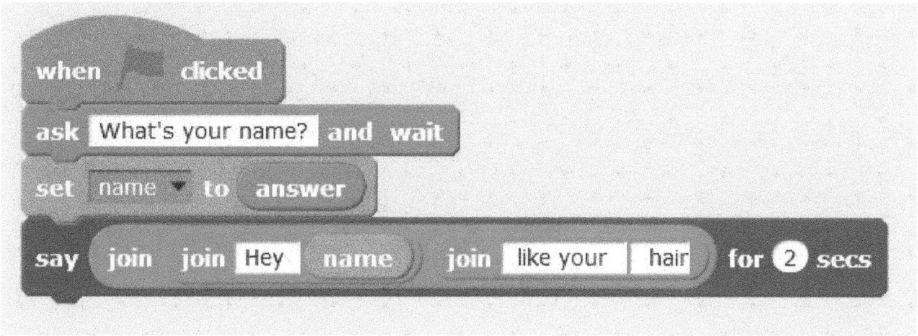
when clicked
ask What's your name? and wait
set name to answer
say join join Hey name join like your hair for 2 secs

You then thought it would be great if every time the program was run it liked something different about the person.

What could you use to randomly choose a different item?

Answer: a list

Point out where you created the list and how you added items to it and how you made sure they all sounded correct in your reply. If you need a refresher on how to create and add to lists, page 184 of the random word module will help.

Explain that you then thought of separating pupils by their answers to an age question and asking them different questions. Add the bottom section and ask them how it works. Where would you put further questions to younger users? Answer: in the else section underneath I am younger than you name.

Add in a list called **item to like** set out like this.

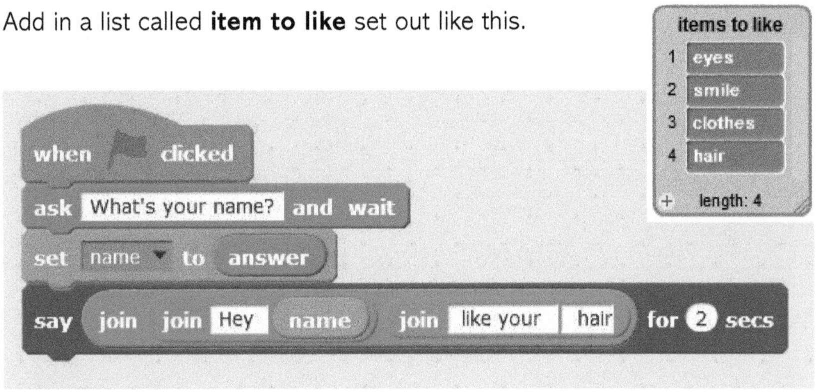
items to like
1 eyes
2 smile
3 clothes
4 hair
length: 4
when clicked
ask What's your name? and wait
set name to answer
say join join Hey name join like your hair for 2 secs

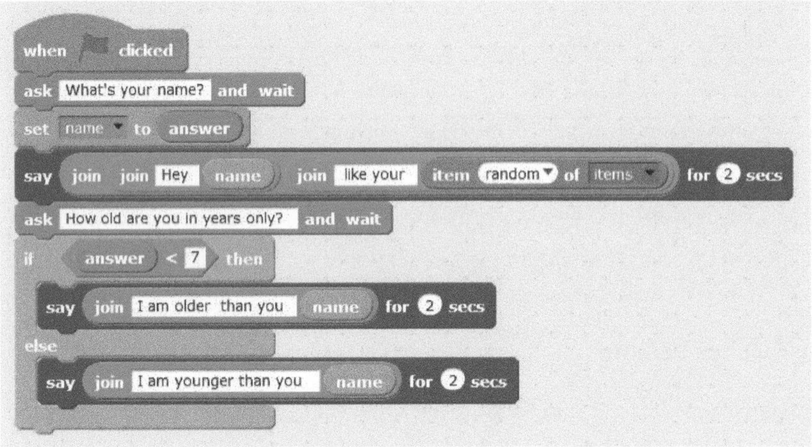
when clicked
ask What's your name? and wait
set name to answer
say join join Hey name join like your item random of items for 2 secs
ask How old are you in years only? and wait
if answer < 7 then
say join I am older than you name for 2 secs
else
say join I am younger than you name for 2 secs

3. How to improve and adapt

Ask pupils to split into twos and turn to page 31 of their pupil work books where there are some focus questions to help them to write their own better version. Explain that they don't need to use any of your ideas. Their only aim is to make the chatbot seem as human as possible.

4. Chatbot Coding

Once they have some ideas proceed to coding.

Sample pupil code to help you understand what can happen and how to help pupils improve.

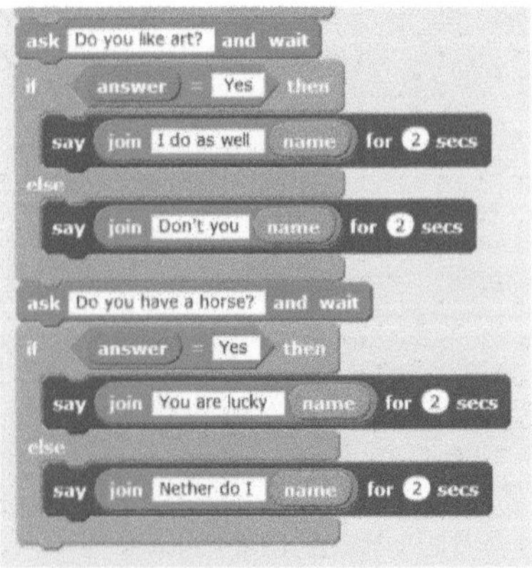
ask Do you like art? and wait
if answer = Yes then
say join I do as well name for 2 secs
else
say join Don't you name for 2 secs
ask Do you have a horse? and wait
if answer = Yes then
say join You are lucky name for 2 secs
else
say join Nether do I name for 2 secs

In this example the pupil is playing it very safe by asking closed questions and commenting on them. They are using the user's name inside a variable which is to be commended. I would ask if they can ask a more open question and collect and use the answer later on.

ask item random of Items and wait

Items
1 Have you had a good day?
2 What is your favourite football team?
3 Do you have a pet?
4 Do you like chocolate?
5 Who is your best friend?
6 How old are you?
7 What is your favourite food?
length: 7

Here the pupil has asked a random question from a list. This is a good idea as it makes the chatbot seem random. However it makes it very difficult to collect and use the answer.

ask So I like hockey too, What's your favourite sport? and wait
set Team to answer

Here a pupil is collecting data to use later. This is to be encouraged.

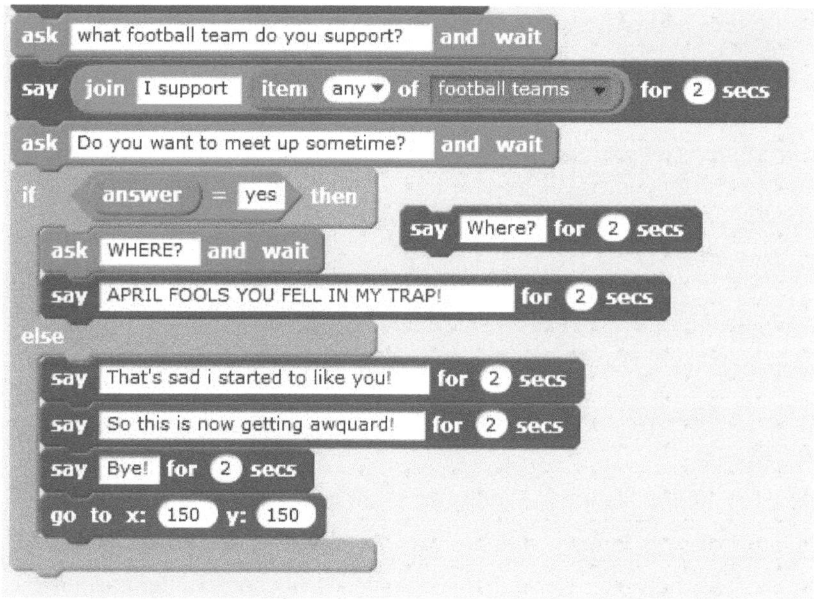
ask what football team do you support? and wait
say join I support item any of football teams for 2 secs
ask Do you want to meet up sometime? and wait
if answer = yes then
say Where? for 2 secs
ask WHERE? and wait
say APRIL FOOLS YOU FELL IN MY TRAP! for 2 secs
else
say That's sad i started to like you! for 2 secs
say So this is now getting awquard! for 2 secs
say Bye! for 2 secs
go to x: 150 y: 150

The last selection block is an example of painting yourself into a corner where there is nowhere the user can go. This is common and pupils need to be encouraged to create questions that carry the conversation on.

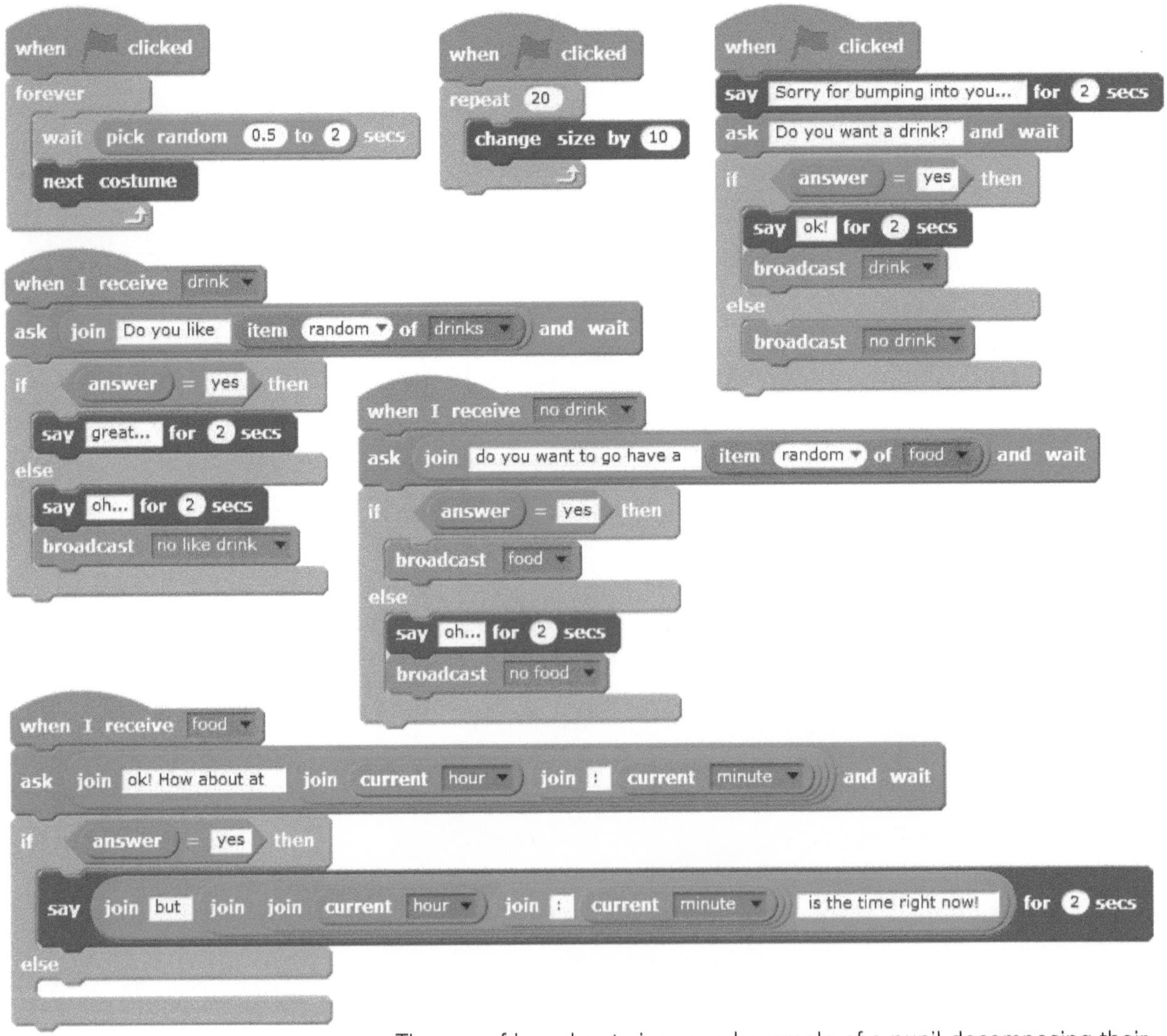
when clicked
forever
wait pick random 0.5 to 2 secs
next costume
when clicked
repeat 20
change size by 10
when clicked
say Sorry for bumping into you... for 2 secs
ask Do you want a drink? and wait
if answer = yes then
say ok! for 2 secs
broadcast drink
else
broadcast no drink
when I receive drink
ask join Do you like item random of drinks and wait
if answer = yes then
say great... for 2 secs
else
say oh... for 2 secs
broadcast no like drink
when I receive no drink
ask join do you want to go have a item random of food and wait
if answer = yes then
broadcast food
else
say oh... for 2 secs
broadcast no food
when I receive food
ask join ok! How about at join current hour join : current minute and wait
if answer = yes then
say join but join join current hour join : current minute is the time right now! for 2 secs
else

The use of broadcasts is a good example of a pupil decomposing their project. You might want to show them how to use or make a block, and there is more information on that in the perimeter planning module in section 4B

Although at first glance this looks excellent there is very little collection of information to interact with the user. An advanced user such as this would respond very quickly to a suggestion they capture information to use later.

This is quite an advanced use of a list. The list is being checked to see if the user's answer is on it.

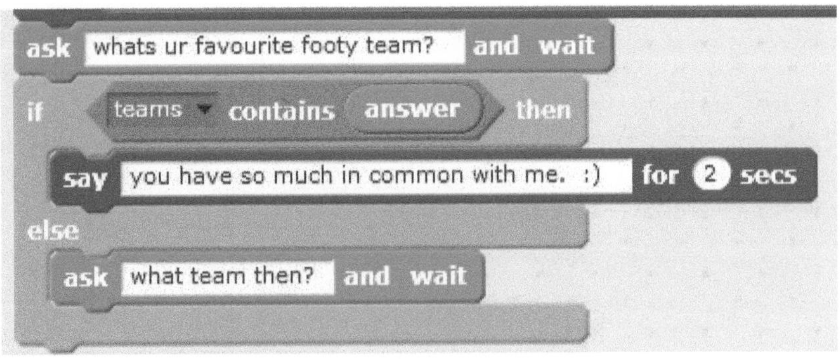
ask whats ur favourite footy team? and wait
if teams contains answer then
say you have so much in common with me. :) for 2 secs
else
ask what team then? and wait

5. Chatbot Evaluation

Instruct all pupils to set their programs to full screen using the icon in the top left hand side of the screen. Now encourage everyone to go round and test each other's programs. Finally at the end ask them to stand by the programs they thought was most like a human. They are not allowed to choose their own. Ask pupils to justify their opinion.

Chapter 5

5A. Additional Computer Science Resources

Code-it Unplugged Resources

Jam Sandwich Algorithm

Age approximately 6-9 year olds **Time Needed** 45 minutes to 1 hour

In this module pupils are asked to write an algorithm to program their teacher to make a jam sandwich. The teacher lays out an open packet of sliced bread, an unopened tub of butter spread, an unopened jar of jam and a knife and plate. The teacher instructs the pupils that they can only use a set list of words, although they can additionally use any small connective words and or any numbers. Working individually or in pairs they write a part of the algorithm before reading it to test it on their teacher. As they encounter errors they fix these before creating more of the algorithm to test on their teacher. To get a flavour of this lesson I suggest the teacher watches the outtakes video but doesn't show this to their pupils before the lesson.

The word list, including an SEN word list and outtakes video can all be found at http://code-it.co.uk/unplugged/jamsandwich.

Playground Games Flowcharts

I discovered early on that if you wish pupils to use flowcharts in algorithm design they need experience of reading them first. This activity introduces flowcharts through play.

Age approximately 6-9 year olds **Time Needed** 45 minutes to 1 hour

In this outdoor activity pupils are given a flowchart of a popular playground game such as Stuck in the Mud. Without any prior instructions on using flowcharts, they are asked to work in a small group to work out what game it is. They are allowed a few minutes to play the game once they have worked out what it is. After they have completed five flowcharts, these are taken away and they are asked to return to class. Here they are presented with a bugged copy of the same games. They are tasked with working in pairs to find where the incorrect line has been placed and draw in where it should be pointing.

Five bugged and five good playground games flowcharts and the solutions can all be found at http://code-it.co.uk/unplugged/playgroundgames/playgroundoverview.

Exchange Sort Investigation

Age approximately 10-11 year olds **Time Needed** 2-3 hour

Computers use lots of different ways (algorithms) to sort numbers. In this module we attempt to understand the advantages and disadvantages a computer has when sorting numbers. Pupils then investigate all the different ways they can think of to compare two numbers before testing which methods will sort the numbers. In doing so they discover certain simple sorting algorithms. You will need dice and number cards to use this resource.

All the investigation sheets and instructions can be found at http://code-it.co.uk/unplugged/sort/sortoverview.

Other Great Resources

Code for Life Rapid Router by Ocado

Rapid Router is a great example of puzzle solving using programming. It was created by Ocado to help teachers with the new computing curriculum. This free resource challenges pupils to program an Ocado truck to reach various depots and homes. Along the way pupils are introduced to new computing concepts. In KS2 (7-11 year olds) we start pupils in class with this and then encourage its independent use through certificates, praise and the occasional lesson in school. In KS1 (5-7 years olds) we dip in for a longer series of sessions in both year groups.

Rapid Router can be found at
https://www.codeforlife.education/rapidrouter/.

CAS Teacher Resources

CAS, Computing at Schools, is a grassroots organisation committed to promoting Computer Science in schools. Many teachers publish planning and schemes of work on the site.

You can register for the site here
http://community.computingatschool.org.uk/door

Training

It still amazes me the amount of primary schools that have decided to muddle through computing without any training or support. It is not an exaggeration to say that the Computer Science and Information Technology aspects of Computing are the biggest change in the new National Curriculum. Nothing beats good training by an excellent practitioner. CAS, Computing at Schools on behalf of the DfE, have appointed primary computing master teachers across England.

You can find out which master teachers are near you:

http://community.computingatschool.org.uk/door. When logged on the list of Master Teachers is linked at the top left of the page.

I can be contacted via my website http://code-it.co.uk/contact/ for help in designing curriculum, staff training and modelled lessons. I lead local training in Hampshire via HIAS, these are open to all teachers both inside and outside the County. You can find these at http://code-it.co.uk/courses . I also lead courses and speak at conferences through Osiris and other training providers. You can find these at http://code-it.co.uk/ukeurocourses I look forward to meeting you in my travels.

5B. Independent Tasks Hints and Answers

Whilst the independent tasks are not designed as teacher marked homework, parents or pupils may ask for help.
Here are some hints and solutions for these activities.

Year 4 Maths Quiz Further Steps Hint

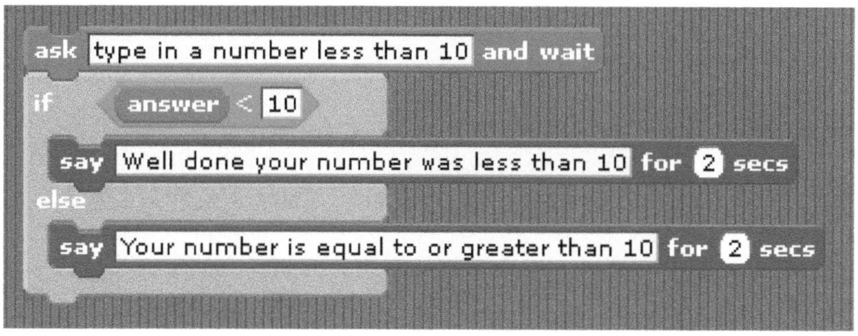
ask type in a number less than 10 and wait
if answer < 10
say Well done your number was less than 10 for 2 secs
else
say Your number is equal to or greater than 10 for 2 secs

Year 4 Music Algorithm to Music Code Next Steps

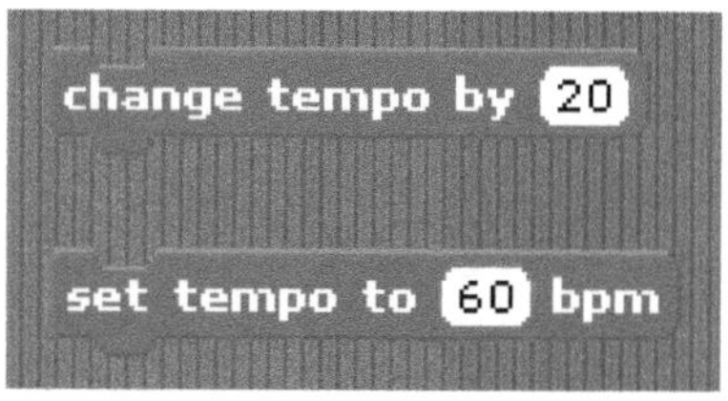
change tempo by 20
set tempo to 60 bpm

Slug Trail Game Further Steps

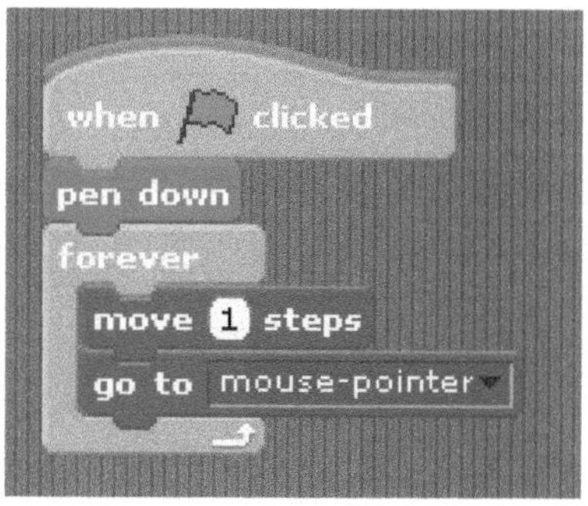
when clicked
pen down
forever
move 1 steps
go to mouse-pointer

Counting Machine First Steps & Next Steps

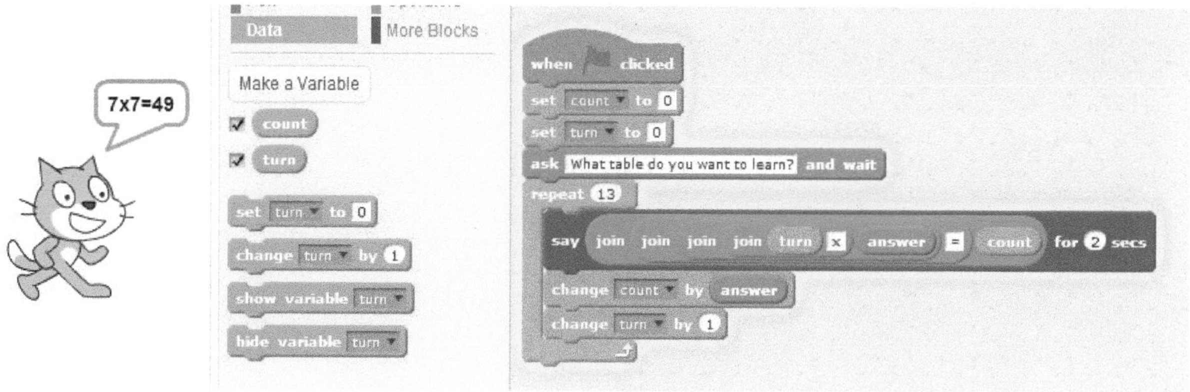
7x7=49
Data
More Blocks
Make a Variable
count
turn
set turn to 0
change turn by 1
show variable turn
hide variable turn
when clicked
set count to 0
set turn to 0
ask What table do you want to learn? and wait
repeat 13
say join join join join turn x answer = count for 2 secs
change count by answer
change turn by 1

Music abstraction further steps

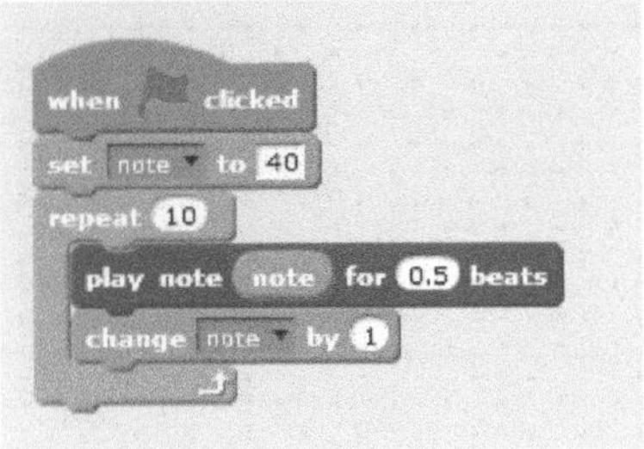
when clicked
set note to 40
repeat 10
play note note for 0.5 beats
change note by 1

Crab Maze Further Steps

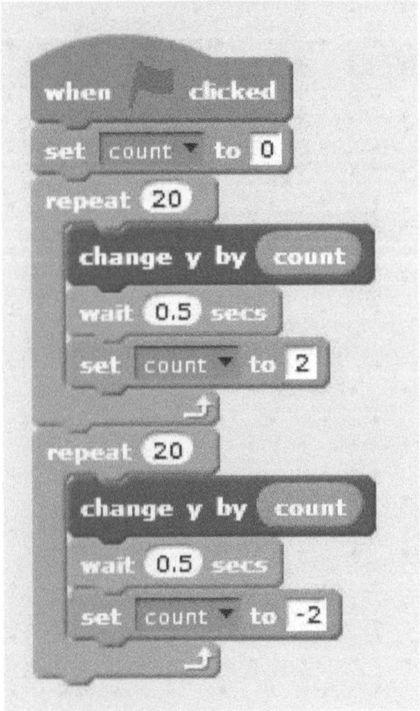
when clicked
set count to 0
repeat 20
change y by count
wait 0.5 secs
set count to 2
repeat 20
change y by count
wait 0.5 secs
set count to -2

Music Abstraction First Steps

Retelling a story in a different context uses abstraction

Random Word Next Steps

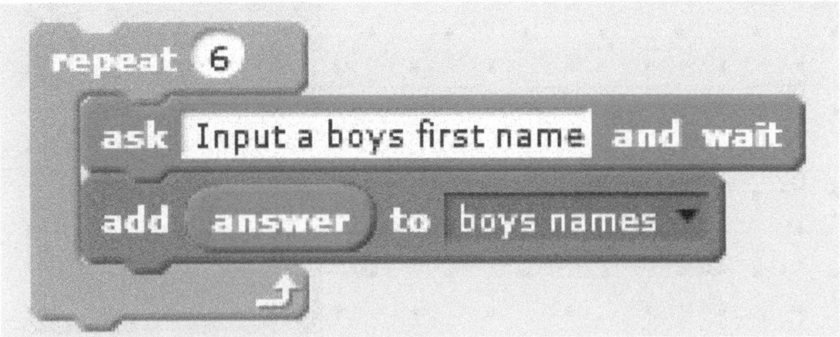
repeat 6
ask Input a boys first name and wait
add answer to boys names

Random Word Further Steps

if boys names contains John then
say Hello John for 2 secs
else
say There is no John here! for 2 secs

Toilet Fan First Steps

A sensor detects a car and triggers the light to change.
A timer sets the length of light time: this could be adjusted at certain times of the day to enable more traffic to cross in one direction than the other.
It could be triggered by a user pressing a crossing button.

Toilet fan Next Steps

The door needs to detect blockages and automatically open again if it does. The door needs to open slowly so it doesn't hurt someone behind the door.

Toilet Fan Further Steps

Zebra Crossings, level crossings, traffic lights, next stop messages on trains

Car Park Barrier Challenge (There are lots of variations and level of detail that could be included or missed).
If train is sensed approaching by distance sensor:

- Start warning noise and flashing lights
- Wait 5 seconds
- Start lowering barriers

If train is sensed leaving by distance sensor:

- Start raising barriers
- Wait until barrier raised
- Stop warning noise and flashing lights

Times Table Game Further Steps

Set random moving sprites and steerable sprite to start in a specific location using go to X and Y blocks

Clock Next Steps

Broadcast Commands

Clock Further Steps

A 100 minute hour day would take 14.4 hours

Cartesian Coordinates Next Steps

Shape translates and draws in a different place

Cartesian Coordinates Further Steps

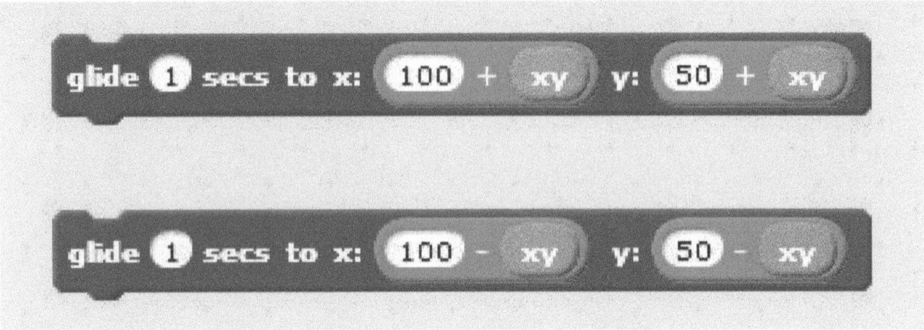
glide 1 secs to x: 100 + xy y: 50 + xy
glide 1 secs to x: 100 - xy y: 50 - xy

Translation, Enlargement & Rotation First Steps

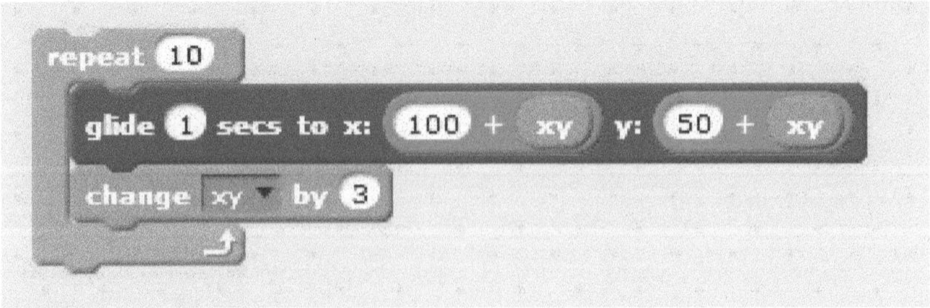
repeat 10
glide 1 secs to x: 100 + xy y: 50 + xy
change xy by 3

Tilt Switch First Steps

Aeroplane, helicopter, drone, train

Tilt Switch Further Steps

This could be set to say how many degrees it is tilting so it can be countered by the rotors or enable it to move in a controlled manner.

Chatbot Further Steps

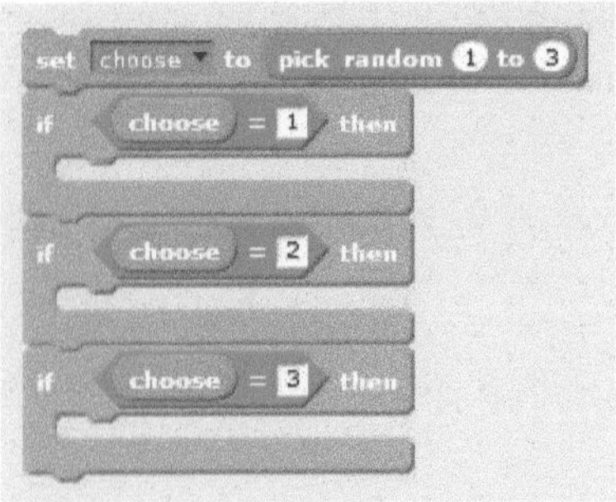
set choose to pick random 1 to 3
if choose = 1 then
if choose = 2 then
if choose = 3 then

Notes

Notes

Notes

Notes